Faces along the Bar

FACES ALONG
Lore and Order in the Workingman's

**HISTORICAL
STUDIES OF
URBAN AMERICA**
A series edited by
James R. Grossman and
Kathleen N. Conzen

THE BAR
Saloon, 1870–1920

MADELON POWERS

The University of Chicago Press • Chicago and London

MADELON POWERS is associate professor in the Department of History at the University of New Orleans, Louisiana, where she specializes in U.S. urban and gender history. Her articles have appeared in the book *Drinking: Behavior and Belief in Modern History,* Susanna Barrows and Robin Room, eds., and in the journals *International Labor and Working-Class History* and *History Today.*

The University of Chicago Press, Chicago 60637
The University of Chicago Press, Ltd., London
© 1998 by The University of Chicago
All rights reserved. Published in 1998
Printed in the United States of America
07 06 05 04 03 02 01 00 99 98   1 2 3 4 5
ISBN: 0-226-67768-0   (cloth)

TX
950.56
P69
1998

Portions of this book, used here with permission, were previously published in slightly different forms as follows: "Decay from Within: The Inevitable Doom of the American Saloon," in Susanna Barrows and Robin Room, eds., *Drinking: Behavior and Belief in Modern History* (Berkeley: University of California Press, 1991), 112–31, © 1991 The Regents of the University of California; "The 'Poor Man's Friend': Saloonkeepers, Workers, and the Code of Reciprocity in U.S. Barrooms, 1870–1920," *International Labor and Working-Class History* 45 (Spring 1994): 1–15; and "Women and Public Drinking, 1890–1920," *History Today* (London) 45, no.2 (February 1994): 46–52.

Library of Congress Cataloging-in-Publication Data

Powers, Madelon.
    Faces along the bar : lore and order in the workingman's saloon,
    1870–1920 / Madelon Powers.
        p.   cm. — (Historical studies of urban America)
    Includes bibliographical references and index.
    ISBN 0-226-67768-0 (cloth : alk. paper)
    1. Bars (Drinking establishments)—United States—History—19th century.
    2. Bars (Drinking establishments)—United States—History—20th century.
    3. Drinking customs—United States—History—19th century.   4. Drinking customs—United States—History—20th century.   5. United States—Social life and customs—19th century.   6. United States—Social life and customs—20th century.   I. Title.   II. Series.
    TX950.56.P69   1998
    394.1'3'097309034—dc21   97-39278
                                                                    CIP

To Nick
who taught me how

Contents

Illustrations

Acknowledgments

Suddenly I sympathize with all those giddy Hollywood folks on Academy Awards night who go on and on trying to thank everyone from the producer to the parking lot attendant. Like their films, my book is most assuredly a collaborative effort to which many kind people have contributed much help over many years. How can I possibly thank everyone? What if I forget someone? Still, the show must go on.

First I wish to thank my mentor and friend, Lawrence Levine, whose wisdom, wit, and wicked martinis have helped keep my spirits up and my pen moving for many a season. From him I learned how to listen to my sources, craft my ideas and language, and trust my own sense of the past. As my project grew from a seminar paper to a Ph.D. dissertation at the University of California at Berkeley, I also benefited enormously from the expertise of Leon Litwack of the History Department, Alan Dundes of the Folklore Department, and Robin Room of the Alcohol Research Group.

Many others have generously agreed to critique my book in its various drafts. My heartfelt thanks go out to Shirley Moore, Mary Odem, Larry Glickman, Bert Peretti, Steve Petrow, and Paul Gorman of the Remedial Dissertation-Finishing Group; Harry Levine, Ron Roizen, and all the gang at the Alcohol Research Group; and Reid Mitchell, Charlie Zappia, Kent Brudney, Peter Busowski, and Timothy Gilfoyle who interrupted their busy schedules to lend me a hand. I am also indebted to colleagues and friends who provided suggestions and helped me search out hard-to-find facts, including Lynn Dumenil, John Lumsdaine, Dan Spitzer, Jennie Lou Mintz, Susan Mann, Sherrie Sanders, and Raymond Sanford.

To Deanie Bowen, my friend and photographer, I owe very special thanks. She created all of the New Orleans photographs for this volume and printed and restored most of the others. Her skill and enthusiasm are deeply appreciated. With regard to Johnny Heinold's

First and Last Chance Saloon, I am very grateful to Rebecca Pulk for permitting me to use several photographs which belonged to her father, Otha D. Wearin. I also wish to thank Libby Hazlett for helping me hunt down the photograph of the Eagle Saloon; Jeannine Hinkel for assisting my research into John Sloan's paintings; and Lea Brown for dragging me to an exhibit of Edward Hopper's paintings, from which she then barely could drag me away.

Everyone at the University of Chicago Press has been most cordial and helpful. I wish to thank especially Jim Grossman, Doug Mitchell, Matt Howard, Jenni Fry, Mike Brehm, and Barbara Fillon. I never could have done it without you.

Though my dear parents, John and Helen Powers, did not live to see the completion of this book, I like to think that their spirit of good fun and hospitality lives on in its pages. To them, as well as to Tom, Jay, and the rest of my family, I offer many thanks for your continual encouragement. I know that you all share my joy and astonishment that this project is at last at an end.

And finally, to all my wonderful bar buddies through the years, I raise my glass in gratitude and fellowship. Here's looking at you, kids, down at Mr. Jones's in Chicago; at the Fairmont Grocery, Land's End, and Bardelli's in San Francisco; at Salerno's in Berkeley and George Kaye's in Oakland; and at Buffa's, the R Bar, the Apple Barrel, Molly's at the Market, and the Napoleon House in New Orleans. We'll tak a cup o' kindness yet, for auld lang syne.

Introduction

Faces along the bar
Cling to their average day:
The lights must never go out,
The music must always play,
All the conventions conspire
To make this fort assume
The furniture of home;
Lest we should see where we are,
Lost in a haunted wood,
Children afraid of the night
Who have never been happy or good.
—W. H. Auden[1]

My first inspiration for this study came while gazing at a photograph of an 1890s saloon and finding that I wanted to know more about the "faces along the bar" staring mutely back at me over the chasm of a century. I had long been interested in the "saloon period," the fifty turbulent years from 1870 to 1920 when the industrial revolution wrenched and reshaped American society and its working-class institutions such as the trade union, the ethnic lodge, and, of course, the saloon.[2] My studies at Berkeley had piqued my interest in the comparatively new field of urban social history. I was curious to learn about the everyday lives of the millions of workers (mostly men, but some women as well) who patronized the saloon so regularly that it became known as the "poor man's club." Further, my first graduate training had been in the field of folklore. I was enthusiastic at the prospect of exploring the rich lore of the barroom with its many games, stories, songs, food customs, and especially its elaborate system of drinking rituals. Finally, as a regular myself in neighborhood bars in San Francisco, Berkeley, Chicago, and now New Orleans, I have long been aware of the sense of camaraderie which develops among people who come to regard a particular establishment as their personal club.

In investigating the literature on the preprohibition saloon, I soon discovered that while observers from the period widely acknowledged the institution as the "workingman's club," historians have only recently scrutinized its role in working-class history. Several factors account for this omission. Until the mid-twentieth century, as Herbert Gutman points out, scholars interested in the working class had a tendency to remain "detached from . . . developments in American social and cultural history," concentrating instead on "the subject matter usually considered the proper sphere of labor history," namely, "trade union development and behavior, strikes and lockouts, and radical movements."[3] This preoccupation led to the neglect of other subjects such as family and gender roles, ethnic heritage, and a wide array of leisure pursuits, including saloongoing.

Historians who did address the subject of working-class drinking tended to focus on the temperance movement rather than the saloon. The sources partly account for this trend. Temperance advocates published a wealth of materials, whereas working-class bargoers seldom recorded their thoughts and experiences for posterity. As a result, historians have produced many fine studies of the temperance movement and its factions, motives, and goals.[4] Yet these studies reveal only one side of the story, while the other side, the working-class drinkers' side, is often lost beneath an avalanche of antidrink propaganda and prejudice. Bar history becomes a mere adjunct of temperance history, and worse, it is perceived through a temperance filter and assessed in temperance terms.

Historians have also neglected to explore drink culture because of their own antidrink prejudices. "[T]hroughout most of American history alcohol has been a taboo subject," as W. J. Rorabaugh observes. "While nineteenth-century librarians filed references to it under a pejorative, the 'liquor problem,' proper people did not even mention strong beverages. Neither did historians, who long neglected the fact that the United States had been one of the world's great drinking countries." Academics, most of them temperate, respectable folk, are often uncomfortable with the world of barrooms and booze which they find distasteful and alien. Unlike the workplace, the church, the family, and other more "worthy" spheres of working-class life, the barroom is to them the black sheep of laborers' institutions. Thus, they tend either to dismiss the subject as too frivolous for serious study, or, at the opposite extreme, to approach the subject with long faces and wagging fingers, narrowly perceiving drinking as "problem behavior" and the barroom as a "problem institution." Certainly it is true that alcohol use is sometimes frivolous and oftentimes problematic. But these observations do not exhaust the subject, nor should they get in the way of exploring other, more complicated and meaningful dimensions of drink culture in American working-class history.[5]

Fortunately, several historians in recent decades have tackled afresh the subject of workers, drinking, and barrooms, producing a rich new literature on the social history of alcohol. Notable contributors include W. J. Rorabaugh and Paul Johnson for the antebellum period, and Roy Rosenzweig, Perry Duis, Thomas Noel, and Elliott West for the postbellum era. The common thread running through these scholars' studies is an effort to concentrate upon drink culture rather than temperance culture. Further, they treat the barroom as a legitimate working-class institution which played a complex and frequently beneficial role in the lives of its constituents.[6]

Scholarship in urban social history emphasizing the process of community building has further clarified the significance of working-class institutions like saloons. Research into immigrant and racial groups has been particularly fruitful. Whereas historians once tended to characterize urban migrants as drifting, dislocated souls bereft of kith, kin, and culture, newer scholarship shows that many families and even whole villages migrated and settled together in American cities. Thus, while Oscar Handlin wrote of *The Uprooted* in 1951, John Bodnar speaks of *The Transplanted* in 1985—people who drew heavily upon family ties and ethnic traditions to fashion new forms of community in the urban setting. Many fascinating studies are now available on urban neighborhood networks, workplace cultures, and leisure subgroups.[7]

This book examines how saloongoers promoted the process of community building in urban America from 1870 to 1920. The scope is national, including saloongoers in larger cities such as New York, Chicago, New Orleans, and San Francisco, as well as smaller but growing cities such as Sioux City, Shoshone, and Oakland. The time period is also sizeable, spanning the five decades from the acceleration of American industrial growth after the Civil War to the achievement of global industrial supremacy by the end of the First World War.

Such a sweeping approach is feasible because of the peculiar nature of barroom culture in which tradition plays such a central and stabilizing role. To appreciate the importance of tradition in this context, it is useful to draw an analogy between the lore of the barroom and that of the schoolyard. Though generations of children come and go, playground lore tends to persist through the years. It is passed on faithfully from one group of youngsters to another as each discovers anew the pleasures of certain time-tested games, songs, riddles, tongue-twisters, jump-rope rhymes, jokes, pranks, scary stories, and the like. Changes and additions do occur, of course. Yet a great many traditions, such as the venerable singing game of "London Bridge Is Falling Down," live on for decades—sometimes even centuries— among successive schoolyard groups growing up through the thick "cake of custom," to use Walter Bagehot's phrase.[8]

Similarly, the barroom was (and still remains) an intensely conservative and traditional place in many respects. Its habitués inherit the lore of drinkers past, make some changes and additions of their own, and then pass it on to the next crop of regulars. This tenacity of tradition makes it possible to study fifty years of saloongoing as a reasonably coherent and continuous whole, as well as to speak of saloongoers in the aggregate even while acknowledging their regional and ethnic differences.

Exploring the inner dynamics of the workingman's saloon requires casting a broad net for a harvest of evidence. Testimony by and about saloongoers is often hidden away in documents devoted primarily to other subjects such as urban machine politics, immigrant assimilation, labor organizing, and tenement housing and household management. Although few eyewitnesses to saloon life survive, those with childhood memories or family stories about it represent an invaluable oral source. Photographers, artists, and cartoonists supply a fascinating visual record. Additional information can be gleaned from the statements of saloonkeepers and their trade associations, and from the various local and state government agencies charged with regulating the bar trade.[9]

Helpful firsthand testimony also comes from the writings of saloon-era journalists, novelists, and playwrights. Particularly valuable are the insights of Jack London, who, despite his continual boasts of drinking prowess and manly derring-do, still provides the most reliable, thorough, and articulate account of saloon life that I have encountered. Readers familiar with drinkers' ways will recognize, moreover, that his very braggadocio has the ring of authentic bar speech. Also essential to this study are Upton Sinclair, Frank Norris, Theodore Dreiser, and other novelists of the "realism school." Their accounts of bar life, though of course appearing in fictional contexts, are so deliberately intended to depict actual customs and conditions that they are tantamount, in my opinion, to direct observation. Regarding journalists such as George Ade, Travis Hoke, James Stevens, and Finley Peter Dunne, the opposite tendency—an inclination to depict saloon life in overly romantic and playful terms—sometimes attends their work. Yet their colorful vignettes and their ironic wit make them indispensable for conveying the spirit of fun and fellowship that often prevailed in the "poor man's club." [10]

The vast literature produced by social reformers is both the boon and bane of the saloon historian's existence. Some of it, especially that issuing from religious circles, is so fanatically antiliquor and so obviously based on wild imaginings rather than careful observation that it is nearly useless except as a foil for the presentation of facts. [11] Yet the literature by progressive reformers such as Jacob Riis, Lincoln Steffens, and Jane Addams is extremely valuable. Many of these did their homework on the facts as well as some fieldwork in settlement projects, urban reform leagues, immigrant assistance programs, and other "hands on" endeavors bringing them in direct contact with saloongoing folk. [12]

Of particular importance is the extensive survey of saloon life conducted in the 1890s by the "Committee of Fifty." This self-appointed group of progressive scholars, clergymen, and other professionals endeavored to ascertain the appeal of the saloon and evaluate possible substitutes ranging from union halls to temperance tearooms. Raymond Calkins, Royal Melendy, and other members of the Committee's survey teams amassed detailed data from some seventeen cities nationwide. [13] Though much of the progressive literature is marred by its unmistakably condescending and judgmental tone, it nevertheless contains a wealth of factual evidence without which the saloon historian's task would be immeasurably more difficult.

Still another rich source of information is the lore of the barroom, the widely embraced folkways of drinking, eating, gaming, storytelling, and singing which helped give saloon life its clublike character and appeal. By adopting the interpretative techniques already developed by folklorists, ethnographers, and popular entertainment analysts, the saloon historian gains many valuable insights into the collective worldview of barroom regulars.[14]

While the existence of these various sources makes an in-depth examination of saloongoers possible, the question remains, what can be gained from such a study? Why should historians or anyone else care about what workers did in their saloons? I shudder to think how many raised eyebrows and embarrassed titters I have encountered when I have tried to explain what my project is about and why it is worth pursuing. "Saloons—you mean, *bars*?" many people have responded incredulously. My usual defense has been to point out immediately that old-time saloons were the places where union leaders first organized their members, machine politicians cultivated the workingman's vote, and immigrants sought the assistance of their countrymen. As such, saloons deserve serious scholarly attention. By thus referring to the "hard" history issues of union activism, politics, and economics—long thought to be "the proper sphere of labor history," as Gutman observes—I have managed to satisfy the skeptical and extricate myself from many an uncomfortable coffee-break conversation.

The time has come, however, to explain my true objectives. This is not primarily an institutional study of the saloon and its role in labor organizing, politics, or economics, though these subjects of course crop up in my discussion. Neither is this an examination of the impact that men's drinking and saloongoing had on wives and children, health problems, violent crime, or the temperance sentiment of nonsaloongoers. These are important subjects, but they are not my subject.

This is instead a study of *saloongoers,* an effort to climb inside their minds, to see the barroom as they saw it and to understand what it did for them as they understood it. They built a community around drink, and it is that community I propose to explore.

There will be those who will take me to task for portraying drink culture in a largely positive light. They will wish my accounts of saloon revelry contained more sober reminders of likely negative consequences. They will claim I am romanticizing my subject. My response is to reiterate my purpose. This is a study of how *saloongoers* viewed the saloon—not wives, not employers, not policemen, not social workers, and certainly not temperance advocates. The fact is, saloongoers liked the life, and this book attempts to show why. It does not attempt to show why they should not have liked it, nor why others did not like it. These antisaloon views have already been exhaustively explored elsewhere, and I provide guidance to such works in the notes. This time, however, it is the saloongoers' turn to tell their side of the story, with an analytic assist from me.

From the regular customers' viewpoint, what made the saloon so attractive that they adopted it as their "club"? How did they go about becoming "regulars," and what were the principal ties that bound them to fellow barmates? What can be learned of their worldview by examining their preferences in drink, food, games, stories, and songs? How did the custom of "clubbing" for drinks, with its underlying code of honor and reciprocity, guide their behavior and promote a sense of comradeship?

Finally, what was the relationship of the saloon club to the larger urban marketplace in which it thrived? Some scholars, focusing on the saloon's communal aspects, have suggested that it constituted an "alternative culture" where workers sought refuge from the dominant American society with its market exchange mentality. From my research, however, I am convinced that marketplace values were much more deeply imbedded in saloongoers' worldview, traditions, and relationships than such an interpretation allows. What are the implications of this finding? Was saloon culture in fact *dual* in nature, reflecting an intricate commingling of marketplace and community orientations? Rather than representing an alternative, was the saloon club instead a complementary and integral part of urban marketplace culture? In that case, did the saloon club differ much from voluntary associations like unions and mutual aid societies which also combined marketplace and community orientations? Indeed, might saloon culture be best understood as an elemental form of voluntary association?

In addressing these questions, I intend to demonstrate that working-class saloongoers in the industrializing years of 1870 to 1920 represented an extraordinary example of ordinary people developing the potentialities of bar life to the fullest. I also intend to show that saloon clublife and lore, far from being trivial or detrimental, constituted instead a major stepping-stone along the road to cultural integration, self-organization, and cooperative effort within the working class. In probing the inner workings of this world, I mean to dispel some of the antisaloon, antidrink prejudices still lurking in many Americans' minds to this day. Moreover, by approaching the phenomenon of saloongoing from the perspective of the participants themselves, I hope to animate and give voice to those engaging but all too often enigmatic "faces along the bar."

Part I

The Criteria for Comradeship

One

The Importance of Being Regular

The poor man's club, the poor man's club!
The man who says that deserves a rub.
The club that takes the Saturday pay,
The club that chases all hopes away. . . .
Takes the price of toil from the laboring man,
That empties the stomach and fills the can. . . .
With the wife out washing, her rub, rub, rub,
Beats time for the songs of the poor man's club.
—Anti-Saloon League[1]

What would possess anyone to return night after night to the same saloon? According to many prohibitionists, Satan himself had a great deal to do with it. "In the late nineties of the last century," observed journalist James Stevens in 1927, "all the evangelists in practice in the United States were picturing Hell as a place much like the American saloon." Indeed, during its heyday from 1870 to 1920, the saloon—or "poor man's club," as the workingman's barroom was commonly called in this period—was continually under fire for being the very agency that kept poor men poor, both materially and morally. Serving as what the Anti-Saloon League called "the devil's headquarters on earth," the saloon allegedly exercised a diabolical hold over its habitués, acting as an irresistible den of iniquity "where the sotted beasts gather nightly at the bar."[2]

In one respect at least, prohibitionists were correct: most saloons did cater to a regular crowd. Just as churches had their congregations, so most saloons had loyal constituencies of perhaps fifty to sixty "regulars" who kept them in business. Most customers were working-class men, though some women also participated in saloon life in ways guided and limited by barroom custom. Unlike the "sotted beasts" of temperance lore, however, the typical customers of working-class drinking establishments were neither drunkards nor slaves to some satanic conspiracy.[3]

Indeed, settlement-house workers who actually surveyed saloon life firsthand reported that only occasionally did outright intoxication occur in workers' barrooms. "Most incredible of the facts which the study of the saloon revealed to me was the relatively small amount of drunkenness," exclaimed Royal Melendy of Chicago Commons. Similarly, Robert Woods of Boston's South End House remarked that "a drunken man is seen with surprising infrequency when the enormous number of saloon patrons is taken into account." E. C. Moore of Chicago's Hull House summed up the issue with his assertion that "it is use, not abuse, that [the saloon] stands for. . . . The exception has been made the rule. . . . That intemperance is an exception can be proved only by careful observation." Certainly there were dives where habitual drunkenness was encouraged, but such "low" saloons were comparatively few, confined to the worst districts, and patronized by unsavory characters who could hardly be considered "working class." To be sure, wage earners were fond of their schooners of beer and jiggers of whiskey, and they did indulge in periodic drinking binges. But "King Alcohol" was not the only attraction that tempted them to become saloon regulars, nor even the most important.[4]

The principal appeal of the saloon lay in the opportunity it afforded ordinary workingmen to cultivate the sort of clublife *they* found most enjoyable and useful during the industrializing years of 1870 to 1920. At a time when various groups from Bible-thumping evangelists to profit-hungry industrialists were busily hatching paternalistic schemes for reshaping working-class leisure habits, the saloon offered its predominantly male clientele a place to work out their own solutions to their needs. As long as the ultimate outcome was income, the bar trade was game for almost any social, economic, or political experiment that its customers cared to try.[5]

But what precisely was the nature of this "club"? Contemporary observers often remarked on the close-knit camaraderie of the "regulars." Yet their headquarters was a commercial enterprise open to the public and selling liquor for profit. How did the community-oriented values of the saloongoers mesh with the market-oriented values of the saloon business? How was the bargoers' desire for intimate drinking company reconciled with the proprietor's desire for maximum profits? A closer look at how saloon culture developed and what the terms "club" and "regular" meant in the context of barlife will suggest some answers.

SALOON CLUBS IN PERSPECTIVE

Even with its controversial reputation, the saloon between 1870 and 1920 was widely acknowledged as the "workingman's club" by friends and foes alike. From beer-loving journalists and liquor sellers to teetotal progressives and religious leaders, most who observed the saloon for themselves were struck by the clublike character of its atmosphere, facilities, and regular clientele. Bar owners were only too happy to encourage this conception of the trade, adopting such friendly sounding bar titles as "The Social," "The Reception," "Ed and Frank's," and often simply "The Club." Episcopal Bishop Henry C. Potter of Chicago even went so far as to compare the saloon to the private men's clubs of the respectable classes, popularizing the phrase "poor man's club," which was soon affectionately taken up by almost everyone but ardent prohibitionists and, one suspects, poor men themselves.[6]

Condescending though the epithet "poor man's club" of course was, still it had the ring of truth for those who had once tasted poverty and turned to the saloon for solace. "The saloon was the poor man's club, as only the poor understood," declared Frederic Howe, a progressive reformer who had needed a place of refuge during his struggling student days in the 1890s. "It was the only friendly place in New York for me; it was my club." At the other end of the continent, author and inveterate bargoer Jack London told of a similar experience from his early years as a penniless unknown in the California waterfront community of Oakland. "They were the poorman's clubs," London insisted, "and they were the only clubs to which I had access." The prestigious "Committee of Fifty," who thoroughly surveyed the nation's saloons at the turn of the twentieth century, came to the same conclusion. Employing the phrase themselves to describe the saloon, the Committee added, "Its hold on the community does not wholly proceed from its satisfying the thirst for drink. It also satisfies the thirst for sociability." Thus, while the merits of the saloon were hotly debated by its defenders and detractors, its status as the chief leisure headquarters for poor men was not. "Bishop Potter was right when he said it was 'the poor man's club,'" concluded George

Ade, "and he might have added that the poor man dropped in every night to pay his dues."[7]

The term "club" had in fact been associated with drink culture since the early seventeenth century. Before then, the only "clubs" among English-speaking people were heavy sticks with a knob or mass at one end, and the verb "to club" meant simply "to beat": the soldier clubbed his enemy to the ground. But sometime in the early 1600s, "to club" also came to mean "to combine" or "to join" into a mass or knot, presumably a reference to the knotted mass of a club's head: the lady clubbed her hair behind her neck; her husband clubbed with other merchants to form a business; husband and wife clubbed in the act of procreation.[8]

This sense of "combining" made its way into tavern parlance in England and America in the late 1600s and early 1700s. Drinkers combining their resources toward the joint defrayal of the bar bill were said to be "clubbing," and the group they formed came to be called a "club." By the early eighteenth century, then, a "club" was "a meeting or assembly at a tavern, etc., for social intercourse; a social meeting the expenses of which are jointly defrayed; later, a periodical social meeting of such an association."[9]

Consider the case of a group of friends, among them a shoemaker, a joiner, a merchant's clerk, and a youthful printer named Benjamin Franklin, who began meeting at a Philadelphia tavern every Friday evening in 1728. Calling themselves the "Junto," they congregated to share, over rounds of ale, their views on morals, politics, and natural philosophy. Further, at Franklin's suggestion, they extended the club idea to their private book collections. He explained that "by thus clubbing our books in a common library, we [had] each of us the advantage of using the books of all the other members." The rewards of this clubbing arrangement so inspired Franklin that in 1730 he helped found the first public library in Philadelphia, which, he later claimed in 1784, "was the mother of all North American subscription libraries, now so numerous." In this way did great libraries from a little tavern club grow, developing naturally and logically out of the concept of clubbing resources toward a mutually agreeable end.[10]

The club idea rapidly spread both within and beyond the context of tavern life, so that by the late 1700s, *any* group formed primarily for social purposes and supported by the combined resources of its members also came to be called a "club." This expansive trend continued into the 1800s, with the result that as the saloon period began in the 1870s, a great many clubs spawned in America had no gestational relationship whatsoever with barrooms. But the club idea itself originated in seventeenth-century places of public amusement like taverns, and so characteristic and fundamental to tavern life did "clubbing" remain that barrooms themselves have been popularly known as "clubs," from that day to this.[11]

The term "club," then, has long been associated with at least three aspects of tavern society. It denotes a *method* of communal drinking, wherein participants make a pact to combine their resources toward the barroom's pleasures. It also refers to a *group* of taverngoers engaging in such a pact. Finally, the term acts as a synonym for "barroom," meaning the *place* where people assemble to make a club of the drinking experience. This centuries-old concept of the club applied in every sense to the world of the saloon. Further, just as tavern clubbing in Franklin's day sometimes led to grander associative endeavors, so saloon clubbing in the industrializing years of 1870 to 1920 often played a pivotal role in the cooperative and self-organizing efforts of the emerging working class.

FROM TAVERNS TO SALOONS

With brewery financing, the workingman's tavern after 1870 was generally better equipped and more attractively appointed than its counterpart in the past.[12] Accompanying this change, it began to be known by the more stylish name of "saloon." While this term made its debut in the American language before the Civil War, its ubiquitous use was a late-nineteenth-century phenomenon. Derived from the French "salon," meaning a large and elaborate social hall, "saloon" caught the popular fancy and no doubt pleased liquor dealers as well. "Only in the United States was a common drinking resort known by such a hifaluting title," remarked Ade on its pretentiousness. "We started out with taverns. . . . Then some enterprising dealer opened a place with mirrors and chandeliers and a picture of Venus arising from the Bath and the whole lay-out was so elegantine that he decided to call it a 'saloon.'. . . It was a high-toned name which very soon began to drag in the mud." Indeed, in the decades to follow, the temperance movement would make the name "saloon" such a dirty word to so many people that even after the prohibition era of 1920 to 1933, some areas forbade the very use of the word in new bar titles.[13]

Like taverns throughout history, the primary function of the saloon was to offer the basic amenities of home in a public place. Drink, food, shelter, and companionship have ever been the tavern's stock-in-trade. Since many saloongoers lived in substandard tenements with few home comforts, the saloon in comparison seemed a most appealing prospect. As Moore explained in 1897, "It is the workingman's club. . . . In it he finds more of the things which approximate to luxury than he finds at home, almost more than he finds in any other place in the ward. In winter the saloon is warm, in summer it is cool, at night it is brightly lighted. . . . More than that there are chairs and tables and papers and cards and lunch, and in many cases pool and billiards. . . . What more does the workingman want for his club?" The basic attractions of the saloon, then, were nothing new in the venerable tradition of tavernkeeping.[14] What was new, however, was the peculiar set of social and economic circumstances which prevailed during the saloon period.

As rural Americans and immigrating Europeans poured into the cities after the Civil War in search of employment in the burgeoning industrial marketplace, the crush of their numbers made even the most basic facilities and services hard to come by. Few specifically working-class institutions had had ample time to develop. Further, many rural, middle-class citizens were reluctant to acknowledge the permanence of the growing American proletariat, an attitude which hindered society's ability to cope with its mounting urban problems. Meanwhile, the breweries had received a considerable boost from British investors beginning in the 1880s. This increased the already intense competition between the newer companies and those owned by old German families such as Pabst, Schlitz, Anheuser, and Busch. In their rush to outsell one another in the retail market, the major companies sought to control existing saloons through exclusive distributorship contracts or direct ownership (known as the "tied-house system"). They also financed the opening of hundreds of new saloons in expanding urban-industrial areas.[15]

Adam Smith himself could not have envisioned a more perfect capitalist dream of supply and demand. The saloon, backed by influential liquor interests and allied with machine politicians, offered the nascent working class a wide array of facilities, services, and contacts often available nowhere else. In time, the saloon also became a principal arena for all manner of working-class movements including labor organization, political action, and immigrant assistance. This is not to ignore the many detrimental effects that the barroom and its wares had on the laboring population. Its role in aggravating alcoholism, disease, violent crime, family hardship, job absenteeism, political corruption, and other social problems has been well documented.[16] Despite the saloon's faults and excesses, however, it earned considerable customer loyalty by serving as both shelter and staging ground for its vast working-class clientele.

In terms of structural features, saloons bore a striking family resemblance to one another. As Ade remarked, "When you had visited one of the old-time saloons you had seen a thousand." This similarity was due partly to longstanding traditions in the tavern trade, but just as importantly to the standardizing influence of the breweries that provided drinking establishments with bar fixtures and decorations in addition to liquor supplies. Yet, while barroom interiors exhibited a certain sameness, this did not mean their facilities were necessarily mediocre. On the contrary, the cutthroat competition among the breweries led them to upgrade the interiors whenever possible to attract a larger and steadier clientele. As a result, saloons offered creature comforts and an aura of opulence that workers could rarely afford in their tenement dwellings or boardinghouses.[17]

Most saloons featured a hardwood bar of oak or mahogany that ran nearly the length of the establishment. The bar constituted both a serving counter and storage cabinet. It was kept clean by the constant swabbing motions of the saloonkeeper, and its front surface was sometimes intricately carved. Behind the bar was a narrow walkway, and behind that, built into the wall, was a back bar consisting of shelves, cabinets, and a large plate-glass mirror. Here a great variety of bottles and glasses were prominently displayed. Paralleling the bar were a brass footrail and frequently a handrail as well, designed to accommodate the custom of stand-up drinking so common in this period. Bar stools were rare, though many establishments provided chairs and tables in the Continental cafe-style tradition. Huge brass cuspidors were usually situated at intervals along the floor, and sawdust was liberally strewn about to absorb spills and prevent slipping. Pictures of nubile nudes and posing prizefighters often adorned the walls, and a pool table sometimes stood in the back. Food, available for the price of a drink, was spread out on a separate serving table. Gas (and, later, electric) lights were suspended from the ceiling, heat was supplied by a stove in the corner, and toilet facilities were located in the rear. Many establishments also offered a back room equipped with tables and chairs to provide meeting space for more organized groups.[18]

Some reformers insisted that such comforts were part of a sinister brewery-saloonkeeper conspiracy to entrap the worker, "the proprietor knowing well what bait will prove most attractive to his customers," as Marcus Reynolds asserted. The bait worked very well indeed. On a typical day in Chicago in 1899, for example, a police precinct report indicated that the number of people entering saloons amounted to half the city's population. A similar tally in Boston revealed about the same ratio of barroom patronage to city population on an average day. Unfortunately, these surveys were merely headcounts which did not record whether the persons observed were male or female, adults or children, local residents or commuters, or onetime or repeat customers. Nevertheless, the sheer volume of daily foot traffic into saloons is impressive. The number of saloons themselves is also striking. Regarding San Francisco, New York, and Buffalo, for instance, maps of working-class neighborhoods published in 1901 were thick with dots representing barrooms. On Howard Street in San Francisco, a single block featured thirteen drinking establishments on one side and eight on the other. It is no exaggeration, therefore, to assert that millions upon millions of working-class people were patrons of saloons from 1870 to 1920.[19]

THE SALOON CLUB REGULAR

In imagining these swarms of saloongoers in working-class neighborhoods, it is important to keep in mind that the relationship among the regulars of any particular saloon was usually a personal one. Thus, the astonishing volume of barroom attendance did not mean that people were going willy-nilly to any saloon that was handy. Although there were always a number of one-time or occasional customers, a great percentage of saloongoers were the steady patrons of some single establishment. As Melendy observed, "The term 'club' applies; for, though unorganized, each saloon has about the same constituency night after night."[20]

Because the saloon was first and foremost a business, there could not be that degree of exclusivity characteristic of formal clubs. A stranger was generally made to feel a stranger, however, until he had

This drinking code included a host of customs regarding what men ought to drink; where and when they should drink it; what special words, gestures, and rituals should accompany it; and what their comportment should be having drunk it. Taken together, these various customs and the sense of camaraderie they fostered had the effect of regulating the regulars, bringing approval and acceptance to those who conformed. Thus, although specifics of behavior differed enormously in the realms of medicine, politics, athletics, and saloongoing, the phenomenon of the "regular" remained fundamentally the same: the trusty good fellow habitually on hand to participate in his group's activities and honor the code of his comrades.

In barroom parlance, then, a "regular customer"—or, more familiarly, a "regular"—was first of all a steady patron who, by consistently drinking his fill and paying his bill, helped keep the bar business afloat. A loyal clientele was the lifeblood of the liquor trade. The proprietor's prosperity depended on encouraging "the spending proclivities of his own little group of bar-flies," as Ade observed.[26] A New York saloonkeeper at the turn of the century described the financial quandary he faced when "a number of the best regular patrons lost their jobs" and requested the right "to drink 'on trust.'"[27] Similarly, Chicago proprietors reported that they could not survive with many charity cases, no matter how deserving, among those who were their "steady regulars," to use their phrase.[28] To qualify as a saloon club member, a customer first and foremost had to be a steady—and solvent—drink-buyer.

Yet a patron's eligibility for full-fledged regular status depended on much more than simply hours logged at the bar. Beyond being a constant consumer, a customer had to meet at least three other criteria, judging from contemporary descriptions of saloon clienteles. He had to conform to the laws of barroom drinking, both written and unwritten, that guided customer interaction. He had to be a reasonably convivial fellow, agreeable enough to be acceptable company for the other customers. Finally, he had to share some common ground with the established clientele, some linking factor such as an occupational or ethnic tie which the group regarded as essential to maintaining their esprit de corps. Constancy, conformity, conviviality, commonality—these appear to have been the principal traits which facilitated the transformation of customers into "regulars" and their saloons into "clubs."[29]

Saloon Dualism

What emerges from this analysis of regulars and clubbing is the saloon's pronounced duality of character. It is both brotherly and businesslike, both communal and commercial. Regulars are comrades in some respects, customers in others. The saloon club seems now an organic community, now a contractual relation. This ongoing dialectic between communal and commercial tendencies is one of the fundamental features of saloon life.

Several scholars have noted a similar dichotomy in urban life and urban institutions generally. Among the first to examine the phenomenon was German social theorist Ferdinand Tönnies, who in 1887 published his seminal ideas on "community" and "society" (*Gemeinschaft und Gesellschaft*). Tönnies observed that in urban settings, people form two kinds of social relationships to meet two different kinds of social needs. The first form of relationship, the "community" (*Gemeinschaft*), involves the personal, face-to-face, emotionally charged bonds that develop among kith and kin. Families, friendship circles, and neighborhood networks are rooted in community relationships. In contrast, the second form of relationship, the "society" or "market" (*Gesellschaft*), involves the more impersonal, contractual, rationally constructed bonds that develop among individuals pursuing practical, self-interested goals. Business ventures and special interest groups are based on society or marketplace relationships.[30]

These two forms of association—the communal and the contractual—are both present in modern society. While Tönnies predicted that increasing urbanization and commercialization would weaken the communal impulse, he nevertheless maintained that "the force of Gemeinschaft persists, although with diminishing strength, even in the period of Gesellschaft, and remains the reality of social life." Many scholars have since expanded on this theme of duality in urban relationships, including Charles Horton Cooley, Max Weber, Émile Durkheim, Talcott Parsons, Robert Redfield, and Eric Wolf.[31]

Thomas Bender applies these scholars' community-society theories to the study of United States history. He rejects the suggestion that historical change in America has involved a unidirectional march away from the closeness of community to the anomie of the city. Instead, he argues that communal and contractual relationships have always represented "two intertwined and simultaneously available repertoires," two options which any American in any era might exercise in meeting this or that social need. To illustrate Bender's point, consider Puritans of the 1660s and counterculture hippies of the 1960s. Both engaged in communal relationships with loved ones and contractual relationships with businesses and governmental bodies. But they did so in drastically different ways, in response to vastly different economic, political, and social circumstances. The challenge for historians is to determine how specific historical circumstances affect the way Americans exercise these options and prompt them to reshape their institutions to accommodate evolving social requirements. "The task of the cultural historian or critic," Bender contends, "is not to date the moment when one of the worlds of social relations is replaced by the other; it is to probe their interaction and to assess their relative salience to people's lives in specific situations."[32]

Further, these two forms of social relationships often coexist within the same institution. Many voluntary associations such as trade unions, ethnic lodges, and mutual aid societies combine elements of both brotherly solidarity and economic self-interest. "Analytically, gemeinschaft and gesellschaft can be completely separated as ideal types, but historians and sociologists must expect to find a good deal of interpenetration in actual social experience," as Bender points out. "There are no completely closed social systems in modern society. External networks impinge upon the family (and all other forms of community), and the ways of community often intrude into larger social networks and institutions." This concept of interpenetration is emphasized throughout the works of Tönnies, Cooley, Weber, Durkheim, Parsons, Redfield, and Wolf. For all their diversity, these scholars concur on at least three points. The urge to form social combinations is fundamental to all human activity. These combinations tend to assume two basic forms. And finally, the interplay of these two types of social combination is a defining characteristic of urban life.[33]

This duality and this interplay permeated all aspects of saloon culture in American cities. Clubbing, for example, incorporated many elements of the commercial marketplace. When strangers at the bar made pacts to combine their nickels toward the purchase of drinks, their actions entailed contractual arrangements, monetary outlay, and the deliberate construction of interpersonal relationships. These are among the classic elements of market relations. At the same time, the main aim of clubbing was camaraderie. The social lubricant of drink, as well as the lore guiding its use, encouraged conviviality and mutuality among participants. Through clubbing tradition, saloon-goers cultivated the kind of intimate, emotionally charged bonds usually associated with "community" rather than "society" or the "marketplace."

Similarly, the status of regular combined elements of both business and brotherhood. As a customer, the regular was a creature of the marketplace who made an implied contract with the proprietor to uphold the code of commerce. As a comrade, the regular was a member of a drinking fraternity who made an unspoken pledge to uphold the code of the club. Regulars, like their clubbing traditions, represented a thorough intertwining of commercial and communal impulses.

To emphasize the saloon's dualistic nature in this way is to run counter to much recent scholarship which concentrates primarily on the communal qualities of barlife. Scholars struck by the evident camaraderie of bargoers have suggested that the workingman's saloon represented an alternative to, and a refuge from, the competitive urban marketplace and its social relations and values. While they acknowledge that the barroom was a business as well as a social center, they view the commercial side of the life as peripheral or even antithetical to the workers' communal culture thriving within. According to this view, the saloon was a kind of cultural Alamo about to be overwhelmed by the hostile forces of industrial capitalism.[34]

There is merit to this "alternative culture" interpretation, for it rightly points up the importance of communal values in saloon life. It also contrasts sharply with the old prohibitionists' view that saloons were little more than vice-ridden liquor dispensaries where people just went to get drunk. This pejorative view no doubt contributed to labor historians' former tendency to downplay the historical role of the workingman's saloon, dismissing it as irrelevant, unfortunate, or simply embarrassing. Recent saloon scholarship, in emphasizing the constructive role of saloongoing and communal values in workers' lives, provides a valuable corrective to a decades-old misconception and encourages historians to take a serious new look at the inner workings of saloon culture.

I am arguing, however, that market values and relations were an equal—and complementary—component of saloon life in American cities. Communal and market orientations were neither incompatible nor mutually exclusive. They could and did coexist in the institution, just as they did in the individuals' lives who patronized it. The two tendencies converged in the figure of the regular as customer-comrade and in clubbing tradition, which combined mercantile and mutualistic objectives. Dualism in the saloon culture of industrializing America made it dynamic, not anomalous. It also made the barroom doubly attractive and relevant to workers whose daily reality in the city involved a similar dialectic between communal and market concerns. The saloon was not alternative culture. It was urban culture.

Two

Gender, Age, and Marital Status

> The character of saloons is determined often by the character of the men who, having something in common, make the saloon their rendezvous. . . . The saloon becomes the natural headquarters of a club which may have no constitution or by-laws, but is still a distinct, compact, sympathetic company of men.
> —Raymond Calkins [1]

In addition to constancy, conformity, and conviviality, a sense of commonality was essential to the "sympathetic company" who made a particular saloon their club. Most fundamentally, the regulars' group identity was rooted in the shared circumstances of their personal lives. Saloongoers were mostly males seeking the fellowship of other men of similar age and marital status. They were also linked by their working-class status and often by their particular occupations as well. Many were members of minority groups struggling to achieve a livable balance between ethnic ways and the American way. Most made their homes in the tenements of working-class districts where, despite overcrowding and poverty, people still developed strong feelings of neighborhood loyalty. Such similarities in gender, age, marital status, occupation, ethnicity, and neighborhood provided the basis for the sympathetic relationship among regulars.

In some cases, one tie so dominated the regulars' relationship that saloon historians have been tempted to apply special labels to such establishments, most frequently referring to "occupational saloons," "ethnic saloons," and "neighborhood saloons." Yet a single barroom might cater to customers who were all steel workers of Slavic origin residing in the same neighborhood. Into which category should this establishment be placed? Such a case points up the difficulty of attempting to categorize saloons by "type." Further, such a labeling system overlooks other factors such as gender, age, and marital status which constitute equally important core elements of the bargoing relationship. The saloongoers themselves, not "types" of saloons, formed the basis of saloon culture. Their world can be best understood by examining the factors which figured most importantly in their relationships, keeping in mind the tendency of one or more of these elements to dominate—but not exclude—the others.[2]

Gender identity, age group, and marital status were factors linking bargoers at the most personal level. In saloons, men defined themselves as men. They established standards of manly comportment and continually reaffirmed their personal and group esteem by observing these standards. They sought out men of the same age cohort whose experiences and interests chronologically paralleled their own. Their marital status also figured in their sense of affinity. Single men, married men, migrating men whose families waited behind—all sought fellowship and solace from barmates in comparable situations. As regulars dealt collectively with these deeply personal concerns, they cultivated the kind of intimate, emotionally charged relationships associated with community.

Yet their attitudes toward masculinity, maturity, and matrimony were also influenced by events and requirements of the marketplace. Industrialization and the slipping status of workers prompted saloongoers to reformulate longstanding concepts of manliness. Urbanization and the challenges of tenement streetlife produced new collective responses among particular age groups, so that saloons now catered to such cohorts as the boys' "push," the adolescents' gang, the young men's pleasure club, and the older men's peer group. Saloongoers' attitudes toward marriage were also affected by the marketplace. Economic dislocations and uncertainties prompted some to postpone or avoid familial commitments and others to juggle work, marriage, and peer group demands in ways unimagined in preindustrial societies. Thus, the regulars' ties of gender, age, and marital status represented a commingling of personal and public concerns. No saloon was an island unto itself.

GENDER IDENTITY

The first thing to be noted about saloongoers is that they were overwhelmingly male, in demeanor as well as numbers. The liberal drink-

ing, raucous talk, and sometimes obstreperous behavior of male customers meant that the barroom proper was anything but a proper social venue for most respectable working-class women. There were,
however, exceptions to this general rule of masculine exclusivity. For
example, some women consumed the celebrated "free lunch" or attended social events in the back room. There were also a few family-
style saloons where parents and children sat together in groups at the
tables, though most of these had moved to the suburban districts by
the 1890s. For the most part, therefore, the everyday world of the urban working-class saloon was a masculine domain, and the regulars'
sense of group identity was powerfully influenced by concepts of
manliness that prevailed there.

Just as the rise of industrial capitalism in the nineteenth century
wrought enormous changes in the nature of men's work, so also it
transformed popular concepts of the nature of manliness. As the century began, the preindustrial apprenticeship system still prevailed in
most urban areas, a system in which adolescent males learned a trade
by progressing from apprentice to journeyman and, if talented and
diligent enough, to independent master craftsman. Master, journeymen, and apprentices toiled, drank, and socialized together in the
master's small workshop. Further, they often lived together under the
master's roof and authority, at least until older journeymen could
accumulate enough savings to establish their own households and
perhaps their own shops as well. Though tensions and jealousies inevitably arose in such workshops, an ethic of mutuality and artisan
pride still obtained among most masters and their charges. Not all
workers participated in the apprenticeship system, of course, but the
large artisan population who did helped establish the standards by
which all workingmen measured their success and self-worth. In this
early era, then, manly status was closely associated with mastery of
craft, control of tools and work pace, and membership in a respected
circle of workmen.[3]

With the expansion of markets and the demand for increased pro-
ductivity after 1820, however, the apprenticeship system began to
break down. Shop masters discovered that rather than training each
man to produce one item from start to finish, it was more expedi-
ent to divide the labor into specialized tasks which anyone could be
quickly trained to perform. In many trades, a journeyman's skill was
no longer needed nor valued. His chances for employment and advancement were further diminished with the growing availability of

cheap immigrant and female labor by mid-century. Having less need to impart complicated skills to workers, masters withdrew from the shop floor and instead devoted more energy to pursuing new markets and bigger profits. As their operations grew, masters also established larger workshops separate from their households, distancing themselves residentially as well as occupationally from their workers.[4]

As mechanization and mass production increasingly became the norm in factories at the end of the nineteenth century, the estrangement of masters and workers from one another and from their artisan traditions was complete in many trades. Though the union movement struggled to restore the waning power and pride of workers, especially those highly skilled, the vast majority of laborers remained unorganized and unable to halt the deterioration of their working conditions. The rise of industrial capitalism had transformed masters into businessmen and journeymen into wage earners. In the process, there emerged new standards of success and manliness shaped by the experience of class.[5]

When men of the middle and working classes employed the term "manly," they meant very different things by it, as scholars of male gender roles in the late nineteenth century have shown. For the Victorian bourgeoisie, to be manly meant first and foremost to possess unwavering strength of character. This was demonstrated by an individual's capacity for self-control, industriousness, acceptance of responsibility, and moral uprightness (including sobriety). Thus, the middle-class test of true manhood was economic success as a boss and breadwinner in the highly competitive capitalist marketplace. This concept of manliness, extolled in advice manuals, Horatio Alger novels, evangelical pulpits, and biographies of successful businessmen, was also embraced by some workingmen who were highly skilled and aspired to middle-class status. For many more working-class men trapped in low-paying, low-skilled factory jobs, however, middle-class manliness with its emphasis on upward mobility through rigid self-discipline had little relevance or appeal.[6]

For many urban laborers in the late nineteenth century, the realm of leisure rather than labor began to offer more opportunities for establishing their worth as men. Here they strongly identified with male peer groups who shared some mutual interest such as following sports, arguing politics, asserting ethnic pride, or defending home turf. For them, to be manly was to display an unflinching sense of personal and group honor. This was observable in a group member's capacity for courage, physical prowess, and loyalty to his fellows. Though these men cared for their wives and children, they were likely to pass many of their free hours outside of their tenement flats, and the companionship they sought was more often male than female. As Jack London once revealingly remarked, "I didn't know anything about girls. I had been too busy being a man." For many working-class men, the test of true manhood was peer recognition for being a reliable ally and comrade in the volatile street culture of urban America.[7]

The saloon's regular crowd constituted just such a working-class male peer group. The essence of being "regular" was to be a recognized group member who was habitually on hand to participate in saloon activities and uphold the code of the club. According to this code, men who did each other the honor of drinking together were also expected to celebrate and reinforce their special bond through the swapping of drinks, favors, small loans, or other gestures of mutual assistance and friendship. Further, by vying with one another in friendly contests of drinking, pool-playing, wagering, storytelling, and the like, they displayed their ability and stamina to one another and reaffirmed their worth as clubmates. Should strangers appear in their midst, the regulars closely scrutinized the interlopers' behavior to determine whether any slight to their group and their code was threatened. If it was, more displays of manly bravado might be required, even to the point of violence. More often, however, rivalries were resolved through conventional forms of barroom interaction.[8]

Bolstering the regulars' ethic of manliness was the ambience of the saloon itself. Indeed, nearly every feature of the saloon's interior seemed designed to promote an aura of freewheeling masculinity. The air was redolent with beer fumes and cigar smoke. The bar's brass footrail was itself "a symbol of masculinity emancipate," according to Travis Hoke. Wall decorations often included photographs of prizefighters such as John L. Sullivan, dubbed "the idol of the barrooms" by the *New York Times* in 1892, as well as depictions of cockfights, horse races, and battleships. Also popular were lithographs of buxom, scantily clad women who posed provocatively and were "shaped like bass viols," in George Ade's words. Other indelicate bar accessories included mustache towels hanging along the bar for the use of one and all. Brass cuspidors stood within convenient spitting distance, with sawdust scattered about to accommodate lapses of marksmanship. For those disinclined to leave their drinking posts to answer calls of nature, a few establishments even featured a urination trough on the floor running lengthwise along the bar counter, built on a slight tilt to facilitate flushing. Thus, it would appear that a major function of the saloon and its accoutrements was to reinforce feelings of uninhibited masculinity and gender solidarity among workingmen. As Hutchins Hapgood observed of McSorley's Saloon in New York, the barroom was a place where men could spend their time "in purely male ways . . . , untroubled by skirts or domesticity." [9]

Much of saloon culture might be considered "sexist" by late-twentieth-century standards. Male exclusivity was the general rule. While prostitutes might be tolerated in some lower saloons, male customers never accorded them regular status and often treated them with disdain. As for respectable women, the regulars made it abundantly clear that the main barroom was strictly reserved for the male peer group. There they enjoyed dirty jokes told at women's expense, ogled suggestive placards on the walls, and from the doorway sometimes verbally harassed female passers-by. Bartenders reported that when liquor loosened their regulars' tongues, they complained at length of failed romances, domestic woes, and other gender-related difficulties. Some bar songs and recitation pieces poked fun at alleged female frailties or told the sob stories of men used and betrayed by avaricious temptresses. [10]

This suspicious and defensive stance indicates that many saloon-goers still embraced a centuries-old conception of females as "daughters of Eve, mankind's ill fortune, prey to vanity, folly, and concupiscence," as Christine Stansell vividly phrases it. Stansell reports the prevalence of this attitude among workingmen from the colonial era to the nineteenth century, its origins of course going back to biblical times. According to this traditional masculine view, women were by nature dangerously passionate and corruptible creatures. They required continual male control and corrective guidance lest their fallibility undermine domestic life and civilization itself. Among middle-class and upwardly mobile people in the nineteenth century, a more positive conception of women's nature and capabilities gradually arose with the influence of republican ideology and evangelical theology. Yet Stansell notes the persistence in many quarters of "laboring men's view that sexuality was a female weapon, the instrument by which women duped men and then took them for all they were worth." [11]

To the extent that saloon culture perpetuated this derogatory stereotype, it represented a formidable obstacle to the fight for justice and equality for women, particularly women of the working class. Further, the saloon denied women the opportunity to counter the stereotype or present their own assessment of male-female relations. "Safe in his saloon, a man boasted of his marital independence, complained of marital injustice. . . , and there no woman dared invade him with drab truths," as Hoke remarked.[12]

Yet saloongoers were not totally anti-woman by any means. Many bar songs and stories portrayed females as merciful and decent and were surprisingly sentimental about mothers, wives, and women friends. Moreover, male customers accepted and indeed welcomed a female presence in certain areas of the saloon under well-defined circumstances. Though bargoers jealously guarded their male prerogatives and commiserated over male-female conflicts, there is no indication that these men as a group reviled or hated the women in their lives. Sexists and chauvinists they were, but not complete misogynists.[13]

While male peer groups dominated the barroom proper, it is important to note that many establishments also had a side door known as the "ladies' entrance." Through this portal passed a considerable number of working-class women, whether alone, in groups, or with male escorts. Very few of these women were prostitutes, the latter's haunts usually being the low saloons and dives of the worst slum districts. Instead, most female customers of ordinary saloons were either wage earners or the wives and daughters of wage earners who participated in barlife in significant though limited ways.[14]

If the "ladies' entrance" demonstrates that saloons did indeed have their female customers, it also reveals that the saloon trade regarded women as a special and separate class of customers. The purpose of the side door was threefold. First, it permitted women to enter inconspicuously and minimize public scrutiny of their comings and goings, an indication that even those bold enough to patronize saloons remained sensitive to the disapproving glances of their more conservative neighbors and peers. Second, women's entry through the side door eliminated the necessity of their running the gauntlet through the establishment's front room—the barroom proper—which in this era was still undisputed male territory. Adventuresome though most saloongoing women were, they were not agitators. Their aim was sociability, not social equality, and their stepping out did not include stepping into bar areas where they were not welcome. Finally, the side door afforded women quick and convenient access both to the far end of the bar, where they could purchase carry-out alcohol, and to a second chamber known as the "back room," where they could feast on free lunches or attend social events hosted there. By means of the ladies' entrance, the saloon trade both facilitated and circumscribed women's participation in saloon culture, inviting them to step in while simultaneously reminding them to watch where they stepped.[15]

Many working-class women participated in the saloon's voluminous carry-out trade, colorfully known in this era as "rushing the growler." A "growler" was a bucket or other container which the customer carried ("rushed") to a saloon to be filled and then hauled away for consumption elsewhere. Growlers were usually used for beer, though wine or whiskey might also be purchased in this manner. Particularly in the daytime, when male household members were off to work, women would enter by the side door, order their growlers filled, and depart. Though some women drank alone in the relative privacy of their tenement flats, others sought the company of female neighbors who gathered on the stoops and in the courtyards to drink together from the beer pail while they monitored the teeming street-life of their neighborhoods.[16]

In the evenings and on Sundays, working-class men and women might participate in growler fests or "can rackets," which often took place in such outdoor venues as tenement rooftops, stoops, and courtyards as well as city parks, alleyways, and waterfront wharves. A mixed-company growler group might include a household of relatives and boarders, or it might be composed of young men and women flirting and courting while they passed the pail around. Though reformers like Jacob Riis deplored the beer bucket's "blighting grip" on tenement dwellers, a great many working-class families, especially immigrants, appear to have regarded growler-drinking by men and women as both acceptable and fun.[17]

More controversial was female drinking on the saloon premises, though this was also acceptable to many working-class people under certain circumstances. When inclement weather made an outdoor rendezvous impractical, a dating couple might pass through the ladies' entrance and proceed to a table in the rear to drink and chat. Couples might seek out saloons offering modest vaudeville shows, which featured comics, magicians, and song-and-dance acts of a reasonably respectable character. Women also accompanied their male friends and kinfolk to social events held in the back room. These included dances sponsored by fraternal and labor groups, and wedding receptions hosted by neighborhood families. Women who drank at such events were usually expected to do so moderately, but then so also were the men; these were heterosexual social occasions, not barroom bacchanals. For women, however, there were two additional rules to observe: they must have male escorts, and they must confine themselves to the back room.[18]

The only circumstance in which respectable women might legitimately linger unescorted on the premises appears to have been in order to consume the saloon's famous free lunch. This hearty midday meal, "free" with the purchase of a five-cent drink, was made possible by brewery subsidies beginning in the late 1880s. Ironically, reformers despaired at the general excellence of these lunches, for they lured many female workers (as well as otherwise nondrinking male workers) into saloons. Even when women did come through the side door for this purpose, however, they seem often to have entered in all-female groups, confined themselves strictly to the back-room area, and engaged in little if any socializing with the male patrons. The men, moreover, appear to have given the women wide berth. Thus, although the lure of the free lunch made the women's presence understandable, the male regulars still apparently regarded them as interlopers in gendered space who might be tolerated temporarily but never accepted fully as members of the club.[19]

Prostitutes were a rarity in ordinary working-class saloons. Bar owners preferred to avoid harassment from bribe-seeking police and from their regulars' womenfolk. Further, the regulars themselves preferred the company of their male peers. Yet, while brothels and cheap hotels handled most of the prostitution trade, there were a few saloonkeepers in the poorest districts who encouraged the "social evil."[20] The affiliation between prostitutes and proprietors was usually an informal one. "There may be no definite business agreement between the women and the keepers of the saloons," observed Calkins, "but as a rule the saloon-keepers are compensated . . . by the increased bar receipts, and the women, in turn, are furnished with a 'hang-out.'" Prostitutes did not usually stand at the bar to solicit customers, but rather kept to the stalls and back rooms where the men could find them if they wanted them. Thus, regardless of whether a woman was a hustling hooker or a hungry free-luncher, she was still relegated to the same saloon back room, well away from the masculine milieu of the main bar.[21]

Female saloonkeepers were also a rarity. By the 1890s, most family-style saloons had relocated to the suburbs. In addition, commercial, brewery-backed saloons and tougher licensing policies had all but crowded out the informal, unlicensed "kitchen saloons" which immigrant women (often widows) had formerly run in their tenement flats. Nevertheless, there were some urban women in the late nineteenth and early twentieth centuries who ran barrooms, either by themselves or as part of a mom-and-pop family business. Those in business for themselves often seem to have been very colorful characters indeed, running places with such unforgettable names as "Peckerhead Kate's" in South Chicago, "Indian Sadie's" in Green Bay, and "Big Tit Irene's" in Ashtabula. More commonly, though, saloonkeeping was a male occupation, with the barman upholding the same code of manly comportment and gender-based camaraderie that prevailed among his regulars.[22]

The wide-open, all-male flavor of saloonlife was perhaps best captured by Jack London, who described his fascination with saloons as a teenager: "In the saloons life was different. Men talked with great voices, laughed great laughs, and there was an atmosphere of greatness. Here was something more than the common every-day where nothing happened. Here life was always very live, and, sometimes, even lurid. . . . Terrible [saloons] might be, but then that only meant they were terribly wonderful. . . . In the same way pirates, and shipwrecks, and battles were terrible; and what healthy boy wouldn't give his immortal soul to participate in such affairs?" In such an atmosphere, it is understandable that most working-class women seldom set foot in saloons. Slouching against the bar with one foot on the rail would have been unthinkable behavior for most "decent" women, let alone spitting into the cuspidors or allowing their skirts to trail in the beer-soaked sawdust. Men's thinking on this issue seems to have involved an interesting mixture of solicitude and defiance. On the one hand, decent women should be protected from the rough world of men; on the other, the rough world of men should be protected from decent women. In the saloon, according to Hoke, "One ceased to be a man among women. One breasted the bar, downed a drink, and became a man among men." To allow women into this working-man's world would not only cramp its style, but defeat its purpose as well.[23]

AGE GROUP

While the rough world of the saloon was ostensibly for adult males only, its bright lights, liveliness, and reputed sinfulness made it intensely interesting to street children and especially to boys eager to learn how men were supposed to behave. "To them the saloon was a place of delight," remarked a New York City saloonkeeper of the children in his neighborhood. "They would linger around my doors all day and all evening, trying to catch a glimpse of the inside." James Stevens confirmed that the fascination with saloons often began in childhood. He recalled that the "terrific smells that poured from the bar-room had a rare aroma of mystery for me; passing by, I would breathe deeply and think of drying blood and dead men's bones." Stevens further explained how he and a boyhood friend regularly "played" saloon just as other boys played soldiers or pirates. "[T]he two out-and-out wicked men of our valley, Bud Winkle and Russ Hicks, always drank in the Copper King. . . . They had never robbed and killed anybody, but they were the best heroes at hand," he recollected. "Ern Saling and I had some grand times pretending we were Russ and Bud. . . , staggering all over the calf corral and cursing like sixty." Unfortunately for the boys, Stevens' mother eventually caught them in their play and severely punished them. Like many other concerned adults, she condemned what she perceived as the barroom's pernicious influence upon youth with its glorification of drinking, profanity, and rowdiness. Nevertheless, the saloon offered a provocative model of manhood to emulate, and some young boys did apparently try to shape their personalities to suit the standards of masculinity they observed there.[24]

When children did set foot in saloons, it was often with growler in hand. Adults frequently sent both boys and girls to fetch their beer for them. Most saloonkeepers readily complied despite signs often displayed on the walls proclaiming that no liquor would be sold to minors. Jacob Riis called these signs a "heartless, cruel joke" and added, "I doubt if one child in a thousand, who brings his growler to be filled at the average New York bar, is sent away empty-handed." He told of once having been roughly ordered out of a saloon after trying to dissuade the barkeeper from filling a little boy's pitcher. One New York saloonkeeper concurred with Riis, asserting, "It was hard for me to understand how these mothers could send their young daughters for beer." Yet when he explained to these girls that they were too young to purchase alcohol, "Then they would be quite mortified, saying they were no longer children, which was perhaps the truth." Indeed, many working-class families did rely on their younger members to earn their keep through scavenging, peddling, and running errands which sent them to all corners of the urban environment and often made them streetwise beyond their years. To these children, fetching beer was merely a family duty, and a comparatively innocuous one at that.[25]

How frequently children actually sampled the contents of the growlers they carried is uncertain, though some no doubt succumbed to the temptation. According to one lurid newspaper story from the late 1880s, a boy who liberally sampled from the growler he carried all day long for his father's workshop was later found dead in a cellar, reportedly overcome and half-eaten by rats. More typically, however, the children who rushed the growler lived to tell about it, and reports of drunken children were few. Rather, the most important consequence of the growler tradition for children was to afford them the opportunity to participate, albeit briefly and peripherally, in the world of the saloon.[26]

If one were to believe the claims of prohibitionists, children also frequently ventured into saloons to fetch another sort of growler— namely, father. The image of the pathetic child begging a drunken daddy to attend to a destitute family was immortalized in that most famous of temperance songs, "Come Home, Father." It was composed by Henry Clay Work in the mid-nineteenth century and was popular among temperance advocates well into the twentieth century. In this tearful lyric, a little girl appears at the saloon door to implore:

> Father, dear Father, come home with me now,
> The clock in the steeple strikes one,
> You said you were coming right home from the shop
> As soon as your day's work was done.
> Our fire has gone out, the house is all dark,
> And Mother's been watching since tea,
> With poor brother Benny so sick in her arms,
> And no one to help her but me.
> > Hear the sweet voice of the child,
> > Which the night winds repeat as they roam,
> > Come home! Come home!
> > Oh Father, dear Father, come home.

Similar depictions appeared in popular novels and melodramas. Perhaps the most famous was Timothy Shaw Arthur's novel, *Ten Nights in a Barroom* (1854), which in the second half of the nineteenth century was outsold only by Harriet Beecher Stowe's *Uncle Tom's Cabin* (1852). Published "with a picture on the cover of a little girl grasping her father's arm and saying, 'Father, come home!'" noted Russel Nye, "the book sold a steady 100,000 a year for twenty years; turned into a play, it stayed on the stage for another fifty." In one of the book's most celebrated scenes (an illustration of which is included in the gallery following page 156), an ailing little girl tries to retrieve her drunken father from the saloon, only to be knocked unconscious by a flying beer glass.[27]

It is difficult to know whether such a scene ever actually occurred in real life. There can be no doubt that alcoholism was a source of misery for a considerable number of working-class families. Numerous studies have chronicled the tragic consequences of excessive drinking in the saloon period, including familial neglect, violence, poverty, disease, and death. Less certain, however, is whether young children tried to retrieve saloongoing parents as routinely as the temperance movement claimed. At least such stories did form an important part of the exoteric (i.e., outsiders') folklore about the saloon, widely embraced by teetotalers.[28]

So well known, in fact, was this antisaloon cliché of drunken father and pleading daughter that it eventually became the object of parody in vaudeville skits. As Sigmund Spaeth has noted, "The pathetic story . . . is hard to take seriously, and a burlesque performance is the usual result." Unfortunately for temperance advocates, these vaudeville parodies may have influenced some young minds more than the sober original. Among his schoolmates in Milwaukee in the late 1910s, for example, John Powers recalled, "The joke was, somebody would speak in the little girl's voice, all high and nasal, 'Is my daddy in here?' And then the same guy would say in a deep, gruff voice: 'Keep away from them swingin' doors, little girl!'" Stevens confided that he was secretly titillated rather than terrorized as a child when he heard a revivalist preacher describe "angel-faced little girls . . . getting struck down by the bottles the lost souls were always throwing at one another." As he later confessed, "I was always and forever catching myself in the wish that I could see one of these Saloon Hells myself."[29]

Another errand bringing children into saloons was that of selling newspapers. Many saloonkeepers purchased a paper for their patrons' use, though customers often wanted their own copies. For newsboys, this sales opportunity in itself made the saloon appealing, but there were other attractions as well. "Whenever we went into Louie Inzio's saloon, it was an experience, at least for me," recalled Powers, who accompanied a seven-year-old friend on his newspaper rounds in Milwaukee in 1915. He remembered vividly the strange beer smells, the sawdust on the floor, and the big men slouching against the bar with one foot on the rail. What impressed him most, however, was the men's kindness. "They were real nice to us kids, you know, and they always had something to say—kidding us, or some such thing as that. And of course they always tipped." For every three-cent copy of the *Milwaukee Journal* the newsboy sold, two cents went to the dealer and one he got to keep. An additional penny received as a tip meant his earnings were doubled. Other customers on his rounds might also tip, but Powers's friend could always count on the men in Louie Inzio's saloon to come through.[30] Thus, whether hawking newspapers, rushing growlers, or just peering under the swinging doors, children were often glad of the opportunity to see the interior of a saloon for themselves with its curious odors, boisterous banter, and intriguing glimpses of adult male comportment.

As boys in working-class districts approached adolescence, they tended to band together into clubs or gangs that in many ways presaged the regular crowd of the barroom. Some gangs were criminally inclined, but most were merely circles of friends who took part in the "street corner society" of the tenement districts. As Raymond Calkins observed, "Nearly every boy in all our cities has his club of intimate friends . . . familiarly called 'the gang' or 'the push;' and these clubs all taken together form the source of that great stream which a few years later fills the saloon." The single greatest problem confronting these boyhood gangs was to find a meeting place where they could indulge in their favorite pastimes without fear of harassment from police, truant officers, or well-meaning reformers. "Driven about the street like dogs. . . ," Royal Melendy observed, "they have recourse to but one of two alternatives: to dodge the police, hiding in underground caves and under sidewalks . . . or to enter the places the saloon has provided for them." Not surprisingly, a considerable number of teenage gangs were quick to establish their headquarters in saloon back rooms. These were often equipped with card tables, gymnastic apparatus, pool and billiard tables, and sometimes even a small bowling alley or handball court. The only catch, of course, was the five-cent beer that everyone was expected to consume from time to time, but this was hardly a burden to the boys.[31]

Unfortunately, some saloon-based gangs did constitute a menace to the surrounding neighborhood. Riis noted the unsavory connection between certain New York saloons and some of the city's worst gangs, including the Rag Gang, the Stable Gang, and the Short Tail Gang. In his words, "By day they loaf in the corner-groggeries on their beat, at night they plunder the stores along the avenues, or lie in wait at the river for unsteady feet straying their way." Sometimes gangs were even known to turn on their former hosts, as in the case of one New York saloonkeeper who was attacked and robbed by a group he had formerly counted among his patrons.[32]

Occasionally, boys' gangs were "redeemed" from saloon back rooms, as in the case of the "Keybosh Club" retrieved by the Northwestern Settlement House in Chicago in the late 1890s. The Keybosh Club was a gang of teenagers whose principal pastimes were playing billiards, making jokes, and speculating about girls. The significance of the unusual name of this club is obscure, but it might have been derived from the expression "to put the kibosh on," meaning "to put out of action; to squelch, especially by violent means; to beat up someone; to quash, cancel, or eliminate." Whatever the case, the Keybosh Club came to the attention of Harry Ward, head of the Northwestern Settlement. Ward opened up a room adjoining the settlement house, furnished it with a billiard table, and encouraged the boys to gather there and do all the things they ordinarily did in the saloon back room, except drink. In time, Ward also encouraged them to take themselves more seriously, hold regular "business meetings," and invite speakers to discuss current social and political issues.[33]

The strategy worked, for the members of the Keybosh Club themselves appear to have regarded as salutary their transformation from a saloon to a settlement club. As one member remarked, "We used to think and talk of nothing but the girls, crack jokes, and plan how to have a good time. Now we have something serious to talk about." Yet, while the results of this and other settlement projects for boys were encouraging, reformers conceded that most boys' clubs met at the settlement only one night a week. Where they went on other nights can be left to the imagination.[34]

As boys entered their late teens and early twenties, they themselves sometimes voluntarily withdrew from saloons—for a time at least—to form what were known as "pleasure clubs." An intermediate stage between the adolescent's gang and the adult's fraternal lodge, the pleasure club was a group of about twenty-five to fifty young men for whom athletic competitions, parties, and young women had now become life's most worthwhile attractions. They frequently adopted playful and outlandish names. In New York, for instance, club names included the Limburger Roarers, the Round-Back Rangers, and the East Side Crashers. These social groups were extremely popular and numerous in urban areas. In Philadelphia in 1899, for example, there were approximately 700 such clubs, and in Cincinnati nearly 1,000. Some met in saloons, though many others preferred to club their resources and rent their own modest meeting room which they could decorate with their chosen pictures, flags, and bunting. There they could loaf about in privacy or invite their girlfriends (or occasionally prostitutes) for parties and amateur talent exhibitions. Saloonkeepers did not have to concern themselves overmuch with the boys' defection, however, for they knew from experience that the pleasure club phase in a young man's life would not last forever.[35]

MARITAL STATUS

"Wedding bells are breaking up that old gang of mine" went the Tin Pan Alley hit of 1929, but this song might well have been written for pre-1920s pleasure clubs as members entered their twenties and began to marry. Such clubs were, after all, a function of the age and drives of the pleasure-seekers who formed them, young men whose primary interests in life were carefree carousing and courting the girls. At marriage, these interests changed, or were supposed to change, so that wife, children, and family relations now became major factors in a man's life, and the support of family his primary obligation. He still sought the company of his fellows, but his priorities had changed from looking for women and excitement to looking for mature friendships and relaxation. There were always those few married men, of course, who would not admit that the party was over, as well as a significant number who remained bachelors and continued to court and carouse. In most cases, however, when young men reached a certain level of maturity and responsibility, and especially when they settled into marriage, the pleasure club died a natural death.[36]

While willing to relinquish the pleasure clubs of youth, many men still felt the need for some form of clublife better suited to their needs.

To belong to a regular crowd of the saloon was club enough for most, though some men also pursued personal interests by joining more specialized groups. One common form of men's organization was the political club, which frequently constituted the basic building block of political machines such as Tammany Hall in New York. Such clubs almost invariably met in saloons, the proprietor himself often being a prominent figure in local ward politics. Trade unions also held their meetings in saloons. This was partly because workingmen naturally gravitated to these places, and partly because no other "respectable" places such as hotels or civic halls would host the then much despised unions. Fraternal, ethnic, and benevolent societies, though often officially dedicated to temperance, found it difficult to enforce this principle when their members were meeting in the rent-free rooms connected with saloons. In addition to clubs with weighty political, economic, and social objectives, there were others conceived in a lighter vein, such as the music and singing clubs especially popular among saloongoing German, Polish, and Danish immigrants. Thus, any married man with a stake in his community and a desire to participate in its affairs was almost inevitably drawn into saloons which played host to nearly every political, labor, fraternal, ethnic, and social organization that a workingman might care to join.[37]

Not all married men were saloongoers, of course. Those with ambitions for upward mobility (with the notable exception of the politically ambitious) sometimes regarded saloonlife as a waste of time, in the spirit of work-ethic apostle Horatio Alger. He maintained that if a man "wanted to succeed in life. . . , he must do something else than attend theatres and spend his evenings in billiard saloons." Also mindful of their time and money were a number of married immigrants who came to this country alone to earn their fortunes and hoped to return to their homelands as quickly as possible. Other non-saloongoers were simply dedicated family men who believed in devoting their full earnings to the well-being of their dependents, as in the case of one father who assured his four young daughters that "all his nickels was for us."[38]

In some cases it was the workingman's wife who wooed her husband away from the saloons by various means. In interviews with the housewives of Homestead, a grim and grimy steel mill community of 25,000 near Pittsburgh, Margaret Byington discovered in 1910 that "thoughtful women are especially conscious that part of the responsibility for keeping the men away from the saloons belongs to them." One housewife's strategy against the barrooms was to strive to keep her home comfortable and herself attractive no matter how hard her day had been. In this way, her husband would not be like "the man next door who was always going off to Pittsburgh 'on a lark.'" Another housewife planned informal card games at home, even though she thought it immoral. Otherwise, she feared that "her husband who was fond of playing would be tempted to go to the back rooms of the saloons for his entertainment," and to her, "the drink evil was the more serious."[39]

Other wives more tolerant of drink might have tried to beat the saloon by joining their husbands in a glass of beer at home. Frank Norris suggested this possibility in his 1899 novel, *McTeague*. For Trina McTeague, in fact, this was not just a concession to her husband, but actually part of an overall effort at reform. "She broke him of the habit of eating with his knife; she caused him to substitute bottled beer in the place of steam beer," wrote Norris. "McTeague no longer spent an evening at Frenna's. Instead of this he brought a couple of bottles of beer up to the rooms and shared it with Trina." Among married men, then, devotion to family might act as a restraining influence on their saloongoing proclivities.[40]

Unattached men, on the other hand, were of course freer to indulge themselves in any manner they saw fit, with the result that they frequently outdid their married peers in the matter of drinking, spending, and carousing in saloons. As Byington noted of Homestead and neighboring industrial communities, the men whose budgets were most taken up by liquor were "the unattached ones, who are the constant tipplers in all towns."[41]

Lone "tipplers" were numerous in the late nineteenth and early twentieth centuries for several reasons. Owing to the large number of male immigrants entering the country unmarried or unaccompanied by their wives, males outnumbered females in several major cities. In Chicago, for example, the ratio of males to every hundred females was 103.4 in 1900, 106.3 in 1910, and 102.9 in 1920. The imbalance was even more striking in San Francisco, where the ratio was 117.1 in 1900, 131.6 in 1910, and 116.6 in 1920. Among some ethnic groups, the preponderance of males was strikingly high. As Timothy Gilfoyle notes, "From 1880 to 1910. . . , 80 percent of the Italians arriving in New York City were male." Further, the proportion of unmarried men in the general population was large, even though there was an increasing tendency for men to marry as the twentieth century progressed. Among males fifteen years of age and older (that is, males of saloongoing age), the percentage of singles was 40.2 percent in 1900, 38.7 percent in 1910, and 35.1 percent in 1920.[42]

During the saloon period, therefore, there was not only a preponderance of males in some urban areas, but also a great number who had neither wives nor families to provide meaningful social contacts and emotional support. In the absence of any real homelife, the camaraderie of barlife was especially appealing to these solitary fellows in lodging houses and tenements. As John Koren observed, the saloon did much to compensate for "the lack of social opportunity which, of course, the unmarried man feels more commonly." In fact, some saloons were almost exclusively patronized by these bachelors, as evidenced by Koren's discovery of urban bars in which virtually all the regulars were over thirty and single. Further, as Thomas Babor and Barbara Rosenkrantz's research has shown, the "prototypical problem drinker" of the late nineteenth century was "a middle-aged, single, unskilled, beer-drinking, foreign-born male." Unmarried saloongoers were perhaps outnumbered but hardly outdone by their wedded counterparts in the barrooms of industrializing America.[43]

For many workingmen—married or unmarried—saloongoing was a lifelong avocation. When a regular did pass on, his fellows might observe the sad event in a number of ways. Among the Irish in Chicago, it was customary after a wake for the male mourners to assemble in a neighborhood barroom and become boisterously intoxicated in honor of the deceased. In Washington, D.C., meanwhile, a departed regular's memory was honored in one case by the placing of black crepe on the door of his favorite saloon. Perhaps the most flamboyant example was the jazz funeral in New Orleans, a tradition especially prevalent in the African-American community. After assembling at a neighborhood saloon, mourners solemnly followed the hearse and a marching band out to the cemetery for the burial. Then they burst into a joyous dancing parade on the way back to the barroom where prodigious amounts of drink, food, and music helped the group celebrate the life of the departed. Thus, even in a regular's old age and beyond, the saloon had its role to play.[44]

From childhood to cemetery, workingmen's lives were touched at many points and in many ways by the ubiquitous and versatile saloon. Whatever the drinking styles and social objectives of particular saloongoers, however, all were similar in that their eligibility for membership in the poor man's club began when they could first competently drink down a beer, and ended only when the big black carriage came and took them away.

A SYMPATHETIC COMPANY OF PEERS

Throughout America's industrializing era, working-class saloons provided gendered space where male peer groups coalesced and thrived. Whether married or single, middle-aged or teen-aged, male bargoers devoted much energy and time to cultivating saloonmate solidarity. What does this say about male-female relations and the saloon's impact on them? Why did bargoers so often opt for the company of men rather than women?

It is important to note at the outset that very few working-class men embraced the notion of "companionate marriage." This middle-class ideal, growing in acceptance through the nineteenth century, mandated that the husband-wife relationship should be a balanced partnership founded on mutual respect and shared emotion. "Marriage partners had once been chosen by parents, whose main considerations were wealth, prestige, and political power," as Suzanne Lebsock notes. "Companionate marriage, however, was for love," so that "emotion moved to the center." Both spouses still had their separate spheres, his the public realm of work and politics and hers the private world of home and family. Many middle-class men also belonged to civic organizations and private clubs which absorbed some of their leisure hours. But husbands were now expected to devote a greater portion of their time and attention to wives and homelife, and the emphasis was on interdependence and complementarity. "The new, companionate ideal of marriage was one based on sympathy, affection, esteem, friendship, and mutual obligation, as opposed to the hierarchical mode of traditional marriage," explains Nancy Woloch.[45]

In traditional marriage, the husband-wife relationship was asymmetrical and patriarchal, with emphasis on male prerogative and female subservence. The separation of spheres was unmitigated by notions of husbands' obligations to share with wives the charms and challenges of domestic life. Husbands might choose to stay home evenings, but it was not their particular duty to do so. Most working-class men, whether anticipating or already participating in matrimony, embraced this older conception of traditional marriage. As long as husbands provided financially for their dependents and occasionally imposed the necessary familial discipline, they felt entitled to venture out in their leisure hours. A study of workingmen in New York City in 1913 found that the majority spent about half their leisure time away from families. Some groups, including less-skilled workers and certain immigrants such as the Irish, English, and Italians, were away much more. When they ventured out, they often headed for their favorite saloons.[46]

Indeed, it appears that many working-class men sought the companionate ideal not in marriage, but in male peer groups. What better words could describe the saloongoers' relationship than Nancy Woloch's describing companionate marriage: "sympathy, affection, esteem, friendship, and mutual obligation"? While most middle-class men were striving to cultivate a sense of commonality with their wives, working-class bargoers were meeting most of their companionate needs within what Raymond Calkins called the "distinct, compact, sympathetic company of men" in saloons.

Was this a bad thing, this opting for the homosocial world of saloons instead of the heterosocial world of families? Many contemporary observers deplored the practice. "Saloons were often pictured by Prohibitionists and middle-class women as competitors to home and family," as Jon Kingsdale observes. Reformers endeavored "to curb the self-assertive, boisterous masculinity of the saloon, to support and protect the family, and to return the husband—immigrant workingmen in particular—to the home." Working-class wives also criticized and feared husbands who overindulged in the saloon's wares, squandered desperately needed wages, and returned home belligerent and violent. In the words of Elsa Marek, an immigrant wife in New York City, some husbands went to saloons "and they started yelling there and getting drunk and come home and the children cry, there was no money, then they start fighting." Yet it must be acknowledged that the majority of saloon regulars did not engage in antisocial or pathological behavior such as habitual drunkenness, wife abuse, or child neglect. Some did, and their behavior was of course indefensible. But to paint all saloongoers with the drunkard's brush is both a distortion and a tiresome cliché.[47]

Most workingmen chose to use the saloon for purposes *they* regarded as legitimate, positive, and even necessary. Men valued gendered space free of heterosexual tensions. They also valued "male culture," just as women valued "female culture" and "female space."[48] The saloon's social ambience answered a need among workers for emphatic reaffirmation of their identity and worth as men. It also reflected and reinforced the working-class version of the doctrine of separation of spheres. Some no doubt came to saloons to get away from wives; some might also have been getting even with them. But to deem all saloongoing irresponsible, as many reformers did, was to miss the point. As bargoers saw it, they had two social responsibilities: their families and their peers. Family support and love were important, but so were peer group honor and esteem. Some may have neglected one for the other, but most tried to strike a balance.

"The average workaday mortal craved, in the evening, a hearty recognition of his merits as a man," remarked George Ade, as well as "lively intercourse with persons of his own social rating, bantering conversation, laughter and song. The saloon naturally attracted a lot of regulars."[49] Linked by ties of gender, age, and marital status, saloongoers cultivated a companionate ideal they deemed requisite to the good life.

Three

Occupation, Ethnicity, and Neighborhood

> [M]en naturally associate according to their own cliques or affilia-
> tions. . . . There are whole blocks of saloons which appeal to men of a
> single nationality. Or the bond that unites them may be their occupa-
> tion, as indicated by the names "Mechanics' Exchange" or "Milkmen's
> Exchange.". . . Politics may be the common bond. . . . In Chicago, one
> saloon is known as "The Democratic Headquarters of the Eighteenth
> Ward.". . . Thus the strongest ties which unite men are effectually used
> by the saloon.
> —Raymond Calkins[1]

Workingmen were understandably selective when it came to the drinking company with whom they shared their few precious leisure hours. With dozens of urban saloons to choose from, they tried to find the best "fit." In the seventeen cities Raymond Calkins surveyed in 1901, he found that workers sought barmates with a similar stake in occupational matters, ethnic heritage, and neighborhood affairs. Subsequent saloon scholars have confirmed the importance of these factors.[2] Along with gender identity, age group, and marital status, they constituted the principal criteria for comradeship in urban saloons.

In examining the occupational, ethnic, and neighborhood ties linking the regulars, the commingling of communal and market concerns in saloonlife is once again strikingly evident. On a personal level, workers cultivated bonds of friendship and mutuality based on the similarity of their livelihoods, national heritages, and local acquaintanceship networks. At the same time, many workers used their saloons as staging grounds for all manner of practical, self-interested goals in the marketplace. Occupational ties became the basis for union organizing, ethnic ties gave rise to immigrant aid societies, and neighborhood ties fostered the growth of ward-based political organizations. Thus, whether workers sought simply sympathetic company or more organized activity or both, the saloon was their connection.

OCCUPATION

The working-class status of most saloongoers greatly promoted customer solidarity in barrooms. Laborers spent a significant share of their day at the workplace, shifts of ten or more hours being typical. Though many men held jobs in smaller workshops and businesses which peppered the tenement districts, a growing number became employees in large factories where they encountered increasing workplace regimentation, specialization, and depersonalization. Difficult though these circumstances were, many laborers still found solace in the company of their co-workers. Even the very disagreeableness of factory labor—the long hours, the hated foreman, the shared personal problems resulting from low wages and poor working conditions—drew workers together. This is not to minimize the divisive effects of job competition, ethnic prejudices, gender conflicts, religious differences, and other alienating factors so often bemoaned by union organizers. Nonetheless, judging from saloon patronage at least, a common bind often produced a common bond.[3]

The relentless timetable of the industrial marketplace produced definite waves and peaks of saloon patronage during an average workweek and on a typical workday. The weekly cycle began spectacularly on paydays—Saturdays for many laborers—and then progressively declined until week's end, when it began anew. As one New York saloonkeeper noted, "[F]rom morning to midnight Saturday my bar was continually wet." By Thursday, however, "Vest pockets and stocking feet were being emptied of their 'chicken feed'; the week's earnings were exhausted. Then came Saturday and Sunday again, with fresh money."[4]

Many temperance advocates, particularly Protestant evangelicals, objected vehemently to saloons doing business on the Sabbath and pushed for closing laws on that day. However, like so many other unpopular temperance measures, the Sunday ordinances were widely flouted. Many immigrants did not share the American Protestant pre-occupation with maintaining a sober Sabbath and regarded the never-on-Sunday rule as unfair and unreasonable. In Chicago, for example, many looked upon the law as an "ethnic insult," according to Perry Duis, and reformers' attempts to enforce it were met by widespread evasion and occasional street protests. Further, workers laboring ten or more hours a day, six days a week, considered it their right to spend their one day off as they chose. As Roy Rosenzweig has noted, sa-loongoers in Worcester, Massachusetts, consistently ignored the Sun-day closing ordinance, asserting "their right to use their leisure time for 'what we will,' even if that meant drunkenness." From the saloon-keeper's standpoint, his Sunday operation was merely a response to a cyclical demand determined by others. It was unfortunate, per-haps, that Sundays followed Saturdays, but from the purely practical viewpoint of the saloon proprietor, "I was compelled to run Sundays to live." [5]

Another difficulty with Sunday drinking was that some workers then invoked the longstanding tradition of "Saint Monday," accord-ing to which they were entitled to slow down or skip work on Mon-days to nurse their hangovers and perhaps indulge in a few more drinks. This tradition of "Saint" or "Blue" Monday had been wide-spread in America since the colonial period. Benjamin Franklin lamented in 1768 that "Saint *Monday* is as duly kept by our working people as *Sunday;* the only difference being that instead of employing their time cheaply at church they are wasting it expensively at the ale house." Monday absenteeism, as well as casual drinking on the job, were holdovers from preindustrial days when men were able to exer-cise more control over the pace and progress of their own workday. [6]

By the late 1890s, however, the workers' "Saint Monday" tradition finally gave way under pressure not only from employers, but also from union leaders who argued that drunkenness and absenteeism undermined the cause of organized labor. "I can well remember when there could be found in no city, from Sunday until Tuesday or Wednesday of the following week, any tailors who were sufficiently sober to work at their trade, or if any, they were very few," remarked John B. Lennon of the Journeymen Tailors Union of America. By the twentieth century's turn, however, he observed, "You can now go to the same cities where our unions have existed . . . and you will scarcely find a single member of the organization that is an habitual drunkard." Similarly, as Edward W. Bemis of the New York Bureau of Economic Research concluded in 1900, "It used to be said that carpenters, cigar-makers, iron-workers, printers, shoemakers, and tailors were always drunk on Mondays. Such a remark is now rarely heard." Most workers gradually accepted the rigid division of labor from leisure hours and now confined their heaviest drinking to Saturday nights, though some still clung tenaciously to their right to drink copiously on the Sabbath as well.[7]

The daily routine of saloon business was greatly influenced by the schedules of nearby factories. According to one New York proprietor, "My saloon, like all the others in that vicinity, was opened at five in the morning" when the bartender was occupied with "cleaning the place, washing dishes and rinsing glasses," and, as the morning continued, "waiting on the early customers." In many establishments, these first patrons of the day were either workers seeking a quick bracer before their morning shifts, or retired or unemployed laborers cut adrift from the bustling world of work outside. More interested in straight shots than sociability, this "parade of Early Birds," as George Ade described them, "came one at a time and partook without delay or ceremony."[8]

At noontime, however, patronage picked up as workers flocked to saloons for the free lunch. In an establishment on New York's East Side in the early 1900s, for example, bartender M. E. Ravage stated, "At the noon-hour, a gang of workmen from a near-by 'job' will trudge in in their heavy boots and grimy overalls to devour a plate of free soup and innumerable hunks of bread with their schooner of beer." Growler (bucket) sales were also heavy to men who remained at the job site to consume beer from the saloon and lunches from home. "One saloon, of which I know," observed Melendy in Chicago in 1901, "sold ninety gallons [of beer] every noon to men in a factory and to a railroad gang that was working near." After the peak lunchtime hours, patronage fell off but by no means ceased. "There was a great deal of transient trade all through the daytime," one New York proprietor observed, "especially from teamsters who passed our place, and came in to get a drink or a cigar, while their horses got their fill of water at the trough outside."[9]

At changes of shifts and at closing time in local industries, saloons also did a brisk business. As an 1891 editorial in a Worcester, Massachusetts, publication stated, "Watch the 'dinner pail' brigade as it files down, at nightfall, from the shops north of Lincoln Square and see how many men and boys drop into the saloons along the north end of Main Street." In New York in 1899, Bowery district saloons also served as "a 'half-way' stopping place where, over a schooner of beer, the men talk over their work of the day and plan for the evening," settlement worker Raymond Spaulding noted. "At nightfall these places are thronged four or five deep along the bar." The same spectacle occurred in the vicinity of the Chicago stockyards. "Around that long and dismal stockade, at every hole from which a human being can emerge, a shop or group of shops sits waiting," remarked George Turner in 1907. At quitting time, even the most exhausted or abstinence-pledged workingman found saloons hard to avoid or resist.[10]

After a meal at home, in a lodging house, or in a cheap restaurant, many men returned to their favorite barrooms for an evening of moderate drinking and socializing with their fellows. Nighttime patronage was common in establishments catering to immigrant workers such as Italians, Poles, and Hungarians. "During working hours these places are half empty," observed Calkins in 1901, "but they fill up rapidly in the evening, when they do their best trade." Yet southern and eastern Europeans were by no means the only nighttime patrons. Among many German, Irish, and native-born American families in turn-of-the-century New York, for example, the "husband comes home at night, has his dinner, and goes out with the 'men,'" according to a contemporary observer. Many working-class wives resented the saloon's competition for their husbands' free hours and discretionary income, and middle-class reformers universally deplored the practice. Certainly it was true that evening saloongoing could result in familial discord and fiscal (not to mention physical) harm. On the other hand, many workingmen exercised more restraint in monetary outlay than reformers gave them credit for. From reports on workers' household budgets in South Chicago, New York City, and Homestead, Pennsylvania, for example, it appears that a customary practice among many married men was to turn over the majority of their weekly earnings to their wives, saving out only a modest, regularly budgeted drinking allowance for themselves.[11]

How late at night the barroom remained open depended greatly on the proprietor's inclination to accommodate customer demand. Municipal regulations often set official closing times, but in New York, Chicago, and many other major cities, these laws were easily flouted by proprietors in good standing with local ward officials and the police. Ade noted that some Chicago saloons "had not been closed for a single minute for years and years." Yet it appears that most establishments did not go in for all-night operations since their wage-earning customers, facing early wake-up calls, did not demand it. Thus, for both proprietors and patrons, it was the workplace regimen, rather than temperance-inspired regulation, which was generally the most decisive factor regarding closing time. This was usually not much later than the midnight hour, though of course the same establishments opened again bright and early the next morning.[12]

Payday, however, was another matter. The Saturday payday celebration was the social highlight of the week for many workers. For some, it approached the character of ritual. "One bricklayer, a man earning good wages, on coming home Saturdays, always provided liberally for his family. Then, his mind free of that responsibility, he would issue forth, dressed in his best clothes, and go on a 'glorious drunk,'" a New York proprietor remarked of one of his customers. "He would return late Sunday night or early Monday morning, with not a cent left. This was his practice, regular as clockwork." Some workers invited their wives or girlfriends to join them in back-room drinking frolics, and saloonkeepers sometimes encouraged such payday parties by hiring musicians and sponsoring dances. For the majority of men, however, the Saturday-night saloon bash was an all-male rite during which they crowded together along the bar to indulge in a riotous communal binge.[13]

The phenomenon of the communal binge dates back to the colonial period when, according to W. J. Rorabaugh, there were two principal styles of alcohol consumption: dram drinking and binge drinking. With dram drinking, the imbiber consumed small amounts of alcohol in almost ritual fashion throughout the day, to accompany such actions as arising from bed, taking meals, completing daily tasks, and retiring for the night. This drinking by drams fit easily into the preindustrial pattern of life in which people's work and leisure hours were not sharply differentiated. Binge drinking was more a periodic public ritual in which imbibers drank to intoxication, often at such events as local elections, militia exercises, and feast days. As the nineteenth century progressed, the custom of dram drinking became ever less common, while binge drinking—communal or solitary—became more frequent. The communal binge, Rorabaugh maintains, had a special ideological significance for drinkers in the postrevolutionary era, symbolizing their new-found feelings of personal liberty and independence as well as their deeply felt need for unity in the new nation. Further, the alternating pattern of abstinence and binges was well suited to the rising market economy of the 1830s in which work and leisure time were increasingly compartmentalized.[14]

The persistence of the communal binge pattern after 1870 was a logical and perhaps inevitable consequence of the worsening economic and social dislocations attending the advent of large-scale industrialization. In its way, the binge was a form of protest and rebellion, albeit inchoate and unfocused. Workers asserted their bid for independence and their right to spend their time and money as they pleased, without attempts by employers, wives, or others to restrain or reform them. Most significant, the payday spree was evidence of the workers' impulse to turn to one another when faced with similar adversities and to counteract alienation by cultivating a sense of community among themselves.[15]

This impulse toward fellowship was also evident during workers' soberer moments in saloons. In establishments catering to those working at the same occupation and often at the same job site, saloongoers reinforced ties of labor solidarity by discussing their workdays, comparing experiences, and swapping tales of the trade. Saloonkeepers, to attract a loyal and steady clientele, frequently encouraged the growth of such occupational bonds among customers by choosing such bar titles as the "Mechanics' Exchange" and the "Stonecutters' Exchange."[16]

Increased employment opportunities were an important side benefit of this tendency of workers in the same occupation to gather together. Employers seeking skilled men for hire had only to inquire at the appropriate saloon. More often, however, workers learned of job openings from other regulars. A New York bargoer explained that "the fellows just kind of talk about jobs when they're sitting 'round in the saloons, and sometimes you pick something up." In his nationwide survey in 1901, Calkins concluded that workingmen everywhere were making use of saloons as informal employment bureaus. "A man out of employment does not go to the charity organization society, but to his club saloon," he noted. "Information concerning positions is gathered by the men themselves and is made common property." In addition to being of practical help to the man out of work, barmates and the club atmosphere they created offered him much-needed moral support. As John Koren observed in 1899, "[A]t the saloon he rids himself, for the time at least, of the horrible sense of isolation which weighs heavily upon workingmen who are in honest search of employment."[17]

As a congregating place where men shared occupational ties and met on a regular basis, the saloon constituted a natural headquarters for labor organizing and union meetings. Some establishments, in fact, catered exclusively to members of unions. H. L. Mencken recalled that his father, a conservative businessman, "avoided very diligently a saloon a bit up the street kept by one William Ruth, for over its door hung a sign reading *Union Bar*." (This same Ruth, incidentally, was the father of "the imperishable Babe," noted Mencken.) Unions often met in the saloon back rooms. Of the sixty-nine union affiliates in Buffalo, New York, in the 1890s, for example, sixty-three utilized saloons for their meetings. "The hotels . . . do not want the man with the soiled clothes and the calloused hands in their rooms," as Melendy pointed out. "They are forced to meet in the saloons, or in rooms above." At the turn of the century, therefore, a great many union chapters assembled in saloons, including approximately 30 percent of the Brotherhood of Boiler Makers and Iron Shipbuilders, 50 percent of the Wood Carver's Association, 75 percent of the Amalgamated Wood Workers, and nearly 100 percent of the United Brewery Workers.[18]

Whether workers assembled in their saloons for union meetings, shoptalk gatherings, or payday binges, on one thing they could rely: their employers would not be joining them. Most bourgeois bosses strongly disapproved of working-class barrooms and the drinking, criticizing, and organizing that took place there. For workers, on the other hand, their barroom gatherings—and their employers' disapproval and eschewal of them—served to strengthen their resolve to cultivate unity and defend their interests. Thus, saloongoing not only encouraged solidarity within particular occupational groups, but also reinforced the workers' sense of class identity.

ETHNICITY

Urban saloons catering to specific ethnic groups were the most exclusive and inwardly directed. In such establishments a shared ethnic tie was usually a necessary precondition for attaining regular status. The clienteles of such saloons were most often of European descent. This was partly because European nationalities dominated the massive waves of immigration to America from 1870 to 1920, and partly because European immigrants by 1890 were mostly settling in the urban-industrial areas. In contrast, Latin-American immigrants (mainly Mexicans) and Asian immigrants (mainly Chinese) were less numerous and tended to settle in the less urbanized areas of the Southwest and Far West. Still, those who did reside in the barrios and Chinatowns of the cities patronized drinking establishments catering specifically to their nationalities. Far more rural were Native Americans, most of whom in the late nineteenth century were either fighting for their land and their lives on the frontier or struggling to adapt to existence on isolated reservations. African Americans, too, were mostly concentrated in rural areas of the South, where alcohol was available mainly at general stores and roadhouses. Nevertheless, most major cities had long contained scattered black neighborhoods with black-run businesses like saloons. By 1900, these neighborhoods were expanding with the first stirrings of the "Great Migration" of rural blacks to the industrial cities. Regardless of the particular group served, however, saloons functioned like beacons in the storm for many urban newcomers seeking the solace of their countrymen.[19]

The flow of European immigration in the nineteenth century was continuous and heavy except for the brief interlude of the Civil War years. During the so-called "old immigration," lasting until about 1890, the majority of newcomers came from Germany, Ireland, England, Scandinavia, and other areas of northern and western Europe. Though these nationalities continued to arrive after 1890, the principal source of immigration then shifted to eastern and southern Europe, producing the "new immigration" of Italians, Slavs, Jews, and others. A great many of these newcomers came to American cities through the process of "chain migration." After a few early immigrants scouted the urban scene to find an acceptable working and living environment, they sent word overseas to family and friends to join them at that particular destination. Following one upon another like links in a chain, these transplanted kinsfolk and villagers clustered together in urban colonies and supported a variety of community institutions, including saloons.[20]

In Chicago, for instance, some sixteen separate "Little Italies" thrived between the 1850s and the 1920s, each established through its own chain of migration and each founding its own local institutions. According to Rudolph Vecoli's research, one Francesco Lagorio was the "founding father" of Italian immigration to the city in the

1850s, spearheading a settlement of Genoese on the Near North Side who for decades were "conspicuous as fruit peddlers, confectioners, saloon-keepers, and restaurateurs." So insular was the Genoese community that compatriots hailing from other regions of Italy, particularly the south, were not welcome in the Genoese streets, housing, or saloons. When Tuscan immigrants settled nearby, they established their own saloons, fruit stores, and other enterprises. Another chain of migrating Toscani, set apart by their passionate prosocialist and anticlerical beliefs, settled slightly westward in Cicero in 1910. Their little enclave of a few hundred residents supported a store and a saloon, but emphatically not a church. Still another group, Calabresi from southern Italy, settled in the southside district of Grand Crossing, where the nucleus of their community consisted of a handful of stores, a barbershop, and a saloon.[21]

These examples demonstrate the strong determination of regional groups of Italians to reconstitute their Old World communities in urban America. Further, they point up the role that saloons played in establishing ethnic territory and preserving cultural distinctiveness. For the first and second generations at least, most Genoese, Toscani, Calabresi, and other *paesani* in Chicago made a deliberate effort to live, work, worship, marry, and drink exclusively with members of their respective subgroups.

Although provincial antagonisms from the Old World persisted among many regional subgroups of Italians, Jews, Slavs, and other European immigrants, powerful forces in their new urban environment also brought them closer together. Estranged though they might start out, subgroups often found their similarities greater than their differences when confronted with other foreign- and native-born populations in the American city. They also discovered that other Americans tended to regard them as a monolithic group, even if they themselves did not. Further, it was sometimes in their best interests to cooperate as though they were a unified group in such ventures as labor unions, fraternal orders, and mutual aid societies.[22] As immigrants embarked on this gradual process of intragroup adjustment and exchange, the saloon once again had its role to play.

In the early 1900s, for example, many Croatian, Serbian, and Slovenian immigrants gravitated to South Chicago to work in the steel mills. These three Slavic groups had long regarded one another with hostility and disdain in the Old World. However, they soon discovered that Americans tended to lump them together and to treat them all with equal contempt. As a result, they began to band together and share many of the same institutions, most importantly the church and the saloon. The latter, according to William Kornblum, "served as the common house, the social and political meeting place, the bank, and the sometime funeral parlor for all the men and what few women were settled in the neighborhood."[23]

Antagonisms did not completely disappear, of course. As one Croatian resident remarked of the pre-1920s era, "You know all us Hunkies were always fighting, especially about what was going on in the old country." Yet he also acknowledged that saloons had helped to bring the warring elements of the community together. "You know old K———, the undertaker? Well his father ran one of the biggest taverns and boarding houses during immigration. They were Slovenians, but plenty of Croatians and Serbians lived there when they first came to South Chicago," he explained. "Lots of our parents and some of us kids had our weddings at his place. Now the son is burying the folks his dad married off." Serving as a focal point for the Slavic community from the beginning, this saloon both facilitated subgroup intermixing and promoted cultural continuity from one generation to the next. "There's still Croatian families who don't get along too well with the Serbians, but things aren't like they were," the Croatian observer concluded. "We'll back the same Hunky politicians, and even the church people are getting along better."[24]

Fraternal lodges and benefit societies meeting in saloon back rooms also encouraged immigrants to put aside Old World regional conflicts and devote their energies to cooperative effort. Thus, in Denver in the late nineteenth century, the Irish Fellowship Association, the Irish-American Progressive Organization, and the Ancient Order of the Hibernians all utilized saloons for both practical and pleasurable purposes. Similarly, in New York at the turn of the century, saloon parties and dances were frequently held by Russian, Polish, Italian, Irish, and German fraternal orders and social clubs. In this way, the saloon encouraged the community life of ethnic groups, offering them a place to cultivate feelings of shared identity and cultural integrity.[25]

A sense of ethnic solidarity also grew out of more informal, everyday barroom activities. Regarding drinking preferences, many Germans shared their longstanding taste for lager beer, while the Irish relished their whiskey, Italians and Jews called for wine, and Swedes

drank their traditional punch and aquavit as well as beer. Ethnic identities also found expression at the free lunch counter, where such
items as German *blut-wurst*, Irish stew, and Italian spaghetti proclaimed the national origins of proprietors and their clienteles.
Saloonkeepers often subscribed to newspapers printed in the native
languages of their customers. In Chicago, *L'Italia* was made available
to customers in Italian establishments, while *Svornost* and *Denni
Hlasatel* were frequently to be found in the barrooms of the Bohemian
district. When in a singing mood, immigrants might render "Ach du
lieber Augustin" in German saloons, "Wearin' of the Green" in Irish
places, or traditional folksongs accompanied by the tamburitza in
Slavic saloons. Immigrants also played games from their native lands.
In Boston, where card-playing was not permitted in barrooms, Italians engaged in a traditional game played with the fingers. Homeland
holidays were sometimes celebrated in saloons. In Irish places,
St. Patrick's Day was the occasion for an exuberant communal binge,
the saloonkeeper sometimes supplying appropriate decorations to increase the festive mood. During one such bash, vaudevillian Tom
Heath (of McIntyre and Heath) was "chased out" by the proprietor
"because he ate the shamrocks on the bar, thinking they were watercress," according to Ade. "He always insisted they were very good,
with mustard." Through a host of such social activities, immigrants
celebrated and revitalized their ethnic heritages in saloons.[26]

The ethnic saloonkeeper often functioned as a cultural magnet for
immigrants, attracting fellow countrymen and promoting the growth
of ethnic ties among regulars. The man behind the bar was in a position to provide valuable help to his clientele. He offered advice to
newcomers and passed along news of relatives and community members. These services as well as the reassuring presence of the saloonkeeper inspired considerable customer loyalty. Bar owners who did
not share the ethnic backgrounds of their clienteles often hired bartenders who did. Settlement worker Robert Woods observed that
while several saloons in Boston's North End were owned by Jews,
"Irish and Scandinavian bartenders are employed in them to draw in
the trade of the Irish and Scandinavians." Further, some ethnic community spokesmen, while wary of the temptations in saloons, also
acknowledged their importance as social centers for young people
who might otherwise grow away from their countrymen. "Would it
not be preferable," argued the Swedish newspaper *Skandinavia* in

Worcester, Massachusetts, in 1888, "to have our young men spend their time in a Scandinavian saloon as opposed to Irish, German, and American saloons, where they now spend their time?"[27]

In their observations on ethnic saloongoers, writers of the period often remarked on the relationship between cultural origins and bar behavior. Sometimes these remarks were complimentary. Ade, for example, referred to "quiet German places on the side streets" and spoke of the wide-open days in Chicago when he "took refuge among the law-abiding Germans." After conducting a field study of New York saloons in 1911, F. D. Laubach noted that Germans and Austrians generally ran respectable saloons. Similarly, John Koren praised German, Jewish, and Italian saloongoers for their overall sobriety.[28]

More often, however, the comments in the literature were thinly veiled ethnic slurs. The Irish, for example, were almost universally described as not only intemperate but temperamental as well. Koren reported that in Irish saloons there was "immoderate drinking and drunkenness in greater measure than any others." Ade remarked that "a couple of drinks never calmed down any good Fenian," especially if the British were mentioned. Similarly, Laubach described the Irish places in New York as "low" saloons, characterized by intemperance and vice. Derogatory comments were not limited to the Irish, however. Royal Melendy noted with disapproval the large number of saloons in the Bohemian district of Chicago; E. C. Moore remarked that the "non-intellectual, non-inventive oriental is devoted to gaming;" Francis Peabody warned that "the drunken Indian is a person it is well to avoid;" and Jacob Riis complained that among Italians the "women do . . . all the work" while the men loaf "in the open doors of the saloons smoking black clay pipes, talking and gesticulating." Thus, the barroom appears to have played a significant role in reinforcing (perhaps even creating) certain familiar ethnic stereotypes, especially those of a negative cast. In this regard, the saloon no doubt did considerable damage to the reputations and therefore the chances for upward mobility of these groups.[29]

No ethnic group suffered more, however, from their association with saloons and drink than African Americans in the South. Southern temperance advocates, like their northern counterparts, often stooped to vicious stereotyping. In a 1908 article in *Colliers*, for example, Will Irwin condemned "negro dives" such as George's Place and Caesar's Place in Shreveport, Louisiana. Their "reeking, filthy" atmosphere and cheap gin featuring "pictures of naked white women on the labels" were allegedly known "to stimulate the low passions" of the "black beast."[30] The provocative power of this stereotype of the drunken, lascivious black was tragically demonstrated in the race riot in Atlanta, Georgia, in 1906. White working-class bargoers, believing rumors of local black men's attacks on white women, "erupted from the city's saloons one Saturday evening and began chasing, beating, and killing innocent and defenseless Negroes," according to James Timberlake. "Before the mob was through, 19 Negroes had perished at its hands." As this example shows, the perceived link between saloon drinking and southern violence applied to whites as well as blacks. "It is realized that in any Southern community with a barroom," remarked Samuel Mitchell in 1909, "a race war is a perilously possible occurrence."[31]

If the saloon's role in aggravating interracial violence was worrisome, its role in promoting interracial fraternization was anathema to many observers in both the South and the North. "Both blacks and whites mix and mingle as a mass of degraded humanity in this cesspool of iniquity," asserted Alabama prohibitionist J. F. Clark of the racially mixed saloon. In New Orleans, establishments catering to interracial clienteles often seem to have combined the functions of barroom and bawdy house. "From Canal to Toulouse Streets virtually every building was a brothel," Herbert Asbury has written of the French Quarter in the 1880s, where "white women and Negresses crowded together indiscriminately and were patronized by men of all races and colors" under conditions "so bad as to be almost unbelievable." Asbury also noted the existence in the 1890s of at least one homosexual bordello-cum-barroom "to which both white and Negro men were invited." In New York City, meanwhile, Jacob Riis also deplored the "black-and-tan saloon" which he claimed "has always been the worst of the desperately bad."[32]

Thus, the twin specters of racial confrontation on the one hand and racial amalgamation on the other were deeply disturbing to many white spokesmen, particularly in the South. Andrew Sinclair argues that white southerners' fear of racial violence was the major reason why there was such widespread antisaloon, pro-prohibition sentiment in the region. In addition to racial motivations, Sinclair attributes the South's "dry" stand to the power of Baptists, Methodists, and fundamentalist sects, the relative lack of large industrial cities with "wet" immigrant populations and worldly attitudes, and the southern "cult of purity and white womanhood" which a drunken lower class, black and white, would threaten. For these various reasons, the South had far fewer licensed barrooms than the North. In fact, there were fewer saloons in the fifteen southern states taken together than there were in the city of Chicago at the turn of the century.[33]

The general store in the South sometimes filled in as a kind of informal saloon. In the early nineteenth century, general stores in rural areas all over the country had commonly sold liquor and doubled informally as taverns. By the turn of the twentieth century in the North, however, the commercial, brewery-backed saloon had taken over much of the liquor-selling activity (off-sale and on-sale) formerly handled by small stores and home-based kitchen enterprises. In the rural South, in contrast, small storefront operations had persisted.[34]

A rare glimpse into the nightlife in one such grocery catering to rural blacks is preserved in the records of the Virginia Anti-Saloon League Papers for 1905. This organization hired Bland's Detective Agency in Richmond to look into a report of illegal hard liquor sales at one Mr. Bagby's general store in the small town of Ellerson, Virginia. In the course of one Saturday evening, the detectives observed "a large number of colored men" who came in, bringing with them two pints of whiskey they had purchased in Richmond and also buying cider from Bagby. They then commenced "having a good time drinking cider, dancing, singing, and playing music" for the rest of the evening. According to the detectives, the black men in this establishment were convivial, not criminal, and there was nothing particularly unusual or reprehensible about their drinking behavior. This was in sharp contrast to the typical appraisal of blacks and drinking in the literature of the Anti-Saloon League and other temperance advocates.[35]

Further, the detectives' report makes it clear that Bagby's was serving as a surrogate saloon. The drinkers' code of reciprocity and communality clearly applied in this setting, the customers clubbing their resources—in this case, two pints of whiskey, a jug of cider, and their musical talents—toward the mutual pleasure of all. The code of the club was also evident in the proprietor's occasional offer to treat his customers to a free drink, and in his customers' offers to him as well. In the South, then, the saloon was perhaps suppressed in form, but not necessarily in spirit or substance.[36]

Like Bagby's customers, many rural blacks who migrated to cities in the early 1900s combined the delights of music and drink in their saloons. "Cabarets and nightclubs rose to preeminence as havens of excitement and exotic pleasure," notes Denise Herd, as migrants adopted "a new cultural image of liquor . . . complete with a folklore of heavy drinking and pleasure seeking." In this burgeoning barroom culture of African Americans in major cities like New Orleans, St. Louis, Chicago, and New York, music was a principal source of ethnic pride, identity, and good times. Here migrants from the Mississippi Delta, Texas, and other southern locales discovered one another's regional music traditions and created new combinations which appealed to a wide spectrum of the urban black populace.[37]

In their city barrooms, then, African Americans appear to have engaged in a process of intragroup adjustment similar to that which European Americans like Italians, Slavs and others were undertaking in their saloons. In both cases, the saloon functioned as incubator for an emerging culture which preserved elements of the past while simultaneously transcending longstanding regional differences. This process among blacks encompassed "not merely the emergence of the new, but the revitalization of the old," according to Lawrence Levine. "It has been a dual process of creation and re-creation, of affirmation and reaffirmation, of looking both without and within the black community for the means of sustenance and identity and survival." Thus, in the early twentieth century, the integration of musical heritages in black saloons helped impart a sense of community among formerly disparate subgroups.[38]

Although both races could be found in "black-and-tan" saloons, and whites (especially fans of blues and jazz) could occasionally be found in black saloons, it was very rare indeed to find a black man in a white saloon. This was owing in great measure to the hostility of whites, of course, who discriminated cruelly against blacks not just in the South, but in all parts of the country. In Chicago, for example, an Illinois civil rights law passed in 1885 ostensibly guaranteed all citizens access to public accommodations in that city. Custom and prejudice meant, however, that blacks who dared enter white saloons in Chicago were coolly received, often refused service, and occasionally caught up in violence. Similar circumstances prevailed in Denver and most other cities of the era.[39]

But these negative factors were only part of the reason why blacks rarely set foot in white barrooms. Just as European immigrants gravitated to saloons where they could find sympathetic fellow countrymen, so blacks, particularly those in northern industrial cities, were drawn to establishments where the clientele, bartender, and cultural atmosphere were familiar and supportive. Further, the black saloonkeeper often had influential business and political contacts in the African-American community. Regular customers in search of advice or favors could turn to him just as immigrants turned to their saloonkeepers in times of need. While blacks had good reason to avoid white saloons, then, they also had good reason to frequent black establishments run and patronized by members of their newly adopted communities.[40]

Thus, saloons were instrumental in enabling urban newcomers from foreign lands and America's hinterlands to preserve their premigration cultures in congenial surroundings. Many middle-class reformers were alarmed at the barroom's role in encouraging such ethnic pluralism. As temperance advocate John Barker asserted in 1905, "The saloon fosters an un-American spirit among the foreign-born population of our country," adding that the urban masses should abandon "any demoralizing custom" from the past, "assimilate American ideals" and embrace the dominant Anglo-American culture. Like many other native-born reformers, Barker was unmoved by the fundamental dilemma confronting all minorities: the urge to preserve a distinctive ethnic identity versus the desire to participate in the benefits of the larger American society. The saloon, by permitting minorities to perpetuate their distinctive folkways, was regarded as a serious impediment to achieving a virtuous, harmonious, and homogeneous America.[41]

Yet it is possible to speculate that saloons catering to ethnic clienteles did in fact facilitate assimilation in one respect. Barrooms were the scene of important intragroup adjustments among people with regional differences to reconcile. This process of adjustment, with its attendant lessons in tolerance, compromise, and social exchange, might be regarded as a first stage of integration in which ethnic subgroups redefined themselves as Italian Americans, Slavic Americans, and so forth. Even though such saloons tended to be exclusive and inwardly directed, they may ultimately have represented an early way station along the road to cultural accommodation and fuller participation in American society.[42]

NEIGHBORHOOD

Despite the efforts of ethnic groups to establish exclusive enclaves in cities after 1870, few maintained much more than a plurality in a local area much larger than one square mile. Instead, most working-class neighborhoods tended toward ethnic diversity and continual flux. This was owing to unending floods of newcomers, high rates of residential mobility, and the polyglot character of many nearby factories, marketplaces, schools, and other urban institutions. While some saloons continued to cater only to a particular ethnic group or subgroup, many more attracted a cross-section of the local populace. As Royal Melendy remarked, the local saloon was "an institution grown up among the people" and was "a part of the neighborhood," where "nationalities meet and mingle, and by the interchange of views and opinions their own are modified." Thus, the saloon provided a neighborhood center where male residents of various backgrounds could fraternize and swap views on local and national events.[43]

Some workers used saloons for organized political activity in their neighborhoods, forming political clubs which met periodically in the back rooms. "It is the exception to find the political clubs without a bar or some visible connection with the saloons," remarked Calkins in 1901. "For a great many of these clubs, it serves as the headquarters." Saloon proprietors, themselves often active figures in ward politics, encouraged these groups by offering meeting space free of charge. The main activity of the political clubs was to promote the election campaigns of neighborhood candidates affiliated with the city's political machine. Once in office, these men were expected to reward their neighborhood constituents with municipal jobs, peddlers' licenses, and other political favors. With the help of club members, politicians also sponsored seasonal balls and banquets in their host saloons to which the entire community, men and women, were usually invited. Most of the year, however, the political clubs were primarily utilitarian affairs. Their debates focused not on weighty philosophical issues, but rather on their candidates' election prospects and the practical assistance they could expect to win for themselves and their neighborhoods.[44]

In addition to offering political and social opportunity, the local saloon with its brewery-supplied amenities provided a vivid and refreshing contrast to the often deplorable physical conditions of urban working-class neighborhoods. Jacob Riis lamented in 1890 that "it is true, worse pity, that in many a tenement-house block the saloon is the one bright and cheery and humanly decent spot to be found." Certainly this was the impression conveyed in Edward Hopper's painting, *New York Corner (Corner Saloon)*, which critics praised in 1913 as "a perfect visualization of New York atmosphere." On a canvas otherwise gray and dismal with its depiction of hulking tenement barracks and towering factory smokestacks, there appears in the foreground a dazzling splash of color and festiveness emanating from the huge, elaborate sign adorning a saloon doorway. Similarly, in her study of Homestead, Pennsylvania, in 1910, Margaret Byington included a photograph entitled "Saloon Corner, Saturday Night," in which the bright, inviting lights of a local barroom dispel the nighttime gloom of an industrial neighborhood. As long as this startling contrast continued to exist, the saloon would persist, as frustrated reformers wearily acknowledged. In Riis's words, "It is a sorry admission to make, that to bring the rest of the neighborhood up to the level of the saloon would be one way of squelching it; but it is so."[45]

The clienteles of many saloons in workers' neighborhoods were both occupationally and ethnically diverse. In the Oakland and Benicia waterfront districts in California, for example, Jack London described saloons catering to longshoremen, fishermen, sailors, and day-laborers who were variously of Greek, Russian, Italian, and French descent. Similarly, a German bar owner in New York City reported, "The population in the neighborhood of my saloon . . . was made up of Irish and Germans in about equal parts, with a good-sized Italian section, and a few Americans thrown in." His ethnically diverse clientele included bricklayers, plasterers, marble-cutters, carpenters, furniture movers, teamsters, and a number of unskilled day-laborers. In another New York establishment, a Rumanian bartender employed by a German proprietor described how he mixed "kosher liquids" for Jewish regulars during Passover. Among this bartender's steady patrons were local merchants often accompanied by their customers, as well as a great variety of artisans and day-laborers, inspiring him to call his East Side saloon "one of the central meeting-places of humanity." It is worthy of note in this connection that Eugene O'Neill chose a 1912 saloon to be a symbol of humanity's crossroads in "The Iceman Cometh" (the same device later used by William Saroyan in "The Time of Your Life").[46]

To promote the loyalty of local residents toward his barroom, the saloonkeeper often extended special financial privileges to his steadiest customers. Many workingmen relied on saloonkeepers to cash their paychecks, with the understanding that they would purchase a drink or two to repay the favor. For example, a manufacturer in Joliet, Illinois, stated in 1908 that of the 3,600 paychecks his firm issued on one payday, 3,599 came back with a saloonkeeper's endorsement (the last one having been cashed in a grocery store selling liquor). It is probably true that this check-cashing custom was the cause of much unconscionable extravagance in saloons on payday. Yet it is also important to note that banks were usually located miles from the factory districts. Moreover, many workers, especially first-generation immigrants, found the stiff institutionalism of banks confusing and intimidating. As Peter Roberts noted in his 1904 study of coal-mining communities in Pennsylvania, the company "pays the laborer and the saloon serves a useful purpose by accommodating these men with change." Thus, the saloon in working-class areas acted as the poor man's bank.[47]

Saloonkeepers also permitted neighborhood regulars to establish a credit account or "tick" (short for "ticket"), an account which they were honor-bound to pay down as soon as they were able. In one Pennsylvania coal-mining town, for instance, Roberts asked a local proprietor what he did to encourage steady patronage. "His answer was, 'I keep good stuff, give good measure, keep a clean place and sell on tick.'" In saloon parlance, the privilege of drinking on credit was known as "getting trusted," a significant thing in the lives of the working poor. Further, a man temporarily short of cash could always treat his neighbors to a friendly round and thereby maintain his status in the community. Jack London recalled his intrigued reaction when he became aware of the credit book kept by the proprietor of the First and Last Chance Saloon in Oakland, California, in the 1890s. "At once I became possessed with a desire to have a page in that book," he remarked. At length he did achieve this coveted status symbol. "And I glimpsed, as through a golden haze, a future wherein that page would be much-charged, and crossed off, and charged again," he reminisced with pleasure. In the eyes of many reformers, this credit arrangement constituted an insidious trap to encourage extravagance and indebtedness. To the bargoing worker, however, the fact that "the saloonkeeper trusts him for drinks" represented both a privilege and "a debt of honor," as E. C. Moore observed.[48]

In addition to offering credit accounts, the saloonkeeper courted and rewarded the loyalty of his neighborhood customers with small loans. London described how he often turned to the proprietor of the Last Chance for loans "without interest, without security, without buying a drink." This was in sharp contrast to the only other place he knew to borrow money, his neighborhood barber shop. There he was charged 5 percent interest every month until the loan was repaid. "And yet—and here is the point, the custom and the code—in the days of my prosperity, after the lapse of years, I have gone out of my way by many a long block to spend across Johnny Heinhold's bar deferred interest on the various loans," he later recalled. "Not that Johnny Heinhold asked me to do it or expected me to do it. I did it, as I have said, in obedience to the code I had learned along with all the other things connected with John Barleycorn." Melendy noted a similar philosophy underlying the loans extended to neighborhood customers in Chicago saloons in 1900. "No questions are asked about the 'deserving poor;' no 'work test' is applied; and again and again relief is given in the shape of money, 'loaned expecting no return.'" But, of course, there was a return: the future patronage of a grateful customer.[49]

Saloonkeepers, particularly those with political ambitions, sometimes extended outright charity to destitute families in the neighborhood even if the recipients were not regular patrons of their saloons. In 1897, for example, Moody Morton, a printer by trade, learned of a desperately needy family in his area. Morton suggested to his wife and a family friend that they solicit help from the Associated Charities. The friend contended, however, that from the charity organizations they would receive "nothing but red tape and blanks and tracts and references," and added, "I'd rather call on a few saloon keepers. They'll do more and do it quick." Deciding to try both avenues, Mrs. Morton and her friend went to the Associated Charities while Mr. Morton approached several local merchants, including saloonkeepers. "So we separate, and the ladies have just the experience predicted," reported Morton, "while I secure . . . a sack of flour from one grocer, bacon and coffee from another, and money from several liquor dealers."[50]

The saloonkeeper's duty to act as the "poor man's friend" in his district was confirmed by a New York proprietor in 1909. "Whenever a case of distress became known in my neighborhood, it was to my place that the first appeal was made." On one occasion, he recalled, "A number of my patrons responded quickly and nobly to an appeal for help," combining their resources with the proprietor's to rescue a destitute neighborhood family. Through such charitable gestures, the barkeeper earned the gratitude of his community and encouraged neighborly cohesiveness among his customers.[51]

Often a political motive prompted the barkeeper's largesse toward his neighborhood regulars. In most urban areas, saloonkeepers depended on the goodwill of voters to elect sympathetic machine politicians, who in turn would fight temperance advocates attempting to restrict or shut down saloonkeepers. Politicians, once in office, depended on saloonkeepers (and the powerful liquor industry behind them) to contribute to their campaign coffers and to help deliver the saloon vote at election time. Saloongoing voters, meanwhile, depended on ward politicians to secure them jobs and licenses, bail them out of jail when necessary, and perform various other favors, as well as keep saloonkeepers in business by blocking passage and enforcement of temperance legislation.[52]

Saloons and politics were so thoroughly intertwined that many saloonkeepers themselves became machine politicians. For example, Michael "Hinky Dink" Kenna ran a Chicago barroom significantly called the "Workingmen's Exchange" and, with his partner "Bathhouse John" Coughlin, ran Chicago's first ward as well from the 1890s to the late 1930s. In that ward, saloonkeepers constituted 50 percent of the Democratic captains at the turn of the century. In New York, the Tammany machine also included a large number of barmen; in 1890, eleven of the twenty-four city aldermen were saloonkeepers. Similarly, in San Francisco, Christopher "The Blind Boss" Buckley conducted his business in the back room of the Alhambra Saloon, which was dubbed "Buckley's City Hall."[53]

Whether a professional politician or not, the saloonkeeper still occupied a pivotal position between the vote-seeking political machine and its liquor-industry allies on the one hand, and the working class with its need for municipal services and assistance on the other. "He knew the inside of things," as Travis Hoke observed, for "the breweries ran the politics of the town, hence he was close to important people and spoke mighty names with familiarity—especially before election, when a word from him was very much to the point." By brokering the interests of these groups in his own little corner of the urban scene, the proprietor of a local saloon could become a key figure in the social, political, and economic affairs of his community.[54]

Saloonkeepers were of course a varied lot. Some preferred to keep their operations small, informal, and neighborly. Others turned their establishments into veritable "reciprocity machines" in which drinks, favors, jobs, and votes were routinely and openly swapped. It was this latter group which particularly outraged the Anti-Saloon League and other temperance advocates. In their view, such favor-swapping saloonkeepers were not only peddling the poison of drink, but also perverting the political process and thereby imperiling the very survival of the republic. To workers in great need of small favors, however, the reciprocal arrangement between themselves and their neighborhood bartenders seemed both legitimate and indispensable.[55]

The Gateway to Comradeship

From this analysis of the linking factors of occupation, ethnicity, and neighborhood, it is clear that saloongoing did not represent a retreat from the outside world. On the contrary, the saloon was thoroughly entangled in the issues and events of the urban marketplace. It functioned as a labor bureau, an immigrant assistance center, and a neighborhood political base. The regulars' sense of commonality was due in large part to market forces acting upon their lives in similar ways. The marketplace did not stand outside of saloon culture; rather, it was an integral part of that culture.

Upon arriving in a city, a worker could approach the saloon as his point of entry into the social, economic, and political life of his new community. The barroom was a reliable place to locate congenial company among men who had already sorted themselves out according to their shared traits and interests. It might take more than one try. When Jack London and a friend "started out to select our saloon" in an unfamiliar part of downtown Oakland, for example, they immediately "voted against" one establishment's clientele on the basis of age and ethnic factors (too old, too German). Instead, they "made several more tries on succeeding nights, and at last found our way into the National" where the mix of linking factors was more appealing.[56]

Reinforcing this function of the saloon as stepping stone into the community was the standardized appearance of most establishments. Just as churchgoers in a strange city could enter expecting to find an altar, pews, statues, and stained-glass windows, so saloongoers everywhere could push through the swinging doors expecting to find a long hardwood bar, brass rails, mirrors, and displays of bottles and glasses.

This rough regularity among saloons, combined with the potential for fellowship they promised, makes it understandable why so many millions of workingmen found the "poor man's club" an attractive and useful entrée into urban life in the industrializing era.[57]

Equally as important as targeting a particular saloon for membership, however, was knowing how to behave once inside, how to cultivate friendships and participate in the activities of fellow customers. While each saloon crowd had its own special character reflecting the individuals who composed it, there was a discernible uniformity in all barroom behavior owing to longstanding folkways of drink culture. A prospective club member had to master this lore of the barroom, and particularly the art of clubbing, before he could realize the full potential of the saloon as the gateway to comradeship.

Part II

The Gentle Art of Clubbing

Four

Drinking Folkways

> As we stepped inside. . . , the great mirror shone gloriously, and at its
> base the glasses sparkled between the colored labels of the stacked
> bottles. Never before had I seen such an array of glasses, or such vivid
> colors, or such a vast mirror, or such huge carved and polished pillars
> and beams, or such enormous vessels of brass as the spittoons. . . . The
> bar-room was strange and wonderful to look at, and even the smells
> were curious and pleasant to breathe.
> —James Stevens [1]

One of the most appealing aspects of clublife is that members
know what to expect. Saloongoers had that assurance. They
knew where and when their fellows would congregate and what the
look and feel of the clubroom would be. The usual allures of barroom
decor greeted the eye, particularly the glittering glassware and colorful bottles with their promise of convivial drinking sessions to come.
In saloons, traditions were observed, faces were familiar, and events
were predictable enough to support the illusion that, for the duration
at least, reality was comfortably under control.

Drinking folkways played an essential role in promoting this sense
of regularity and ease. Of course, governments passed scores of liquor
laws, temperance advocates demanded compliance, and saloonkeepers protected licenses by curbing the worst excesses of transgressing
customers. But what ultimately kept barlife on an even keel was the
bargoers' voluntary observance of the saloon's unwritten laws and
lore of drink.

Workers' drink culture drew upon a number of sources. Some customs were of American origin, either invented during the saloon period or inherited from Anglo-American taverns of the colonial era.

Others were contributions from the millions of European immigrants arriving in the nineteenth and early twentieth centuries. From 1870 to 1920, this lore of drink increasingly resembled the metaphor of the "melting pot" as native and immigrant traditions blended in the barrooms of the working class. Meanwhile, two other segments of society were producing their own drink lore. First, there were the traditions of well-to-do "wets." These drinkers of the middle and upper classes shared the saloongoers' antipathy toward prohibitionist "drys" and yet embraced what might be called a "cocktail culture" far different from the beer-and-whiskey world of saloongoers. Second, there was the "anti-drink culture" of reform-minded "drys," abstainers who harbored nightmarish visions of the Demon Rum and its attendant evils. Both cocktail culture and teetotal tradition had some impact on workers' patterns of alcohol use. For the most part, however, laborers adhered to their own system of drinking preferences, practices, and precepts.[2]

THE CULTURAL SIGNIFICANCE OF CLUBBING

At the center of working-class drinking lore was the custom of clubbing, the combining of resources toward a communal drinking session. During the saloon period, two forms of clubbing were popular: the treat, in which participants took turns buying drinks for the group, and the collection, in which participants chipped in toward a drinking fund for the group.

Jack London noticed this distinction upon his introduction to drink culture in California in the early 1890s. Determined to win acceptance among the hard-drinking seafaring men of the Oakland waterfront, he carefully examined their drinking behavior both in saloons and on fishing sloops. "As I pondered this, I recollected that several times other men, in couples, had entered the Last Chance, and first one, then the other, had treated to drinks," he observed. "I remembered, on the drunk on the Idler, how Scotty and the harpooner and myself had raked and scraped dimes and nickels with which to buy the whisky." The underlying philosophy of mutuality and fellowship was always the same, regardless of which method of dues-paying the drinking partners adopted. "There was more in this buying of drinks than mere quantity," London concluded after numerous experiences with both methods of clubbing. "I got my finger on it. There was a stage when the beer didn't count at all, but just the spirit of comradeship of drinking together."[3]

Clubbing by treat was particularly appropriate for informal, spontaneous barside encounters in which participants wished only to swap a few rounds (sometimes quite a few rounds) and depart. Clubbing by collection, on the other hand, was better suited to more formally organized groups, such as singing or sporting clubs, whose members met regularly and wished to maintain a dues-supported fund to cover recurring drinking expenses. A third option might have been to run up a bar bill together and then split it among participants at party's end. But this practice seems not to have been much employed. Perhaps the saloonkeeper preferred his payment up front and assured. Perhaps the postparty accounting process was too vexing, as anyone who has ever tried to divide up a bar bill among inebriates knows. In any case, the "pay-as-you-go" plan prevailed in the saloon era, whether by taking turns treating or by taking up collections.

Why should methods of drink-buying have been so influential in shaping barroom encounters? To begin with, drink-buying was of course the one absolutely required activity in every bar. As Upton Sinclair remarked, "According to an unwritten law, the buying a drink included the privilege of loafing for just so long; then one had to buy another drink or move on." With drink-buying being the most basic and enduring fact of life in barrooms, it is logical that some traditions would have built up around it. Beyond this, buying drinks necessarily involved money, and money could be a socially ticklish subject in any setting, let alone the beery atmosphere of bars. Rules guiding its disposition helped people avoid misunderstandings and reduce social tensions, ever primary functions of tradition.[4]

Drink-buying also drew significance from longstanding cultural attitudes toward drink itself. Since colonial times, drink had traditionally been associated with good health in American culture. Even the straight-laced Puritan preacher Cotton Mather called it the "good creature of God," as long as used in moderation. Drink was regarded as food, despite temperance advocates' efforts to portray it as "poison" (a term which saloongoers soon playfully took up as their own synonym for alcohol). In addition, drink was regarded as medicine: a remedy for physical ailments, an aid to digestion, and a bracer for physical labor. Thus, the buying of drinks for others was a tribute to their well-being, as the well-known toast "to your health" attests.[5]

Drink was also valued as a social lubricant. The tendency of alcohol to break down inhibitions, loosen tongues, and produce feelings of euphoric camaraderie has long been acknowledged among the peoples of Europe and America. Among alcohol researchers today, this phenomenon is known as "disinhibition"—admittedly a clumsy term, but useful in summarizing the effects of alcohol on social behavior. Precisely why alcohol should produce such disinhibiting effects remains a subject of great controversy. Some researchers insist on physiological or even genetic explanations, while others emphasize the influence of sociological and cultural factors. Three thousand years ago, a religious explanation also would have been suggested by the members of Dionysian, Bacchic, and Orphic cults in ancient Greece, convinced as they were that inebriation was a form of "divine madness" inspired by the gods. Whatever the cause of disinhibition, however, the fact remains that alcohol in the saloon era was popularly perceived as a powerful and desirable stimulant to the emotions and imaginations of men.[6]

In addition to being valued as a promoter of health and sociability, drink was prized as a commodity of exchange, a thing intrinsically valuable that could function like money in all manner of transactions among men. When politicians, businessmen, employers, union recruiters, or others wished to curry favor or reward jobs well done, they often did so not with cash, but with drink. Cash was valuable but crass; drink was both valuable and pleasurable. The practice dates back to the colonial era in America, when alcohol was very commonly used as an item of barter and remuneration. For many immigrants fresh from the peasant cultures of Europe, alcohol was also a familiar item of barter as well as a widely accepted form of reimbursement for labor or favors rendered. The gesture of drink-buying, then, could represent an economic offering, a token of gratitude and repayment for the efforts of others on the donor's behalf.[7]

Thus, both drink and drink-buying played a highly symbolic and functional role in the lives of American saloongoers. The purchase and consumption of alcohol was, after all, the heart and soul of the saloon trade. When customers invoked time-honored drink-buying customs, they signaled that such purchasing and consuming were to proceed in an orderly manner, one of the important social guarantees which tradition provides. Further, the offer of drink was an offer of health, sociability, and mutual esteem. In view of these several factors, it becomes clear why there was no more significant gesture among saloongoers than the invitation to drink *with* others.

Yet did customers never simply buy their own drinks? Of course they did, and many a saloongoer did just that if he lacked the time, money, or inclination to join in a communal drinking session. Similarly, customers might each buy their own drinks individually and then consume them side by side with other customers, engaging in conversation and making a lively party of it. Then as now, this practice was known as "going Dutch treat," defined as "each of two or more persons paying his own way or for his own refreshment and entertainment."[8]

But this was not "clubbing." Drinking *alongside* others was not at all the same thing in drinking parlance, practice, or philosophy as drinking *with* others. In Dutch treating, no pledge to institute a binding drinking partnership was made. No one had any particular responsibility to anyone else, financial or otherwise. In the drinkers' rite of the club, in contrast, participants literally owed one another, for in the last analysis it was the commitment to commingle finances that transformed drinking into clubbing. Money added a modicum of formality to the hilarity, rigidifying the group outline and imposing mutual obligations on the members, financial and otherwise. Further, according to lexicographers, "'Dutch' slang words, such as 'Dutch act,' 'Dutch treat,' and 'Dutch uncle,' all have some connotation of disaster, dislike, and cheapness." In the saloon milieu, then, the "Dutch treat" had a somewhat negative connotation of cheapness and unsociability, in contrast to reciprocal treating, which was associated with generosity and comradeship. With the Dutch treat, it was every man for himself; with clubbing, it was all for one and one for all. As London remarked of his extensive clubbing experience, "[T]he buying of drinks for other men, and the accepting of drinks from other men, devolved upon me as a social duty and a manhood rite."[9]

TOWARD AN AMERICAN TASTE IN DRINK

What men drank was also a matter of barroom tradition. By 1870, working-class drinkers had settled on beer and whiskey as their principal drinks of choice, preferences that would prevail until the end of the saloon era. Both beverages had of course been available in America long before 1870, but they had shared the limelight with several more popular forms of alcohol. The reign of rum came first, bolstered by the colonial traffic in molasses and slaves from the 1600s to the Revolutionary War. Cheaper and more plentiful than whiskey, gin, or brandy, rum was by far the most popular distilled beverage of that period. Fermented beverages such as beer and ale were available, but inadequate brewing and preserving techniques yielded a product so notoriously mediocre, bitter, and flat that many people simply opted for cheap rum instead. Domestic wine was even more unpalatable, and imported wine was too scarce, expensive, and exotic for all save the likes of Thomas Jefferson and other connoisseurs among the sophisticated rich. The only serious competitor to rum was hard cider, produced domestically from the apple orchards of the northern colonies.[10] W. J. Rorabaugh estimates that among drinking-age persons (15 years and over), the per capita consumption rate in 1770 was 7.0 gallons of distilled spirits (predominantly rum), 34 gallons of hard cider, 0.2 gallon of wine, and a negligible quantity of beer. One hundred years before the saloon period began, then, rum and hard cider were the most heavily consumed alcoholic beverages, with whiskey (usually made from corn or rye), wine, and beer merely distant also-rans.[11]

Just as the Revolutionary War ended the reign of George III in America, so it ended the reign of rum with the ensuing disruption of the molasses trade, the imposition of stiff import duties on rum, and the tendency of many Americans to associate rum-drinking with English colonialism and dependence on foreign manufactures. Whiskey and hard cider, on the other hand, were produced domestically. They became ever cheaper and more available after the war as farmers greatly expanded their grainfields and orchards. Whiskey in particular enjoyed a meteoric rise in popularity, boosted by Irish and Scottish immigrants arriving in the late 1700s. They brought to America their taste for good whiskey and especially their superior distilling techniques, to which Americans then added their own refinements.[12]

From the 1790s to the 1830s, Americans increasingly found themselves up to their breeches in inexpensive, plentiful, good-quality whiskey, making it possible for them to indulge in what Rorabaugh has called a "veritable national binge." Regarding distilled spirits, the per capita rate of consumption among persons aged fifteen and older recovered from a postwar low of 5.1 gallons in 1790 to 7.2 gallons in 1800 (about the same quantity as in 1770, though the proportion of whiskey was rising as the popularity of rum fell). After that point, however, Americans seemed to go whiskey-mad, the consumption rate for distilled spirits climbing to 8.7 gallons in 1810 and finally reaching a peak of 9.5 gallons in 1830. As the popularity of whiskey rose, consumption of hard cider gradually slipped from 32 gallons in 1800 to 27 gallons in 1830, though the latter was still a decidedly impressive quantity. Wine and beer consumption, meanwhile, remained low through the 1830s. The rate for wine hovered at about 0.5 gallon (mostly Madeira, a sweet wine often fortified with distilled spirits), while the rate for beer continued to be statistically negligible.[13] Thus, in the early years of Andrew Jackson's presidency, Americans were drinking whiskey at levels never equaled before or since, hard cider at a still prodigious rate, and beer so very little that no one then would have dreamed of its glory days to come in the saloon era.

After 1830, American drinking habits underwent still more significant changes. One major force for change was the temperance movement, which had greatly increased in strength and numbers since the founding of the American Society for the Promotion of Temperance in 1826. This national organization spearheaded a growing coalition of clergymen, women's benevolent societies, professional men, and employers. Reformers pressured farmers to convert less of their corn and rye crops into whiskey, as well as to limit hard cider production by chopping down apple trees in a kind of perverse reversal of the Johnny Appleseed legend.[14]

Tackling the problem of demand as well as supply, reformers issued a flood of pamphlets, lectures, and sermons denouncing alcohol consumption as physically harmful, morally degrading, and economically counterproductive. Their arguments and denunciations were especially effective among middle- and upper-class drinkers, many of whom became abstainers or began mixing their alcohol with water, soda, and other diluents in a foreshadowing of the "cocktail culture" of the late nineteenth century. Reformers' arguments also reached many working-class drinkers, particularly the more upwardly mobile artisan elite who embraced the evangelical Protestant creed of industry, sobriety, and thrift. One of the favorite tactics of the early temperance movement was to encourage people to take public abstinence pledges, a phenomenon which bewildered foreign travelers like Alexis de Tocqueville. In his words, "The first time that I heard in America that one hundred thousand men had publicly promised never to drink alcoholic liquor, I thought it more of a joke than a serious matter and for the moment did not see why these very abstemious citizens could not content themselves with drinking water by their firesides."[15]

By the mid-1830s, over half a million people had made such public pledges, and by the 1840s, the runaway consumption rates of whiskey and hard cider had dropped dramatically. Consumption rates for distilled spirits among persons aged fifteen years and older dropped from 9.5 gallons in 1830 to 3.7 gallons in 1845, where the rate hovered until after the Civil War. Then it dropped even further to between 2.8 and 1.8 gallons from 1875 to 1920. The consumption rate for hard cider fell even more precipitously, from 27 gallons in 1830 to 4 gallons in 1840, and thenceforth to rates so low that they became negligible.[16]

Yet, while the temperance crusade against hard liquor claimed much of the credit for these plummeting consumption rates, the drinking habits of many "wet" workingmen in the cities were at least equally influenced by the arrival of German immigrants after 1840. The influx of Germans had a threefold impact on American drinking habits. They brought to America their fondness for beer, a taste shared by contemporary immigrant groups such as the Scandinavians and, to a lesser extent, the Irish (who preferred whiskey). More important, Germans introduced sophisticated brewing techniques that revolutionized the American brewing industry, in much the same way that Scottish and Irish immigrants had transformed the distilling industry several decades before. Moreover, Germans opened hundreds of new taverns in urban areas where their customers were further encouraged to drink beer. Through their tastes, techniques, and taverns, Germans had a tremendous influence on American drinking patterns.[17]

By mid-century, a number of master brewers bearing such names as Schlitz, Pabst, Anheuser, Busch, and Müller (Americanized into "Miller") were prepared to offer a superior product that would appeal to both natives and immigrants alike. Not only was beer becoming more palatable, plentiful, and inexpensive, but also its alcoholic content (5%) was far less than that of hard cider (10%), wine (18%), or distilled spirits (45%). It was thus a safer and more temperate drink for laborers facing the rigors of an increasingly industrialized workplace. As a result of these various factors, consumption rates for commercial beer among persons aged fifteen years and older rose from next to nothing in the 1830s to 6.4 gallons in the 1860s. After the Civil War, with further improvements in methods of production, preservation, and distribution, the rate skyrocketed from 8.6 gallons in 1870 to 20.6 gallons in 1890, finally reaching a peak for the saloon period of 29.7 gallons in 1915.[18]

When the saloon period began, therefore, Anglo-American drinking patterns had already been heavily influenced by immigrants' tastes and production techniques, particularly those of whiskey-drinking Irish and Scots and beer-drinking Germans. These immigrant preferences had by 1870 become American drinking preferences, thereafter reinforced by the arrival of millions more northern and western Europeans during what historians have termed the "old" wave of immigration before 1890. So prevalent did this American taste for beer and whiskey become that it in turn influenced the drinking habits of Italians, Jews, and other southern and eastern Europeans arriving during the "new" wave of immigration after 1890. Among these latter groups, the drink of choice had traditionally been wine, but preferences were changing by the turn of the twentieth century. "Among the Jews and Italians alike, beer has displaced to a very large extent the . . . light wines of Europe; but among the Italians especially, stronger liquors are beginning to displace both," observed settlement director Robert Woods in 1902 of the North End population of Boston. "[T]his change in the direction of more intoxicating drink is due more or less to mere imitation of American ways."[19]

This is not to argue that members of the "new" immigration completely abandoned the consumption of wine. On the contrary, so typically did Italians consume Chianti (and other dry red wines of the claret type) that other Americans of the early 1900s often referred to *all* wine by the crude but common epithet "dago red," defined as "Italian red wine; any cheap red wine. . . ; specifically red Chianti." Many Italians kept a large quantity of wine in their homes for family consumption. This fact became very evident in San Francisco during the earthquake and fire of 1906 when, according to Walton Bean, the "Italian residents of Telegraph Hill saved their homes by using barrels of wine to wet down a strip in the path of the flames." In the larger cities, some establishments catered especially to Italians and to Jews where wine was the principal beverage consumed. Raymond Calkins noted that the "Italians have their wine-shops," just as the *Daily Jewish Courier* observed that "Jewish neighborhoods have their saloons and wine-joints." Moreover, wine-drinking newcomers had some influence on American drinking habits. London recalled consuming wine by the demijohn (as well as great quantities of beer and whiskey) when he and other American-born friends drank in the company of French, Greek, Russian, and Italian fishermen in California in the 1890s and early 1900s.[20]

Thus, immigrants from southern and eastern Europe continued to drink wine and sometimes influenced others to drink it as well. The fact remains, however, that wine consumption in America stayed comparatively low and restricted throughout the saloon era, even taking middle- and upper-class drinkers of Madeira, port, and sherry into account. The per capita consumption rate for persons aged fifteen and over ranged from only 0.6 gallon in 1900 to 0.9 gallon in 1910, dropping back to 0.7 gallon in 1915.[21] Compared to the rate of two gallons of hard liquor and twenty to twenty-nine gallons of beer consumed per capita during the same period, wine was not what could be called one of the "national drinks" of America. Instead, for those immigrants striving to imitate American folkways, the glass of wine had to be replaced by the schooner of beer and the jigger of whiskey.

Given saloongoers' obvious and well-known preference for beer, whiskey, and occasionally wine, it is a quaint and curious fact that temperance advocates were forever pointing to rum as the great destroyer of American society. In the antidrink songs popular in the early 1900s among members of the Woman's Christian Temperance Union (W.C.T.U.), for example, rum was repeatedly singled out as the beverage which must be banned if the nation would be saved:[22]

> Hear the happy voices ringing
> As "king rum" is downward hurled,
> Shouting vict'ry and hosanna
> In their march to save the world.
> ("We'll Take the World")

> Save the boy, save the boy,
> Save him from the curse of rum;
> Fill the mother's heart with joy,
> Save our country, friends and home.
> ("Marching Onward")

Decked out in their white temperance ribbons, the musical militants of the W.C.T.U. urged the public to agitate against the "rum sellers" whom they held responsible for this alleged scourge of "king rum":[23]

When worn by the W.C.T.U.
Of the District of Columbia so true,
The white ribbon makes the rum-sellers tremble,
When worn by the W.C.T.U.
("District of Columbia W.C.T.U. Song")

We've tried to stop this curse of rum,
We've tried both pray'rs and tears;
We ask for home protection laws,
They answer us with sneers.
("I'll Be There to Vote")

Despite the fact that rum had not been a major factor in the liquor trade for nearly a century, this rum fixation on the part of temperance advocates persisted. The explanation, according to H. L. Mencken, was that the "Prohibitionists . . . kept on using *rum* to designate all alcoholic drinks, including even beer. . . . Some of its derivatives dated from the Eighteenth Century: *rum seller* from 1781, *rum guzzler* from 1775, *rum house* from 1739 and *rum shop* from 1738." [24]

The term "rum" also appears to have had a special symbolic significance for prohibition advocates. Just as working-class "wets" and well-to-do "wets" each embraced a drink lore rich in cultural meaning and historical precedents, so temperance folk embraced a "lore of abstinence" that supplied them with time-honored guidelines for belief and behavior. Replete with songs, stories, proverbs, symbols, superstitions, taboos, and legendary heros and heroines, teetotal tradition provided a compelling subculture for its adherents. In the context of this heritage, rum had an archetypal significance for abstainers, representing the original sin and thus the original taboo in their interpretation of American moral history and development. Regarding use of the pejorative "rum shop" instead of the more stylish "saloon," for example, the remarks of temperance advocate Richard O'Flynn in 1880 are instructive. "I must be pardoned for the use of the word 'Rum Shop,'" he asserted. "I cannot conscientiously give any other name no matter how magnificent the surroundings." [25]

Prohibitionists were not blind to contemporary consumption habits, nor were they merely mimicking past antiliquor pronouncements, nor were they carelessly misusing the language. Instead, "rum" had a resonance for them that other names did not. It invoked powerful, timeless images of sin and destruction that went straight to the heart of their creed. Prohibitionists hurled the name "rum" at their opponents because the label was so laden with cultural meaning that just to speak it created an electrifying sense of mission, urgency, and righteous solidarity. When temperance advocates railed against rum, rummies, and rum sellers, they were speaking from within a longstanding abstinence tradition that was internally coherent and deeply meaningful to them, even if it bore little relation to the actual drinking practices of the period.

For the vast majority of working-class drinkers, then, beer and whiskey were the drinks of choice on most occasions, despite the variety of liquor bottles adorning the back-bar shelves of many saloons which were "displayed but seldom used," according to Travis Hoke. "Thirsts were simple in the neighborhood," he explained. "A man usually drank beer or whiskey, and only beer or whiskey." Similarly, Ade remarked that workingmen's saloons were not "the happy hunting grounds for cocktails, cobblers, fizzes and sours," adding that "only two staples were in steady demand by the regular trade of the common or garden variety of saloon. These were beer and whisky." Proprietors usually kept a supply of other liquors on hand, partly because it was "just one of the traditions of the trade," explained Ade, and partly because customers did sometimes call for other drinks under special circumstances. Thus, one New York saloonkeeper reported in 1909 that he customarily supplemented his basic stock with assorted bottles of brandy, gin, cordial, kümmel, vermouth, champagne, wine, and other beverages. When on one occasion he ran out of beer, however, his business fell off so much that he decided to shut down for the day, his fancier stock being of little interest to his predominantly beer-drinking, working-class clientele.[26]

DRINKING CUSTOMS AND COMRADESHIP

To many workers, liquors other than whiskey and beer were to be drunk only on specific occasions. Believing in the medicinal qualities of alcohol, many drinkers maintained that gin was beneficial to the kidneys, rum was a cure for bronchitis, and Rock and Rye was the best remedy for the aches and pains of the common cold. "It might be peppermint in whiskey for cramps, or hoarhound, honey and rye for a cold in the chest," remarked Hoke. "A little jalap in whiskey was good for one kind of trouble, Jamaica ginger or wild cherry cordial for its antithesis." Hoke also noted that a stale beer or a sloe gin fizz was recommended for hangovers, and "a raw egg in sherry was esteemed as soothing to a roiled stomach." Some drinkers maintained that the best hangover remedy was another drink of whatever had made them drunk the night before, proclaiming "their need of a hair from the dog that had bitten them."[27]

But if unusual liquors were warranted when men were feeling under the weather, they were also appropriate when men were feeling joyous, such as during holidays and celebrations. At Christmas and on New Year's Eve, for example, popular drinks included eggnog made with rum, as well as a "gooey confection" known as a "Tom and Jerry" which called for cream, beaten eggs, sugar, nutmeg, and "the addition of rum or brandy or whisky or all three," according to Ade. "A huge white bowl with their names entwined in gilt stood on the bar at Christmas time," confirmed Hoke.[28]

Similarly, champagne was seldom consumed. "New Orleans, and to a lesser extent San Francisco, were about the only towns where a champagne cocktail might easily be had; there was enough demand for them to use up a bottle of champagne before it grew flat," claimed Hoke. The bubbly beverage was appropriate on New Year's Eve, however. It was also called for at wedding celebrations, as illustrated by a passage in Frank Norris's novel of 1899, *McTeague*. "When all their glasses had been filled, Marcus proposed the health of the bride, standing up. The guests rose and drank," Norris wrote. "Hardly one of them had ever tasted champagne before. The moment's silence after the toast was broken by McTeague exclaiming with a long breath of satisfaction: 'That's the best beer *I* ever drank.'"[29]

As the *McTeague* example shows, special occasions were observed not only with special drinks, but also with traditional verbal salutes known as "toasts." The purpose of the toast was to honor drinking partners by acknowledging some past accomplishment or by wishing success, prosperity, and good health in future endeavors. Often the wording of a toast was set by tradition, called a "fixed-phrase blessing" by folklorists. Typical examples from the saloon era, cited by Ade, included "Here's hopin' your shadow'll never grow less" and "May the skin of a gooseberry make overcoats fer all o' your enemies." According to Hoke, saloongoers were also heard "to mutter exorcisms such as 'Looking at you!' 'Over the river!' 'Here's how!' or to exchange benevolent greetings such as 'Here's mud in your eye,' 'Hope you choke,' etc." Free-phrase toasts were also common, however, since the speaker frequently wished to tailor the blessing to the specific deeds and virtues of the honoree. To reinforce the solemnity of the occasion, drinkers might accompany their verbal tributes with traditional gestures. These included such physical rituals as coming to a standing position, raising and clinking glasses, intertwining drinking arms, draining the glass dry in one great swallow, and smashing all glasses afterward to ensure that nothing would ever disrupt the sanctity of the drinking circle. While special beverages like champagne or brandy added a touch of class to the event, ordinary potables like beer or whiskey often served just as well. The most important thing was to symbolize the drinkers' sense of solidarity and mutual regard through the toasting ceremony.[30]

Just how little acquaintance many laboring men had with drinks other than beer and whiskey was vividly illustrated by an awkward incident in the life of Jack London. In the early 1900s when his reputation as a novelist was on the rise, he was invited by some well-to-do admirers to join them at the very exclusive and elegant Bohemian Club in San Francisco. "[A]t that time in my life I did not know what a cocktail was," he confessed. "We sat in the most wonderful leather chairs, and drinks were ordered. Never had I heard such an ordering of liqueurs and of highballs of particular brands of Scotch." Accustomed to the rough-and-tumble saloons of the Oakland waterfront where sailors and longshoremen were his drinking partners, he had no idea how to proceed. "I didn't know what a liqueur or a highball was, and I didn't know that 'Scotch' meant whisky," he recalled. "I knew only poor men's drinks, the drinks of the frontier and of sailor-town—cheap beer and cheaper whisky that was just called whisky and nothing else." Although London was in the company of "wets" who enjoyed drinking and who rejected the antiliquor tirades of prohibitionist "drys," he now found himself in what seemed another drinking universe altogether. "I was embarrassed to make a choice," he admitted, as he desperately cast about for something, anything that might be appropriately sophisticated for the occasion, "and the waiter nearly collapsed when I ordered claret as an after-dinner drink."[31]

London had erred on two counts. By calling generically for claret when others were naming premium brands of Scotch, he inadvertently revealed just how far out of his element he was in such sumptuous surroundings. He compounded his error by ordering dry wine as an after-dinner drink, making his selection doubly inappropriate for the occasion. In these two ways, London transgressed the drinking code of well-to-do "wets," a fact painfully brought home to him by the horrified reaction of the waiter.

Why was there such a considerable gulf between the drinking preferences of working- and middle-class "wets"? The difference was in part a matter of monetary outlay. Beer and whiskey were cheap and readily available, making them favorite "poor men's drinks" since the mid-nineteenth century. Yet price and plentifulness alone cannot fully explain the popularity of such plain potables among workingmen. It did not require any great additional outlay to put some water in the whiskey, add a dash of sugar and bitters, and produce what has been known since at least 1806 as a "cocktail." Workers generally eschewed such mixed concoctions, however, from the time of their invention straight through to the prohibition era, when mixers became popular to disguise the often revolting taste of bootleg liquor.[32]

Probably the principal reason why workers rejected "cocktail culture" was that such potables struck them as sissy drinks inconsistent with their norms of manly behavior. Thus, saloon regulars not only insisted on beer and whiskey for themselves, but also looked askance at the manhood of any customer who dared order otherwise. Ade claimed that the scotch highball, which "seemed to arrive with golf," was scorned as the height of dandified pretension. Similarly, because gin was usually diluted with mixers, it was considered "fit only for dudes and weaklings." (Very different, however, was gin's reputation in the South, where whites alleged that it worked as a powerful aphrodisiac on blacks.) "Not to drink your liquor straight was considered a sign of effeminacy," Ade explained. "The idea was to uphold a reputation as a he-man, no matter what happened to the lining of the stomach." Some men drank their whiskey with a "chaser" of seltzer, soda, or plain water. "But the real die-hards drank chasers of beer. They would let no charge of effeminacy be lodged against them," observed Hoke. "They diluted alcohol with more alcohol, and their stomachs seldom knew the softer beverages which they termed belly wash."[33]

Not only what men drank, but how much they were capable of consuming was regarded as a measure of manhood. In Margaret Byington's study of the steel mill town of Homestead, Pennsylvania, in 1910, she found that municipal fines imposed on Slavic men for being drunk and disorderly did not always discourage excessive drinking. "It is indeed currently said that some are proud of having a large fine imposed, as they feel that it indicates increased importance," she observed. Official acknowledgment of a man's prodigious drinking sprees became a status symbol.[34]

Tests of drinking capacity were also a way of establishing manly status in the saloon. For example, John Powers recalled a story about a preprohibition drinking contest in a St. Louis saloon between "Ol' Louie," a whiskey-drinking regular, and "some Irishman," whose drinking preference was beer. "Anyway, the Irish guy was bragging about how well he could hold his liquor, but everybody in the bar knew that Louie could drink anybody down," Powers asserted. "The Irishman offered to give Louie an edge by drinking two beers to every whiskey Louie drank, but Louie scorned this idea, insisting it should be one to one." The regulars eagerly gathered around the two men while the bartender readied the beer tap and the whiskey bottle. At last the bout began. "As the contest went on, the Irishman kept talking endlessly, while Louie just kept hanging on the bar. Then, all of a sudden, the Irishman just fell on his face. He had talked himself out of it," Powers explained. "The idea was, when you're drinking, don't talk—you can't hold your liquor that way. So the Irishman talked himself drunk, and Ol' Louie beat him." Thus, Louie outdid his competitor not only in terms of quantity, but also in terms of style and savoir faire, to the delight of his fellow saloonmates. Further, he sealed his victory with one last gesture of barroom aplomb. With the humiliated Irishman still sprawled at his feet, according to Powers, "Ol' Louie casually turned to the bartender and asked him to pour him another whiskey, drank it right down, and then proceeded to stroll nonchalantly out the door."[35]

To be able to drink and talk and still outdo one's competitors was an even greater feat, according to London. He recalled many occasions "when I engaged in drinking-bouts with men" because "it was a matter of pride . . . to show as strong a head as they." Particularly he recalled when a "wild band of young revolutionists" in Berkeley, California, impressed by London's involvement in the socialist movement, invited him to a "beer bust" which they intended as an "endurance test." "I'd show them, the young rascals," he bristled. "I'd show them . . . who could make most of a swine of himself and show it least. These unlicked cubs who thought they could out-drink *me*!" When their drinking session was over, he remembered the sight of "one of them in indignant tears on the street corner, weeping as he pointed out my sober condition." As London admitted in later years, however, "Little he dreamed the iron clutch, born of old training, with which I held to my consciousness. . . , kept my voice unbroken and easy and my thoughts consecutive and logical." [36]

Despite the pleasures of victory, London woke up "sick and poisoned" the next morning and vowed never again to become entangled in any sort of drinking bout. "Oh, I have drunk ever since," he acknowledged, "but . . . never in a competitive spirit." In all subsequent encounters with fellow imbibers, his drinking was "wholly a matter of companionship." [37]

In this sentiment, most saloongoers apparently concurred. Though competitive drinking was an enjoyable challenge on occasion, most workers adopted a more companionable and moderate approach in their everyday barroom encounters. The idea was to stay even with one's drinking partners in terms of quantity, monetary outlay, and degree of intoxication. Sociability was the object, while drunkenness was "a sort of accident," in Hoke's words. Rather than trying to outdrink their companions, most men sought simply to drink *with* them in the congenial and even-handed spirit of the saloon club. [38]

WHAT'S IN A DRINK

Drinking folkways lay at the heart of saloonlife. Bargoers employed drink to toast one another's good fortune, restore and salute sound health, and repay favors and debts. Alcohol enlivened some occasions and solemnized others. It embodied the spirit of many holidays, for what is more Christmas than eggnog, more New Year's Eve than champagne? In many instances, drink also symbolized a bargoer's solidarity with saloonmates. Some drinks, like Chianti, communicated ethnic loyalties. Others, like straight whiskey, confirmed standards of masculinity. Still others, like champagne, signaled high regard for present company. The many symbolic and practical uses of drink served as a kind of universal language for workers, promoting communication among strangers, solidarity among regulars, and stability in a setting of potential anarchy. Beneath all the surface noise, saloonlife involved a good deal more conformity than chaos due to longstanding links between lore and order.

If drink lore was the heart of saloonlife, clubbing was its heartbeat. The formation of drinking circles through elaborate rituals of acquisition and consumption was basic to barroom society. This fact becomes evident upon closer examination of exactly how bargoers employed clubbing rituals as they clustered along the bar, gathered in friendship groups at the tables, or assembled for meetings of their voluntary associations in the back room. When the centrality of clubbing is recognized, many seemingly miscellaneous aspects of barlife begin to fall into place. Whether by treat or by collection, clubbing was the driving force behind customer interaction, making saloongoing the social adventure that it was.

Five

Clubbing by Treat

We had been seven months together, and our paths were separating.
One last farewell rite of comradeship remained. (Oh, it was the way, the
custom). "Come on, boys," said our sailing-master. There stood the inevitable adjacent saloon. . . . And the nineteen of us drank the sailing-
master's treat. Then the mate looked at us with eloquent eyes and
called for another round. . . . There were six hunters, and each insisted,
in the sacred name of comradeship, that all hands drink with him just
once. There were six boat-steerers and five boat-pullers and the same
logic held with them. There was money in all our pockets, and our
money was as good as any man's, and our hearts were as free and
generous.
—Jack London[1]

The convenient thing about tradition is that it often requires
people to do what they want to do anyway, but in an orderly
and time-honored fashion. For Jack London and his shipmates in that
San Francisco waterfront saloon of 1893, seafaring tradition demanded one last glorious drunk before disbanding, and bargoing tradition defined how this "rite of comradeship" was to proceed. No
question who belonged to this impromptu drinking club, for the ritualistic buying of drinks defined the membership and reinforced group
identity with every round. No squabbling over who was to pay, for
seasoned saloonmates like these already knew that every man was expected to contribute equally to the buying of rounds. Even the order
of drink-buying was guided by tradition. Once the dominant male
in the assembly—the ship-master—had offered to treat all hands, it
was incumbent on the next man in the "pecking order" to do the
same, and so on down to the last lowliest boat-puller. No matter that

nineteen men buying nineteen rounds was outrageously excessive, even for sailors. On such occasions, "[I]t was no time to make invidious distinctions—to drink with this shipmate and to decline to drink with that shipmate," explained London. "We were all shipmates. . . . So we drank with all, and all treated. . . , and knew one another for the best fellows in the world."[2]

Treating tradition has an extraordinarily long and venerable lineage. It was a feature of American colonial tavern life from the first, brought over by English immigrants in the 1600s. They inherited their attitudes toward drink, reciprocity, and treating from distant Saxon ancestors of the fifth century (or perhaps even from the more remote cultures of ancient Egypt and Assyria). In antebellum America, the treating ritual thrived in workers' taverns, where it was customary for men to purchase half-pints of whiskey in turn to be passed around their drinking circle. By the beginning of the saloon period in the 1870s, treating was already a centuries-old custom that constituted an integral part of barroom social interaction.[3]

THE HONORABLE TREAT

The first rule of barroom treating was that the recipient was expected to reciprocate, in drinks or favors or some other mutually acceptable manner. Once a man joined a circle of treaters, explained Travis Hoke, "naturally he couldn't desert them. That would be the trick of a short-sport, a quitter—unmanly, in fact." The term "treat" is somewhat misleading in this regard, for it tends to imply a one-way favor, and language purists might wish that saloongoers had used the more precise term, "reciprocal treat." But bar folk well knew the point of honor involved in accepting a treat. As London remarked of a drinking episode involving a friend and some regulars in the National Saloon in Oakland, California, "They treated, and we drank. Then, according to the code of drinking, we had to treat."[4]

This "code of drinking" was further articulated in the grittily realistic novels of London's contemporaries, most notably Upton Sinclair and Frank Norris. In Sinclair's *The Jungle* of 1906, Lithuanian immigrant Jurgis Rudkus was introduced to the code in the saloons of "Whiskey Row" (Ashland Avenue) outside the Chicago stockyards. Sinclair described how easily Rudkus's fellow workers were drawn into barroom society, "for there was pretty sure to be a friend who would treat you, and then you would have to treat him. Then some one else would come in—and, anyhow, a few drinks were good for a man who worked hard." But Rudkus preferred to put family before camaraderie and bought only one drink for himself each day at noon-time, "so he got the reputation of being a surly fellow, and was not quite welcome at the saloons, and had to drift about from one to another."[5]

Years later, however, after Rudkus had lost his family and strayed west, his perspective on saloon clublife changed. "On a Saturday night he drifted into a town with his fellows . . . to a saloon. And there would be some who treated him and whom he had to treat, and there was laughter and singing and good cheer." Jurgis Rudkus had learned to accept the drinkers' code of reciprocity as the price of barroom pleasure, and in return he gained the acceptance and fellowship of his peers.[6]

The barroom rule of honor that a man "had to treat" when treated also featured prominently in Frank Norris's *McTeague* of 1899. The destitute protagonist, a self-taught dentist now enjoined from his practice for lack of credentials, was at wit's end trying to find work and appease his penny-pinching wife Trina. One day he found himself unemployed, broke, and rain-drenched in front of Joe Frenna's Saloon on Polk Street in San Francisco. His old friend Heise, shocked at McTeague's sorry appearance, offered to buy them both a whiskey. "Take it as medicine," Heise insisted. "You'll get your deatha cold if you stand soaked like that." McTeague accepted in the name of good health and old friendship, but still he felt obligated to apologize for his inability to reciprocate. " 'I'd—I'd ask you to have a drink with me, Heise,' said the dentist, who had an indistinct idea of the amenities of the barroom. 'Only,' he added shame-facedly, 'only—you see, I don't believe I got any change.'" The oafish McTeague knew enough of "the amenities of the barroom" to sense that both his honor and manhood were diminished by his breach of clubbing etiquette.[7]

Determined never to lose face that way again, McTeague took to confronting Trina over her hoarded earnings and lottery winnings. But Trina, little knowing or caring about barroom amenities, fiercely resisted his demands for club money. And so one day, full of whiskey and fury, McTeague finally cornered his miserly wife and strangled her.[8]

Fortunately, not every man embarrassed by lack of club money went to such extremes. Lurid enough for a temperance tract, Norris's scenario of McTeague's barside humiliation and its aftermath was nevertheless rooted in an ethic of drinking and manhood that was widely embraced in the saloons of his day. An honorable man down on his luck might accept a treat from a sympathetic barmate, but always with the expectation that he would return the favor when circumstances permitted. "Whoever was treated must treat in turn, of course," as Hoke explained regarding what he called "the code of treating." Further, he observed, "No one must take a more expensive drink than that ordered by the treater." Otherwise, the equilibrium of the relationship was disturbed, with one man indebted and beholden to another, thus defeating the spirit of barroom clubbing in which each man freely and equally contributed his fair share to the whole.[9]

Though treating episodes were usually spontaneous and casual, they could at times exhibit a degree of formality and solemnity that underscored the strongly ritualistic character of the custom. According to a Colorado newspaper of 1883, for example, one saloon customer's invitation to his fellows to drink with him precipitated a highly orchestrated response. "Each man waits, says nothing, and eyes every motion of the bartender. The silence is impressive. All is ready," the newspaper reported. "Each glass is grasped and raised, and then from each to each, and . . . from all to the drink donor, there is a nod, that incantory phrase is uttered, 'Well, here's luck,' and the poison is down." As soon as the drinks were consumed, another member of the circle called for more drinks all around, and so on until every participant had gone his turn. These Colorado saloonmates elevated treating to a ceremonial rite, each man dutifully doing honor and being honored until the ritual was complete.[10]

The Unrequited Treat

What happened when a bargoer violated the code of drinking by accepting a treat without reciprocating? Consequences depended on intent, but always there was a loss of face involved, whether for the donor or recipient or both. Often the failure to reciprocate was due to poverty, as in the case of the pathetic "sitters" who besieged urban barrooms in the poorer districts in wintertime. In saloon parlance, a "sitter" was a destitute man permitted to loiter in the barroom so long as some paying customer occasionally treated him to a drink. "The bartender permits them to sit about the stove and by shivering invite the sympathy of transient customers. . . , especially about Christmas and election time," Jacob Riis observed of these men in New York City in the 1880s. "In some saloons 'sitters' are let in at these seasons in fresh batches every hour." The arrangement was beneficial to the saloonkeeper, for he was able to bolster his charitable image and make a nickel simultaneously. The benefactor too could feel the warm glow of charity. As Sinclair wrote of such sitter-treaters in Chicago, "A workingman would come in, feeling cheerful after his day's work was over, and it would trouble him to have to take his glass with such a sight under his nose."[11]

For the "sitter," however, treats and sympathy came at the cost of utter humiliation in the eyes of his fellows. Just how lowly and precarious his standing was in the barroom was dramatized by his fate if caught napping at his post, asserted Riis. "A tramp placidly dozing at the fire would not be an object of sympathy. To make sure that they do keep awake, the wily bartender makes them sit constantly swinging one foot like the pendulum of a clock. When it stops the slothful 'sitter' is roused with a kick and 'fired out,'" he explained. "It is said . . . that habit has come to the rescue of oversleepy tramps and that the old rounders can swing hand or foot in their sleep without betraying themselves." Such demeaning treatment was anathema to any self-respecting man. In Riis's words, the acceptance of the "charity drink" put "a brand on the able-bodied man," so that he "seldom recovers his lost caste." Thus, a charity case could never a clubber be. Without the resources to reciprocate, the "sitter"—or any other man habitually unable to pay his dues—had no hope of attaining full membership or respectable status in the clublife of the workingman's saloon.[12]

If a bargoer failed to reciprocate out of ignorance of the treating ritual, he might be forgiven and indulged—for a time. Eventually, however, he would have to pay either by making proper restitution or by suffering permanent damage to his barroom standing, as Jack London learned at the age of fifteen. His misadventures began in 1891 in the First and Last Chance Saloon in the waterfront district of Oakland, California, where he had high hopes of proving his manhood. The regular clientele consisted of longshoremen, fishermen, and "oyster pirates" whose felonious poaching of oyster beds could mean a prison term if caught. Determined to become an oyster pirate himself, London had negotiated the purchase of a sloop from local oysterman "French Frank," who then invited London to the Last Chance "to complete the deal." For the eager teenager, it was his first chance to participate fully in the society of men along the bar, not as a curious child imagines it, but as grown men knew it. Unfortunately, he blew it.

London was baffled when French Frank concluded their business agreement in the Last Chance by offering to treat the house to drinks. "He and I drank, which seemed just; but why should Johnny Heinhold, who owned the saloon and waited behind the bar, be invited to drink?" he wondered. "I could, in a way, considering that they were friends and shipmates, understand Spider and Whisky Bob being asked to drink, but why should the longshoremen, Bill Kelly and Soup Kennedy, be asked?" After witnessing this display of seemingly needless extravagance, London was anxious to inspect his new boat. He noticed, however, that everyone was still hovering at the bar. "No hint broke through my obtuseness of why they lingered," London later recalled. "I have often thought since of how they must have regarded me, the newcomer being welcomed into the company, standing at bar with them, and not standing for a single round of drinks." By failing to reciprocate, he had unwittingly committed an egregious breach of barroom propriety.[13]

To make matters worse, London soon repeated his gaffe in the company of another Last Chance regular, "Young Scratch" Nelson. Again, he accepted drinks from Nelson without realizing he was expected to reciprocate. Later that day, as he mused over the curiousness of Nelson's generosity, he had a sudden flash of insight from his childhood days. "Then came my boy code: when on a day a fellow gave another a 'cannonball' or a chunk of taffy, on some other day he would expect to receive back a cannonball or a chunk of taffy." At that moment the awful truth of the matter dawned on him. "That was why Nelson had lingered at the bar. Having bought a drink, he waited for me to buy one. *I had let him buy six drinks and never once offered to treat.* And he was the great Nelson!" London recalled with anguish, "I could feel myself blushing with shame. I sat down on the stringerpiece of the wharf and buried my face in my hands. And the heat of my shame burned up my neck and into my cheeks and forehead. I have blushed many times in my life, but never have I experienced so terrible a blush as that one." Nelson had treated to test him, test his mettle as a drinking man. He had failed so miserably that it still made him wince a quarter century later when writing his autobiography. "He wanted to find out just what kind of a gink I was," London concluded ruefully. "He wanted to see how many times I'd let him treat without offering to treat in return." [14]

At length, the mortified would-be oyster pirate returned to the Last Chance, explaining feebly that he had left only to get money stashed on his boat. To redeem himself once and for all for his sins against barroom honor, he decided he had better treat the entire house into oblivion, noting, "I had achieved a concept. Money no longer counted. It was comradeship that counted." By rectifying his treating blunders, London salvaged his standing and achieved full welcome in the Last Chance, a status he retained to the end of his days. [15]

But what if a bargoer's failure to reciprocate were intentional, a deliberate rebuff of someone's treating overture? Then loss of face could be devastating for the donor, as James Stevens discovered during a painful saloon experience in Shoshone, Idaho, in about 1905. Stevens had been greatly impressed in his childhood by the largesse of two local ranchers who had always treated everyone upon entering the wildest of his hometown's eleven saloons. Looking forward to the day when he too could cultivate a warm welcome from barroom peers, Stevens thought he saw his opportunity in his mid-teens when he got work in a reclamation camp outside Shoshone. First chance, he headed to town, bent on "performing in some Shoshone saloon as Bud Winkle and Russ Hicks used to do in the Copper King." When he found a barroom with familiar faces from camp, he embarked on his plan to treat his way into their good graces. "A gang of them in the Horseshoe Saloon welcomed me as if I was an old friend, one of their kind," he recalled. "The bartenders wouldn't allow me to drink anything but a few small beers myself, but they didn't object to me spending my money in the style of Russ and Bud as I set up the drinks for the team-hands." But somehow, something was wrong. Certainly the team-hands accepted every treat Stevens offered. After they drank down the rounds he purchased, however, they turned their backs, ignored him, and seemed little inclined to reciprocate. Embarrassed and disillusioned, he realized that his bid for membership in this drinking club had been rejected. [16]

In short, Stevens had been the victim of a club snub. In this nonverbal and symbolic way, the barroom gang had informed him that they did not think him qualified for full membership in their drinking circle. How had he failed? To start, he was too young to be taken seriously as a peer, as symbolized in drinkers' terms by the "few small beers" the bartenders would permit him to drink himself. Further, he was too much an underling in occupational status. He served only as a self-described "flunky" in the reclamation camp, washing dishes while these men moved mountains. He might also have failed to meet other criteria, for many factors contributed to the cohesiveness of bar groups. The point is that on grounds of age and occupation alone, Stevens did not measure up as an equal in work or play. Thus, the team-hands, having no intention of embracing him as a permanent member of their group, did not feel obligated to reciprocate his un-solicited treating spree beyond politely tolerating his presence for the duration of his rounds.

It is instructive to compare the treating tribulations of Stevens and London. Both were teenagers eager to gain acceptance into barroom society, though woefully ignorant of its subtler rules and cues. In London's case, however, the regulars recognized him as a potential equal on the waterfront, a sloop owner who was about to engage in similar work on similar footing. They offered to treat him first, a clear sign of welcome to their drinking circle. And they kept on treating and humoring him, apparently confident that soon he would realize what a "gink" he was being and start reciprocating. But in Stevens's case, he treated first, as though making application to the club. The team-hands let him go on with his unrequited treating, apparently to see just what kind of a "gink" *he* was. And while no one black-balled him outright by refusing his treat, his application to the club languished since he could not meet this group's basic membership criteria, no matter how desperately he tried to buy his way into their company.

If the team-hands felt so little inclined to reciprocate, why did they not simply refuse Stevens's treat in the first place? This might seem the logical thing to have done, but the symbolism of drink rendered such action out of the question. It was one thing to fail to reciprocate; it was quite another to refuse to drink altogether. Both were gestures of rejection, but the first was comparatively passive, a slight by omis-sion, whereas the second was unmistakably aggressive, a slight by commission. Only if circumstances clearly prevented a man from ac-cepting, as when he had pressing business elsewhere or had already had too much to drink, might he be forgiven for demurring. As Hoke remarked, "It was insulting to refuse to be treated—so much so that a weak (or hardy) soul who could not endure the thought of more liquor down his gullet would order a cigar, even if he put it in his pocket." Such refusals were socially neutral, not reflecting on men's relationships or the degree of their regard for one another. Out-and-out rejection of a treating offer was, however, a definite personal affront and was not an action to be taken lightly by either party.[17]

There were those so hungry for a listening public that they were willing to treat just to buy one, settling for the presence of a captive audience as reciprocation enough. A New York saloonkeeper described a customer of this type who frequented his establishment in 1909. "When intoxicated, this man button-holed everybody, paid for drinks for his auditors, and told rambling stories that had neither beginning nor end," he reported. "By his baleful eye he held men spellbound, like the Ancient Mariner, for hours and hours." Similarly, Stevens observed a man in the Horseshoe Saloon, one Poker Tom Davis, who adopted the same tactic of buying drinks to hold his audience. He was reputedly an ex-Mississippi River gambler who intimidated everyone with his erudite air as well as the gun on his hip. One night, Poker Tom commanded the barroom's undivided attention by treating all present three times in succession while he regaled them with tales from the Trojan Wars. Like the eerie "Ancient Mariner," Poker Tom Davis approached the saloon not as a general marketplace for ideas, but rather as a private lecture hall which he rented by the glass.[18]

These men used treating not to initiate the flow of friendly conversation, but rather to arrest it, to seize a temporary position of power from which to pontificate on matters chiefly of interest to themselves. An element of the clubbing spirit was present, for both treater and treated did contribute and derive something of value from the arrangement. But the unevenness of the exchange, the substitution of monologue for dialogue, and the absence of shared intent all conspired to make such encounters fall short of the club ideal.

THE CELEBRATORY TREAT

Most people who treated the crowd to drinks were not barroom megalomaniacs, of course. Often a customer "called up the house" when he had good fortune to celebrate. "The birth of another infant," for example, ". . . called for the immediate purchase of a round of drinks," according to George Ade. The treat was a bid for attention, but the intent was also to make a party of the occasion, to spread the cheer around by providing drinks (and, traditionally, cigars) to all. In fact, almost any excuse could be used to start a round of celebratory treating, observed Hoke. "The neighborhood stood treat on a variety of occasions: births, deaths, funerals, weddings, betrothals, on meeting friends, on meeting strangers, on perpetrating a joke or becoming the butt of one, or for no reason at all except the desire to be friendly and have a drink." [19]

A sudden windfall might prompt the buying of drinks all around, as when London's waterfront friends earned a sizeable reward for locating a missing salmon boat. "They couldn't wait a moment to celebrate the fifty dollars they had so easily earned," he recalled. "It was the way of the devotees of John Barleycorn. When good fortune comes, they drink." The upstanding drinking man remembered his barmates in times of good fortune, knowing that they would do the same when their good times came, and also that they would not forget him should misfortune follow. Meanwhile, immediate reciprocity came in the form of communal jubilation and recognition. [20]

Legendary for celebrating pugilistic triumphs in this fashion was John L. Sullivan, the "Boston Strong Boy." "He was idolized as a man-killer and also because he was the ideal customer," Ade explained. "He slapped a large bill on the counter and called up the house and often tried to slug the bartender who pushed any change back to him. A man's man!" For Sullivan, his generous treating enabled him to enhance his heroic image and assert his dominance in nearly any barroom assembly he chose to join. At the same time, it enabled him to pay tribute to his public, acknowledge their worthiness as drinking partners, and prove himself a "regular fellow" at heart who appreciated his barmates' esteem. On the bargoers' part, they received free liquor and the considerable honor of being invited to drink with John L. Sullivan, repaying him with the adulation and deference due a great man who retained the common touch. The trade was an equitable one to all parties concerned, as dramatized by Sullivan's indignation at the thought of receiving change back from the bartender. He had contributed what he considered his fair share to the occasion and would not countenance having his magnanimity quantified. Besides, by leaving the change to the keeper, Sullivan cultivated his good will and did honor to the clubhouse that honored him by prominently posting his portrait on the barroom wall. [21]

Celebrating good fortune by treating the house was a custom so universal that even total strangers could employ it to cultivate instant barroom camaraderie. In New York City in 1909, for example, a saloonkeeper recalled an occasion when two strangers from the Far West came into his establishment. "One of them, a man of about fifty-five, baldheaded but very active, pulled out a big wad of five and ten dollar bills, and declared his intention of leaving this roll at my place," the proprietor reported. "He invited everybody to drink with him and . . . proposed champagne, called for the best in the house." As strangers in the big city who wished to celebrate with others, where else were these two men to go but to a saloon? Here was a place where people often did their celebrating, with a tradition in place that guided the course of the celebration. Had these men entered a barbershop or butchershop and ordered haircuts or lambchops for everybody, they would have been adjudged lunatics. But two strangers could enter a saloon and order drinks for the house, in which case they were thought very fine fellows indeed. Moreover, in a further demonstration of good treating form, the bald-headed benefactor insisted that no change come back to him. Like John L. Sullivan, he apparently disdained the notion of counting small change at so grand a moment, preferring instead to include the bartender in his newfound circle of drinking comrades.[22]

Another rather bizarre example of celebrating good fortune by treating the house was offered in Frank Norris's *McTeague.* When the protagonist and his friend Marcus Schouler stopped for a drink at the Cliff House in San Francisco, Marcus astonished McTeague with the feat of popping a billiard ball all the way into his mouth and then out again, betting his friend a quarter that he could not do the same. In the sporting spirit of the barroom, McTeague accepted the challenge and inserted the same ball into his mouth, where it promptly lodged and refused to budge. Pandemonium ensued. With McTeague frantically flailing about, the commotion attracted a group of frightened on-lookers. And then, suddenly, inexplicably, the ball just popped back out of McTeague's distended jaws, and the emergency was past. There was but one thing to do after that. "On the strength of the occasion Marcus Schouler invited the entire group to drink with him."[23]

Marcus's group treat was a fitting gesture for several reasons. It was of course customary to celebrate fortunate outcomes of any sort in a saloon. It was also fitting that Marcus should treat, for he was ultimately responsible for the trouble and had the greatest reason to celebrate, next to the relieved McTeague. Further, his treating compensated the crowd for the upset they had suffered and rewarded them for their kind concern. In this way, treating helped restore calm and camaraderie after crisis. Though the whole episode was of course fictional, Norris's insistence on realistic detail in his novels might indicate that he had drawn upon actual experience in recording the incident. In any case, the friendly wager on a dare and the celebratory treating of the house were certainly common elements of the barroom scene.

Even stranger than fiction was the true episode of treating the house—in this case, a frontier courthouse—witnessed by labor leader Frank Roney in the early 1870s. Roney was traveling in Iowa at a time when Sioux City was still little more than a row of tents. One of the largest served as a saloon, where he was startled to discover a court in session behind a curtain rigged up to create a makeshift back room. Being tried on a charge of murder was a man who had in fact greatly pleased the local townsfolk by eliminating a notorious troublemaker from their midst. The trial adjourned for lunch. Then, to Roney's astonishment, "The prisoner, with nonchalance as perfect as it was innocent, addressing the judge said, 'Well, Judge, I guess the drinks are on me this time,' and as no objection was raised we all, prosecutor, judge, sheriff, and a few others, drank at his expense. . . . For a prisoner on trial to treat the prosecuting lawyer and the judge trying him was so novel a proceeding that it rather charmed me." [24]

Was this not an outrageous bribe and an affront to the solemnity of the court? Not at all, apparently; on the contrary, the participants behaved as though there were nothing wrong or ridiculous in the situation whatsoever. To them, the prisoner's treat was just a friendly gesture of thanks in advance for his certain acquittal to follow that afternoon. The treat was a symbol of their mutual accord and a celebration of good fortune all around, except of course for the deceased, that "bad man and desperado of whom the community appeared to be well rid," in Roney's words. The prisoner had inconvenienced everyone by necessitating the formality of a trial. To compensate them for their time and support, it was fitting that he should treat the house. By accepting the treat, the crowd demonstrated that there were no hard feelings. He was still one of their company, and they intended to follow through on their unspoken pact to reward his civic service with freedom. [25]

Sealing pacts, business contracts, and agreements of every description was a barroom practice dating back to colonial days when merchants, employers, and others often used taverns as informal business offices. Such dealings in saloons usually involved treating, for as Melendy observed, "The glass of beer in a business transaction has a function similar to that of the cigarette in diplomacy." Customarily, the treating was done by the promoter of the deal, so that the merchant treated his client, the salesman treated his buyer, and the man with a scheme treated his prospective partner. According to a bartender on New York City's East Side, it was to his humble neighborhood barroom that many a local merchant would "resort with his customer when both [were] jovial over a particularly satisfactory bargain." Similarly, *Fortune* magazine reported that the establishment of what eventually became Warner Brothers Studios began in 1917 in a Los Angeles barroom. Harry Warner lacked the necessary facilities to produce his first major film, but "by taking the old-time movie speculator Mark Dintenfass to a stand-up lunch in a saloon he secured the studio and laboratory in which he made the picture." Further, since the promoter of deals made use of the saloon premises to achieve personal gain, his buying of drinks compensated the saloonkeeper for providing congenial surroundings in which to do business. As London explained, this was "an evident custom, and a logical one—the seller, who receives the money, to wet a piece of it in the establishment where the trade was consummated." The promoter might also include the bartender and other regulars who could then join in celebrating the successful realization of his schemes.[26]

THE KEEPER'S TREAT

Treating the barkeeper might at first glance appear a peculiar custom, since he had easy access to the bar stock and could presumably help himself to free drinks whenever he chose. For many barkeepers, however, their "first rule of conduct was not to do any nipping while 'on watch,'" according to Ade. This claim was corroborated by George Washington Plunkitt, a powerful Tammany machine politician in New York who often dealt with bar owners in organizing the saloon vote. In Plunkitt's words, "The most successful saloonkeepers don't drink themselves and they understand that my temperance is a business proposition, just like their own." Further, many bar owners strictly forbade their employees to imbibe on the job, under threat of immediate dismissal. Oddly enough, then, the bartender, who was seemingly in the best position to drink freely and for free, was often the one person not drinking at all—not unless, that is, he was offered a treat.[27]

For the bartender, just as for any other barroom denizen, a treat was an offer he could not refuse. This lesson was learned the hard way by Rumanian immigrant M. E. Ravage when he began tending bar for one Mr. Weiss in New York in the early 1900s. "From him I first learned . . . that bar-men never drink," Ravage stated, "except at a customer's invitation, which is another story and is governed by a special ethical rule." Yet, though the young bartender had been told to accept customers' treats, he was reluctant to comply. He disliked beer and detested hard liquor. To resolve his dilemma, he suggested to one customer that the man simply give him the money for the treat instead. In terms of drinking tradition, however, Ravage had refused a treat, a grave personal affront to the customer. In addition, he had audaciously suggested money in place of drink, an action which struck both his customer and his boss as a baldly unsociable solicitation for personal gain. Moreover, because the treat was supposed to be rung up on the cash register like any other sale, he had in effect proposed robbing the proprietor of his drink-selling revenue.[28]

Ravage might have lost his job over this violation of the "special ethical rule" that governed bartenders and treating, except that Mrs. Weiss intervened on his behalf. Thereafter, however, "My employer constantly impressed it upon me that it was my duty to his firm to accept every treat that was offered me," Ravage reported. "It pleased the customer, he explained, and it increased the sales." Thus, the bartender, who often was forbidden to drink on his own during business hours, could accept a drink—indeed, was obligated to accept—when a customer invoked the ritual of the treat.[29]

Had Ravage but known, there were some diplomatic dodges that the saloonkeeper could employ to give the appearance of accepting a treat without actually imbibing large quantities of alcohol. He might take a cigar instead, which was acceptable because it cost the same as beer (generally five cents) and because treating with tobacco was recognized as a sociable gesture roughly comparable to treating with alcohol. Otherwise, if a customer insisted the bartender drink with him, he might use a special glass called a "snit," which according to Ade was "about the size of an eyecup and the supposed drink was all foam." Snits and cigars enabled the bartender to fulfill the requirements of treating tradition without incapacitating himself or insulting his customer. Such ruses point up the highly symbolic nature of barroom treating. The customer could make the offer, the bartender could pretend to accept, and both were satisfied as long as the spirit, if not actually the letter, of treating law was observed.[30]

Bartenders customarily treated big spenders from time to time, to cultivate good will and to reciprocate treats offered him. "Once in so often, if a group of enthusiastic buyers had been pushing important money across the moist mahogany," observed Ade, the barkeeper "was expected to announce, smilingly and suavely, 'Gents, this one is on the house,' thereby establishing himself as one of nature's noblemen." A bartender might also treat his regulars on special occasions, such as St. Patrick's Day. As Arizona saloonkeeper George Hand remarked in his diary entry for 17 March 1875, "Treated all the boys. Everyone drunk. . . . Got tight myself." Another Arizona bartender, M. E. Joyce of the Oriental Saloon in Tombstone, made a daily ritual of treating and storytelling. First he treated his morning customers to a round and a joke. After that, he reciprocated each customer's offer to treat with another anecdote, and so on all day until well past midnight.[31]

Temperance advocates complained that such treating by bartenders was simply a ploy to entice and obligate customers to spend extravagantly, particularly when business was bad. As Robert Bagnell asserted, "[O]ften when the sales lag the saloon keeper himself treats to start business going again."[32] In part, reformers were correct, for the saloonkeeper's treat was of course a tactic calculated to stimulate sales. At the same time, however, it was a gesture of gratitude and goodwill, a way of recognizing and reciprocating the regulars' loyal patronage. Like many other aspects of saloon culture, the barkeeper's treat represented a commingling of business and brotherly impulses.

THE POLITICIAN'S TREAT

In addition to social and economic motives, the saloonkeeper often had strong political motives for treating his clientele to drinks and other favors. In cities nationwide, the saloon was a principal arena of local politics, with the saloonkeeper serving as liaison and power broker between the machine politicians and the barroom voters. "By his position he is a leader," as Raymond Calkins observed. "He is the man to whom the politician must go before the realization of his schemes. If there is any bribery, it concerns the saloon-keeper, who is asked to treat 'the boys' in return. Such are the varied functions of the barkeeper; such is his social position; such is his influence." [33]

Ward politicians were familiar figures in city barrooms where they frequently came in person to cultivate the saloon vote. To keep up his image as the poor man's benefactor, according to San Francisco boss Martin Kelly, the politician must "swagger into a saloon, slap down twenty dollars, call up the house, and tell the barkeeper to freeze onto the change. . . . He must never forget his lowly retainers, for whom he must find jobs, kiss their babies and send them Christmas presents." Similarly, across the nation in New York City, Tammany boss George Washington Plunkitt dutifully made the same effort to curry favor with his constituency. As he observed in his diary in 1905, "Went to a church fair. Took chances on everything, bought ice cream for the young girls and the children. Kissed the little ones, flattered their mothers and took their fathers out for something down at the corner." [34]

By the late nineteenth century, such generous treating was refined into seasonal rituals designed to remind voters of their representatives' beneficence on their behalf. Tammany district leaders in New York, for example, customarily sponsored two picnics every summer, and in winter, a steak dinner and an elaborate annual ball. After these events, the district leader publicized an exact accounting of the food and drink he had so liberally provided. "The drinking records, as given out, are . . . phenomenal," reported William Riordon. Further, "[W]hen he excels all others in this particular, he feels, somehow, that he is a bigger man and deserves more patronage than his associates in the Tammany Executive Committee." [35]

Treating by politicians was not limited to the saloon premises, nor was it limited to voting males. Rather, entire districts were included (and corrupted, reformers charged) in Tammany's communal extravaganzas. Moreover, for "Bathhouse John" Coughlin of Chicago, the flamboyant First Ward boss famous for his flashy dress and expansive manner, the scope of his treating even included nonresidents and out-of-towners. As his biographers noted, "Coughlin, usually surrounded by a noisy crowd of friends, delighted to dash upon open-mouthed strangers. 'I'm John Coughlin,' he would shout. 'I'm th' alderman of the ward. Come on, I'll buy you a glass of beer.'" For machine politicians, campaigning was a year-round, district-wide activity in which treating played a central role both on and beyond the saloon premises.[36]

What was it like to be a saloongoer swept up in the treating net of vote-hungry politicians? London provided a vivid firsthand account. He and "Young Scratch" Nelson deliberately planted themselves in the path of free-spending office seekers in 1892 in Oakland's Overland House saloon. In his words, "One is sitting at a table, in a dry condition, wondering who is going to turn up and buy him a drink . . . when suddenly the saloon doors swing wide and enters a bevy of well-dressed men, themselves usually wide and exhaling an atmosphere of prosperity and fellowship." These politicians would heartily greet all bargoers present, regardless if they were penniless or shabbily dressed. Even homeless hoboes were warmly received, for they could be temporarily put up in cheap lodging houses and become qualified voters almost overnight. Such "floaters" or "lost nerves" were lured into cities in huge numbers at election time. They jammed the lodging houses and saloon back rooms at the politicians' expense until they could cast their ballots. No man was too lowly for consideration, and everyone might expect at least civil treatment and a treat. Thus, London and Nelson loafed at the Overland, "broke, thirsty, but with the drinker's faith in the unexpected drink," waiting like two Dickensian Micawbers "for something to turn up, especially politicians."[37]

Suddenly, their friend Joe Goose burst in to inform them that a group of politicians were organizing a trainload of supporters for a march in a nearby town. It was supposed to be a parade of the Hancock Fire Brigade, but "the politicians who ran it were short of torchbearers, and anybody who would parade could get drunk if he wanted to." No one cared, apparently, that London, Nelson, and Goose were not firemen, nor were they residents of the town they would march in, nor were they even sure what political party they were representing. For the three drinking cronies, all that mattered was that the politicians had already bought out the stocks of the town's saloons for treating purposes. Meanwhile, all that mattered to the politicians was that enough men marched with enough enthusiasm to impress the local townsfolk with the strength and generosity of the political machine. And so the thirsty trio rushed off to change into firemen's shirts and helmets in time to catch the political gravy train to a place where drinks and drinking men would run free.[38]

When the train delivered them to the parading point, they were told that no drinks would be forthcoming until after they had marched. "Oh, those politicians had handled our kind before," remarked London. "Parade, first, and earn your booze, was the order of the night." So they dutifully paraded, completing their end of the bargain. Then it was time for the politicians to reciprocate. The parched marchers descended on the saloons, overwhelming the bartenders who could not keep up with the demand. "This method of jamming and struggling in front of the bar was too slow for us," London recalled. "The drink was ours. The politicians had bought it for us. We'd paraded and earned it, hadn't we? So we made a flank attack around the end of the bar, shoved the protesting barkeepers aside, and helped ourselves."[39]

Finally it was time for the train ride back to Oakland, so "Nelson and I were hustled out of a saloon, and found ourselves in the very last rank of a disorderly parade." London fell and lost consciousness on the way, but his drunken partner managed to carry him to the train. There London came around and decided to smash a window for air. Somebody mistook this for an act of aggression and knocked him out cold, whereupon a terrific "free-for-all fight" ensued, with London unconscious on the floor beneath a heap of bodies and broken glass. He awoke seventeen hours later in some strange lodging house in Oakland, desperately hung over but relieved to be alive.[40]

All in all, in London's estimation, it had been a very satisfactory evening. The politicians had gotten their parade, the marchers had gotten their drinks, and no real damage had been done except for a little broken glass, some sore jaws, and London's reluctant realization "that there were limits to my gorgeous constitution, and that there were no limits to John Barleycorn." Reformers of course deplored this sort of boisterous bacchanalia, although street parading and communal bingeing at election time had in fact been characteristic of working-class political participation since the colonial era.[41]

Pre-election treating was prodigious, but it was on election day itself that the activity reached its frenzied crescendo. In Chicago, according to George Turner, the political troops who got out the vote were dispatched at first light with huge firecrackers to awaken lodging-house boarders. They bought them a drink, known as giving them "a scrub of the brush." This essential ritual performed, they hustled the voters off to the polls—sometimes with ballots already helpfully filled in for them—and then paid the going price for voting. This was usually from ten to fifty cents, though sometimes as much as three dollars. Politicians employed a similar system in New York City, especially in the immigrant and black neighborhoods. Regarding the latter, Riis observed that "the black tramp . . . at least exhibits some real loyalty in invariably selling his vote to the Republican bidder for a dollar, while he charges the Democratic boss a dollar and a half." Lesser operators in smaller towns usually relied simply on treats and favors to secure votes. As a carpenter in Janesville, Wisconsin, observed of politicians seeking the immigrant vote, "I knew men to take 35 of these new comers to the county clerk's office, get out their 'papers' at 35 cts. per head, next take them to a saloon, give them a drink, take them to the polls to vote, while the crowd laughed over the matter, and that's the end."[42]

Thus, the election process, and particularly election day, could be an exhausting and expensive proposition for the office seeker. He had all the "floater" voters to satisfy in addition to his regular constituency. On the other hand, his outlay would be amply repaid later by the power and money-making opportunities he gained upon becoming an officeholder.

Reformers charged that the politically motivated treat was a bribe and that workers were being tricked and manipulated in a gross perversion of the American political process. In the context of drinking tradition and symbolism, however, the politician's treat was more accurately a bid for mutual support and favor swapping, something that bargoers did among themselves all the time. Saloongoing workers did not regard this use of treating as dishonorable or perverse, nor did it seem to them that they were being defrauded or duped. On the contrary, the treat sealed a pact between political leader and constituent that each would contribute and derive something of value from the arrangement. It was not subversion or trickery at all, but rather a very practical and mutually beneficial implementation of the barroom ideal of reciprocity.

TRICK OR TREAT

Outright subversion of the club ideal, in which donor or recipient cynically and underhandedly manipulated the treating ritual to achieve some crassly self-serving or illicit end, was rare but not unknown in working-class saloons. For the most part, hustlers, confidence men, parasites, and other "low-life" characters did not fare well in the workingman's club. The clientele was too regular and thus too quick to find out and ostracize offenders of the code. In addition, most ordinary customers had too little money to make them interesting quarry to predators. Moreover, the proprietor had a license and a neighborhood reputation to protect, both of which could be jeopardized by the machinations of sleazy troublemakers. There were always some disreputable establishments that paid bribes to the police to stay in operation and accommodate customers in search of big stakes gambling, professional prostitutes, or other attractions of the shadier side of barlife. Most workers' saloons did not operate in this manner, however, for as Calkins noted, "[T]he demand is not great enough for a large number to thrive and pay the 'tax,' that is, the hush money."[43] Still, people in ordinary barrooms did occasionally resort to manipulating or subverting the honor code of the club for their own purposes, most often in the pursuit of money, sex, or power over others.

Treating trickery touched the life of labor leader William "Big Bill" Haywood in an incident illustrating how a trusting soul might be entrapped by the unscrupulous treater pursuing power over his victim. In Denver in 1908, Haywood attended a convention of the Western Federation of Miners, an organization torn by warring factions headed by Haywood and by his rival, Charles H. Moyer. Before the meeting, at which Haywood was scheduled to make an important speech, several convention members offered to take him out for drinks in an apparent gesture of comradeship and support. Only later did Haywood learn from an ally that the treat was a scam. "'That is exactly what Moyer likes to see you do,' he told me. 'At the last convention I know that Moyer gave members money and told them to go out and have a good time with Bill; get him good and drunk.'" Haywood managed to deliver his speech (though Moyer walked out on him when he rose to speak), for heavy drinking in barrooms had long been part of his normal routine. When he learned of Moyer's treating treachery, however, he realized his vulnerability to betrayal at the hands of those who would twist the traditions of drink to their own advantage. "My friends and family had often begged me to stop drinking; I had made many promises which I knew I wouldn't keep," he confessed in his autobiography. "But now I was mad, mad clear through, under the eyes, deep down in the stomach. . . . I did not touch intoxicating liquor after that for many years."[44]

Haywood's abrupt decision to abstain from hard liquor reveals how deeply he was shaken by this incident. He had come to rely on the brotherhood of labor and the traditions of drink to make workers' barrooms a safe haven wherever he went. Both labor groups and drinking groups embraced the code of reciprocity, solidarity, and fair play, or so Haywood had assumed. Henceforth, however, he would always have to wonder whether the generosity of fellow bargoers was trick or treat.

Another sort of treating trickster was the professional gambling "sharp" who wangled free drinks or money out of unwary regulars.[45] In barroom games involving cards, dice, pool, billiards, and slot machines, it was common for participants to gamble for small stakes. As Calkins remarked, "[P]laying for drinks or for the cost of a game . . . is a common matter of courtesy," the loser paying tribute to the winner(s) by the gesture of the treat. The technique of the gambling hustler, however, was to subvert the friendly game either by cheating or by misrepresenting his talent to lure his victims into making extravagant sucker bets. Such ploys might have kept the gambler in drinks and money for a while, but he ran the risk of being discovered and punished by irate regulars (as symbolized several decades later by the broken thumbs of pool shark "Fast Eddie" Felson in the 1961 film classic, *The Hustler*). Like most aspects of saloonlife, gambling conduct was guided by the code of the club. Each participant expected to contribute and derive his fair share of drinks and pleasure over the long run. By maneuvering others into one-way treating, the unscrupulous gambler betrayed the code and laid himself open to rejection, retaliation, and expulsion from the drinkers' fold.[46]

In addition to power and money, sex was occasionally the object of treating, introducing its own peculiar elements of tension and manipulation to the barroom scene. John Dos Passos provided an illustration in *Nineteen Nineteen,* a novel detailing the customs and morals of preprohibition Americans. While protagonist Joe Williams, a penniless young sailor, was loafing outside a bar, a stranger "who said his name was Jones" invited him in for a drink. "Joe looked at him suspiciously. 'All right,' he said finally, 'but I might as well tell you right now I can't treat you back.'" Jones seemed unconcerned. He bought a round, then another, then a flask to share while the two explored the local sights, and still another for a nightcap in his rooms. To this point, Joe had contributed only his companionship to their clubbing arrangement. When he got up to leave, however, he discovered that Jones had more meaningful reciprocation in mind after all. "'You can't go away like this, now you've got me feeling all sort of chummy and, you know, amorous,' cried Jones. 'I'll do the handsome thing. I'll give you fifty dollars.'" Shocked and distressed, Joe Williams fled the scene, no doubt leaving Jones shocked and distressed as well. For though a solicitation for sex might have exceeded most ordinary expectations of reciprocity, Joe knew full well he had been violating the code of drinking with this stranger whom he had no hope of repaying. Perhaps he had been "hustled," but he had been doing a little hustling himself, taking advantage of his host's generosity without thought to proper reciprocity.[47]

Of course, most working-class girls going out on dates in this era would have found much that was familiar in Joe Williams's story. They had to deal with the thorny issue of treating and reciprocity all the time. Dating was, after all, just a heterosexual form of treating in which the male paid for food, drinks, and entertainment in exchange for the pleasure of the female's company. In reality, though, the female was often pressured to yield more. Many girls felt obligated to do so, as illustrated in a statutory rape case brought before the Alameda County Superior Court in Oakland, California, in the early 1900s. A young girl was asked why her teenage sister had gone to a hotel with a young man she had only met a few hours earlier in an amusement park. The girl explained, "She didn't like to turn him down, he had given us lunch and paid our way into the rink and she didn't like to turn him down."[48]

In New York City, such accommodating dates were called "charity girls," an expression denoting young women who gave away their sexual favors for gifts, nights on the town, or other treats (as opposed to professional prostitutes, who preferred hard cash). The pressure on young women to reciprocate treats was intensified when young men's "charity" included alcohol, which it often did when fellows brought drinks to their dates in parks, on tenement rooftops, or in the cozy back rooms of saloons. The gift of drink, at once disinhibiting and obligating, was in fact the perfect date treating ploy, if a man's motives were ulterior. This was apparently the strategy of Dos Passos's "man who called himself Jones," mistaking Joe Williams for a "charity boy" who would understand that such generous barroom treating carried with it the expectation of reciprocity, one way or another.[49]

In the case of the professional prostitute, there was seldom any confusion over her motives in accepting treats, for hustling drinks as a prelude to sex was one of the most universal and time-honored tricks of her trade. It was, in fact, the prostitute's ability to persuade prospective customers to spend freely in saloons that earned her the proprietor's tolerance, when he would tolerate her presence at all. "To set up the drinks to 'the girls' is a custom; the women calling for 'small beer' urge the men 'to set 'em up' again and again; hence they are a source of revenue to the saloon," as Royal Melendy remarked. It might be said that the prostitute's manipulation of the treating ritual was at least straightforward. There was no doubt about her intent or what form her reciprocation would eventually take. But this did not do much to improve her barroom standing, for no amount of forthrightness could overcome the social stigma of turning tricks for treats.[50]

The stigma attached to letting oneself be sexually bought through treating was especially intense in the case of the "tango pirate." This fancy-dancing gigolo haunted cabarets in search of women willing to pay for male company at their tables, on the dance floor, or elsewhere. The cabaret, an upscale version of the saloon popular in large cities after 1910, featured music and dancing and welcomed both male and female patrons. Different though it was from the typically male-dominated, hard-drinking saloon, the cabaret was nonetheless a "club"—more precisely, a "nightclub"—where the general conventions of American drinking culture still obtained. Flying in the face of all convention, however, were the tango pirates who were generally "ignorant, ill-born fellows who have acquired a mere veneer of good manners and smart talk," according to New York criminal lawyer John F. McIntyre. "How women can endure men who are palpably, serenely, and obviously parasites is hard for an old-fashioned man like me to understand." The tango pirate's idea of reciprocity was to flatter and dazzle his benefactress with his erotic charm, flashy clothes, and sensuous dancing. Such behavior was regarded as weak and effeminate by most working- and middle-class males of the era, who were already suspicious of any man who spent a great deal of time in the company of women. Historian Lewis Erenberg has pointed out an odd inconsistency in the charge of effeminacy lodged against the cabaret gigolo. "Here was a man who, by nineteenth-century standards, spent too much time with women; ironically the penalty for such action was loss of manhood."[51]

The tango pirate did not dare, nor did he care to set foot in the typical workingman's barroom, violating as he did every tenet of the saloon's manly code of drinking. Still, his example is instructive. Like the gambling sharp, the hooker, and every other variety of hustler hovering at the saloon's periphery, his violation of the clubbing code helps bring its underlying rules and values very much into focus. Such aberrations, however, were rare. For the most part, treating was practiced honorably and straightforwardly by working-class saloongoers of the era.

TREATING AND THE SALOON CLUB

Treating was a complicated and delicate business. All episodes had an outward similarity: men bought drinks for others in ritualistic fashion. But treating episodes in fact differed greatly according to the inner motivations of participants. The principal difference between one instance of treating and another ultimately came down to the extent to which community or marketplace values were uppermost in the participants' minds.

Most frequently, the regulars' motivations were purely sociable. Men swapped rounds with peers in a spirit of equality and mutuality. This arrangement was financial as well as fraternal, of course. Every man had to contribute. In barlife, there were few fates worse than getting a reputation as a "short-sport" or "moocher." When that happened, brotherhood evaporated. A man short of cash might run a tab with his saloonkeeper, but eventually he either paid his dues or faced the street. The bar club was a business, and drink-buying was an integral part of it, as every regular knew. Treating was primarily a communal ritual, but it had its commercial side as well.

Sometimes a regular's motivation for treating was more practical and self-interested. He might treat to procure information, promote a project, or pave the way toward asking a favor. This use of the saloon treat displayed more elements of the marketplace than purely sociable treating. The donor's offer was a deliberate, calculated act of the rational will. His goal was comparatively selfish and narrowly defined. Further, the treating pact looked a little more like a marketplace contract, the treat representing payment in advance for a service rendered. Yet the underlying relationship was still that of two regulars, two social equals who shared a sense of commonality. The treat recipient complied with his drinking partner's request as much out of communal feeling as contractual duty.

On still other occasions, regulars received treats from persons who might be termed saloon "operators." The term "operator" is defined as "[o]ne who figures in many exchanges of favors; one who plays petty politics to achieve minor goals."[52] Politicians, sports celebrities, and saloonkeepers who treated the regulars belonged to this category. Saloon operators manipulated the treating ritual, but their motives differed greatly from saloon hustlers. Operators worked the crowd as a matter of good public relations, building loyalty and support through various means, including treating. They were after something— votes, fame, profit—but they were also offering something in return: patronage favors, reflected glory, recognition as a valued regular. The saloon hustler, in contrast, was an underhanded cad motivated strictly by self-interest, his actions representing market-oriented values at their impersonal worst.

Saloon operators were the special target of temperance advocates who deplored the treating system in general and its manipulation by self-interested parties in particular. The saloonkeeper's treat, they charged, was a coldly calculated ploy to stimulate sales and encourage extravagance. The politician's treat was an equally repugnant scheme to bribe workers for their votes. Both parties allegedly tried to cloak their base motives in a mantle of brotherhood and reciprocity, which reformers regarded as deceitful, exploitative, and morally reprehensible. Or, to put the matter another way, they accused saloon operators of cynically disguising their cupidity with a pretense of community.

What reformers overlooked, however, was that marketplace values could play a legitimate role in barroom interaction as long as they did not crowd out communal values altogether. Treating for practical and even mercenary purposes was acceptable if motives were clear and the principle of community was not violated. But were the motives of the operators clear? Were they deceiving the regulars, thus transgressing the communal ethic? The regulars were not that gullible, nor were the operators that devious. They had a deal. Everyone recognized the asymmetrical power relations involved and understood that the operators were not treating solely out of the kindness of their hearts. Workers well knew about "pecking orders" in life—the social, economic, and political hierarchies that dominated the larger urban marketplace. The idea was to establish a niche for themselves within that pecking order. One way to do that was to cultivate a powerful ally, and the most convenient and congenial way to do that was to engage in the quid pro quo of the saloon operator's treat.

Moreover, the arrangement included many genuine elements of community. Often politicians, saloonkeepers, and sports figures had grown up in the same neighborhood, or at least they shared comparable socio-economic backgrounds with the regulars. They were aware of the sense of commonality that prevailed in saloons and indeed they shared in it with their similar gender attitudes, ethnic heritages, occupational experiences, and the like. Clubbing, with all the cultural resonance of drink lore behind it, conferred a quality of sociability and mutuality on their encounters. Finally, politicians and saloonkeepers made a point of looking after the regulars in a most personal way. Jane Addams noted in 1898 that the immigrants in Chicago's nineteenth ward looked upon Johnny Powers, their saloon-owning alderman, as "a big, warm-hearted friend . . . who will stand by them in an emergency. . . . The Alderman is really elected because he is a good friend and neighbor." Even Lincoln Steffens, the vociferously antimachine author of *The Shame of the Cities* (1904), acknowledged when writing of New York that "Tammany kindness is real kindness, and will go far, remember long, and take infinite trouble for a friend."[53]

Thus, the saloon treat was many things to many people. To reformers, it was an abettor of extravagance, corruption, and drunkenness. To hustlers, it was a tool of the confidence game. To bartenders, it was a promoter of sales and customer goodwill. To politicians and sports celebrities, it was an instrument of public relations. But to most saloongoers most of the time, treating was a rite of comradeship that reaffirmed their status as regulars and made a club of the drinking experience.

Six

Clubbing by Collection

Here groups are naturally formed from among those habitually meeting in the same place. Hither groups already formed come to meet because they have no other shelter. The saloon has been quick to see its advantage and to make the most of it. The process by which its hold is increased through the club instinct which it fosters and satisfies is an interesting study.

—Raymond Calkins[1]

Groups of many descriptions drank in saloons. Some took shape spontaneously along the bar as one individual's offer to buy drinks for others set the stage for reciprocal treating all around. Other groups were more organized. They arrived at the saloon already committed in advance to their drinking partnership. They might be as informal as a circle of amateur singers; they might be part of a 250-member trade union. Whatever their size or purpose, these more organized groups were similar in at least one regard: clubbing by collection, rather than by treat, was their drink-buying method of choice. In most cases, all members chipped in their shares at the outset of the gathering, paying the saloonkeeper up front for the cost of alcohol for all.

Groups clubbing by collection were not tied to the main barroom as were treaters, the latter tending to hug the bar counter where each man's glass could be replenished swiftly and easily. In contrast, after clubbing collectives purchased their quantity of alcohol, they could retire to a table, to a back room, or to some off-premises site to begin consumption. Depending on their level of organization, such groups might even choose to establish regular meeting times and places, restrict the membership, and develop a dues-paying system to ensure a consistently adequate drinking fund. Thus, while the spirit of comradeship lay behind both methods of clubbing, groups taking up collections often exhibited a greater tendency toward exclusivity, formal structure, and permanency than their treat-swapping brethren.

RUSHING THE GROWLER

One advantage of clubbing by collection was that groups were freer to choose their drinking venues. Certainly a great many elected to enjoy the facilities and comforts offered by the saloon. Others, however, opted to carry their alcohol away to some other place for consumption. So common was the practice, in fact, that one New York proprietor estimated in 1909 that "the enormous sale of pitcher beer" in tenement districts "amounts to two-thirds of the whole amount sold" in many saloons, including his own.[2] Strictly speaking, of course, this was not *bar* drinking. But the phenomenon was so important to the bar trade, so widespread among drinkers, and so closely related to on-premises collective drinking, that it warrants attention.

Why, when the saloon had so many allures, did people so frequently opt for off-premises drinking? A principal reason was that it was much cheaper to buy take-out beer by the pailful, called "rushing the growler" in bar speech. Saloonkeepers were by custom expected to charge no more than ten cents for a "growler," defined as a "bucket, can, pitcher, or other large container used to carry beer home from a saloon." Regardless of the actual dimensions of the vessel, the price did not exceed a dime in most working-class establishments for the full fifty years of the saloon period. "Customers come in all day, and during the evening as well, with tin cans, big pitchers, and other vessels of huge size, and invariably call for a 'pint,'" as one barkeeper observed. "And for the ten cents that is the price of a nominal pint, they expect their cans to be filled to the brim." George Ade corroborated this assessment of the great bargain that beer by the pailful represented. "The can customers who 'rushed the growler' and came in to get their malt product in pitchers and buckets, expected to get and did get about four liberal helpings for a dime," he observed. Since four liberal helpings cost twenty cents when consumed glass by glass inside the bar, it is understandable why saloon customers so often indulged in growlers.[3]

Saloonkeepers bemoaned the unprofitability of this practice. As one liquor retailers' association in Chicago lamented in 1889, to sell beer in buckets was practically to sell it wholesale. Yet, for decade after decade, barmen continued to honor the growler trade, so pervasive was the tradition and so adamant the drinking public's insistence upon it.[4]

Though off-premises drinking by the pailful was a custom that predated the saloon era, it was not until the late nineteenth century that the practice became known in America as "rushing the growler." According to H. L. Mencken, the phrase made its first appearance in print in 1888, though he suspected its oral circulation began considerably earlier. The peculiar term "growler," some have speculated, came from "the growling noise made by the can or bucket sliding along the top of the bar."[5]

Several variants of the phrase were also in circulation by the 1890s. Both Mencken and Travis Hoke noted that "to rush the can" was widely used. According to Brander Matthews in 1893, "In New York the act of sending this can from the private house to the public house [for beer] and back is called *working the growler.*" On the Oakland waterfront in the 1890s, Jack London stated that "I would rush Spider, or Irish, or Scotty, or whoever was my crew, with the can for beer and the demijohn for wine," while on other occasions "we rushed the growler or got stronger stuff [whiskey] in bottles." The phrase was still very much current in 1914, as illustrated by Sinclair Lewis's use of it, to wit: "I hope you know growler-rushing"; "I'll match you to see who rushes a growler of beer"; and, in an interesting departure from the usual, "Got a growler of ice-cream soda for the ladies!" From these examples, it is apparent that the phrase "rushing the growler" and its variants were ordinarily used in connection with beer purchases, though buying in quantity for off-site consumption also applied to whiskey, wine, and even ice-cream soda.[6]

Whatever form the growler trade took, it was generally deplored by the liquor industry for bringing in too little profit and condemned by the temperance movement for bringing on too much drunkenness. Among working-class folk, however, it remained a widely embraced custom until at last technology achieved what temperance tirades and liquor sellers' laments could not. With the increasing availability of cheap bottled beer and improved home refrigeration in the early decades of the twentieth century, the cumbersome if copious growler was gradually rendered obsolete.[7]

Among the most persistent participants in the growler trade were immigrant families hailing from both western and eastern Europe. In

Worcester, Massachusetts, for example, Irish immigrants arriving throughout the nineteenth century brought with them their long-standing custom of buying take-out beer from informal, home-based grog shops known as "shebeens." In Ireland, these enterprises had constituted a thriving cottage industry, often carried on by needy widows. After the first influx of Irish families into Worcester in the 1830s, shebeens immediately cropped up in their neighborhoods and customers popped up with their pails in the traditional way. Some lingered for a time at the kitchen table to drink and socialize with neighbors passing to and fro. Others hurried back to their homes where family and friends awaited their bucket of communal cheer. Either way, according to Roy Rosenzweig, the shebeens exhibited "their close connection to the home and the everyday patterns of Irish immigrant life" as they "casually dispensed liquor at all hours to friends and neighbors, men and women alike, for both on- and off-premises consumption."[8]

These generally unlicensed and unregulated home dispensaries survived in numbers well into the 1880s, despite increasing efforts of state and local governments to drive them out of business in favor of the more easily regulated—and more lucratively taxable—commercial saloons. Yet continual harassment did eventually take its toll. By the turn of the twentieth century, formally licensed and brewery-backed saloons in Worcester and other cities nationwide outnumbered and overshadowed, though never completely replaced, shebeens and other "blind pigs" (unlicensed liquor sellers) in working-class neighborhoods.[9]

By popular demand, however, saloonkeepers found themselves obliged to carry on the growler trade, for the Irish were by no means alone in their liking for off-premises drinking among family and friends. In her study of Homestead, Pennsylvania, in the early 1900s, Margaret Byington discovered that Slavic, Hungarian, and Lithuanian families and their boarders made a regular practice of pooling resources to buy beer for group consumption. "On the Saturday after pay day the household usually clubs together to buy a case of beer which it drinks at home," she noted. Men were the heaviest drinkers at such gatherings. Yet women sometimes partook liberally as well, particularly when commemorating significant family and community events. "On most of these occasions," Byington noted, "whether weddings, christenings or funerals, joy and grief and religious ceremony are alike forgotten in a riotous good time."[10]

Often these sessions occurred indoors, where the "group gathers around the stove gossiping of home days, playing cards, drinking, and playing simple musical instruments." Weather permitting, however, residents frequently resorted to the tenement courtyard which served as the principal center of immigrant homelife in the hot summer months. The typical court was surrounded by "smoke-grimed houses" accommodating over one hundred people in some twenty households. "The open space teems with life and movement," Byington observed firsthand. "Children, dogs and hens make it lively under foot; overhead long lines of flapping clothes must be dodged." Thus, this outdoor arena served not only as a setting for socializing, but also as a barnyard, a laundry, and a children's playground. Families might also find fun and recreation in an occasional church outing, lodge dance, or trip to the nickelodeon. Men always had the option of patronizing one of the fifty-odd saloons in the city. For most Homestead residents most of the time, though, their homely beer fests, in the courts in summer and by the stoves in winter, constituted their main opportunity for community contact and entertainment.[11]

Like most progressive reformers, Byington disapproved of such family drinking, though she recognized the compelling factors that motivated Homestead residents to indulge in it. One reason was the physical wretchedness and mental monotony of their worklives. The men performed punishing labor in the hellish atmosphere of the steel mill, while the women strained to keep large households running on meager budgets. "From quiet villages they come to this smoky town; from labor in the open fields to heavy work in the yards and thundering sheds of the mill," she observed, circumstances that prompted most men to drink and many women to join them.[12]

Just as important, however, was the immigrants' desire to preserve something of the village life they had enjoyed in their homelands, a life in which drinking blended easily with agricultural patterns of work and play. Longstanding folkways having been disrupted by the regimen of the American factory, the populace struggled to graft the old onto the new. They coordinated play days with paydays and attempted to recapture the flavor of rural community life in the midst of the harsh industrial environment. "Indeed, the cheerful gossip about the hydrant. . . , like the card playing in the court on a summer evening, suggests the neighborliness of village days," Byington noted. In this setting, Old World drinking customs fit smoothly and naturally. Both to fight exhaustion and to follow tradition, Homestead households clubbed together week after week to buy beer for their social gatherings.[13]

In working-class districts nationwide, much of the growler's appeal arose from the dual opportunity it presented to drink "al fresco" in the warmer months and to include women in the drinking circle. In New York City in the 1880s, for example, Jacob Riis noted the popularity of outdoor, mixed-company "can rackets" which formed an integral part of tenement neighborhood life in summertime. "It is in hot weather, when life indoors is well-nigh unbearable with cooking, sleeping, and working, all crowded into the small rooms together, that the tenement expands, reckless of all restraint," he remarked. "Then a strange and picturesque life moves upon the flat roofs. In the day and early evening mothers air their babies there, the boys fly their kites from the house-tops. . . , and the young men and girls court and pass the growler." Like the courtyards of Homestead, the rooftops of New York were transformed into neighborhood gathering spots where young men and women seized the opportunity to enjoy a breath of air and a bucket of beer together.[14]

Similarly, on the westernmost edge of the continent, Jack London described his participation in wharfside drinking parties, such as one that occurred aboard the sloop Razzle Dazzle in Oakland, California, in 1891. In addition to London, then fifteen years old, and a "grizzled man of fifty" known as "French Frank," the group included "two sisters, Mamie and Tess; a Mrs. Hadley, who chaperoned them; 'Whisky' Bob, a youthful oyster pirate of sixteen; and 'Spider' Healey, a black-whiskered wharf-rat of twenty." In the same spirit as their rooftop and courtyard counterparts in the East, this mixed company "went upon deck to take the air" and share a big bottle of wine purchased at a local saloon. "And we sat there, glasses in hand, and sang, while the big demijohn went around," he recalled. Meanwhile, in cities all over the country, young men who had banded together into self-styled "pleasure clubs" chipped in for beer for their "picnics or outings in the summer," according to Raymond Calkins, events to which girls were often invited.[15]

Precisely how the financing was handled in mixed-company gatherings was usually left unspecified in the literature. Certainly the men were expected to donate their fair share, but whether the women contributed to the collection remains unclear. In the case of whole households or married couples, income was probably pooled so that expenditures for beer, like those for food or clothing, all came out of the shared family budget. Regarding single women unaccompanied by family members, however, it seems likely that they were invited to drink gratis in accordance with dating customs of the era. Technically, then, such gatherings were a combination of clubbing by collection and by treat, young women reciprocating with the pleasure of their company or other favors.[16]

Sometimes women engaged in growler-drinking in all-female gatherings as well. "It is false to assume the women do not share the moral standards of their country, their class, and their neighborhood," as Philadelphia social worker Mrs. Robert Bradford remarked. "The men drank at night and the women drank by day, gathering in this one's and that one's kitchen, supplied from the corner saloon where they carried their kettles." Similarly, Boston settlement director Robert Woods reported in 1898 that Italian women in the tenements were known to share a bucket of beer in the daytime while their menfolk were away at work. Women in New York tenements also indulged in growler get-togethers, some residents claiming that "with the women it was a constant parade of beer kettles from early morning until late at night."[17]

Even more frequently, off-premises drinking sessions were all-male affairs. In the first decades following the Civil War, before workplace regimentation began to stamp it out, jobsite drinking by the clubbing method was common. In the cooperage trade, for example, "Several of the coopers would club together, each paying his proper share, and one of them would call out the window to the driver, 'Bring me a Goose Egg,' meaning a half-barrel of beer," observed Franklin Coyne. "Then others would buy 'Goose Eggs,' and there would be a merry time all around."[18]

By the turn of the century, many employers forbade the centuries-old tradition of drinking in the workshop itself, and particularly of drinking and working simultaneously. At lunch breaks, however, laborers stubbornly continued to consume beer by the growler. In Chicago in the early 1900s, for example, factory workers turned their midday breaks into group drinking sessions. "Several of their number are detailed to 'rush the growler,'" Royal Melendy observed. "Hanging several dinner-pails on a pole, they go to the nearest saloon and return with their pails full of beer." Hoke confirmed that this was a widespread practice. "It was the privilege of the apprentice or the youngest man in every crew to collect the beer buckets, borrow a wiping of lard from the nearest housewife so that the collar of foam would not lie so thick as to cheat an honest workingman of his beer, and get back from the saloon by the time the workers knocked off for lunch."[19]

Clubbing by collection was also common at purely social male gatherings. London cited many instances in the 1890s and early 1900s when his California seafaring friends scoured their pockets for coins to purchase whiskey, beer, or wine for communal consumption. In New Orleans, meanwhile, Louis Armstrong described how flattered he was to be invited to join groups of black men singing and drinking together in the early 1900s. "I thought I was really somebody when I got so I could hang around with those fellows—sing and drink out of the can with them," he recalled. Even very young boys sometimes participated in the growler tradition. In 1890, Riis described an incident in which a truant officer inspecting a New York tenement building "came upon a little party of four drinking beer out of the cover of a milk-can in the hallway." The children demonstrated their good manners in the matter of clubbing "by offering him some," to the consternation of the officer.[20]

Sometimes men's groups clubbed together toward the purchase of an entire keg of beer for mutual pleasure. Ade recalled that " 'keg parties' were popular" in the 1880s, in which "the large, perspiring keg was surrounded by 'weenies,' pretzels and young men who were preparing themselves to face the stern responsibilities of life." A similar phenomenon was reported by Robert and Helen Lynd in their study of "Middletown" (actually, Muncie, Indiana). A workers' singing society in the 1890s "met every Sunday afternoon and Thursday evening with a 'keg of beer' and a hired 'instructor,' " they noted. Bicycling clubs also pooled their resources for a communal barrel, according to Calkins in 1901. "A member of one club said that when runs are held a keg of beer is opened, as a rule, for from thirty to thirty-five riders."[21]

Reformers found the growler trade repugnant precisely because it so completely democratized the drinking experience, and also because it was difficult to regulate. "The sway of the excise is not extended to these back alleys. . . ," Riis complained. "There are secret by-ways . . . along which the 'growler' wanders at all hours and all seasons unmolested." For many working-class folk, however, the growler represented an opportunity for everyone—males and females, young and old, people at work, at home, or "al fresco"—to indulge in a pastime with a long tradition and a short price tag. Moreover, according to Judge Adolph Sabath of Chicago who opposed antigrowler legislation in Illinois in 1903, family ties were actually strengthened by the custom of staying home evenings to share a communal bucket of beer. This view, though no doubt outrageous to many reformers, seems supported by Byington's evidence regarding the households of Homestead. With few other cheap amusements for whole families to enjoy, it may well have been true in many cases that the household that clubbed together, stayed together.[22]

THE BOYS IN THE BACK ROOM

Though rushing the growler was popular, the saloon could still offer a great many advantages, particularly to larger organized groups, that off-premises drinking sites could not. The saloon supplied comfortable, dependable shelter in all seasons with its heat, light, and furniture. It had sufficient alcohol and food on hand to meet the needs of sizeable gatherings. Further, its interior layout was specifically designed to accommodate group drinking, providing within its walls a variety of venues for gatherings to take place. In these several ways, the saloon offered attractions that made it the chief rendezvous for laborers' organizations in tenement districts.

Like all Gaul, the premises of most saloons were divided into three parts. Nearly every establishment featured a hardwood bar with space immediately in front where customers could rest a foot on the brass rail and engage in the "perpendicular drinking" so common in this period. Functioning as a "mixer" area, this barside space permitted customers to circulate in ever-shifting groups, sometimes standing three-deep by the counter at peak patronage hours. With the barkeeper so conveniently close by, drinking here was done by the glass, and drinking partnerships were formed by treating.[23]

As space permitted, many saloons offered an alternative to barside action by setting out tables and chairs in the area adjacent to the serving counter. Among the 163 saloons in Chicago's seventeenth ward, for example, 147 (90%) featured barroom seating in 1900. Similarly, a St. Louis survey in 1901 reported that the "great majority" were furnished with tables and chairs. This tableside space functioned as a lounging area where customers could informally segregate themselves into friendship groups to participate in mutually agreeable pastimes such as talking shop or playing cards.[24]

Occasionally men congregating at tables bought beer in quantity for communal consumption. In Silver City, Nevada, in 1896, labor leader William "Big Bill" Haywood encountered a group of about ten miners "sitting about a big round table in the Brewery Saloon." He overheard one man named Tussy utter a mock prayer regarding a local mine superintendent, imploring him to honor the men's group work contract. "All were pleased with the prayer," Haywood reported, "and bought another gallon of beer in Tussy's honor." From this remark, it seems reasonable to conclude that the group had already been drinking from a gallon bought in common before the mock prayer was offered. Afterward, all chipped in (with the exception of the honored Tussy) for a second gallon.[25]

Yet it appears that ordering gallon-sized pitchers of beer was relatively rare among tableside drinking groups. Most saloonkeepers were not inclined to honor the ten-cent price ceiling on growlers consumed inside their establishments. By tradition and competition they were saddled with out-the-door sales at a dime. But indoor sales were another matter, where the going price was five cents a glass (or ten cents a pint). With no particular economic advantage to buying by the growler, customers at tables understandably preferred making purchases by the cold, frothing glass, often treating their tablemates in the same way as stand-up customers did at the bar nearby.[26]

It was in the back room, the third arena of on-premises bar drinking, that clubbing by collection most often took place. The saloon back room, as the name implies, was a separate chamber accessible from the bar proper through a doorway in the rear. Many establishments offered at least one such room, and a few featured several which might also be located above, beside, or in the basement below the barroom. Customers used the back room to gather informally to chat, play games, consume the free lunch, or attend parties or shows. More formally organized groups of all varieties also utilized this space to assemble with greater privacy than was possible in the barroom. Organization members often made use of both the back room and the main barroom in the course of a single evening. As one Chicago observer reported, groups held "meetings above the saloon and after-meetings in the saloon below."[27]

Many hundreds of Chicago saloons hosted such groups as trade unions, fraternal organizations, political clubs, and even wedding parties in the back room. "It is, in very truth, a part of the life of the people of this district," Melendy concluded. Similarly, Calkins noted that the Casino Saloon in New York City hosted twenty-eight groups each week in its several back rooms. It supplied mailboxes for their correspondence and encouraged them to display members' photographs on the walls.[28]

To repay the proprietor for the use of his back room, most workers' groups turned to the venerable tradition of clubbing by collection. Sometimes group members amassed their drinking dues in advance. For instance, Christine Stansell observes that as early as the 1850s, youthful social groups in New York were financing saloon dancehall parties through collective drinking funds. "Indeed, sometimes young women sponsored dances of their own," she writes, "clubbing together for food and liquor, while male guests provided the music." Other groups sold tickets to finance these occasions, while still others drew upon their general dues fund to cover expenses. As settlement worker Robert Chapin noted in 1909, "The voluntary societies often furnish means of recreation. . . , and expenditure for recreation is sometimes not differentiated from dues and payments to the society."[29]

Instead of collecting drinking dues in advance, some workers' organizations simply trusted their members to buy their drinks by the glass directly from the bartender. Each man was expected to spend from five to twenty cents apiece to keep his group in the proprietor's good graces. "For example," noted Melendy in Chicago in 1900, "a certain German musical society, occupying one of these rooms, fully compensates the saloonkeeper with the money that passes over the bar as the members go in and out of the club-room." Similarly, the secretary of a 250-member trade union estimated in 1901 that "probably on an average the members would drink two glasses of beer per meeting," amounting to sales of about $25 per week (representing $12.50 in profit) for the proprietor. Even more lucrative were the revenues from clubs associated with the socialist labor movement. "They gather each evening and on Sunday by the hundred," reported Calkins. "Their meeting-place, like that of all the other clubs of which we have spoken, is often in or over the saloon, where they are expected to 'drop' fifteen or twenty cents a night per member."[30]

At first glance, the individual's "dropping" some change in the host saloon might not seem "clubbing" or "collection" at all. Instead, this practice might seem "Dutch treating." The essence of the Dutch treat, however, was that the individual paid his own way without regard or obligation to anyone else.[31] Clearly, the organization member was in no such position. He was part of the group, and his drink-buying was a matter of group duty. Yet the fact remains that some organizations' leaders did no collecting of drinking dues. Instead, they delegated this task to the saloonkeeper. But from the members' standpoint, what did that matter? It was much the same to them whether the saloonkeeper collected their drinking dues, or whether the organization's treasurer collected dues for delivery to the saloonkeeper. Members were still drinking as a group; they were still chipping in their fair share to the whole. They were clubbing by collection, no matter who played the role of collections officer.

Indeed, saloon-based organizations delegated a great many tasks to the proprietor besides the collection of drinking dues. He equipped and maintained their clubrooms, providing seating, lighting, heating, and clean-up duties after participants departed. Groups meeting on the premises suffered no interference from police or trouble-making strangers, the saloonkeeper making sure his steady paying customers were not disturbed. Thus, the saloonkeeper acted as both clubhouse custodian and sergeant-at-arms. His role as ad hoc treasurer was simply part of this general symbiotic relationship. With accommodations, security, and refreshments handled in this fashion, the organizations themselves collected whatever additional dues were necessary to carry out their objectives (usually ten to twenty-five cents per week). In this way, workers' saloon life and organizational life were intricately intertwined, with the custom of clubbing at the heart of both.[32]

Citing saloon surveys conducted in seventeen cities nationwide, Calkins concluded that the practice of organization members repaying proprietors for their back rooms by buying drinks en masse was apparently universal. Sometimes proprietors also charged a small rental fee for the room, but the custom of club members "dropping" some change was always the centerpiece of the arrangement as well as the biggest money-maker for saloonkeepers. This practice could actually cost workers more than if they had rented higher-priced rooms with no saloon connections. When a labor leader was confronted with this fact, however, he responded that the rank and file of his organization "were so much accustomed to the scheme of indirect taxation by collecting most of the actual room rent from trade in beer that they would be alarmed to be directly taxed for a sum actually much smaller than that which they were then paying."[33]

Thus, organized groups in the back room had a collective deal with the proprietor which members were bound to respect. Outside the back room, a man's failure to buy his fair share of drinks brought dishonor on himself as an individual; in the clubroom, it brought dishonor on his organization as well. How powerful the pressure was on members to uphold the group's drink-buying obligation was illustrated by the remarks of a Chicago labor leader, himself an abstainer. According to Melendy, "Mr. Thomas J. Morgan, speaking of the early days of the Socialistic Labor Party, said that for years they met in the back room of a saloon, the churches and schoolhouses being closed against them, and that he felt a sensation akin to shame coming over him as night after night he passed the bar without paying his 5 cents for a drink."[34]

And shame he should have felt, for in the context of barroom society, he was a freeloader and a reneger on a deal. The saloon clubroom was "free" only in the sense that the free lunch, for example, was free: a customer who honored the barroom imperative of drink-buying was welcome to enjoy the facilities. The same code applied to organized groups.

Thus, the venerable practice of clubbing, part of tavern culture since the seventeenth century, had by the saloon era become the core concept in a constellation of customs and moral principles guiding barlife at every level. By requiring that each participant in a drinking collective contribute and benefit equally, clubbing tradition promoted stability and even-handedness in barroom encounters. It also helped define the status of a bargoer. It identified him as a member in good standing with his favorite drinking company, a peer, an insider, one of the "we" rather than the "they." Clubbing was a measure of his personal integrity as well. It established him as one who could be trusted to pull his own weight. Each member knew it was a matter of honor to uphold his group's code of reciprocity by paying his fair share to his brothers' keeper.

CLUBBING AND COOPERATIVE EFFORT

Historians have remarked upon the extraordinary number of voluntary associations which formed and met in saloons. They have noted that saloons provided meeting space that was comfortable, convenient, and cheap. Saloons also provided a ready pool of recruitable members. But historians have not asked how the values and mechanisms of drink culture *itself* might have shaped the operation of voluntary associations or contributed to their success.

On the contrary, historians have portrayed the impact of drink culture in a largely negative light, as an obstacle and a drag on organizing efforts. Drink meant fuzzy brains, disorderly meetings, and a poor public image. To an extent, all this was true. Indeed, leaders of voluntary associations sometimes cited these problems as reasons for vacating the saloon premises for independent headquarters as soon as they could.

But saloon culture in fact had some positive influences on the growth of voluntary associations. It provided the communal cohesiveness upon which organizations could build. It encouraged workers to deal cooperatively and honorably with their fellows. It promised the proprietor's assistance in custodial, security, and monetary matters. Perhaps most important, the saloon's tradition of clubbing made the early survival of many voluntary associations possible.

Clubbing for drinks provided the mechanism by which nascent organizations could collect dues and cover costs without scaring workers off. Saloongoers were accustomed to buying drinks as a collective endeavor. They understood that their monetary outlay represented commitment to their fellows and compensation to their saloonkeeper. These expenses and obligations they took in stride. If the group moved in the direction of greater formality with regular meeting times, elected officials, fixed agendas, and specific goals, this might still be acceptable to saloongoers as long as the cost, procedure, and setting of collective drinking remained undisturbed. Voluntary associations that adopted clubbing tradition as a dues-paying method therefore had an improved chance for success. They also benefited from the spirit of camaraderie that attached to the clubbing ritual. Clubbing took the pain out of paying dues. It was easy, familiar, even fun.

Thus, voluntary associations grew and thrived at least in part because they seized upon saloon clubbing and turned it to their own advantage. Eventually, as organized groups continued to meet in the back rooms, members' attendance became more habitual, organizational structure became more stable, and goals became more attainable. Reaching that stage, associations were often ready to try life on their own. Then they left the saloon behind like a cradle they had outgrown. But they left the stronger for it, and they also carried away something of the character of it.

The ease with which organizations incorporated clubbing into their routine operations points up how compatible the custom was with market-oriented endeavors. Through clubbing, a web of contractual relationships arose among proprietors, organizations, and individual members. These market-style relations were deliberately constructed, motivated by self-interest, and underpinned by monetary transactions. Yet many elements of community were present as well. Many organization members were regulars in the host saloon who had already established close personal ties with one another and with the saloonkeeper. Others new to the saloon had the opportunity to establish similar ties as they socialized and swapped drinks during "after-meetings" in the main barroom. It is often difficult to say where their market relationships ended and their community relationships began. Instead, their experience seems to have mirrored the duality inherent in saloon culture generally: partly contractual, businesslike, instrumental, and market-oriented; partly communal, fraternal, expressive, and community-oriented.

By schooling saloongoers in the ways of cooperative effort and group commitment, clubbing helped prepare its adherents for membership in more formal, highly organized voluntary associations such as mutual aid societies, unions, and political groups. Once this fact is grasped, it becomes clear why workers from 1870 to 1920 made saloons the hub of their club activity—not simply because barrooms were available and comfortable, but also because saloon drinking *itself* was an elemental expression of the club tendency. Many factors affected barroom behavior, but the fundamental drinkers' rite of the club was the engine that made saloonlife go.

Part III

More Lore of the Barroom

Seven

Games and Gambling

> "Did ye see annywan th' other day that wasn't askin' to know how th'
> fight come out? . . . Father Kelly . . . said it was a disgraceful an' cor-
> ruptin' affair. . . . But late Winsdah afthernoon he came . . . an' says he:
> 'Be th' way, how did that there foul and outhrajous affray in Carson
> City come out?' 'Fitz,' says I, 'in the fourteenth.' 'Ye don't say,' he says,
> dancin' around. 'Good,' he says. 'I told Father Doyle this mornin' at
> breakfuss that . . . I'd bet a new cassock— Oh, dear!' he says, 'what am
> I sayin'?' 'Ye're sayin',' says I, 'what nine-tenths iv th' people, laymen
> and clargy, are sayin',' I says."
> —Mr. Dooley, on the 1897 Fitzsimmons-Corbett bout [1]

As pointed out by Mr. Dooley, the fictional bartender-
philosopher created in the 1890s by columnist Finley Peter
Dunne, many millions of American men would have readily sympa-
thized with Father Kelly's secret desire to "bet a new cassock" on
"Ruby Robert" Fitzsimmons' ability to defeat "Gentleman Jim"
Corbett in their heavyweight championship fight of 1897. Spectacular athletic contests, whether involving boxing, horse racing, or other
intensely competitive sports, were events which stirred tremendous
public interest during the saloon era. They remained popular despite
the protests of many upstanding citizens against the gambling, drunkenness, violence, and social disorder often associated with such
contests. Further, many working-class men would have instantly understood why Father Kelly turned to Mr. Dooley, a saloonkeeper, to
learn the outcome of this "disgraceful an' corruptin' affair." In a tradition dating back to the colonial period, drinking establishments of
the late nineteenth and early twentieth centuries played a central role
in the sporting life of their working-class constituencies. They served

as clearing houses for sporting news and betting action as well as recreational centers for customers wishing to try their own hand at games played on the premises. When Father Kelly wanted to indulge his interest in sporting matters, then, it was to Mr. Dooley down on the corner that he turned.[2]

THE PLAY'S THE THING

The games associated with saloonlife were so diverse that the task of analyzing them systematically is a daunting prospect indeed. It might seem reasonable, for instance, to begin by distinguishing spectator sports from participant sports, or outdoor amusements from indoor amusements, or team competitions from individual competitions, or physical contests from intellectual contests, or ball games from those using other implements such as cards, dice, or boxing gloves. Though these various distinctions are important to note, they focus on some particular attribute of this game or that, while largely neglecting the human element in game-playing. To fathom the full meaning of games to saloongoers, an approach is needed that delves more deeply into the reasons people engaged in play, what led them to prefer certain amusements, and what these preferences reveal about the participants' worldview.

Many games popular among saloongoers were, like boxing, highly competitive affairs. Yet, as Roger Caillois pointed out in his cross-cultural study of mankind at play, people's desire to compete is but one of their fundamental motivating factors, each of which produces a very different form of amusement with its own strategies, goals, and rewards. "After examining different possibilities, I am proposing a division into four main rubrics," he explained, "depending upon whether . . . the role of competition, chance, simulation, or vertigo is dominant." To make sense of the profusion of sporting activities popular in saloons, it is useful to apply Caillois's system of classification to the matter, a system which focuses on the motives and desires of the game-players themselves.[3]

Many of the amusements in saloons were games of *competition,* such as boxing, pool, and chess, which were based on interpersonal conflict and settled by merit. In these games, saloongoers adopted an active and aggressive stance in the course of play, relying upon such internal resources as skill, strength, memory, and ingenuity to vanquish their opponents. But games of *chance* were also popular, including dice, roulette, and lotteries, which were based on the impersonal dictates of fate and settled by luck. In these games, saloongoers adopted a comparatively passive stance in the course of play, relying upon the external forces of destiny and good fortune to carry them to victory. Of course, some games contained elements of both categories. In many card games, for example, hands were dealt at random (chance), then played by skill (competition). Yet, in most instances, either one or the other element dominated the play, so that even hybrid cases might be legitimately classified as primarily games of competition or of chance.[4] Clearly, these were two very different forms of game-playing, with very nearly opposite psychological and social impulses behind them, and their simultaneous presence in saloonlife raises several interesting and difficult questions.

Also present in saloon culture was a form of play which, to adopt Caillois's terminology, featured the element of *vertigo*. Temporary loss of bodily equilibrium and perception is ordinarily associated with amusements like swinging, sliding, somersaulting, and twirling. Amusement park rides, such as those to be found at Coney Island in New York during the saloon era, exemplify the search for vertigo in which participants willingly subject themselves to dizzying, disorienting, and yet exhilarating sensations.[5]

In saloons, drink itself most often satisfied the desire for the pleasures of vertigo, permitting saloongoers to feel transported beyond the sober confines of daily life and to indulge in the physical and mental joys of intoxication and euphoria. Their enjoyment of the experience was expressed in the playful language they used to describe the state of alcoholic befuddlement. Fuzzled, flushed, cockeyed, and pigeon-eyed were among the most popular terms used by saloon-era drinkers, according to H. L. Mencken; other old favorites included balmy, bamboozled, bent, jingled, slopped, squiffy, tangle-legged, and woozy.[6]

In addition to the drinking experience, the dances and parties hosted by saloons sometimes provided occasions for the enjoyment of vertigo. In *The Jungle* (1906), Upton Sinclair described a Lithuanian wedding celebration held in a saloon back room in which an ecstasy-producing dance was the highlight of the evening. "The climax of it is a furious *prestissimo*, at which the couples seize hands and begin a mad whirling," he explained. "This is quite irresistible, and every one in the room joins in, until the place becomes a maze of flying skirts and bodies, quite dazzling to look upon." Such exuberant dancing was also a chief amusement at the annual parties held in saloon back rooms by fraternal lodges, union chapters, and youthful pleasure clubs. Indeed, the activity had been a facet of the musical heritage of American taverns since the early 1700s. As popular venues for drinking and dancing, saloons provided a congenial setting for working-class people to indulge their desire for vertiginous play.[7]

Saloons also hosted a fourth category of play, which Caillois labeled *simulation*. In pursuing this variety of amusement, participants temporarily assume another identity or persona, often reinforced with special modes of dress, speech, and demeanor. They then play at their adopted roles just as a child plays pirate or an actor plays Hamlet. In saloonlife, this impulse was expressed on St. Patrick's Day, for example, when customers might wear green, drink Irish whiskey, speak in an Irish brogue, and generally play at being Irish for the day. "But ivrybody is an Irishman on St. Patrick's Day," as bartender Mr. Dooley observed of his German, Jewish, and Chinese acquaintances in his Chicago neighborhood. "Schwartzmeister comes up wearin' a green cravat an' a yard long green badge an' says: 'Faugh-a-ballagh, Herr Dooley,' which he thinks is Irish f'r 'Good Mornin'.'. . . Me good frind Ikey Cohen jines me an' I observe he's . . . wearin' emeralds in th' front iv his shirt. Like as not will come little Hip Lung fr'm down th' sthreet with a package iv shirts under his ar-rm, an' a green ribbon in his cue." A principal pleasure of the masquerade is the opportunity it affords to adopt startling new identities, poke fun at social pieties, and upset the established hierarchies of class, race, and gender. In Idaho in 1882, for instance, the *Wood River Times* reported an uproarious scene in Joe Pierceson's saloon in the all-male mining camp of Sawtooth. One cold night in January, the monotony turned to hilarity when four of the miners burst through the swinging doors dressed as "a Chinawoman, negro wench, Irish market woman and Eastern esthete." Probably the most spectacular illustration of simulative play occurred during the annual Mardi Gras celebration in New Orleans, during which bargoers donned outlandish masks and costumes and playfully frolicked and caroused in the centuries-old spirit of carnival.[8]

Simulative play brought theater to workers' lives in an immediate and personal way. It provided them with an outlet for their creative energies, stimulated their imaginations, and encouraged them to experiment with unusual and unaccustomed roles. By permitting such ordinarily unacceptable activities as impersonating people of a different social rank or ethnic group or even cross-dressing to impersonate women, such play afforded working-class men a rare opportunity to act out their fantasies and dabble daringly in what would otherwise be regarded as bizarre and taboo behavior.

In many respects, saloon amusements involving simulation closely resembled those involving vertigo. Both were disinhibiting forms of play, permitting participants to shake off everyday constraints, step temporarily outside of themselves, and engage in hilarious and often licentious activities. Amusements featuring simulation and vertigo were also largely unstructured and spontaneous modes of play, having few fixed rules and granting participants wide berth for improvisation and adventure. For many working-class saloongoers, such diversions offered a welcome relief from the boredom and regimentation of their work lives. Further, through prodigious drinking, exuberant dancing, and outlandish masquerading, they were able to express their resentment against employers, clergymen, and other authorities intent upon subduing and reforming working-class leisure habits and inculcating the middle-class values of moderation, sobriety, and self-control.[9]

In contrast to these more flamboyant and unregulated forms of play, saloon amusements featuring competition and chance were far more rule-bound and methodically pursued. Yet they were no less exciting for this because they offered something the others did not: the considerable allure of *winning*. Here, the object of play was to outshine fellow participants through diligent effort, sheer good fortune, or some combination of the two. This form of amusement constitutes what most people then as now understand by the term "game," with its fixed rules, prescribed course of play, and unpredictable yet ultimately clear-cut outcome.[10] The tremendous popularity of games of competition and chance indicates that while workers found satisfaction and meaning in free-form amusements featuring simulation and vertigo, they also derived pleasure from more structured play with specific goals and rewards. This was no contradiction, but rather evidence of the many different functions of recreation in workers' lives.

TAKING A GAMBLE

One of the principal similarities between games of competition and of chance is that both yield a definite outcome, though that outcome remains uncertain until the game is completed. This quality of uncertainty stimulates the appetite for gambling, for each participant will want his own assessment of the outcome to be vindicated and rewarded. In saloons, workers often placed wagers on the outcome of contests held both on and off the premises, although their gambling was usually informal and small scale. High-stakes gambling was beyond the resources of most laboring men, particularly those with families to support. As Robert Woods noted of poor Italian immigrants in Boston saloons in the early 1900s, "Necessarily, the stakes are small, but the play seems to lose none of its zest on this account." Further, gambling was illegal in a great many areas, and most saloon proprietors were not prepared to pay the necessary bribes or "hush money" to police and city officials to get away with hosting big-time gambling on their premises.[11]

Thus, sporting men intent upon high-stakes wagering went not to ordinary workers' saloons, but rather to the few thriving though illicit gambling houses to be found in the larger cities. Typical examples included Bose Cobb's gaming casino in Boston in the 1880s and "Big Jim" O'Leary's Horn Palace in Chicago in the 1890s. While civic reform groups largely succeeded in closing the most notorious gambling houses by the early 1900s, the truly determined sporting man could still participate in many clandestine games. "General open gambling is not in evidence," as George Turner noted of Chicago in 1906, "but there are large games, in a few specially favored places, and many smaller ones, open to those who have inside information, throughout the city." As a rule, however, the fast and risky world of high-stakes gambling was too expensive and exotic to attract many working-class wagering men on a regular basis.[12]

In addition to financial and legal considerations, what kept most saloon gambling low stakes and low key was the fact that sociability was the primary aim of game-playing bargoers. Unlike professional gamblers with their coldly mercenary motives or compulsive gamblers with their obsessive need to risk and win, most ordinary workingmen wagered among themselves for the fun and fellowship which such friendly in-group rivalry provided. The best evidence for this assessment is the fact that drinks and cigars—ever potent symbols of masculine camaraderie—served as the stakes of saloon wagers just as often as did money. As Raymond Calkins observed in 1901, gambling "may take the harmless form of tossing [dice] for drinks or cigars; it may be the almost universal playing for the game in billiards, by which the loser pays the expense for the whole company; it may be playing for stakes at cards, which is very common, or it may be the use of . . . a penny-in-the-slot contrivance to be played for drinks or cigars, or for money." Since beer and cigars sold for a nickel apiece in most workers' barrooms, it seems safe to conclude that wagers involving currency were similarly modest.[13]

The role of alcohol in saloon games and gambling is important to appreciate, for though "playing for the drinks" represented a comparatively insignificant monetary outlay, the activity itself was full of significance for saloongoers. It was not just that game-playing happened to be popular in places where drinks were sold. Rather, drinks were an integral part of the play. As the principal stakes of the game, they lent a symbolic note of congeniality and goodwill to the occasion. Even when money was wagered instead, the participants usually drank together as they competed, reaffirming the camaraderie of their gaming circle. Drinking itself even entered into the rivalry, for it was an additional test of manhood to hold one's liquor and continue playing competently under its vertigo-inducing effects. Moreover, though the stakes might be cash, it was still considered good form at competition's end for the loser to treat the winner(s) to a drink, as a gesture of respect and continuing fellowship. In this way, game-playing, gambling, and drinking—an unholy trinity in many reformers' eyes— were to bargoing workers the three cardinal principles of sporting life during the saloon era.

PERCHANCE TO DREAM

While social reformers frowned upon all forms of barroom gaming as idle wastes of time and money, their greatest wrath had traditionally been directed against games of chance. Many believed that hard work, frugality, and the exercise of reason were virtues essential to building a moral and prosperous nation. For them, the idea of men acquiring wealth by the luck of the draw, the spin of the wheel, or the toss of the dice was not only repugnant, but dangerous and subversive. Such activities contributed nothing to the social good, corrupted the individual character, and challenged the work ethic which lay at the heart of the nineteenth-century middle-class value system. For these reasons, games of chance and the gambling associated with them were increasingly stigmatized and outlawed in many cities by the 1890s.[14]

From the standpoint of the working poor, on the other hand,

games of chance were appealing precisely because they offered participants an equal opportunity for gain regardless of social position, natural abilities, training, or sweat of the brow. "[D]estiny is the sole artisan of victory, and where there is rivalry, what is meant is that the winner has been more favored by fortune than the loser," as Caillois noted. In games of competition, the participant's "only reliance is upon himself," whereas in games of chance the player "counts on everything, even the vaguest sign, the slightest outside occurrence, which he immediately takes to be an omen or token—in short, he depends on everything except himself."[15] For laborers trapped in unfulfilling jobs with little security or hope of advancement, the allure of instant and gratuitous gain was understandably great. Further, the notion that life and dreams might be full of omens, and that fortune might at any moment confer favor upon those daring enough to play their hunches, meant that even the most wretched and downtrodden folk could still regard the world as a place rich with meaning and promise for *them*. Thus, while middle-class reformers disparaged games of chance and instead preached the virtues of hard work and thrift, many working-class people stubbornly continued to take their chances with dice cups, roulette wheels, slot machines, and lottery tickets.

Of all forms of game-playing and fortune-telling equipment, dice are among the oldest and most widespread in the cultures of the world, and working-class saloongoers did their part in carrying on the tradition of their use. Dice sometimes functioned as adjuncts to other games such as backgammon, itself having a lineage traceable to Ancient Greece. More often, however, dice were used alone, or sometimes in conjunction with dice cups which facilitated the shake and the toss (accompanied by much vigorous slamming of cups upon the bar). As Calkins observed, much of the gambling associated with dice took "the harmless form of tossing for drinks," an illustration of which was provided by Frank Norris in *McTeague* (1899). While McTeague and a group of working-class friends were taking a ferry trip across the San Francisco Bay, one of them suggested they go to the bar on the lower deck and "shake for the drinks." "Have to see you on that," responded one; "By damn, we'll have a drink!" exclaimed another; "Sure, sure, drinks, that's the word," agreed a third. In Norris's example, it seems clear that while these men found the idea of tossing dice appealing, they were not so much interested in the game itself or who might win as they were in the pleasures of drink and camaraderie that would follow. Sociability was their principal objective, with dice-tossing a convenient means to that end.[16]

Norris did not specify what particular dice game his characters played, and indeed a great many writers of the saloon period referred simply to "playing dice." It might well have been, however, that the game in question was "poker dice" which rewards players who throw matching numbers (pairs, three of a kind, and so forth). As Travis Hoke noted in 1899, "There was much shaking of dice—poker dice or 'horses,' whence came the expression, 'That's a horse on you,' to decide who should pay for drinks." Poker dice grew in popularity with the rise of the card game of poker after the Civil War. It was well-suited to what might be called "social gamblers" who, like social drinkers, approached the activity casually for the mutual pleasures it brought to congenial company.[17]

Another dice game popular among the more dedicated saloon gamblers was "craps," in which each "shooter" in turn threw two dice while he and other players placed wagers on whether those dice would turn up in particular combinations. While the shooter had no control over the outcome of his roll, his chances of winning bets were much improved if he understood the odds, making craps a game of ability as well as fortune. Yet, though knowing the odds was helpful, many players still ardently believed in the overriding importance of luck, the notion that fate might somehow be "for" or "against" them on some particular roll, no matter the mathematical odds. This belief added to the excitement of the play and wagering. But it could also lead to foolhardy risk-taking, extravagance, emotionalism, and sometimes even violence, as immortalized in saloon-era murder ballads such as "Stagolee." This potential for excess and disorder made craps a special target of reformers and police. Despite efforts to suppress the game, however, it continued to be widely played by the tenement poor in the streets and in saloon back rooms. In a barroom owned by Chicago alderman Johnny Powers, for example, a mixed crowd of poor whites, blacks, and Chinese regularly congregated to play craps in the 1890s, in this case secure from police interference owing to the proprietor's political connections.[18]

Craps dice, then, was less a game for "social gamblers" than it was for those who took their wagering and winning seriously. On the other hand, there was clearly a strong social component in the play. The sheer intensity and speed of craps tended to bind participants tightly together into a compact gaming circle. Further, the often boisterous and flamboyant behavior of both shooters and onlookers indicated that they played the game for fun as well as financial gain.

Even more vulnerable to police raids and reformers' exposés were games of chance requiring bulky and conspicuous equipment such as roulette wheels and slot machines. In Boston in the early 1900s, for example, Robert Woods noted that police harassment had all but eliminated roulette games in West End saloons. Similarly, Peter Roberts observed in 1904 that slot machines had once been prevalent in Pennsylvania coal mining communities, but "the authorities of our counties have in recent years raided saloons having gambling devices, so that . . . those which remain are kept in back rooms of prominent hotels or transferred to places outside of the city or borough limits." [19]

According to Calkins, however, gambling machines were still "quite prevalent" in the saloons of St. Louis, Cincinnati, Chicago, and many far western communities at the turn of the century. "Often one can see men crowded around these machines," he stated, "waiting a turn to try their luck." The more liberal attitude prevailing in the West was succinctly expressed by San Francisco political boss Abraham Ruef when reformers in 1906 suggested banning slot machines from saloons and cigar stores. Cutting through the hypocrisy of their stance, Ruef remarked, "I cannot see any difference . . . between the poker games at the Pacific Union Club and the gambling in a saloon, or the playing of a slot machine." Yet fear of reformers' crusades and police raids did lead many proprietors to eschew mechanical gambling devices in favor of more portable and easily disposable gaming implements such as dice.[20]

Of all the games of chance associated with saloonlife, perhaps the most interesting for its brazen challenge to the American middle-class ideology of productive work, prudent investment, and the rational pursuit of wealth was the renegade lottery side-game known as "policy" or "numbers." Policy had coexisted with legitimate lotteries since colonial times. In the mid-1700s, the sale of lottery tickets was widely regarded as a legitimate revenue-raising scheme through which colonial governments as well as Protestant churches might finance the construction of buildings and other worthy projects. Policy, in contrast, was an unsanctioned side-betting scheme catering to the lower classes who could not afford to buy an official lottery ticket. Instead, the poor wagered a smaller sum on a favorite number through an illicit policy broker. If their number matched the official lottery result, they would win from the broker a proportionately smaller return. To bet on a number was to "insure" it; hence, the bettor was obtaining a "policy." This scheme both circumvented and mocked the purpose, promoters, and beneficiaries of the official lotteries, and respectable folk condemned it as gambling pure and simple. In the antebellum period, however, so many supposedly legitimate lotteries had been rocked with fraud scandals that many northeastern states outlawed them as well. By the saloon era, lotteries (as well as most other forms of gambling) were illegal in all but a few states such as Kentucky and Louisiana.[21]

Policy, on the other hand, could and did continue to flourish as long as some lottery someplace could be cited as the source of winning numbers. In New York in the 1890s, for example, many "writers" (policy brokers) who hawked their tickets in saloons, on the streets, and in clandestine "policy shops" claimed to base their payoffs on the outcome of lotteries held in Kentucky, the results coming to them by special telegraph. According to Jacob Riis, however, the policy game in New York constituted a "bogus business" based on "alleged daily drawings, that are supposed to be held in some far-off Western town." In fact, the whole operation was "the meanest of swindles" with "the winnings apportioned daily with due regard to the backer's interests." Similarly, Robert Woods described the policy game in turn-of-the-century Boston as an "evil" and noted that while numbers could always be purchased "in and around the hotels and saloons and on the street," the nefarious business was deservedly "kept well 'on the run.'"[22]

Both Riis and Woods especially deplored the fact that policy appealed most to the very people who could afford it least, asserting that the African-American populations in New York and Boston seemed particularly prone to squandering their pennies in this fashion. W. E. B. DuBois acknowledged that the same situation prevailed among poor blacks in Philadelphia in the 1890s, noting that not only men, but also women and children were reportedly succumbing to its allures. Similarly, Perry Duis has noted that policy was particularly popular in the black neighborhoods of Chicago, arguing that the game was "an import from the South" brought northward by migrating blacks. Members of many other ethnic groups also played the numbers, of course. Woods observed that while the game in Boston "has peculiar attractions for the Negroes, it is by no means confined to them." In New York, Riis noted the success of "policy sharks" who swarmed around the Irish barrooms of the twenty-first ward, men who made themselves welcome to the saloonkeeper by guaranteeing him a percentage of the take. Thus, policy appealed to many urban tenement dwellers, the common denominators among all devotees seeming to be their poverty and their faith in "luck."[23]

If the numbers game was a snare and a delusion, as its critics claimed, why did policy writers do such a booming business on the streets and in the saloons? To understand the appeal of the game, particularly within the black urban community, it is helpful to consider how most participants went about choosing their lucky numbers and what this activity represented in their lives. Fundamental to the players' attitudes was the belief that the course of destiny could be divined in advance, if only they could learn to recognize and interpret its forewarning signs. These omens might occur in ordinary waking life, as when a dog howled or a mirror shattered. But more often they were thought to come to people in the magical world of their dreams. Yet dreams were open to many interpretations, and the problem still remained for policy players to translate these vague omens into specific lottery numbers.

To resolve this dilemma, a great many people in the saloon period turned to what were known as "dream books," pamphlets published with such beguiling titles as *Old Gypsy Madge's Fortune Teller and Witches Key to Lucky Dreams* (1889), *Aunt Sally's Policy-Player's Dream Book and Wheel of Fortune* (1889), and the *Gypsy Witch Dream Book and Policy Player's Guide* (1903). Many of these dream interpretation manuals drew heavily upon the venerable folk wisdom of plantation slave communities. They offered explicit advice on the meaning of dreams and what numbers corresponded to these meanings (though how they arrived at these numbers was left shrouded in mystery). Ann Fabian has cited some fascinating examples from these dream books. She notes, "For the Gypsy Witch, to dream of being abandoned 'by influential people signifies happiness,' to dream of a 'NEGRO—Denotes happiness, many powerful friends. 6, 14, 19, 78.'" Further, "'To see a Negro in your sleep denotes an honorable and successful career. 121. To quarrel with him denotes disaster. 321.'"[24]

From this glimpse into the dream world of policy players, the popularity of the numbers game among poor and powerless blacks becomes more understandable. Not only did dream books offer the promise of financial gain, but also they turned the social order on its head, bringing dignity and hope to the oppressed and even deeming it "lucky" to be among the despised and abandoned. By encouraging bettors to regard even the smallest details of their lives as deeply significant clues to the operation of powerful supernatural forces, policy play enabled marginalized people to believe destiny had singled them out as favored, chosen, and special. "Penniless, but with undaunted faith in his ultimate 'luck,' he looks forward to the time when he shall once more be able to take a hand at 'beating policy,'" remarked the exasperated Riis of the player's philosophy. "When periodically the negro's lucky numbers, 4-11-44, come out on the [winning] slips. . . , intense excitement reigns in Thompson Street and along the Avenue." It was nothing but scam and superstition, he insisted. However, to those whose horizons were limited to tenements, sweatshops, pawnshops, and saloons, a penny for their dreams apparently seemed well worth the price.[25]

THE COMPETITIVE EDGE

Though games of chance such as policy, roulette, and dice had their loyal devotees, many saloongoers also took pleasure in games of competition which permitted them to exercise a much more direct influence over the outcome of the play. Further, because competitive games required participants to develop their individual abilities and strive for excellence, such amusements did not as a rule come under as much fire from middle-class reformers as did games of chance. The play was still unproductive, in the sense that no worldly goods resulted from the activity (unlike work and art). But at least the participants drew upon their own resources and cultivated a competitive mentality which might prove beneficial in other spheres of life. Nevertheless, the physical brutality of some sports such as boxing, as well as the gambling associated with most competitive games, meant that even these amusements were regarded as controversial and undesirable by many who preferred to see workers in alcohol-free gymnasiums, libraries, and lecture halls.[26]

From his survey of saloon recreations in 1901, Raymond Calkins concluded that the category of game most commonly played by bargoing workers was cards. In New York, for example, he reported that "out of fifteen representative saloons in the Fourteenth Assembly District, nine have rear rooms used for card-playing." Workers who enjoyed cards sought out saloons not only because proprietors supplied the basic equipment necessary for the game, but also because there were few other indoor public venues available to them for the purpose. As a contributor to the Freemason's *Trestle Board* magazine remarked in 1891, "But where can a dozen men congregate for the purpose of spending a social hour or two? These working men are not patrons of the hotels and they are not wanted there. Where else? The Y.M.C.A.? Would a working man be welcomed and allowed to smoke or play an innocent and purely social game of cards? If any one thinks so let him try it, and see how soon he would be invited out." Card games were regarded with suspicion and distaste by many reform-minded Protestants who founded such organizations as the Young Men's Christian Association to promote more wholesome recreational opportunities for the poor. A few Catholic groups were more tolerant, such as the Young Men's Institute in Chicago which permitted workers to play cards, billiards, and pool, as well as to smoke if they chose. Some settlement houses also offered such amenities.[27]

Yet, though cards and tobacco might be allowed in recreational venues other than saloons, drinking and gambling were still firmly forbidden in most. Even the sympathetic contributor to the *Trestle Board* drew the line when it came to alcohol and wagering. While he argued that philanthropic organizations should offer workers most of the saloon's amenities, including "cigars and tobacco" and such gaming equipment as "cards, or dominoes, or checkers, or chess, or backgammon," he still insisted that such organizations should serve only "temperance drinks" and permit "no gambling in any shape, not even playing games for the drinks."[28] For workers who wanted to enjoy the full gaming experience, then, the saloon with its card tables and other amenities was often the best available rendezvous.

Poker was among the most popular card games in saloons, particularly in the West. While working in Nevada mining camps in the 1890s, for example, William "Big Bill" Haywood noted that poker, along with faro, were "the favorite games" of bargoing miners and were usually played in "a card room in the rear." Some men made poker-playing into a profession. In an Idaho saloon in the early 1900s, for example, James Stevens observed a colorful character known as "Poker Tom" Davis, who stood out for his extensive book-learning, his meticulous appearance, and his gun strapped on his hip. "For some mysterious reason he had turned from his educated life and become a Mississippi river gambler," Stevens remarked. "For another mysterious reason, he had turned from that life and drifted West with the team-hands." Standing at the bar one night in his usual "dignified and solemn style," Poker Tom made a "grand speech" about the gambling trip he had recently made to Boise, the five hundred dollars he had won in a week-long card game, and the "venerable and benignant Bourbon" he had drunk in celebration of his triumph. In all, this man exemplified the legendary frontier figure of the well-groomed, gun-toting, poker-playing gambler, a character type immortalized in many dime novels and travelogues, and later in Hollywood movies and television programs.[29]

But it was not just in the West where poker games were prevalent. In Boston in 1902, Robert Woods noted that although "gaming has been nearly stamped out" in the saloons of the West End, card-playing "behind closed and carefully guarded doors" continued to be common. "The game is invariably poker," he observed, "since the implements for roulette or faro could not be concealed quickly and effectually in case of a visit from the police."[30]

Many other card games were popular in saloons. Faro, a western favorite, involved wagering on cards drawn from a dealing box. Euchre, casino, and Sancho Pedro were preferred barroom pastimes of Jack London in Oakland, California, in the 1890s. Among the Chinese in New York, according to Riis, "Fan tan is their ruling passion," an enthusiasm shared by the Chinese community in San Francisco. Among Jewish immigrants in Boston, meanwhile, " 'Pinnacle' [pinochle], the favorite of their card games, seems never to lose its fascination for old or young," observed Woods in 1902. The game was also popular in the saloons of the San Francisco waterfront in the 1910s. As sailor Fred Klebingat remarked of one local character, "He was a great pinochle player. Daytimes he used to take all the old-timers playing pinochle."[31]

Card-playing was a particularly popular pastime among ethnic groups of the "new wave" of immigration after 1890. Not only were cards portable, inexpensive, and versatile in their uses, but also they had been an important component of Old World leisure patterns and therefore provided a measure of continuity for immigrants. In her study of the steel mill town of Homestead, Pennsylvania, in 1910, Margaret Byington reported that Slavic, Hungarian, and Lithuanian immigrants spent a great deal of their leisure time playing cards in saloon back rooms, lodge clubrooms, and tenement flats and courtyards. These games sometimes assumed the proportions of a neighborhood event, as revealed in a photograph of five card-players in a tenement courtyard who were surrounded by a crowd of fourteen avid spectators, including eight men, four women, and two young children.[32]

Similarly, in Boston at the turn of the century, Woods asserted that "the Jews and Italians are habitual gamesters." When Woods was writing in 1902, card-playing was officially banned in Boston saloons, though games were still played there clandestinely and were "very generally played elsewhere." In their games of "pinnacle," Jewish men often retreated to "the privacy of their homes, shops, and club-rooms," with the result that passers-by on Salem Street could "see in the rear of one shop after another a group of men, some of them quite venerable in appearance, engaged in this game."[33]

In contrast, Italians in Boston preferred the more public venues of the saloon and the tenement courtyard for their game-playing, according to Woods. In barrooms, where "gaming rather than drinking seems to be their main attraction," Italian men got around the card-playing ban in a novel way. "Every evening during the week, and many an afternoon, especially in winter," Woods reported, "any one of these saloons is crowded with men sitting at the tables over their wine or beer, intent upon a game of chance played with the fingers." Outdoors, where men quickly abandoned finger games for cards, the players often became part of an open-air community gathering reminiscent of the Slavic immigrants in Homestead. Woods observed, "Here the bits of bright drapery flung over the galleries of the surrounding houses, the plants in the windows, and the gayly colored head-coverings of the women moving about give a foreign air to the scene." Riis noted analogous customs in the Italian community in New York, where "the entire population seems possessed of an uncontrollable impulse to get out into the street." In the courtyards and near the open doors of saloons, the Italian "settles down to a game of cards" and demonstrates that he is a "born gambler," according to Riis.[34]

Another game in vogue in many saloons was billiards, or more particularly "pocket billiards," which in the saloon era was almost universally known as "pool." Yet, while billiards and pool were popular, they were not to be found in every saloon. The bulky though indispensable green felt table took up a great deal of space and required, on the saloonkeeper's part, a considerable investment to obtain and maintain. Of the 163 working-class saloons in the seventeenth ward in Chicago, for example, only 44 (27%) featured billiard tables. Further, the game was prohibited or severely restricted in some eastern cities. In Boston, where laws governing tavern amusements had traditionally been very strict, saloonkeepers had to obtain a special police concession to maintain a pool table on the premises. In many areas further west, however, laws were more liberal and customer demand was greater, so that billiard and pool tables in cities like St. Louis were "very common" at the turn of the century, according to Calkins. Moreover, while a particular saloon might not itself contain a pool table, next door or nearby there was often a poolroom with several tables which coexisted in a symbiotic relationship with the barroom.[35]

Many saloongoers first became acquainted with billiards and pool in their adolescent years. "A low price is charged for a game of billiards, and five cents will always pay for a glass of beer. Thus the boys begin the drink habit, and become frequenters of the saloon," as Calkins observed. Upon reaching adulthood, many men continued their interest in the game, often engaging in modest gambling with the table rental serving as the stakes. Some men became part of what Ned Polsky has described as a "confirmed-bachelor subculture" whose social life revolved around the green felt tables in saloons and poolrooms in the late nineteenth and early twentieth centuries. Many married men also played the game regularly, of course. In Polsky's view, however, it was this core group of bachelor players who made the tables a paying proposition for many proprietors. In addition, these men brought style and gamesmanship to the play, creating the colorful argot of pool players which included such expressions as "hustler" and "never give a sucker an even break."[36]

Some of these men were themselves hustlers, players who made their livings by gambling on the games and by engaging in "deceitful practices," in Polsky's words. These included misleading opponents about their true expertise and luring the gullible into sucker bets. A few also became exhibition players who performed in professional tournaments held in exhibition halls, arenas, and occasionally in saloons. In Chicago in 1901, Royal Melendy described one such tournament held in a very sizeable saloon with a bar "brilliant with lights and flashing mirrors" as well as a 300-seat amphitheater. Regarding gambling, Melendy explained, "When the stakes on either side are equal, the game is played; those having bet on the winner receive back from the general fund their sum doubled, less 10 per cent., the commission charged by the house." This betting scheme was known as the "pari-mutuel system," a plan also adopted by many racetracks at the turn of the century to regularize the wagering process and ensure a steady income for the hosting institution. Barkeepers in western frontier communities of the late nineteenth century also sponsored billiard competitions. In Virginia City, Montana, for example, two accomplished local players vied for a $500 prize in a contest arranged by one enterprising proprietor.[37]

With urban growth and the increasing concentration of saloons in tenement districts, many outdoor amusements previously associated with colonial and antebellum taverns became impracticable. Bowling and handball games, formerly played in the tavernkeeper's yard, now had to move indoors to rooms fitted with special apparatus which not all saloonkeepers could afford. Nevertheless, there were some proprietors who converted their back rooms into handball courts, bowling alleys, or general exercise areas, sometimes even including showering facilities. In fact, some of these places were actually more like gymnasiums with a bar attached. Though physical exercise was much emphasized in such establishments, drinking remained an equally important element in customers' activities, even among the youngest players. In Melendy's words, "The boys must pass out by the bar of the adjoining saloon, where, heated by the game and feeling somewhat under obligations, they patronize the saloonkeeper." Such drink-buying served the multiple purposes of relieving thirst, cultivating the proprietor's goodwill, celebrating athletic victories, and perhaps also settling wagers.[38]

Urban proprietors who could not provide outdoor recreation space for their athletically inclined customers could still encourage groups to congregate in their establishments after their outings. One New York saloonkeeper remarked in 1909 that the "young fellows who had been playing tennis or baseball in the park close by or on the 'boulevard'" came into his saloon on Sundays to consume beer or "soft stuff" after their competitions. For more mobile groups such as bicycling clubs, however, drinking establishments encountered during countryside runs received the majority of their business. "When the cycling season begins," as Calkins observed in 1901, "the road-house or the brewery profits where the saloon loses."[39]

Outdoor sporting events featuring animals also became more difficult for saloonkeepers to stage in the city. Turkey shoots were obviously out; men interested in marksmanship now went to shooting galleries in penny arcades. Horse races were likewise problematic to arrange. By the close of the nineteenth century, fans went to racetracks constructed specially for the purpose by professional sports promoters. The blood sports of cockfighting (with gamecocks fitted with metal spurs) and bearbaiting (with chained bears beset by dogs) also became ever more rare. This was due partly to increasing urbanization and partly to decades of agitation by humanitarian reformers. Yet illicit cockfights did still occur. In Worcester, Massachusetts, for example, a saloonkeeper and his customers journeyed to a secret countryside spot most Sunday mornings in 1886 to witness such spectacles. Similarly, when Johnny Heinold opened the First and Last Chance Saloon in Oakland, California, in 1883, cockfighting was a favorite though increasingly clandestine sport of the waterfront area, immortalized in pictures of gamecocks still displayed on the old barroom walls to this day. By the early twentieth century, however, many amusements appropriate to a more rural way of life were disappearing from working-class barrooms.[40]

To many reformers, boxing was another "blood sport" just as brutal, repugnant, and archaic as cockfighting and bearbaiting. The sport had been controversial since the eighteenth century when combatants, particularly those in the southern colonies, had routinely resorted to such gruesome tactics as eye-gouging, nose-biting, and testicles-crunching. By the 1830s, however, fighters more often observed the London Prize Ring Rules. These outlawed mutilating, kicking, and striking a man already down, but they still permitted bare-knuckled fighting. Further, the bout could drag on for over a hundred rounds until one man was at last unable to go on. The turning point came in the 1880s when the swaggering but skillful John L. Sullivan rose to fame. He helped convince fight promoters to adopt the Queensberry Rules which mandated boxing gloves, timed and limited rounds, and many other reforms.[41]

Yet the fight game never did achieve true respectability and indeed was outlawed in many parts of the country. There was still too much brutality, gambling, and chicanery associated with it to suit middle-class sensibilities. As Elliott Gorn notes, boxing might have been called the "manly art" by some, but the term "manliness" meant very different things to middle- and working-class people. For the bourgeoisie, the "manly" individual was one who was socially responsible, productive, forthright, and mature. For the working class, to be "manly" was to exhibit toughness, physical prowess, and a prickly sense of personal and peer-group honor. "As exemplars of the manly art, pugilists resisted all slights," Gorn explains. "They avenged with blood insults to themselves and their cliques, and upheld a masculine ideal of elemental virility." Boxing was thus intimately tied up with what Michael Isenberg calls the working-class "cult of masculinity," often figuring importantly in the ethnic gang activity of the streets and the saloons. Some middle-class men insisted that the "manly art," with proper rules and restraints, could be regarded as a physical "science" appropriate for college and country-club gymnasiums. However, most boxing matches in the late nineteenth and early twentieth centuries were associated with the sporting life of the ethnically diverse tenement districts of the working class.[42]

Many of the most famous fighters of the saloon period hailed from minority groups. As Isenberg notes, there was an "ethnic succession" in professional boxing which paralleled the successive waves of migrants to nineteenth-century cities: first the Irish, then Jews and Italians, and finally African Americans from the South. Further, the physical, non-verbal nature of the sport made it easy for non-English-speaking immigrants to join in and for the little-educated to compete. These factors, combined with the longstanding link between boxing and barrooms, meant that most of the stars of the fight game were ethnic saloongoers.[43]

While most boxing matches were prearranged affairs, spontaneous bouts also occasionally occurred, particularly among the Irish. For example, an acquaintance of William "Big Bill" Haywood described an impromptu match which took place in a Irish coal miners' saloon in Pennsylvania in the 1870s. A newcomer named McKenna came into the barroom one night. "McKenna . . . said, buying another drink, 'I'll sing a song, dance a jig, or fight with any man in the house for the whisky for everybody.'" By invoking the treating ritual and advertising his worthiness to join in it, the stranger made his bid for acceptance. In response, the regulars designated their champion, and the group immediately retired to the back room, for they were "all Irish, and nothing tickled them more than a good fight." After they chose a referee, the fight began. "The miner . . . landed a slam on Mac's [McKenna's] nose. The blood spurted as Mac swung and got the young fellow at the point of the jaw, keeling him over. The fight was finished. Every one had been highly pleased." Then, in a gallant show of sportsmanship, the victorious McKenna acknowledged the worthiness of his defeated adversary. "Shaking hands with the young miner, he said, 'Yez was a better man than I thought ye wuz.'"[44]

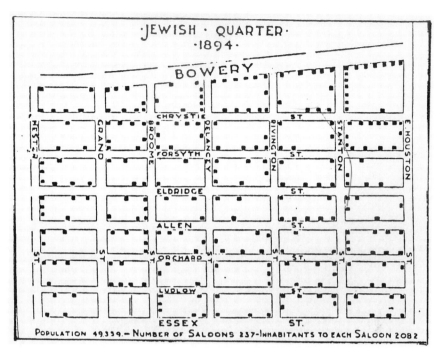

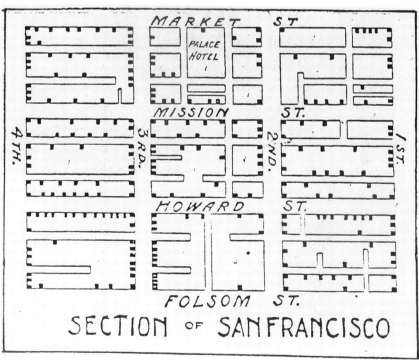

Maps from 1894 illustrate the remarkable density of saloons in working-class districts of New York and San Francisco. Reprinted from R. Calkins, *Substitutes for the Saloon* (Boston, 1901), 386, 387.

Legendary saloonkeeper Johnny Heinold inspects Jack London's dictionary in the First and Last Chance Saloon, Oakland, California, circa 1919. Note the sign referring to Carrie Nation, the nineteenth-century prohibitionist notorious for smashing bar counters with an ax. Photo courtesy of the Otha D. Wearin Trust.

Heinold's First and Last Chance Saloon. Top: Back bar bedecked with historic memorabilia. Bottom: Tables, a pot-bellied stove, and a nickel-in-the-slot stereograph. Photos courtesy of the Otha D. Wearin Trust.

Gambling and singing were among the regulars' preferred pastimes. Left: A gambling machine from 1902 in Bruning's Bar and Seafood Restaurant, New Orleans, Louisiana. Photo by Deanie Bowen. Below: Turn-of-the-century saloon-goers render the Tin Pan Alley favorite, "Sweet Adeline," in a cartoon by H. T. Webster.

Top: Indelicate barroom accessories included urination troughs like this 1902 example in the saloon of the Ernst Cafe, New Orleans, Louisiana. (Note the tile floor with its centuries-old sun symbol—a symbol later appropriated by Hitler's Nazis in the 1930s.) Photo by Deanie Bowen. Bottom: Women might bypass such masculine indelicacies through the "ladies' entrance" to the back room, as illustrated by this nineteenth-century sign from Bruning's Bar and Seafood Restaurant, New Orleans, Louisiana. Photo by Deanie Bowen.

Faces along the bar of the Eagle Saloon, Davisville, California, circa 1910. Note the elaborate cash register and carved counter, the less elegant spittoon and mustache towel, and the coquettish young woman peeking in from the right. Photo courtesy of the Yolo County Archives, Woodland, California; restoration by Deanie Bowen.

With manly status reaffirmed and social equilibrium restored, the crowd returned to the barroom where drinks for everyone, presumably at the defeated young champion's expense, served to consecrate the newly delineated drinking circle and uphold the creed of the club. Bloody though it was, this bout was no unruly barroom brawl. On the contrary, the confrontation was as orderly and comradely as drinkers' sporting lore could make it.

More often, boxing matches were organized in advance by saloonkeepers. In New York City from 1854 through 1886, for example, Harry Hill's notorious concert saloon featured not only risque vaudeville performers, but also a great many boxing matches. The ring was set up on the stage while wagering customers, male and female, looked on from their tables with drinks in hand. Pugilists often included men of the caliber of John L. Sullivan, who in fact made his New York boxing debut in Hill's saloon. Less celebrated but similarly popular bouts were held in many western mining towns. "They might be held in drinking houses, public halls, or outdoor rings," as Elliott West notes of frontier prizefights, "but in most of them a saloonkeeper was involved in some capacity." [45]

In these prearranged matches, bar customers were usually spectators rather than participants, though very active spectators they were with their frenzied wagering and loud shouting throughout the fight. Jacob Riis reported on crowd behavior during one such bout in New York in 1899, which pitted a local fighter against a man from Delaware. The "rough and noisy crowd" at first cheered the New Yorker and made "hostile demonstrations" against the "foreigner." As the bout continued, however, the local fighter aroused increasing "scorn and contempt" as he "struck one foul blow after another," until at last "the audience rose in a body and yelled to have the fight given to the 'foreigner,' until my blood tingled with pride." Riis was deeply impressed by the crowd's sense of honor and justice, particularly as this meant they would all lose their wagers. "'He is a good man,' I heard on all sides, while the once favorite sneaked away without a friend. 'Good' meant fair and manly to that crowd." Riis came away convinced that boxing, though a brutal sport, was perhaps not so pernicious an influence on the morals of the poor as many of his contemporaries believed. [46]

No so charitable, however, were Calkins's remarks regarding the exhibitions of boxing, wrestling, and other sports presented in vaudeville saloons. "They are an unmitigated nuisance, a public misfortune of such dimensions that no time should be lost in absolutely prohibiting them," he declared. To support his charge against these entertainments, he reprinted the program from one such establishment, a portion of which read:

PROGRAMME

Week Beginning
Monday, August 14, 1899 . . .

BESSIE RAYMOND.
She is Handy with Her Mitts.

Jeffries' Next Opponent,
MR. FRED HAWLEY . . .

The Misses
GOLDIE VS. RAYMOND
Will Meet All Comers.

The Modern Atlas
GEORGE WILSON
In Feats of Heavy Lifting, etc. . . . .

MISS TOPSEY TURVY
In Training for a Rough House . . .

A Grand Wrestling Match.
MR. WILSON
Will Meet a Different Man Each Evening.

From these examples, it is clear that the pugilistic talents of women as well as men were on display, and that audience participation was enthusiastically encouraged. Since the audience was predominantly male, the performance must have been uproarious indeed. Certainly Calkins found the spectacle scandalous. "The least that any American city can do for its people," he insisted, "is to prohibit immoral liquor sellers from debauching the minds of its citizens." From the standpoint of the workingmen in the audience, on the other hand, the chance to be a participant-observer and to box playfully with two female sparring partners was no doubt too tempting to pass up. In fact, it might have been an even more titillating experience than Calkins let on. In the same era, Frederick Van Wyck, a wealthy bon vivant in New York, reported witnessing a saloon boxing match "between two ladies, with nothing but trunks on." [47]

TECHNOLOGY ENTERS THE GAME

Thrilling though such vaudeville performances and saloon boxing matches were, many workers might have traded them gladly for the chance to witness firsthand such spectacular but usually far-distant events as major championship bouts, baseball games, and horse races. Yet advances in communications technology meant that at least the latest news of these events could now be brought directly to customers as they lounged in the barroom. Some proprietors installed telegraph (and later, telephone) connections to receive up-to-the-minute bulletins on faraway competitions. In some urban saloons, telegraph operators posted the latest baseball and racing results on large blackboards overhead. In barrooms of the Rocky Mountain mining frontier, customers congregated for blow-by-blow reports on prizefights held in the East. "On the night of a well-known prize fight, the saloons of the entire country are commonly packed," Calkins observed in 1901. "During the baseball and racing season, it is very common to have score cards given out free of charge. As the game progresses and the results are announced, the score can be kept as accurately by one sitting at a table with his drink as if he occupied a seat on the 'bleachers.'"[48]

Saloonkeepers also supplied sports publications to their customers. Beginning in the 1870s, sports statistics, gossip, and human interest stories became available in periodicals such as the St. Louis *Sporting News*, the Philadelphia *Sporting Life,* and the New York *National Police Gazette* (the latter being offered to saloon proprietors at bargain subscription rates). Newspapers also provided detailed sports information, with Joseph Pulitzer's *World* introducing the sports page in the 1880s, and William Randolph Hearst's *Journal* innovating the sports section in the 1890s. Finally, for those bargoers anxious to see the action for themselves, vaudeville saloons sometimes showed films of notable contests as fillers between live acts on the bill. In 1901, for example, Melendy reported that a Chicago establishment "was reproducing with the cinematograph the Jeffries-Fitzsimmons fight." In these various ways, barkeepers used the latest developments in communications media to make their saloons a chief headquarters for working-class sports enthusiasts.[49]

Following spectator sports in saloons was not the same as attending the actual event, of course. The rise of the professional sports industry in the 1880s and 1890s, with its big-time promoters, nationally known athletes, and huge stadiums full of thousands of cheering fans, guaranteed an experience that no smoky saloon with its blackboards and score cards could duplicate. Further, the greenery and open air of the baseball park and the racetrack were amenities which most barrooms could not supply, but which many city dwellers craved as almost the last vestige of pastoral pleasures that remained in their lives.[50]

Yet the saloon did offer a few advantages which the stadium experience could not. Following sports in barrooms was convenient and cheap. There was no streetcar to catch and no admission ticket to buy. Of course the obligatory drink or two had to be purchased, but this was an everyday expenditure for many millions of workingmen in any case. More important was the social atmosphere of the barroom itself. Regulars relaxed at the tables in familiar drinking company and entered easily into discussions of the game. They made friendly wagers on the current contest or on the finer points of sporting lore. Often the proprietor kept well informed on athletic matters so that, according to George Ade, he could act as the "fair-minded referee when it came to deciding wagers concerning the dates and details of major sporting events." Sometimes the saloonkeeper was himself a former athlete. "An ex-prizefighter or baseball champion sets up a saloon which becomes the clearing-house for all kinds of athletic and sporting intelligence," as Calkins observed.[51]

Thus, what the saloon lacked in greenery and open air, it made up for in intimacy and camaraderie. Over time, the same men might congregate many times in the same setting, making a tradition of their gatherings and building their own repertoire of favorite shared moments and stories. In this way, regular gatherings in barrooms during major sporting events produced a quality of relationship among fellow enthusiasts which the stadium experience, with its crush of ever-shifting crowds, could not duplicate.

For workingmen interested in games of competition, then, the saloon offered a wide array of choices appealing to spectators as well as participants and ranging from the cerebral to the visceral. For those who enjoyed a challenge to their powers of quiet calculation, memory, and other intellectual skills, there were many varieties of card and board games available. For those who also sought a physical challenge, there were billiards, pool, handball, bowling, and boxing. Finally, for those interested in following events in the burgeoning professional sports industry, there were horse races, baseball games, and prizefights brought to saloons through the latest communications technology. Accompanying all these amusements was ample opportunity for customers to discuss the progress of games, argue the odds, and gamble on the outcomes. The amount and intensity of such activity varied from one establishment to another, of course, but most saloons offered workingmen several options for expressing their interest in sporting matters.

The Play Community

In many respects, competitive games paralleled everyday experience by encouraging participants to engage in a kind of Darwinian struggle for the survival—or, more accurately here, the triumph—of the fittest. Yet competition in games differed in one very important way from competition in day-to-day living. As Caillois noted, competitive games involved "an attempt to substitute perfect situations for the normal confusion of contemporary life."[52] In games, the rules were well defined, indisputable, and systematically applied to every player. Each man stood equal before the laws and had an equal chance to demonstrate his abilities. In contrast, the rules in "real" life were not always clear, and privileged people evaded or flouted the law. Meanwhile, others of the "wrong" ethnic background, gender, or religious persuasion frequently encountered unfair treatment and blocked opportunities. Further, hard work did not always mean success or a sense of achievement. Many men worked shifts of ten to twelve hours in jobs that stifled creativity, paid poorly, and offered little hope of advancement. For them, saloon games provided a chance to demonstrate their competence, ingenuity, and expertise, as well as to be compensated through such symbolic rewards as drinks, cigars, and small wagers. Everyday life might be plagued with injustices, but games represented a separate reality where every man might have an occasional opportunity to shine.

This quality of separateness from everyday life was in fact characteristic of all forms of saloon play whether involving competition, chance, simulation, or vertigo. As Johan Huizinga noted, play in its many manifestations "is not 'ordinary' or 'real' life. It is rather a stepping out of 'real' life into a temporary sphere of activity with a disposition all its own." When saloongoers shook dice, shot pool, drank, danced, or donned costumes in the spirit of carnival, their actions denoted a departure from one kind of reality into another. In effect, they made a voluntary pact to engage in a communal act of the imagination which generated what Caillois called the "universe of play." A second reality replaced everyday living which involved its own peculiar boundaries of time and space and its own set of rules, goals, and rewards.[53]

Further, as Huizinga argued, "A play community generally tends to become permanent even after the game is over." When people share this experience of "stepping out" of ordinary life into the "temporary sphere" of play, they often create an enduring social bond. "Of course, not every game of marbles or every bridge party leads to the founding of a club," he noted. "But the feeling of being 'apart together' in an exceptional situation, of sharing something important, of mutually withdrawing from the rest of the world and rejecting the usual norms, retains its magic beyond the duration of the individual game." This concept of the "play community" brings added significance to Calkins' remark that "many men find their athletic club within the saloon." By congregating for game-playing on a steady basis, saloongoing workers engaged in a form of group recreation which imparted a special and enduring sense of comradeship.[54]

Barroom games and gambling well illustrate how saloon culture comprised a mixture of marketplace and communal values. Many games were intensely competitive, pitting individual against individual in a struggle for success and dominance. At the same time, ideals of fraternity and sportsmanship tempered the rivalry, producing a "play community" which strengthened the ties among regulars. Gambling involved a spirit of acquisitive individualism as each player vied for personal gain. Yet the stakes were usually small and largely symbolic: a beer, a cigar, a few nickels. Acquisition of such rewards bolstered an individual's worth, but the pleasures of group gambling were also part of the players' motivation. Thus, the goal of the saloon wager was sociability as well as profit.

Further, many games represented a "purification" of marketplace conditions with their prescribed order of events, incontrovertible rules, and clear outcomes. When workers retreated into saloons to compete and gamble, therefore, they were not seeking to escape the marketplace so much as to improve upon it. By applying communal values to marketlike situations in their games, they constructed their own version of reality which combined competition, chance, and camaraderie in ways not commonly encountered beyond the swinging doors.

Eight

Talk and Storytelling

As you step in, you find . . . men are seated about the tables, reading, playing cards, eating, and discussing, over a glass of beer, subjects varying from the political and sociological problems of the day to the sporting news and the lighter chat of the immediate neighborhood. . . . In many of these discussions, to which I have listened and in which I have joined. . . , [t]he names of Karl Marx and leaders of political and social thought are often heard. . . . The saloon is, in short, the clearing-house for the common intelligence—the social and intellectual center of the neighborhood.
—Royal Melendy[1]

The role of the saloon as a popular forum for the exchange of news and views was a continuation of a centuries-old function of tavern culture dating back to medieval England and before. When Geoffrey Chaucer wrote *The Canterbury Tales* in the late 1300s, he made the Tabard Inn the setting for his characters' tale-swapping pact. Even in his early day, storytelling constituted an integral part of everyday life in inns and taverns. In succeeding centuries, with the growth of commerce and cities, people of all classes made increasing use of drinking establishments as marketplaces for ideas. For example, Samuel Johnson, the noted literary critic, was an habitué of the Turk's Head Tavern in London in the eighteenth century. In his words, "[W]ine there exhilarates my spirits, and prompts me to free conversation and an interchange of discourse with those whom I most love: I dogmatise and am contradicted, and in this conflict of opinions and sentiments I find delight."[2]

This English tavern tradition of lively conversation and intellectual candor continued in the New World in the colonial and antebellum periods. As American tavern regular Jonas Green remarked of his drinking circle in the mid-eighteenth century, "We meet, converse, laugh, talk, smoke, drink, differ, agree, philosphize, harrangue, pun, sing, dance, and fiddle together, nay we are really in fact a club." Similarly, in the antebellum period, travelers in Wisconsin reported that when they were gathered around the tavernkeeper's hearth, they "were expected to contribute to the general entertainment by narrating their own or their friends' adventures." By the beginning of the saloon era, then, barrooms were already well-established centers for the spirited swapping of thoughts and lore in the communities they served.[3]

Equally significant, however, were the changes that overtook barroom society and its verbal culture after 1870. In the nation's industrializing phase, economic and social schisms widened between the middle and working classes. An important consequence for drink culture was that saloons became more and more the exclusive domain of laboring men. Saloongoers' discussions were now likely to include references to such marketplace issues as union organizing, radical political philosophies, and other matters important to an increasingly industrialized, urbanized labor force. These newer themes blended with older ones from the preindustrial era to produce the expressive culture of the saloon period.

The Daily Exchange

Much of the talk in saloons consisted of the "lighter chat" of the surrounding community, as Royal Melendy noted. Regulars dropped in to learn the latest gossip and to exchange opinions on happenings of local and municipal interest. In this endeavor, they were often aided by the saloonkeeper who kept himself well informed on current events. "He reads the papers," observed Raymond Calkins, "and makes a point of being a leader in discussion, an arbiter in debate." In many cases, the barman purchased a paper for his patrons' use on the premises. Of the 163 saloon proprietors in Chicago's seventeenth ward in 1900, for example, 139 (85%) supplied newspapers. In addition, an accomplished saloonkeeper was skilled at recycling the choicest conversational tidbits coming across the bar. "[T]here is an accretion of intelligence that comes to him in his business," as E. C. Moore remarked. "He hears the best stories. He is the first to get accurate information as to the latest political deals and social mysteries.

The common talk of the day passes through his ears and he is known to retain that which is most interesting."[4]

One of the most colorful and talented saloonkeepers in this regard was the legendary Jim McGarry of Chicago. This sardonic Irishman was famous in the 1890s for his expertise as a raconteur, social critic, and lampooner of the pompous. According to one of his admirers, George Ade, "His hard-boiled philosophy and caustic sarcasm provided the first inspiration for the inimitable 'Dooley' pieces by 'Pete' Dunne." Finley Peter Dunne adopted McGarry and his customers as models for his newspaper columns from 1893 to 1930 which featured bartender-philosopher Martin Dooley and his regulars. Dooley, like his real-life counterpart, made a point of learning the latest developments through customers' conversation, newspaper accounts, and his own powers of observation from behind the long mahogany. He was therefore well versed on many subjects. He knew all about local marriages, births, and deaths. He discussed citywide sensations like the 1897 trial of Adolph Leutgert, accused of disposing of his murdered wife with a sausage grinder. He also spoke knowledgeably about nationwide controversies such as the country's involvement in the Spanish-American War in 1898. Like both Dooley and McGarry, the most successful saloonkeepers kept their regulars up to date on the talk and tales circulating the neighborhood.[5]

In his role as host of the saloon club, the bartender often facilitated conversation among his customers. One memorable example was Johnny Heinold, proprietor of the First and Last Chance in Oakland, California, in the 1890s. He was reportedly a master at easing newcomers into friendly exchanges with more established members of his clientele. He made a point of introducing them and, "like a true host, made the tactful remarks that enabled us to find mutual topics of conversation," remarked Jack London. Then Heinold "drifted out of the conversation" while his customers carried on the exchange.[6]

The talk in saloons was frequently rough, uninhibited, and at times obscene. In Ade's words, a compilation of "all the talk ever spilled in all the saloons . . . could never get past the censor." Rough talk among working-class men was not limited to saloons, of course. On the job, bawdy stories and speech were a way of establishing one's status within the group, according to James Stevens's observations of teamsters, railroaders, and other laborers. Off the job, meanwhile, noisy profanity was commonplace among adults as well as young newsboys and bootblacks in urban lodging houses, observed Jacob Riis. This was the case even though some reform-minded proprietors posted warning signs, such as "No swearing or loud talking after nine o'clock" and "Boys who swear and chew tobacco cannot sleep here."[7]

The rough talk in saloons, then, was part of a widespread style of language characteristic of many working-class men, though the overtly masculine atmosphere of the barroom no doubt encouraged the tendency. One New York saloonkeeper remarked on the routinely vulgar utterances of his regulars. "My patrons were not choice in their language. They used habitually terms and phrases that elsewhere would not be permissible," he observed. "But they were so used to them that they were scarcely aware, I think, of their original meaning." Indeed, the customary use of strong language in saloons constituted a kind of oral ritual through which bargoers identified themselves as "one of the boys." It was rather the absence of strong language in a customer's speech that would have drawn attention.[8]

Sometimes saloon speech was bombastic and self-aggrandizing. Ade recalled overhearing "the babble of loud and foolish talk" issuing from many midwestern saloons in the 1870s and 1880s. The "picturesque vocabulary" of the "noisy braggart" was particularly memorable. "I can outwrassle, outrun or outfight any skunk in this here town" was the typical boast of the barroom blowhard. "I got two rows o' nipples an' holes bored for more. . . . That's ole Bud for you — the idol o' the women an' the envy o' the men." This exaggerated talk seems reminiscent of the frontier tall tale tradition in which backwoods (and, some might say, backwards) Americans first "turned the ridicule of high-toned English and eastern travelers to glory in brags about themselves," as Richard Dorson noted. Further, according to Constance Rourke, the tall-talking man "shouted in ritual. . . , like savage efforts to create strength . . . by exhibiting strength." To boast so fantastically of personal prowess was to project a superhuman image, a ploy perhaps designed to bolster the speaker's courage as much as to impress his audience. Such a man was "a sore trial for any barkeep," remarked Ade, for sometimes his "brash and insolent talk" provoked arguments and barroom brawls. "More often he was permitted to vapor," however, it being a longstanding custom to tolerate some amount of barroom braggadocio from men whose tongues had been loosened by alcohol.[9]

Another subject inspiring saloon hyperbole was the virtue and beauty of women of the saloongoers' acquaintance. Females might have been largely excluded from the saloon environment, but certainly not from its talk. "Men left their families to loiter in saloons, but this did not mean that they ceased to love their families," Ade noted. "It was right in front of the bar that the fond husband announced to the wide world that his wife was the best damned housekeeper in town and her kitchen floor was so clean that you could eat off of it. And, as Charley Case once remarked, they often did." Similarly, Ade recalled an occasion in a Louisville saloon in the 1890s when a colonel bragged of knowing "the most beautiful girl in Kentucky," declaring grandly that "you could span her waist with your two hands but she couldn't sit down in a tub."[10]

The expansive tone of much of the saloon's expressive culture was particularly well illustrated in the recitation pieces that some regulars were fond of delivering. Throughout the saloon period, Americans exhibited tremendous enthusiasm for oratory in general and narrative poetry in particular, whether in the newspapers, on the stage, or in the barroom. During Fourth of July celebrations, for example, it was common for crowds to "stick to their seats without turnin' a hair while, for four solid hours, the Declaration of Independence is read, long-winded orators speak, and the glee club sings itself hoarse," according to Tammany politician George Washington Plunkitt. William Shakespeare's works, not yet "kidnapped" by polite society into the realm of "higher culture," were popular and well known among working-class audiences. Lesser bards were also embraced by the public, including James Whitcomb Riley, Edgar Guest, Hugh D'Arcy, and Robert W. Service. Often a verse with a vivid plotline found its way into variety theaters and vaudeville saloons, such as Ernest Thayer's baseball epic of 1888, "Casey at the Bat." These and scores of other specimens of poetry and prose enjoyed wide circulation.[11]

Given this background, it is understandable that recitations ranging from Shakespeare to Service formed an important part of the oral culture of saloons. "Every regular place had a few patrons who spouted Shakespeare and had some smattering of the classics," observed Ade. Many saloongoers acquainted with Shakespearean verse were fond of parodies, such as Hamlet's lamenting "the slings and dregs of outrageous whisky" or telling Ophelia, "Get thee to a brewery." Another example spoofed *As You Like It:*

> All the world's a bar,
> And all the men and women merely drinkers;
> They have their hiccups and their staggerings . . .

Such parodies offer evidence of Shakespeare's popularity, since, as Lawrence Levine has pointed out, "It is difficult to take familiarities with that which is not already familiar; one cannot parody that which is not well known."[12]

Some bargoers were acquainted with classical literature. James Stevens described a rousing rendition of Homer's *Iliad* delivered by one "Poker Tom" Davis in an Idaho saloon in 1905. Commenting on the impact of the piece, Stevens wrote, "I felt mightily shaken. It had stirred me all up inside. I felt as if I could listen to Poker Tom tell about the Greeks all night." For the rest of the saloon crowd, how-ever, "It was just another story to them, something like the ones they had lived through themselves, with all of its drinking and carousing, fighting and woman-stealing, rambling away from home, and so on." Stevens's remarks provide a valuable insight into the appeal of Homer, Shakespeare, and other classical poets to saloongoers. Homer's ac-count of the clash between Menelaus the Greek and Paris the Trojan over the beautiful Helen, for instance, addressed familiar themes de-spite the exotic setting. Many could identify with stories featuring fights over personal and group honor which resembled their own life stories, writ large.[13]

Saloon talk of a more practical sort often focused on local politics. Political clubs loyal to the neighborhood "ward heeler" (sometimes the saloonkeeper himself) adopted saloon back rooms as their head-quarters. The primary purpose of such clubs was to marshal votes for the campaigns of machine candidates. Thus, as Calkins observed, the political club "is not a forum for the discussion of current issues so much as a convenient means for 'bunching' votes for the next elec-tion." Nevertheless, with political favors and payments at stake, many workers attended meetings faithfully and spread the good word among saloon regulars about the talents and benevolence of their chosen candidates.[14]

Perhaps the most popular topic of everyday conversation was the sporting news. For many customers, the pool table more than the beer stein had originally attracted them to saloons in their youth. Their interest in competitive games was thereafter fueled by the presence of cards, dice, and other diversions as well as the casual banter that accompanied a friendly contest. Saloongoers' truly impas-sioned discussions of athletics, however, seem to have focused on the more spectacular feats of professional players in prizefighting, base-ball, and horse racing. By following professional sports, they had the opportunity to take sides, brag, criticize, and engage in vehement arguments all without imperiling the ego as they might in more personal exchanges. For beleaguered laborers in industrializing America, moreover, there were few other areas of endeavor in which the Horatio Alger formula of rags-to-riches was so vividly and inspiringly illustrated. Here were the clear heroes, the success stories, and the models of manliness with whom urban laborers could identify. Especially important as symbols of success were athletes with strong ethnic backgrounds, as exemplified by prizefighters Jack Johnson for the black community and "Gentleman Jim" Corbett for the Irish. Thus, as a means of promoting ethnic pride, releasing explosive emotions, and reaffirming gender ties, the discussion of sporting news was a favorite pastime in saloons.[15]

Up Close and Personal

The saloon sometimes served as a forum for the airing of deeply personal grievances, disappointments, and regrets, as many a bartender cornered into playing the poor man's psychiatrist could attest. The atmosphere of fellowship and trust in the barroom, coupled with the disinhibiting effects of alcohol, apparently encouraged many regulars to lay bare their innermost feelings. "All the drinkers at my place, with very few exceptions indeed, opened their hearts to me and George, the 'barkeep,' even when not encouraged to do so," remarked one proprietor. "They would tell their secrets, their troubles, their entanglements, their domestic woes, their afflictions. And the drunker they got, the more confidential they became." Similarly, Travis Hoke observed that a saloonkeeper's regulars "told him their domestic difficulties and their affairs of the heart," and he acted as "counsellor in all the ways of life, recipient of confidences, disburser of advice." Beneath their tough exterior of vulgar language and noisy bravado, many saloongoers seem to have had an anxious, vulnerable side that periodically surfaced when their guards were down. Certainly there were few other places besides saloons where workingmen could openly vent their emotions—including an occasional "crying jag," according to Hoke—and expect a sympathetic hearing.[16]

This penchant for pathos helps explain the great popularity in saloons of two recitation pieces, Robert W. Service's "The Shooting of Dan McGrew" and Hugh D'Arcy's "The Face upon the Floor." As Ade remarked, "No large party, with all the faucets running, was complete without 'the face on the bar-room floor,'" adding that it was a "stand-by which was worn threadbare before the boys got through with it."[17] The same was true of "Dan McGrew." The two narratives were widely performed both within and outside saloons in the early 1900s (and indeed still persist in the oral culture of some late-twentieth-century barrooms).[18]

Service's "The Shooting of Dan McGrew" took place in the Malamute saloon one cold Alaskan night. "A bunch of the boys were whooping it up" while Dangerous Dan McGrew played solitaire under the attentive eye of "the lady that's known as Lou." Suddenly, a stranger entered. He was a "dog dirty" miner down on his luck, whom the regulars scrutinized with curiosity and suspicion. When he offered to treat the house, however, they accepted and drank to his health, though Dangerous Dan was ominously slow to raise his glass. Then, noticing the piano, the mysterious stranger wordlessly sat down to play. As he did, it seemed that his deepest secrets poured out in the haunting music. First his playing conjured up the terrible isolation of his life in the Alaskan "Great Alone." Next it revealed his longtime hunger for hearth and home "crowned with a woman's love." But long ago his dreams for these joys had been shattered—and here the music grew wrenchingly sad—when someone stole his woman away, whose love proved a "devil's lie."

With this, the music "stopped with a crash." The stranger turned and announced that "one of you is a hound of hell . . . and that one is Dan McGrew." All at once the lights went down and two shots rang out. When the lights went up again, Dangerous Dan lay "pitched on his head, and pumped full of lead." And so too lay the hapless stranger in a last embrace with his rouged and faithless Lou, who calmly "pinched his poke" of gold dust as she kissed him goodbye.

In contrast to the faraway Malamute saloon in Alaska, D'Arcy's "The Face Upon the Floor" was set in Joe's barroom down on the square. There a "goodly crowd" was joking and singing one balmy summer night. In the midst of this merriment, a dirty vagabond crept in through the open door, drawing laughter and insults from the regulars. But the vagabond took the abuse "with stoical good grace," and at length the gang agreed to treat him to drinks in exchange for the "funny story" that he promised to tell. "God bless you one and all," he said, as he drained his glass and solicited another. Then he began his tale. Though now he might be just a "dirty sot," at one time he had been a noted painter whose canvas entitled "Chase of Fame" had sold for a considerable sum. But then came Madeline, "with eyes that petrified my brain and sunk into my heart." After two blissful months with her, he was working on a portrait of a friend one day when Madeline admired it. She asked to meet this "fair-haired boy" who had "such dreamy eyes." Before very long, they met, they loved, they ran away, and within a year the "jewel" that had been Madeline "had tarnished, and was dead."

After a pause, the vagabond called upon the hushed crowd for another drink and a piece of chalk. On the barroom floor he began to sketch the face of the "lovely Madeline." He was just adding the final touches when suddenly, with a "fearful shriek," the poor vagabond "leaped and fell across the picture—dead." ("All very dramatic and with the perfect alcoholic finale," as Ade wryly remarked.) [19]

The parallels between these two narratives can be clarified by adopting a method that folklorists use in studying versions of folktales. Stories are broken down into morphological units, called "incidents," "functions," or "motifemes," which are like slots occurring in a prescribed order into which analogous story elements can be inserted. [20] Applying this method to the two narratives, a pattern emerges:

1. A degraded outsider confronts the barroom peer group.
2. He initiates treating and toasting rituals.
3. He makes his "drunkard's confession."
4. He reveals his tragic flaw: his weakness and loss of honor regarding a faithless woman.
5. He attempts a heroic effort to regain his lost woman and masculine honor.
6. He fails and dies in a final embrace with his female nemesis.

The poems exhibit several striking similarities. Both begin by emphasizing the difference in status between the speaker and his audience. The latter is a convivial, comfortable, and united group of peers; the former is a sorrowful and solitary outsider. His degraded condition clearly makes him ineligible for club membership, much like the pathetic, charity-seeking "sitters" who besieged the late-nineteenth-century saloons of New York and Chicago in wintertime. Nevertheless, the outcast makes a bid for sympathetic attention by invoking the familiar clubbing rituals of the treat and the toast. This

puts the regulars in the uncomfortable position of having either to reject him overtly or accept him temporarily as a participant in their
activities.[21]

What then follows is the "drunkard's confession," the same sort of
emotional and personal narrative which regulars often confided to
their bartenders in the later stages of inebriety. The difference here,
of course, is that the confession is public. Further, the audience,
while perhaps empathetic, is not personally known to the speaker. In
this regard, the stranger's speech strongly resembles the ritual of the
public confession employed by temperance groups such as the Washingtonians in the early nineteenth century and Alcoholics Anonymous in the twentieth. According to this technique, the drunkard
stands before other drunkards (now reformed) and makes an open
admission of his weaknesses and failures in an attempt to cleanse his
soul and counsel others. Unfortunately for the poems' protagonists,
though, their efforts to regain their lost caste end in disaster and
death.[22]

The appeal of these narratives, beyond their reference to familiar
barroom conventions and their use of dramatic plotlines, lay in their
cautionary message which directly addressed the emotional concerns
of working-class males. The saloongoers' concept of manliness demanded that no man should tolerate any action which diminished his
sense of personal honor. In the narratives, however, here were two
cuckolds who had permitted their terrible humiliation to drag them
down into degradation and despair. From the time of their dishonor
to the moment they entered the saloon, they had taken no action to
restore their pride. Moreover, they still longed pathetically for the
fallen women who had ruined them. This was, of course, intolerable.
At wit's end, they came at last to the barroom—the locus of manliness and manly confrontations—and made one final tragic effort to
regain their sense of honor. By then, however, it was too late. They
had already sacrificed what mattered most, and for that they had
to die.[23]

The narratives also touched on the sensitive area of male-female
relations. Though married saloongoers did not generally embrace the
middle-class ideal of "companionate marriage," they still believed
that family ties and domestic stability represented what was normal
and respectable in life. For those who were unmarried or separated
from their families, domestic life often consisted of a crowded board-

ing house full of other unattached, rootless men, and it could be a lonely life indeed. Thus, most men well recognized the importance of female companionship and fidelity, not to mention the pleasures of physical intimacy. At the same time, they recognized that this need made them vulnerable to betrayal, heartbreak, shame, and loss. Yet there they all were in the saloon, spending time and money away from women and perhaps putting their chances for domestic happiness in jeopardy. The tension between these conflicting impulses produced anxieties that were not always easy for these men to confess or resolve.[24]

It was here that the recitations under consideration made their appeal. Both poems set forth the ideal of monogamous love. They then relentlessly portrayed the inevitably catastrophic consequences attending violations of that ideal. For Madeline and Lou, their acts of betrayal brought degradation and ruin, ending with Madeline dead and Lou, in terms of Victorian morality, "as good as dead" in her sinful existence as a barroom harlot. The failure of the protagonists to prevent this calamity was a reflection on their deficiencies as men. Indeed, many workingmen still subscribed to the centuries-old view that it was men's duty to control and discipline women, who were all "Eve's daughters." This chauvanistic attitude, though injurious to the cause of women's rights at the time and repugnant to late twentieth-century sensibilities, nevertheless held sway among many saloon-goers. The poems probed these sore spots in gender relations, suggesting that perhaps if the protagonists had been more vigilant, swift, and forceful in curbing their women's corrupting passions, the tragedy could have been averted.[25]

In articulating these cultural imperatives of manly honor and feminine virtue to be defended at all costs, the narratives conjured up a kind of collective fantasy—or, perhaps more accurately, a collective nightmare—all within the safe parameters of a story formula that was familiar and predictable. "Formulas enable the audience to explore in fantasy the boundary between the permitted and the forbidden," as John Cawelti has observed in his study of popular culture, "and . . . to express, explore, and finally to reject those actions which are forbidden, but which, because of certain other cultural patterns, are strongly tempting."[26] Through these imaginary scenarios, men could envision the worst, toy with disaster, and yet emerge in the end unscathed and rededicated to the threatened cultural ideal.

SHOPTALK

Much of the conversation in saloons centered on the worklives of the customers. For example, Jack London recalled his first encounter with a "cantankerous old cuss" known as "Old Scratch" Nelson, a Scandinavian sailor so nicknamed by the seaside community in Oakland, California, for "a Berserker trick of his, in fighting, of tearing off his opponent's face." Both "Old Scratch" Nelson and London gravitated one day in 1891 to Johnny Heinold's First and Last Chance. There the regulars were mostly seagoing men linked by strong occupational ties. The fifteen-year-old London, himself a fledgling sailor, had heard "many weird tales" about Nelson and had "worshipped him from afar." He was therefore delighted when he and "the old sea dog," with Heinold's help, discovered they shared a particular interest in the lore of "the savage old sailing days." "The more beer Captain Nelson and I drank the better we got acquainted," London reported. "So he drifted back to his wild young days, and spun many a rare yarn for me, while we downed beer, treat by treat, all through a blessed summer afternoon." Further, as London pointed out, "It took the saloon to bring us together," the kind of place where men had been congregating for centuries to discuss their work and spin their yarns.[27]

James Stevens also recalled work-related conversations full of bravado and hyperbole in the Horseshoe Saloon in Shoshone, Idaho, in 1905. "In the saloons [the team-hands] talked about horses and beef, and told how to handle them and bragged about how good they were at it. It was the same with . . . railroaders and loggers." William "Big Bill" Haywood encountered similar talk when he began work in the silver mines of Nevada in 1884 at the age of fifteen. "[A]ll the old tales of the different mining camps would be related by men who had been on the scene of the action, or who had heard the stories at first hand." Frequently their talk also turned to workplace hardships and injustices. In 1896, for example, Haywood observed a group of Cornish miners discussing their circumstances in the Brewery Saloon, one of seventeen barrooms in Silver City, Nevada. Their boss, Simon Harris of the local Poor Man Mine, had decided to abolish the leasing arrangement under which these men had worked as a group and earned a superior group wage (an arrangement known as "tributing"). In the midst of their "complaining and lamenting," Haywood heard one man turn to another and demand, "See 'ere, Tussy, can't thee pray? Can't thee pray for we tributes?" In response, Tussy in-toned, "Dear Lord, dost thee know Simmon 'Arris, superintendent of the Poor Man mine? If thee know en, we wish for thee to take en and put en in 'Ell, and there let the bugger frizzle and fry, until 'e give us back we just tributes. And when 'e do, dear Lord, we ask thee to take en out of 'Ell again, an' grease en up a bit and turn of en loose. Amen." Delighted with this irreverent entreaty, the miners drank a round of beer in their comrade's honor. "Like all prayers, however, it was ineffective," Haywood dryly noted.[28]

Sometimes militant saloon talk could be dangerous, as Haywood learned from legends still circulating in the 1890s about the Molly Maguires of Pennsylvania and their barroom betrayal twenty years earlier. The Molly Maguires in such tales were a radical, under-ground labor group who earned the enmity of the coal-mining inter-ests in the 1870s for their obstinate resistance to wage cuts, layoffs, and other employer outrages. It must be emphasized that such stories were *legends*, tales told as true even though they might not be his-torically accurate or verifiable. Some scholars now doubt, for ex-ample, that the Molly Maguires ever really existed as an organized group or performed the many deeds associated with them. For pres-ent purposes, however, the actual facts about the Molly Maguires are less important than the saloon lore about them and especially the role attributed to unguarded saloon talk which allegedly led to their undoing.[29]

Haywood recounted a version of the Molly Maguires' legendary downfall which he heard from a Nevada miner who had been in Penn-sylvania in the 1870s. One of the group's leaders, Barney Hogle, ran a saloon in Pottsville where the members regularly congregated. Un-beknownst to them, a powerful mine owner hired the Pinkerton De-tective Agency to send a "stool pigeon" into their midst. This spy proceeded to "wiggle his slimy way into the organization" with his jovial talk and liberal spending in the bar. Hogle even helped the imposter find work and in time he was invited to join the Molly Maguires. "Through the skulduggery of this detective, a number of young miners were involved in a murder; at least they were mixed up in it to such an extent that they were charged with murder," accord-ing to Haywood. The twenty-four men implicated by the infiltrator's testimony were brought to trial in 1876. Ten were executed and four-teen were sent to the penitentiary. The mine owners triumphed by us-ing the group's bargoing customs against them. According to legend, it was the men's talk in Barney Hogle's saloon in Pottsville that helped bring the fighting Molly Maguires down. Haywood vividly remembered every detail of the old miner's story, which may have served to curb his own propensity for discussing incriminating incidents in saloons.[30]

Like Haywood, Eugene Debs was mightily impressed as a young man by the saloon talk of railroaders in the 1870s, men whom John Dos Passos described as "the big men fond of whiskey and fond of each other, gentle rambling tellers of stories over bars in small towns in the Middle West." By 1880, Debs was an official in the Brotherhood of Locomotive Firemen. Further, he gained widespread fame among railroaders when he triumphed in a heated shouting match with a vice president of the Pennsylvania Railroad. "The story was repeated . . . over beer in a thousand junction towns," according to Ray Ginger. With this feat, as well as his leadership in the bitter Pullman Strike of 1894 and his presidential campaigns on the Socialist ticket from 1900 to 1920, Debs earned an honored place in the railroaders' saloon lore that had been his first inspiration.[31]

Like both Debs and Haywood, many men interested in the cause of labor found the barroom to be a ready-made forum for union organizing. The saloon "is the principal place in which ideas underlying the labor movement originate, or at any rate become consciously held," as Hutchins Hapgood remarked of McSorley's bar in New York. "It is there where men talk over, think, and exchange feelings and ideas relating to their labor and their lives." Most, according to Hapgood, were "quiet workingmen who sip their ale and look as if they are philosophizing." Some, however, had more extreme programs in mind.[32]

CONTROVERSY

Workers profoundly displeased with the socio-economic status quo met in saloons to debate radical alternatives. In these discussions, the ideas of Karl Marx and the socialist movement received frequent mention. In *McTeague* (1899), Frank Norris offered a portrait of such heated debate going on in Frenna's saloon in San Francisco. "Marcus . . . discussed it at the top of his voice," wrote Norris. "'It's the capitalists that's ruining the cause of labor,' shouted Marcus, banging the table with his fist till the beer glasses danced." The militantly dissatisfied also joined socialist clubs bearing names such as the

Working Men's Educational Club, the Socialist's Educational Club, and the Socialist Literary Club. Like most workers' associations of the era, these clubs usually met in saloons to recruit new members and to discuss their views. Such activities alarmed many conservative employers, whose fears were fueled by the great number of immigrants in the club memberships. This was clear proof, they claimed, that foreign radicals were plotting the destruction of America. Thus, when railroad mogul George Pullman founded the company town of Pullman, Illinois, in the late nineteenth century, he banned not only unions, but also saloons. He was determined to squelch both intemperance and subversiveness among his employees, many of whom were immigrants.[33]

Not just radical political views, but also ideas challenging various other cultural and religious norms were heard in saloons. Ethnic fraternal lodges and mutual aid associations meeting in the back rooms frequently encouraged their members to keep their cultural heritages alive. There they discussed, in their native languages, their Old World customs, poetry, and history. In New York City, for example, the "98" Club for the Preservation of the Irish Language met regularly in the Clarendon Hall barroom. This penchant for preservation, nurtured in saloons, struck many native-born Americans as both disloyal and dangerous to the national social fabric.[34]

The tenets of organized religion were sometimes challenged in barrooms as well. In Chicago, for example, Czechs and Slovaks involved in the Free Thought movement discussed their anti-Catholic views in saloons. This practice caused upset in their own neighborhoods as well as in the city at large. Proponents of Marxism also attacked organized religion as the "opiate of the masses" which interfered with the task of raising workers' class consciousness. Even men with no particular class or ethnic ax to grind might use saloons as forums for expressing unconventional opinions on religion. In Dalles, Oregon, for example, Stevens recalled how a local farmer "stood at the bar and orated about Evolution, and about Darwin and Huxley, who had proved through their science that Genesis was all wrong" and "had been blasted to pieces, as he said." Such controversial discussions of religion, ethnic culture, and politics convinced many old-stock, middle-class citizens that saloons were veritable hotbeds of un-American ideas and tendencies.[35]

The trend toward more class-conscious bar talk did not burst forth full-blown as the saloon period opened, of course. Rather, it developed gradually and unevenly with the slow and asymmetric spread of industrialization. In comparison with earlier eras, however, much saloon conversation was striking for its class-specific content, militant undertone, and preoccupation with marketplace issues as workers struggled to meet the exigencies of the emerging industrial order.[36]

Somewhat ironically, male saloongoers' talk well illustrates the late twentieth-century feminist maxim that "the personal is political." According to this view, women who share personal experiences and problems in consciousness-raising support groups soon discover that their individual difficulties are, in Jo Freeman's words, "common problems with social causes and political solutions." Men in saloons had a parallel consciousness-raising experience. Comfortable in their face-to-face, communal relationships, saloongoing laborers confided their personal problems which frequently involved being overworked, underpaid, and underappreciated. As they compared notes, they realized their difficulties were actually the result of larger forces and conditions in the urban marketplace which acted upon their separate lives in similar ways. The saloon provided a setting in which men analyzed their shared personal problems as political phenomena. As Melendy succinctly put it, "Here men 'shake out their hearts together.'"[37]

THE WORKINGMAN'S SCHOOL

After amply sampling barlife in the western states of California, Oregon, and Idaho in the early 1900s, Stevens concluded that most saloongoers were not at all the evil-tongued "lost souls" that religious revivalists of his childhood had led him to expect. On the contrary, he was surprised and even a bit let down to discover that most of the bar talk and storytelling he encountered was "so infernally educational." Not that such talk was boring. Quite the opposite, he was often fascinated by his barmates' wide-ranging discussions of everything from homelife to worklife to the afterlife, as well as their boastful tall tales, adventure yarns, humorous anecdotes, and occasional forays into formal recitation and oratory. The difficulty for Stevens was that almost none of their discussions seemed to measure up to the damnable deviltry that the revivalists promised. Instead, what he received from his exposure to saloon talk was a clear sense of what mattered in life to working men and, in his words, of "what was really going on in the world."[38]

Many others echoed these sentiments. For example, there were the observations of M. E. Ravage, a Rumanian immigrant who tended bar in New York in the early 1900s to earn money for college. "The lessons I learned while standing behind the bar . . . instilled into me more of the rich wisdom of life than I got out of all the labeled and classified knowledge imparted to me afterward in my three universities," he asserted. "A barroom—even an East Side barroom—is . . . as good a start toward a well-rounded education as you could desire." Other firsthand observers of the saloon concurred. "It [has] more influence on more men than all the colleges from Harvard to Stanford," declared Hoke. "It is center of learning, books, papers, and lecture hall to them. . . ," remarked Moore, "the place where their philosophy of life is worked out and from which their political and social beliefs take their beginning." "Nothing short of travel could exert so broadening an influence upon these men," Melendy claimed. Or, as Stevens wistfully concluded, "Instead of proving to be a Hell, the saloon was a fine school for me."[39]

Nine

Songs and Singing

> [T]he orchestra has once more been reminded of its duty. The
> [Lithuanian wedding] ceremony begins again. . . . [S]oon the
> [*acziavimas* dance] is over. . . . Then . . . an American tune this time,
> one which they have picked up on the streets; all . . . hum to them-
> selves, over and over again without rest: "In the good old summer-
> time—in the good old summertime! In the good old summertime—in
> the good old summertime!" . . . [T]hey have danced out all . . . the
> strength that unlimited drink can lend them—and still there is no one
> among them who has the power to think of stopping.
> —Upton Sinclair [1]

In his portrait of a Lithuanian wedding reception held in a Chicago saloon in *The Jungle* (1906), Upton Sinclair showed how
immigrants combined both traditional and commercial music to
heighten the pleasures of their back-room celebration. First they engaged in the traditional *acziavimas,* a four-hour, uninterrupted circle
dance. Each man, after a turn twirling the bride in the center, was expected to deposit a few dollars into the collection hat which would
compensate the saloonkeeper as well as provide the newlyweds with
a nest egg. A lull followed this clubbing ritual, during which some
gathered "in groups of two or three, singing, each group its own
song." The vocalizing interlude ended when violinist Tamoszius
Kuszleika struck up a Tin Pan Alley tune so that guests might engage
in the "promiscuous" (couple) dancing style of the Americans. Orchestral and vocal, commercial and traditional—this hodgepodge of
musical styles in the saloon's back room effectively symbolized the
immigrants' effort to adjust to life in urban America. [2]

Many saloongoers similarly enjoyed a potpourri of musical forms drawn from both folk communities and the urban marketplace. Some compositions, like the rallying songs of the labor movement and the sentimental verses of Tin Pan Alley, were products of the city. Laborers heard them in the workplace, in vaudeville shows, and in the streets, some men later repeating them in informal barroom songfests. Other songs were rural transplants, brought to the city by American migrants in the same way that European folk music accompanied the immigrants. Vaudeville performers sometimes picked up these songs in their travels, popularizing them in concert saloons nationwide. From there, working-class men in the audiences transported the songs back to their own local saloons to sing. In this manner, saloons acted as conduits through which songs of many kinds—indigenous folk tunes, immigrant airs, labor anthems, and popular hits—were passed along from group to group in cities across the continent.

INDIGENOUS FOLKSONGS

As rural whites and blacks poured into America's expanding towns and cities in the late nineteenth century, they and their folksongs often found their way into barrooms. Of the many songs that made this journey, four examples are particularly noteworthy both for their popularity among saloongoers and for their lyrics which concerned barroom incidents and nightlife. The first is probably best known today in its Texan incarnation, "The Streets of Laredo," though this was only one of dozens of versions popular with cowboys, miners, and other frequenters of frontier-town saloons. One version, "St. James Infirmary," was also popular among African-American bargoers. Another example is "Stagolee" (also known as "Stackolee," "Stacker Lee," and "Staggerlee"), which was in wide circulation in St. Louis, Memphis, and New Orleans as well as many rural areas. "People would sing it, neighborhood characters, barroom balladeers, see? They'd add more lyrics and dramatize it," jazz musician Danny Barker stated of the song in New Orleans in the early 1900s. Similarly, "Ta-ra-ra-boom-der-é" (spellings vary) and "Frankie and Albert" (also known as "Frankie and Johnny") became nationally known favorites after blues singer "Mammy Lou" performed them at Babe Connor's Castle Club, a "high-brown bawdy house in St. Louis in the '90s," according to Alan Lomax. A content analysis of these songs reveals why they captured the imagination of so many saloon-going men.[3]

Regarding "The Streets of Laredo" (also known as "The Dying Cowboy" or "The Cowboy's Lament"), many will recognize its familiar opening lines:

> As I walked out in the streets of Laredo,
> As I walked out in Laredo one day,
> I spied a poor cowboy wrapped up in white linen,
> Wrapped up in white linen as cold as the clay.

Musicologists have shown that the original song upon which this version was based is in fact very old, dating back to eighteenth-century England and Ireland.[4] In British versions, variously known as "The Unfortunate Rake," "The Rakish Young Fellow," and "St. James Hospital," the protagonist was usually a hapless young sailor. The lyrics detailed how his wild carousing with prostitutes in seaport barrooms brought him to ruin with a fatal case of syphilis. Some versions referred to the supposed purgatives of "salts and pills of white mercury" which, had they been administered in time, might have saved the poor wretch now laid out in a bandaged and putrescent condition in the hospital morgue.[5] Most versions described the funeral procession subsequently held in the victim's honor, as illustrated in the following verses collected by Lomax in Dorset, England:

> One day as I strolled down by the Royal Albion,
> Cold was the morning and wet was the day,
> When who did I meet but one of my shipmates,
> Wrapped up in flannel yet colder than clay.
>
> . . . .
>
> His poor old father, his good old mother,
> Oft-times had told him about his past life,
> When along with those flash girls his money he'd squander,
> And along with those flash girls he took his delight.
>
> And now he is dead and he lies in his coffin,
> Six jolly sailors shall carry him along,
> And six jolly maidens shall carry white roses,
> Not for to smell him as they pass him by.

The song continued to be an English public house favorite from the 1700s until at least the 1940s. One old seafarer told Lomax that singing sailors had to beware during World War II, however, since "the naval police would not permit it to be sung in a pub," presumably because of its more risque verses.[6]

When the song made its way across the American continent in the nineteenth century, people soon adapted the lyrics to suit their own circumstances. In various parts of the country the victim was transformed into a cowboy, a lumberjack, or a miner. Further, though the theme of barroom dissipation usually persisted, references to venereal disease and venal women were dropped or muted in many American versions. This was not universally the case, Lomax has observed. One version collected in Virginia featured a female victim who piteously lamented, "My poor head is aching, my sad heart is breaking, / My body's salivated and I'm bound to die." The phrase "my body's salivated" referred to the abnormal flow of saliva caused by the ingestion of mercurous chloride, an oblique allusion to the girl's syphilitic condition and its treatment. Significantly, however, in this version the function of the roses on the coffin changed from fumigation to decoration. More explicit was a version popular among African-American honky-tonk singers. "St. James Infirmary," noted Lomax, "retains more of the hospital stink of the original song than any other American form."[7]

Among cowboys, for whom the ballad "became the most popular of all songs, with a score of versions," according to Lomax, the victim's death was usually attributed not to disease but to murder, accident, or generally reckless living. Consider the following example, which was in wide circulation among saloongoing cowboys by 1900:

> As I rode out by Tom Sherman's bar-room,
> As I rode out so early one day,
> 'Twas there I espied a handsome young cowboy,
> All dressed in white linen, all clothed for the grave.
>
> . . . .
>
> "'Twas once in the saddle I used to go dashing,
> 'Twas once in the saddle I used to go gay,
> But I first took to drinking and then to card-playing,
> Got shot in the body and I'm dying today.

"Let sixteen gamblers come handle my coffin,
Let sixteen young cowboys come sing me a song,
Take me to the green valley and lay the sod o'er me,
For I'm a poor cowboy and I know I've done wrong."

Once again, the themes of excessive barroom indulgence, painful death, and a funeral procession with a full complement of appropriate pallbearers are much in evidence. Gone completely, however, are references to the scourge of syphilis, the grotesque side effects of mercurous chloride, or the malodorous state of the body in the coffin. "These cowboy versions seldom if ever ascribe the cowboy's death to the cause so lucidly stated in the British stall print," H. M. Belden observed. The cowboy "has indeed taken to bad courses, has drunk and gambled; and now he has been shot. And the scene, naturally, is not a hospital. Some location is almost always given, most often a barroom."[8]

Several explanations might be suggested for the changes the lyrics underwent on American shores. Lomax has argued that the stern legacy of American Protestantism, with its emphasis on sexual restraint and propriety, undoubtedly made some singers reluctant to refer so graphically to diseased prostitutes and the smell of a syphilitic corpse. Yet just as important as what was omitted was what was added and emphasized. People prefer to sing about what they know. For men fresh from the frontier, including cowboys, lumberjacks, and miners, violent death was a grimly familiar reality, whether resulting from the perilousness of their work or the lawlessness of their towns and saloons. "Teddy Blue" Abbott, himself a cowboy who drank, sang, and caroused in the barrooms of Dodge City and Cheyenne in the late nineteenth century, confirmed the frontier wranglers' penchant for violence. "They were out there for months on end. . . ," he wrote in his memoirs, "and when they hit the bright lights of some little cow town, that looked like gay Paree to them, they just went crazy." Thus, as ballad scholar G. Malcolm Laws observed, "Death, the favorite subject of all balladry, occurs time and again in the ballads of the West." Under these circumstances, a song describing a drunken, murderous altercation over a barroom card game was something with which many could identify.[9]

Further, by specifying the saloon as the scene of physical violence, people were bringing the song in line with several other murder ballads of the era. Lurid barroom homicides fired the imaginations of many American folksingers in the late nineteenth century (and of many Hollywood western filmmakers in the twentieth). Certainly the saloon was occasionally the site of real-life violence, and such incidents sometimes found their way into song. In addition, the setting was colorful and familiar. Conventions of saloon decor including the long hardwood bar, the sawdust floor, the glasses, the mirror, and the swinging doors all helped conjure up a vivid mental image in the listeners' minds. A tinge of potential danger already hung in the atmosphere of beer and whiskey fumes and of raucous voices along the bar. Most rousing of all was the primal spectacle of two individuals—at times two men, at others a man and a woman—facing off in a deadly confrontation over some unforgivable wrong while the hushed bar crowd looked on. As a setting for elemental struggles with dramatic outcomes, the barroom was a natural.

Other murder ballads popular among saloongoers focused on the same motifs of drinking, gambling, and gunslinging found in "The Streets of Laredo." One of the best known in African-American barrooms was "Stagolee," in which a craps-shooting "bad man" became embroiled in a spectacular barroom shoot-out. The protagonist's historicity has been the subject of considerable scholarly debate. Some suggest he was a member of the Lee family in Memphis, while others offer alternative family lineages and crime venues. Scholars who have thoroughly combed newspapers from the turn of the century have failed to turn up any written account of the shooting itself. In barrooms, however, Stagolee became a legendary folksong outlaw and a favorite among "barroom balladeers," according to bluesman Danny Barker.[10]

Stagolee was convinced that, in a late-night craps game, Billy Lyons had cheated him out of his money and his prized Stetson hat. He tracked his quarry down in the local saloon. As one version of the ballad described the incident,

> He shot him three times in the shoulder,
> Lawd, and three times in the side,
> Well, the last time he shot him
> Cause Billy Lyons to die.
>
> Stagolee told Mrs. Billy,
> "You don't believe yo' man is dead;

> Come into the bar-room,
> See the hole I shot in his head."

Like many figures in murder ballads, Stagolee expressed no remorse for his crime. To him, Billy Lyons was the dishonorable villain of the piece who had asked for trouble and gotten just what he deserved.[11]

Some murder ballads focused on romance betrayed and avenged. In "Frankie and Albert," for example, the outrageous barroom philandering of Frankie's wrongdoing man brought on the tragedy. Whether the incident was rooted in reality is questionable, though one woman swore that she was the original Frankie in a defamation of character suit she brought against Republic Pictures in 1938 for their movie based on the ballad. In any case, by the 1890s the song had become a staple in Mississippi rivertown barrooms and in concert saloons like the Castle Club in St. Louis. "Here the relatively relaxed racial attitudes . . . brought about frequent contacts between whites and Negroes in sporting-house areas," according to Lomax, "and thus a number of Missouri Negro ragtime songs ('Bill Bailey,' 'Ta-ra-ra-boom-de-ay,' 'Frankie,' etc.) became known to the whole country."[12]

In the ballad, the trouble began when Frankie stopped at the local saloon to inquire about her lover's whereabouts, whereupon the bartender passed along some very unwelcome news:

> Frankie went down to the bar-room
> And called for a glass of gin,
> She asked the man called the bartender,
> "Has my cheatin' man been in?
> He's my man, I b'lieve he's doin' me wrong."

> Says, "Frankie, I'll tell you no story,
> Good gal, I'll tell you no lie,
> I saw your man pass here an hour ago,
> With a girl called Alice Fry,
> He's your man, I b'lieve he's doin' you wrong."

Frankie, a "good gal" who invariably handed over most of her street-walking profits to her man, was stunned by the bartender's revelation. Not only was her lover betraying her, but also he was blatantly carrying on his affair in the very public arena of a neighborhood bar. Consumed with humiliation and rage, Frankie hunted down and shot her "cheatin' man," a crime subsequently ruled justifiable homicide in many versions of the ballad because, as the refrain relentlessly insisted, "He was her man, but he done her wrong." [13]

What conclusions might be drawn from the fact that the saloon was so often implicated in murder ballads such as "The Streets of Laredo," "Stagolee," and "Frankie and Albert"? At first glance, such depictions might seem to constitute a damning indictment of the American barroom, portraying it as a place where disreputable characters gathered to sin, cheat, brawl, and murder one another in reckless abandon. Upon closer examination, however, it becomes clear that the violence, though deadly, was not random. On the contrary, the murderers focused on particular victims and, in the latter two cases, made public declarations of their grievances before taking action. In "Stagolee" and in several versions of "Laredo," the murder victims stood accused of publicly swindling and humiliating their adversaries in a crooked game. In "Frankie," the victim committed the unforgivable sin of openly cuckolding his lover in front of the local drinking fraternity. In all cases, the victim had deeply wounded the perpetrator's sense of personal honor. To let such transgressions go unpunished was to suffer a devastating loss of face. On the other hand, to take action was almost certainly to risk facing the gallows. Most ordinary folk might shrink from such a prospect, but the protagonists of these ballads refused to tolerate any treatment that tended to diminish them.

Thus, the saloon emerges not as a place where disreputable people wantonly go about murdering one another, but rather as a place where personal honor is valued and defended regardless of the cost. Viewed in this way, the protagonists' drastic actions involved a certain courageousness and commitment to principle, even if they were outlaws by nonbarroom standards. The public's taste for sensationalism and tragedy was amply satisfied by such murder ballads following the basic formula of barroom betrayal, confrontation, and retribution.

Not all the songs that rural Americans brought to their urban barrooms were murder ballads, of course. Many were conceived in a lighter vein, and some were rollickingly risqué. For example, there was the humorous and immensely popular "Ta-ra-ra-boom-der-é" (alternative spellings abound). This ditty devoted verse after verse to describing a woman of great beauty if questionable virtue who enjoyed the nightlife of concert saloons and cabarets. In barroom renditions, singers often placed hip-swinging emphasis on the "boom":

A smart and stylish girl you see,
Queen of swell society,
Not too strict but rather free
When it's on the straight Q. T.
But the very thing I'm told,
Not too timid, not too bold,
Just the kind you'd like to hold,
Not too hot and not too cold.

Ta-ra-ra-boom-der-é! Ta-ra-ra-boom-der-é!
Ta-ra-ra-boom-der-é! Ta-ra-ra-boom-der-é![14]

Though scholars dispute the song's origin, some suggest that it began as a slaves' work song (though with significantly earthier lyrics, one suspects). On the shipping docks of antebellum New Orleans, some scholars maintain, slave crews hoisting sails or raising anchors would all pull together upon the word "boom." In the 1870s and 1880s, the song entered the repetoire of black performers in southern honky-tonks, according to affidavits filed in an 1890s lawsuit over publishing rights. By 1890, it was popular in Basin Street resorts in New Orleans. It also accompanied blacks northward to St. Louis, where it became a favorite at Babe Connor's Castle Club. From there, it was cleaned up and incorporated into Henry Sayer's traveling minstrel comedy of 1891, *Tuxedo*. Soon it became a sensation among white audiences in vaudeville houses and concert saloons from New York to London. By 1893, the song had made its way back into the humbler "late-hour hideaways on Sixth Avenue" in New York, according to George M. Cohan. As part of the 1890s "ragtime craze," Isaac Goldberg asserted that " 'Ta-Ra-Ra-Boom-De-Ré' arrived at the precise moment it was needed to herald the new spirit of popular music."[15]

Much African-American music followed a similar path from the barrooms of southern cities like New Orleans to those of northern metropolises like Chicago and New York. The reminiscences of Louis Armstrong illustrate this trend. Recalling his days in New Orleans in the early 1900s, he told of joining in with groups of black men "who hung around the saloons with a cold can of beer in their hands, singing up a breeze while they passed the can around." Later, with trumpet in hand, he began performing in countless urban barrooms of both the South and the North. There he encountered other professional musicians hailing from many parts of the country who played ragtime, blues, and jazz for mostly black audiences who were likewise diverse in their origins and tastes. Performers such as Armstrong, Jelly Roll Morton, Willie "The Lion" Smith, and many others found the convivial, freewheeling atmosphere of saloons an important stimulus to developing their musical styles as well as their rapport with the urban black population.[16]

Most whites heard this music only in diluted form through the intermediaries of blackface minstrels, vaudeville performers, and Tin Pan Alley song publishers, as was the case with "Ta-ra-ra-boom-der-é." Nevertheless, in places like Peter Lala's in New Orleans and Babe Connor's in St. Louis, the adventuresome and the avant-garde sometimes mixed with predominantly black clienteles to hear the exciting new music developing there. Such flouting of longstanding racial barriers did not become a widespread phenomenon until after World War I, however, when establishments like Harlem's Cotton Club and its imitators began to capture the public fancy.[17]

Why did indigenous African-American music, even in diluted form like blackface minstrelsy, appeal so strongly to urban white audiences? "I think in part what they were watching was more complicated than merely whites masking themselves as blacks. They were watching whites *release* themselves as blacks," Lawrence Levine has speculated. Whites pretending to be black "could dance, and sing, and show emotions openly, and cry, and laugh—and I think there was something cathartic about this. I think blacks have played that role in this society. They have been a kind of surrogate." In an era dominated by Victorian standards of restraint and self-control, whites of all classes found a welcome emotional escape in the comparatively uninhibited music emanating from black barrooms and cabarets. For African Americans, meanwhile, the music of Louis Armstrong, Jelly Roll Morton, and other barroom performers helped strengthen their sense of community and ease their adjustment to urban society.[18]

Tracing the travels of folksongs from their points of origin to their eventual and often multiple destinations is a daunting task indeed, as both folklorists and copyright lawyers will attest. Songs arise, catch on, and then quickly carom off in all directions. They undergo many permutations as well, with a clean-up here and an embellishment there. While the specifics of dissemination are difficult to pinpoint, however, it is evident that saloon customers and performers played an important role in facilitating the overall process. All four songs examined here seem to have disseminated horizontally, from saloon to local saloon. Two of them, "Frankie" and "Ta-ra-ra-boom-der-é," also traveled vertically from local barrooms to the celebrated St. Louis Castle Club to the national vaudeville circuit. The latter song then traveled down the line again to smaller establishments in New York City. These several examples illustrate how saloons facilitated the multidirectional spread and often nationwide appreciation of the indigenous music of various native-born American groups.

IMMIGRANTS' MUSIC

Like rural migrants from the American hinterlands, European immigrants also found urban saloons a congenial setting for enjoying and perpetuating their native music traditions. This was true of "old wave" immigrants from northern and western Europe who predominated until about 1890, as well as of "new wave" immigrants from southern and eastern Europe whose numbers increased from the 1890s until World War I. Gravitating to establishments known to cater to their particular ethnic or nationality groups, immigrants used saloons to stage everything from impromptu barside songfests to formally organized concerts and dances.

Among "old wave" immigrants, both the Irish and the Germans were noted for their spontaneous saloon singing which usually featured patriotic and sentimental favorites. In Irish establishments in Chicago in the 1880s and 1890s, for example, George Ade recalled the popularity of songs bristling with Irish nationalism and hatred for the British. Typical selections included "Wearin' of the Green," "The Harp that Once through Tara's Halls," and "Where the River Shannon Flows."[19]

Equally fond of mixing drink and song were the Germans, whose *Sangerfests* in saloons included such melodies as "Ach du lieber Augustin," "Hi-lee! Hilo!" and "Die Wacht am Rhein." German immigrants were also active participants in organized singing societies which met regularly in the back rooms. During these meetings, Royal Melendy noted that "beer-drinking is almost universal among these people," though music-making remained their primary focus and was seldom marred by "excessive drinking."[20]

Instrumental as well as vocal music was enthusiastically performed and supported by the German community. In the steel mill town of Homestead, Pennsylvania, Margaret Byington remarked in her 1910 study that on Friday paydays, "The streets are filled with music, and the German bands go from saloon to saloon reaping a generous harvest when times are good."[21] Orchestras were also familiar fixtures in the many German beer-gardens situated in the suburban districts of major cities like Chicago. Appealing to a cross section of the population, these establishments helped introduce German musical culture to their non-German patrons and promote social interaction among people of various ethnic and economic backgrounds. Though these establishments were often too expensive and distant to draw many working-class customers, some "ten-cent and free gardens" offered a mixture of orchestral music and vaudeville acts designed "for the poorer classes," according to Melendy. At one such open-air establishment "at a terminus of several north-side car lines," for example, the people "sit drinking and smoking about the tables placed in front of the stage. Others stroll about, visiting the booths, which make the whole place resemble the old country fair."[22]

"New wave" immigrants from southern and eastern Europe also utilized the saloon premises to nurture and perpetuate the music of their homelands. Poles, for example, were as active in organized singing societies in Chicago as were Germans, congregating in the back rooms of saloons to pour the songs out and the beer in. Similarly, Poles as well as other Slavs in the anthracite coal communities of Pennsylvania in the early 1900s flocked to saloons that hired musicians and sponsored dances on payday each week. In major cities like New York, meanwhile, the ethnic lodges and benevolent associations of Hungarians, Italians, Jews, and other groups often featured their native music in the parties and balls they held in saloons. As New York settlement worker Michael M. Davis asserted, the saloon dance-hall was a "veritable neighborhood rallying-place, where young and middle-aged of both sexes crowd in the stuffy room together; where English is little spoken; and mental and physical atmosphere suggest a medieval inn."[23]

The South Chicago neighborhood of Irondale offered a particularly striking example of the importance of barroom music fests to immigrant communities. In the early 1900s, Serbian and Croatian immigrants regularly gathered in the local saloons to listen to the music of the mandolin-like tamburitza, dance the traditional *kola,* and sing songs of life in the old homeland as well as of the immigrant experience in America. Itinerant tamburitza bands often supplied the music, following a circuit of Slavic saloons in various towns. These traveling bands helped link far-flung Slavic settlements together, "bringing news to South Chicago people about their cousins and ethnic peers in Pittsburgh, Aliquippa, Steubenville, Hibbing, and other industrial areas where South Slavs settled," according to William Kornblum.[24]

Such communal celebrations of turn-of-the-century Slavic folkways continued to be well attended in Irondale taverns until the mid-twentieth century. The participants made every effort to preserve their native music exactly as it was when the first-generation immigrants left the old country. Ironically, Slavs still in the old country had no such preoccupation with preservation; there, the accordion and the electric guitar had long since replaced the tamburitza. Folklore scholars refer to this phenomenon as "marginal survival": bits of culture are preserved on the margins of migration which would be regarded as archaic at the cultural center.[25] In this way, the Slavic saloons of Irondale acted as a kind of shrine to the past, a time capsule in which immigrants and their American progeny lovingly if artificially shielded their cultural heritage from all change. Monuments to the determination of immigrant groups to cherish their ethnic identities, these saloons also symbolized the difficulties American society faced in attempting to absorb newcomers with radically divergent cultural heritages.

LABOR ANTHEMS

If the ethnic music in saloons tended to divide immigrant groups from one another and from American-born workers, the songs of the labor movement were designed to have the opposite effect. Though the mostly English lyrics posed an obstacle for some recently arrived immigrants, the rousing themes of camaraderie, solidarity, and workingmen's rights that pervaded the music had a wide and immediate appeal for many workers experiencing the upheavals of the emerging industrial order. In the 1880s and 1890s, for example, saloongoers sang the following rallying cry of the Knights of Labor:

> Your attention, friends, I'll now invite,
> While I will sing to you
> In regards to the cause of the working man
> Which, no doubt you'll find is true;

> For, the noble Knights of Labor
> Are doing the best they can
> To elevate the condition of
> The noble working man!

There was some irony in the fact that this song was sung in saloons, incidentally, since the Knights of Labor organization was an aggressive advocate of temperance and banned all saloonkeepers from its membership. Apparently dismissing this inconvenient fact, bargoers enthusiastically embraced this and other workers' songs which, as Ade wryly observed, extolled "the organized workingmen and their nobility of character as compared with millionaire employers." [26]

Among the most memorable songs produced by and for the labor movement were those associated with the Industrial Workers of the World (I.W.W., also known as the "Wobblies"). Founded in 1905, this radical and militantly anticapitalist union sought to unify the vast legions of semi-skilled and unskilled laborers who were neglected or shunned by more conservative, craft-oriented organizations like the American Federation of Labor. In their efforts to inspire and organize this most downtrodden segment of the workforce, I.W.W. activists like Harry "Mac" McClintock, Jack Walsh, and Joe Hill seized upon the medium of music. They lampooned the pieties of the American socio-economic order and voiced the discontents of the exploited and the unemployed. Because saloons in the poorer districts were favorite congregating places for the very constituency that the Wobblies' leaders hoped to reach, the songsters of the movement often deliberately performed within earshot of the swinging doors.[27]

As a runaway teenager hopping freight trains through the South in the mid-1890s, Wobbly-to-be McClintock learned early that his penchant for singing was often warmly shared, as well as generously rewarded, by the saloon crowds he encountered from town to town. "It was in New Orleans that I found singing in saloons could be profitable," he later recalled. "A bunch of Limey sailors were having a bit of a sing-song and I ventured to join in one of the choruses. I was immediately invited to grab a glass and sit in. They kept dropping coins in my pockets." McClintock found most barroom music-making to be a casual, spontaneous affair in which a congenial youngster like himself could easily join. Further, he found that the code of reciprocity in barrooms usually worked in his favor, his entertainment efforts being amply repaid with drinks and tips from his new-found saloon-mates. "In a strange town I searched for sounds of 'revelry by night,' and there were few saloon crowds that would refuse to listen to a kid who wanted to sing."[28]

Though his singing ability enabled him to change from a "moocher" to a "producer," as he put it, McClintock felt great sympathy all his days for the hoboes and drifters he met on the road. These men, he maintained, had had to resort to mooching because they could not find decent work at decent pay. His understanding of their plight, coupled with his flair for satire and sarcasm, enabled him to compose several delightful yet bitterly insightful tunes which quickly passed into oral tradition. One of his most memorable contributions was "The Big Rock Candy Mountains":

> In the Big Rock Candy Mountains
> You never change your socks,
> And little streams of alcohol
> Come a-trickling down the rocks.
> The box cars are all empty
> And the railroad bulls are blind,
> There's a lake of stew and whisky, too,
> You can paddle all around 'em in a big canoe
> In the Big Rock Candy Mountains.
>
> > O—the buzzing of the bees in the cigarette trees
> > Round the soda-water fountain,
> > Where the lemonade springs and the bluebird sings
> > In the Big Rock Candy Mountains.

Gently poking fun at the foibles and pipe dreams of his vagabond brethren, including their notorious fondness for alcohol, McClintock created this hobo's vision of utopia which soon echoed in railroad camps and poor men's saloons nationwide.[29]

When McClintock became involved in the I.W.W. in the early 1900s, he encountered two other avid believers in the unifying power of music, Joe Hill and Jack Walsh. Hill was a remarkably prolific songwriter who composed much of the music for which the Wobblies were famous. His songs were brought to the fore when I.W.W. speakers in the Northwest repeatedly experienced difficulty in making their remarks heard over the din of the Salvation Army bands which were always situating themselves near saloon doorways. The Wobblies resolved to beat the evangelists at their own game. McClintock teamed up with Jack Walsh and others to form their own street band. "Then," according to Lomax, "they convulsed their hard-boiled audience with irreverent parodies of favorite Salvation Army tear jerkers," many of them Joe Hill's compositions.[30]

Perhaps the best known of all the Wobblies' songs was Hill's parody of the Salvation Army standard "In the Sweet Bye and Bye," which he entitled "Pie in the Sky":

> O the starvation army they play,
> And they sing and they clap and they pray,
> Till they get all your coin on the drum,
> Then they'll tell you when you're on the bum:

> > "You will eat, bye and bye,
> > In that glorious land above the sky,
> > Work and pray, live on hay,
> > You'll get pie in the sky when you die."

In San Francisco in the 1910s, the Wobblies had their headquarters in a room situated over the Bulkhead saloon, where sailor Fred Klebingat was a regular. He had one vivid memory of their presence. "I recall their song: 'Sing and Pray, Live on Hay, You'll Have Pie in the Sky When You Die,'" he reminisced some seventy years after the fact. With memorable songs like "Pie in the Sky" and with headquarters situated close by saloons, the I.W.W. endeavored to attract the interest and sympathy of the working population. Further, by focusing on two pastimes already dear to many laborers' hearts—singing and saloongoing—the Wobblies encouraged workers to overcome alienating differences in language and ethnicity and instead cultivate the common culture crucial to labor solidarity and success.[31]

TIN PAN ALLEY HITS

Elsewhere in American society, meanwhile, another very separate effort was being made to provide the masses with a common musical culture. In this case, however, the chief motivation was profit for the purveyors rather than power for the people. The epicenter of this song boom was New York City, and its name was Tin Pan Alley.

Named for the "tinny" effect which tunesmiths like Harry Von Tilzer achieved by threading newspaper through their piano strings,

Tin Pan Alley was a cluster of music publishers, composers, and promoters on Fourteenth Street. In the early 1890s, they transformed songwriting into a mass-market commercial enterprise. Songs had of course been written and hawked for profit long before that time. Broadsides, songbooks, and piano sheet music had all sold well throughout the nineteenth century. In the middle decades, minstrelsy shows, featuring white performers in blackface, provided a considerable market for songs by composers such as Stephen Collins Foster ("Swanee River," "Camptown Races") and James Bland ("Carry Me Back to Old Virginny," "Oh Dem Golden Slippers"). After the Civil War, minstrelsy was gradually eclipsed by the rise of vaudeville. Its more varied fare typically consisted of comedy skits, acrobatic feats, trained animal stunts, magic tricks, dance numbers, and a great many musical acts requiring a constant supply of new songs. The increasing demands of vaudeville performers, coupled with the growing home market for piano music, set the stage for the rise of Tin Pan Alley.[32]

In New York in the 1870s, when vaudeville was still in its formative phase, hosting institutions were often similar in function but known by various names. "Whether called dime museums, theaters, or concert saloons, most of these establishments differed only in label," Timothy Gilfoyle has explained. All shared four basic characteristics. "Each of them served liquor. Stage performers attracted patrons. Performers intermingled with spectators. And prostitutes solicited potential clients in the audience."[33]

By the 1880s and 1890s, vaudeville establishments in New York became more differentiated by class and bill of fare. Some, like Tony Pastor's, were enormous, elaborate, and highly respectable theaters which attracted the middle and upper classes. Others, still known by sundry titles but usually called "concert saloons," catered to the less genteel. Within this category, there were numerous gradations. Harry Hill's establishment, for example, was big, flashy, and wild. Places like his catered to sporting men of various stations and featured bawdy stage performers and "waiter girls" who often doubled as prostitutes. Other establishments, like Miner's in the Bowery, were smaller and sleazier with near-naked women performing lewd and suggestive dances. But a significant number of concert saloons in New York were neither wild nor obscene, though prostitutes might hover at the periphery. Gunther's Palm Garden, Theiss's Alhambra, and the Globe Dime Museum were establishments of this type. They featured standard, mostly unobjectionable vaudeville acts and attracted a respectable clientele of workingmen, sometimes accompanied by wives and children. By the 1890s, these were the kind of places where many workers became acquainted with the Tin Pan Alley product.[34]

Most concert saloons resembled regular saloons except for their large back rooms with a stage added. "Indeed, it is often hard to tell whether we are dealing with a saloon or with an amusement enterprise," as Raymond Calkins remarked of the saloon-cum-vaudeville arrangement. "The two meet and mingle. Is it a theatre saloon, or a saloon theatre? Is it a concert hall where drinks are served, or a saloon where music is furnished? There is little upon the surface to determine." In contrast to the fancier theaters which charged up to twenty-five cents admission with refreshments costing extra, concert saloons often charged no entrance fee. Instead, as was the case with food, games, meeting space, and other saloon amenities, customers were trusted to purchase a few five-cent beers to compensate the proprietor. The show might be amateurish and mundane, but the price was right.[35]

In Chicago, where an array of concert saloons similar to New York's thrived by 1900, Melendy provided a firsthand account of the vaudeville fare offered to predominantly working-class clienteles. He distinguished between programs designed for all-male audiences and those aimed at families and dating couples. Regarding the former, he noted, "The boot-black and the street boy is there, the clerk and the office-man, and in the most prominent places may be seen the cheap and flashy aristocracy of the city." In one such establishment, Melendy reported with approval, "At first a stereopticon [slide show] of good quality throws upon the canvas pictures illustrating songs sung by a gentleman . . . usually in a dress suit. Thoughts of home, of mother's love, of woman's purity, of personal honor, are received with hearty applause and cheers." Changing his tone, he added, "Next follows a cinematograph reproduction of a prizefight, and then, in striking contrast with the first, a 'leg show' of the most shameless character."[36]

Interestingly, much of the music that appealed to this masculine, streetwise audience was the same sort of wholesome fare one might expect to hear sung around the parlor piano in a middle-class Victorian household. Home and mother, purity and honor—these were ideals and values which persons of all classes and backgrounds could embrace, a fact well appreciated by the sales-conscious songsmiths of Tin Pan Alley. Further, it was not necessarily incongruous that such songs should be popular with an audience also receptive to a boxing match and a "leg show." These various elements were all part of the vital, heterogeneous popular culture of America. They reflected the eclectic tastes of the urban masses who, in contrast to progressive reformers like Melendy, were more interested in variety and excitement than gentility and uplift.

Other concert saloons in Chicago catered to the working-class family trade. In these establishments, the "hard-worked men and women . . . with their families . . . can enjoy an evening of pleasure," according to Melendy. The entertainment fare included the usual assortment of acrobats, comics, singers, and dancing girls, the latter still too "bawdy" to suit Melendy's tastes but by and large presenting "little that is suggestive of evil." In such places, musical numbers were especially popular, and the audience often sang along with the performers as familiar refrains of patriotic and sentimental songs rolled around. "Patriotic songs are never missing, and I have heard them join heartily in the chorus," Melendy reported. "Cheer after cheer greets the names of our heroes, as they appear in the songs of the girls." The emphasis on patriotic songs at the century's turn was probably owing to continuing public fervor over the Spanish-American War. Like most wars, it inspired songwriters to compose appropriate verses. Among those most popular were Paul Dresser's "Break the News to Mother," Cobb and Barnes's "Good-Bye, Dolly Gray," and Harry Von Tilzer's "I Want to Be a Military Man."[37]

After hearing songs of all kinds in concert saloons as well as theaters, park concerts, and other venues, workers brought their favorites back to their neighborhood saloons where, by all reports, they did a considerable amount of singing. Most saloons did not offer formal musical entertainment except on special occasions such as parties and dances. Some did offer mechanically reproduced music. "A music box is occasionally found," Calkins noted, "or a graphophone, or a nickel-in-the-slot machine, or other device for reproducing sentimental songs." Unfortunately, the sound quality of these machines left much to be desired. As Hoke wryly remarked, the "mechanical piano" in the saloon was usually "an instrument with strings of tin which played selections thought to be 'Good Old Summer Time,' 'Hiawatha,' 'Alexander's Rag Time Band,' 'Red Wing,' etc., when a nickel plumbed its vitals." Not until the eve of World War I would recorded music become a major factor in the entertainment industry or in the saloon. Thus, if customers wanted music, they usually had to make it themselves.[38]

Sentimental songs appear to have been the music of choice for most saloongoers with a penchant for singing. To begin with, the ballads of Tin Pan Alley were far easier to sing than the ragtime numbers which, though increasingly popular after 1890, were often too complicated rhythmically for amateurs to render comfortably. In contrast, the sentimental songs were specifically designed for singing, with their languid tempos, flowing musical phrases, and limited tonal ranges.[39]

Yet it was also the content of the lyrics that appealed to barside songsters. Just as all-male vaudeville audiences responded enthusiastically to songs of home, mother's love, and woman's purity, so most saloongoers favored these themes. As Hoke observed, whenever a saloon group was inspired to sing, there were "soul-stirring harmonics through which permeated occasional accessory words recognizable as silvery moon, you wouldn't dare insult me sir, she may have seen better days, dear old girl, blinding tears are falling, etc. and etc." Even sailors on a drunken lark were susceptible to the typical Tin Pan Alley tear-jerker and "luxuriated in the pathos and tragedy of it," according to Jack London. George Ade concurred on this point. "You might think that the saloon, established for drinking purposes, would have specialized on convivial choruses which lauded the grape or the foaming tankard, but they did not go in for anything jolly," he noted. "The sons of toil and the mercantile slaves who flocked to the bars every evening took their pleasures seriously and wallowed in the most abject sentimentality." Fortunately for the saloon historian, Ade made the effort to note some of the titles he knew to be barroom favorites from the 1880s to the early 1900s. A sampling of the lyrics of these songs, as well as of the circumstances of their creation, will help clarify how and why they made their way into the saloongoers' songbag.[40]

Maudlin and saccharine though they often seem by late-twentieth-century standards, songs extolling motherhood were the ones most often taken to heart by bargoers, according to Ade. One enduring favorite was "A Boy's Best Friend Is His Mother," composed by Joseph P. Skelly in 1884:

> Then cherish her with care
>   and smooth her silv'ry hair;
> When gone, you will never get another;
>
> And wherever we may turn,
>   this lesson we will learn—
> A boy's best friend is his mother!

Skelly was himself a notorious drunkard who, though having composed nearly four hundred songs between the 1870s and the 1890s, was perpetually broke and bleary in the tradition of his predecessor and model, Stephen Collins Foster. Sigmund Spaeth maintained that there was a direct correlation between Skelly's alcoholism and the tearful lyrics of his tunes. "Hard-drinking songwriters of the Skelly type," Spaeth suggested, "seem to turn almost automatically to sentimental thoughts of their mother's graves, girls' names and tender associations with mills, lanes, gates and other possible rendezvous." Spaeth's reference to maternal burial plots had to do with another Skelly composition of 1891, "A Violet I Picked From My Mother's Grave." Skelly shamelessly lifted the theme of this song from a much earlier hit, "A Flower From (My Angel) Mother's Grave," which Ade cited as another barroom perennial. It was written in 1878 by Harry Kennedy who, according to Spaeth, also "lived up to the best songwriting traditions of intemperance," spending much time in saloons where he kept up a pretense of gentility by "always insist[ing] that his drinks be brought to him at a table."[41]

It seems significant that these deeply sentimental songs, which enjoyed much popularity among saloongoers, were composed by men who were themselves inveterate saloongoers. As Isaac Goldberg has observed of typical Tin Pan Alley lyrics, "Often they read—and sound—like the sentimental admonitions of a drunkard in his self-pitying, weepy stage. There is the faint aroma of alcoholic hysteria about them."[42]

Several other "mother songs" also found favor among musically inclined saloongoers in the 1890s. In 1893, for example, Joseph Flynn, who would later compose such Irish-flavored favorites as "The Night Maloney Landed in New York" (1888) and "Down Went McGinty" (1899), scored a hit with bargoers with "Little Hoop of Gold":

Just a little band
From my dear old mother's hand,
Far dearer to me now than wealth untold;
Though it's hardly worth a shilling,
Still to die I would be willing,
Ere I'd part with mother's little hoop of gold.

Similarly, David Marion touched a responsive chord in 1894 with "Her Eyes Don't Shine like Diamonds" which, it might be argued, had some interesting Freudian overtones:

With a smile she always greets me,
From her I'll never part;
For, lads, I love my mother
And she's my sweetheart.

Finally, to round out Ade's sample of maternal melodies, there was Ellsworth's "Mother and Son" of 1895:

Never despair, dear mother,
Trust in our Father above,
When you're sad, dear mother,
Think of your son and his love.[43]

It is noteworthy that the "father" mentioned in the latter verse referred to God. The ballads of Tin Pan Alley almost never mentioned fathers in the same loving way as they did mothers. "Where were the father songs? Father, dear father, come home with me now. . . . The relative absence of the father song can hardly be an accident," as Goldberg observed. "When father does appear, it is either as a reprobate—now repentant, now unrepentant—or as a good-natured scalawag." Similarly, Ade remarked, "Only two songs regarding the male parent are now remembered—'Everybody Works But Father' and 'The Old Man's Drunk Again.'" Speculating on why this should be, Goldberg noted, "Father is an unromantic figure. Motherhood is holy; fatherhood, in some dim way, is a joke. There is no money in it. . . . When there is profit in fathers, Tin Pan Alley will sing them."[44]

In the context of saloon culture, the absence of "father songs" and the omnipresence of "mother songs" might well be related to gender roles and child-rearing practices prevalent in the late nineteenth and early twentieth centuries. As Kathy Peiss has noted, many working-

class fathers in New York City, particularly the semi-skilled and unskilled, were absent from the home most of the time. Spending their
days at the jobsite and their evenings out with their peers, they had
little contact with their children except at dinnertime. Though this
situation was changing at the turn of the century as many workers,
especially the skilled and upwardly mobile, were beginning to adopt
middle-class "canons of domesticity," mothers continued to loom
largest in the everyday lives of most children of working-class families. Boys raised in this manner might naturally identify most strongly
with songs glorifying nurturing mothers. Inhibitions regarding the
overt expression of affection between males might have also played a
part. Add to this the disinhibiting effects of alcohol which brought
emotions to the surface, and the laborers' difficult and often lonely
existence in the industrial metropolises, and the result, in Ade's
words, was the saloongoer "who broke down and wept like a child
while listening to a maudlin tribute to 'dear old Mother.'"[45]

After mothers, the next most popular subject for barroom vocalizing was "the poor girl who was tempted and who either fell or did not
fall," according to Ade. The fate of one who fell was described in
Charles Graham's song of 1891, "The Picture That Is Turned toward
the Wall":

> There's a name that's never spoken,
> And a mother's heart half broken,
> There is just another missing
>   from the old home, that is all;

> There is still a mem'ry living,
> There's a father unforgiving,
> And a picture that is turn'd
>   toward the wall.

Graham, ever vigilant like his Tin Pan Alley colleagues for new song
ideas, got the inspiration for this composition when he witnessed the
same symbolic gesture performed in a play by Joseph Arthur called
Blue Jeans. Also like his Alley cronies, according to Spaeth, Graham
was a "staunch supporter of alcoholic ideals and, with his brother
Howard, a regular member of the poker-playing group presided over
by Monroe H. Rosenfeld." (It was probably Rosenfeld who coined
the term "Tin Pan Alley;" his own song credits included "Johnny Get
Your Gun" of 1886 and "Take Back Your Gold" of 1897.)[46]

Another case of sullied virtue was the hapless lass described in the 1895 hit, "Just Tell Them That You Saw Me." The composer of this song was Paul Dresser, brother of author Theodore Dreiser. Brother Paul was inspired to write the song, according to Spaeth, after "an actual encounter with a girl whose life had seemingly if not actually gone to wreck on the shore of love." The lyrics told the story of a small-town girl who had succumbed to big city sin, and who was now too ashamed to face her family. Meeting an old acquaintance on the street one day, she simply said, "Just tell them that you saw me / And they will know the rest." The first time composer Dresser sang this song for author Dreiser, he had to pause midway through the chorus when his voice choked up with emotion. "Tears stood in his eyes and he wiped them away," recalled Dreiser. Soft-hearted, generous, and jovial when not in tears, Paul Dresser was still another Tin Pan Alley man who loved the nightlife and, Spaeth reports, was "a welcome visitor at the bars of New York, where he was always accompanied by a retinue of admirers." His song also had many admirers among saloongoers who, like Dresser, were well aware of the pitfalls awaiting the naive newcomer in big city life.[47]

Sometimes feminine virtue won out in the songs that saloongoers favored. One example cited by Ade was the 1896 composition by Edward B. Marks and Joseph W. Stern, entitled "My Mother Was a Lady" (also known as "If Jack Were Only Here"). According to Marks, the inspiration for this song was an actual incident in a New York restaurant. Some customers were teasing a waitress new on the job when all at once, through streaming tears, she burst forth with words to the following effect:

> My mother was a lady
>   like yours, you will allow,
> And you may have a sister,
>   who needs protection now,
>
> I've come to this great city
>   to find a brother dear
> And you wouldn't dare insult me, Sir,
>   if Jack were only here.

It is not known whether the poor waitress ever actually found her brother. But Marks and Stern knew they had found a gold mine in her story, and the song they composed went on to become a smash hit. It was popular among saloongoers because it celebrated so many cherished virtues all at the same time: motherhood, woman's purity, brotherly love, and personal honor. Further, it was eminently singable, with the result that for years it would continue to be sung "at congenial gatherings," according to Spaeth.[48]

Perhaps the most popular of all Tin Pan Alley compositions sung in saloons was the barbershop quartet favorite, "Sweet Adeline." Harry Armstrong and Richard Gerard composed it during what Ade called "the later Lachrymose Period" of the saloon era:

> In the evening when I sit alone a-dreaming
>   Of days gone by, love, to me so dear,
> There's a picture that in fancy oft appearing
>   Brings back the time, love, when you were near;
> It is then I wonder where you are, my darling,
>   And if your heart to me is still the same,
> For the sighing wind and nightingale a-singing
>   Are breathing only your own sweet name.
>
>> Sweet Adeline, my Adeline,
>> At night, dear heart, for you I pine;
>> In all my dreams your fair face beams,
>> You are the flower of my heart,
>> Sweet Adeline.

This "hackneyed classic" was "a perfect specimen of the love-laden verse which was so popular in the saloons" and was "a prime favorite of the working classes," according to Ade. Like many other Alley hits in the saloongoers' repertoire, the song's lyrics dripped with sentimentality and longing for an idealized love beyond reach. Indeed, one wonders if it was not Adeline's very absence and unattainability which made her so "sweet" to bargoers who, in the last analysis, appear to have actually preferred the easy camaraderie of male drinking partners.[49]

The song's appeal also lay in its music. Its chorus was perfectly suited to amateur quartets, for the lead singer could hold on steadily to the last note of each line while his comrades echoed a harmonizing response: "Sweet Ad-e-line . . ." ("Sweet Ad-e-line . . ."). Informal singing groups of this kind, though known as "barbershop quartets," could well have been called "barroom quartets" for the apparent frequency of their impromptu saloon songfests. "About ten o'clock . . .

and especially on lodge nights, there were deep, complicated, soul-stirring harmonies" in many saloons of Hoke's acquaintance, for example. "[T]hese arias . . . not infrequently went sour on a minor swipe. . . , but they met with profound appreciation from simpler and sadder souls."[50]

FROM SONGSTERS TO LISTENERS

One of the most significant aspects of the music in saloons was that it was so much the customers' own. Unlike the vaudeville show in which performers sang a prearranged song list in a prearranged manner and, if there was to be audience participation, decided and directed that too, the singing that customers did in the average barroom was strictly a do-it-yourself proposition. *They* picked the songs. *They* chose the style of rendition. And, most important, *they* did all the singing. It was an active, participatory, self-created form of entertainment, consisting of song combinations and singing styles entirely of their own choosing.

What saloongoers chose to sing was also significant, for their eclectic repertoires revealed how profoundly they were influenced both by the urban marketplace and by their traditional community loyalties. Like the Lithuanian wedding party that Upton Sinclair described in *The Jungle,* most saloongoers embraced a mixture of current hits and age-old folksongs. Popular tunes and labor anthems addressed the joys and jolts of modern city life, while traditional music assuaged nostalgia for a simpler but receding past. Taken together, these songs became the basis for a new sense of community among saloon regulars, one which reflected the same interplay of market and communal orientations discernible in so many other aspects of saloon culture.

Further, in this atmosphere of community, surrounded by familiar drinking partners and stimulated by strong drink and sentimental lyrics, the workingman might sometimes let down his guard and display emotions he would not ordinarily permit himself to show. Songs provided a socially acceptable vehicle for the expression of frustrations, disappointments, and regrets. And, though it was not an everyday occurrence, the occasional shedding of tears was a barroom reality. Few other settings in workingmen's lives permitted such behavior. Recognizing the importance of this emotional safety-valve, and the catalytic role of music in making it possible, is essential to gaining an understanding of the significance of the saloon in workers' lives.

Yet great changes would soon overtake the barroom and its tradition of song. By the late 1910s, the musical culture of bargoers, as well as most other Americans, had begun to undergo the most dramatic transformation witnessed since the rise of Tin Pan Alley in the 1890s. The cause of this change, which would alter the character of musical entertainment in America forever, was the rise of the commercial recording industry. Though Thomas Edison had designed his first phonograph in 1877, and though "nickel-in-the-slot" music boxes were available in some turn-of-the-century establishments, it was not until a few years before World War I that record players and recording techniques were sufficiently perfected to influence the popular music market. Thereafter, the changes wrought were drastic and swift. "Songs of the nineties and the early 1900s were written for playing and singing by amateurs at home; now songs were written for performance by experts on recordings to be listened to by a non-participating audience," as Russel Nye has observed. "Since professionals did the recordings, the music they used could be much more complicated, arrangements more intricate, harmonies and ranges suited to better-trained musicians."[51]

Not only were the newer songs increasingly harder to sing, but also the availability of perfected studio recordings tended to dampen people's desire to make the effort. This tendency would become more pronounced after World War I with the rise of radio and the development of the jukebox (though by then, of course, the old-time saloon had already been legislated out of existence).

Despite these changes, however, music remained a significant feature of saloonlife. Vaudeville performances and community dances continued to be held, though movie houses and municipal halls were steadily drawing away business. While popular music did become increasingly sophisticated, still a considerable number of new songs were amenable to singing by ordinary mortals. Further, the impetus to sing persisted among drinkers long accustomed to mixing drink with song. Yet the fact remains that the singing habits of bargoers, and indeed of all Americans, were undergoing a radical and lasting transformation by the eve of the First World War. As music of the people and by the people increasingly became music *for* the people, the great era of spontaneous barroom singing drew to a slow but inexorable close.

Ten

The Free Lunch

Especially I liked the San Francisco saloons. They had the most delicious dainties for the taking—strange breads and crackers, cheeses, sausages, sardines—wonderful foods that I never saw on our meager home-table. . . . Stores, nor public buildings, nor all the dwellings of men ever opened their doors to me and let me warm by their fires or permitted me to eat the food of the gods from narrow shelves against the wall. Their doors were ever closed to me; the saloon's doors were ever open.

—Jack London[1]

The "free lunch" to which Jack London referred was an interesting combination of eighteenth-century innkeeping tradition and nineteenth-century capitalist innovation. From the past came the tavernkeeper's traditional role as victualler as well as drink dispenser. Since colonial times, tavern hospitality had customarily included snacks or meals in addition to alcoholic beverages. Echoes of this tradition were what London encountered in the barrooms of San Francisco in the 1880s through the early 1900s. Their general atmosphere of warmth and largesse contrasted sharply with the inhospitable coldness of most other contemporary institutions. Further, the congenial surroundings suggestive of home comforts helped promote a sense of fraternity and community among workers who regularly congregated there to break bread with their fellows.

Yet, while the idea of serving food in drinking establishments was by no means new in the saloon period, the idea of serving it on a massive scale using the latest marketing and distribution techniques was most definitely an innovation of late-nineteenth-century industrial capitalism. In one of the most successful public relations schemes of the era, the powerful liquor industry used its resources to supply saloons with vast quantities of food at extremely low prices. As a result, in barrooms from San Francisco to New York, any poor man who bought at least one five-cent beer could help himself to whatever "free" edibles the proprietors had to offer. In this way, the free lunch epitomized the dualism of saloon culture, with proprietors capitalizing on the mechanisms of the marketplace to produce the pleasures of a communal feast. By deftly combining age-old tavern culinary hospitality with modern marketing techniques, the saloon trade provided an almost gratis repast which swiftly became the chief daytime source of sustenance for much of working-class America.

Origins of the Free Lunch

The custom of offering food as well as liquid refreshment dates back to English monastic inns of the late Middle Ages. The monks regarded it their Christian duty to provide hospitality to strangers on religious pilgrimages. The practice was later taken over as a commercial enterprise by English taverns of the 1500s and 1600s. Yet a lingering aura of hospitality and welcome was still associated with partaking of the innkeeper's "table." This tradition was carried on in colonial American drinking establishments, then variously known as taverns, inns, or ordinaries. Particularly with the expansion of stagecoach routes and the growth of new towns in the 1700s and early 1800s, taverns responded to the increasing demand for meals from travelers and townsfolk alike.[2]

Many early taverns offered an "ordinary," defined as "a public meal regularly provided at a fixed price in an eating house or tavern." Part of English tavern tradition since the 1500s, the "ordinary" became so common a feature of American establishments that the term was often used as a synonym for "tavern," particularly in the southern colonies. Establishments generally served their main meal or "ordinary" between the afternoon hours of one and three (a repast known in this era as "dinner" rather than "lunch"). As a public meal offered every afternoon at a set time and price, the "ordinary" in colonial and antebellum taverns was the precursor to the "free lunch" of the saloon era.[3]

After the Civil War, as the nation embarked on its industrializing phase, the rapid growth of the liquor trade brought dramatic changes in the way that food was supplied and sold in most drinking establishments. As more barrooms opened in urban areas to cater to the expanding working-class population, proprietors groped for ways to attract the largest and steadiest clienteles. Some, like Chicago saloonkeeper-politician Joseph "Chesterfield Joe" Mackin, believed that the way to men's hearts was through their stomachs. According to journalists Lloyd Wendt and Herman Kogan, "Mackin was a former saloon owner who, by giving an oyster with every beer, introduced in Chicago the saloon free lunch." The story went that he cooked up the free lunch idea in the early 1870s as part of a campaign to endear himself to local voters and thus realize his political ambitions. Like so many popular legends, which folklorists define as tales told as true, the story of Mackin's pioneering food feat has been often repeated if never conclusively proven.[4]

By the early 1880s, individual saloonkeepers in other parts of the country had also adopted the strategy of offering free food as a customer incentive. Not until the major breweries became fully involved in the endeavor in the late 1880s and 1890s, however, did the free lunch begin to assume the proportions of a celebrated nationwide saloon institution.[5]

THE BREWERIES TAKE COMMAND

From the 1880s onward, the liquor industry, and particularly the breweries, gained increasing control of urban saloons through direct ownership or exclusive distributorship rights. As a result, these companies had as much interest as the saloonkeepers in attracting steady clienteles. At the same time, the breweries worried about rising temperance sentiment against the saloon for its role in promoting public drunkenness. When temperance advocates began demanding that barrooms offer food to counteract the intoxicating effects of alcohol, the liquor industry went them one better by arranging to supply huge amounts of good, cheap food to all their constituent saloons.[6] "Thus the cost of not only the beer, but the meat, bread, and vegetables, bought in vast quantities, is greatly reduced," remarked Royal Melendy of the free lunch in Chicago in the late 1890s. Further, he asserted, "I believe it is true that all the charity organizations in Chicago combined are feeding fewer people than the saloons." Even saloonkeepers independently procuring their own lunch items benefited from the bulk merchandizing arrangements that grew up between food suppliers and saloonists. As one New York proprietor reported in 1909, he bought pork and beans from an Indiana firm, pretzels from a New York company, and meat and sausages from a variety of regional suppliers.[7]

By the turn of the twentieth century, therefore, the time-honored custom of serving food in drinking establishments had come a very long way from the generally modest operations of the antebellum period. No longer strictly dependent on local farming and hunting to provide the provender, saloonists could now order food in bulk from a variety of specialized suppliers, some of them located many hundreds of miles away. Certain of a constant supply, they could regularly offer a large repast at midday as well as smaller snacks at any time of the day or night.[8]

In offering so much food so cheaply, the liquor industry was able to satisfy simultaneously the hunger of the working poor and the demands of nutrition-minded progressive reformers. This triumph the latter regarded with considerable ambivalence. "Some provision of food by the saloons is required by law for hygienic reasons: it is bad for a man to drink upon an empty stomach," wrote Raymond Calkins in 1901. Then, with a note of dismay, he added, "But it is a long cry from this to becoming, as the saloons now are, the base of the food supply of thousands of men of all classes in our cities." So successfully had the liquor trade made a virtue of a necessity that some poor men depended utterly on the free lunch for survival. "With ten cents—five cents for a bed and five cents for a glass of beer, and access to the free lunch—a man may cover the space of twenty-four hours and pay his way," George Turner observed 1907. "A 'town bum' in Chicago said recently: 'I have not had my legs under a table for six years.'"[9]

And it was not just men who were coming in for the lunch. Some women also found that their budgets and their appetites drove them into drinking establishments for meals. "I know girls who have entered a saloon because they could there get a bowl of soup as well as a glass of beer for five cents, receiving in that bowl of soup better nourishment than any other expenditure of such five cents could bring them," remarked labor activist Margaret Dreier Robbins in 1913. Similarly, as Kathy Peiss found in her study of New York working women in the early twentieth century, "They commonly saved their allowances for lunch by eating the free food served in saloons or skipping the meal altogether."[10]

A firsthand description of both the lunch and the social circumstances surrounding it was provided by Dorothy Richardson in 1905, a young working woman performing back-breaking labor in a commercial laundry in New York City. One afternoon when another young laundress collapsed "with nausea and exhaustion," middle-aged co-worker Mrs. Mooney declared that it was "them rotten cold lunches you girls eat" and urged them to try the free lunch at nearby Devlin's saloon. "We go there every day . . . and you can go along if ye have a mind to," she and a friend offered.[11]

The following day, Richardson, Mooney, and four others "filed in the 'ladies' entrance'" of Devlin's, seated themselves in the back room, and ordered "Six beers with the trimmins'!" Greatly enjoying the hearty meal, Richardson declared, "I instantly determined never again to blame a working man or woman for dining in a saloon in preference to the more godly and respectable dairy-lunch room." Soon, she and her female co-workers were daily patronizing Devlin's where, Richardson noted, "I had become a regular patron."[12]

The reaction of Devlin's male patrons to the presence of an all-female group drinking, eating, and chatting in the back room was interesting. At lunchtime a number of workmen usually lounged about the tables, smoking cigars and drinking beer. Upon the women's arrival, however, Richardson reported that "when they saw us each man jumped up, and grabbing his glass, went out into the barroom." Was this a gesture of annoyance and disapproval? Not at all, according to the knowledgeable Mrs. Mooney. "Sure, and what'd ye expect!" she explained. "Sure, and it's a proper hotel ye're in, and it's dacent wurrkin'-men that comes here, and they knows a lady when they see her, and they ups and goes!" In her view, it was a simple matter of propriety. Saloon chivalry demanded that decent workingmen surrender their seats and give wide berth to respectable women with whom them were unacquainted and who might feel uncomfortable dining in the presence of beer-drinking, male strangers.[13] Another possibility, of course, was that the men were thinking more of their own comfort than the ladies', preferring to withdraw to the male milieu of the barroom where they would not be inhibited or distracted by a female presence.

It might also have been that the men vacated the back room for neither chivalrous nor chauvinistic reasons, but rather out of sheer confusion. They recognized that the working women's desire to take advantage of the free lunch was legitimate. But no clear social guide-lines had yet evolved regarding proper male behavior when groups of respectable female strangers invaded previously male-dominated space. The free lunch had been a feature of saloons since the 1880s, but female use of it was still a comparatively new and controversial phenomenon. Had the women been prostitutes, the men might have flirted with them; had the women had male escorts, the men might have respectfully acknowledged them. Confronted with a group of working women merrily drinking and chatting over lunch at a back-room table, however, the men were very possibly uncertain how to proceed and might have decided that the safest course was a swift exit.

Richardson and her cohorts of course had the advantage of being guided and chaperoned by the unflappable Mrs. Mooney. They also had access to an establishment that offered a back room, a waiter, and an obliging male clientele. However, not every working woman could or would flout social proprieties in this way. Many preferred to pa-tronize cheap restaurants or bring lunches from home, no matter how mediocre the fare. Yet, for those women in larger cities like New York or Boston who did dare to partake of the free lunch, the bargain was often worth the disapprobation of shocked onlookers. As Richardson observed, she and her female co-workers had to face far worse hard-ships during the course of their long working days, "their torture re-lieved by such comforts as we could find in the gossip of the table, and in daily excursions to Devlin's." [14]

Not all saloonkeepers made a big production of their food-dispensing role. Indeed, there were some establishments that offered no *free* lunch whatsoever. Surveying the 634 saloons in Minneapolis and St. Paul in 1899, Calkins found free lunches to be "elaborate in 3 saloons; excellent in 8; good in 50; fair in 88; poor in 77; 56 saloons provide no free lunch; the rest simply crackers and cheese." In the seventeenth ward in Chicago, he observed that 111 of its 163 saloons served a free lunch, 28 offered no food, and 24 offered a fancier lunch for a price (usually ten to fifteen cents or more, called a "business-man's" or "merchant's" lunch). In Atlanta, meanwhile, where laws strictly regulated what fare could be offered, only 19 of the city's 106 saloons offered free lunches. [15]

On the other hand, those barrooms that did provide food were of-ten far more generous and attractively appointed than the cheap lunch counters and restaurants of the larger cities. According to Melendy's investigation of food-dispensing establishments along Madison Avenue in Chicago in 1901, for example, "In this distance of four miles there are . . . but eight restaurants for the poor man, and all of these are unattractive." Of the three offering a five-cent lunch, Melendy reported, "The air of poverty about these places is intolerable." One served meat that was "unfit for even a dog," in a physical environment "too indescribably dirty for mortal man to endure." The five restaurants offering a ten-cent lunch were slightly better, but these "furnish lunches about equal to those which can be found in the saloon with a glass of beer" for only five cents. In contrast to these eight restaurants catering to workers, "In this same four miles there are 115 saloons, nearly all of which furnish free lunches, together with all the other attractions of the Chicago saloon." Given this choice, it is understandable why all but the most adamantly abstinent working people opted for the beer and cheer of the barroom.[16]

ETHNIC AND REGIONAL INFLUENCES

Though the free lunch was a nationwide phenomenon, regional and ethnic touches distinguished most saloon offerings. Barrooms in the Midwest, Far West, and South generally offered a greater abundance than those in the East. This was owing partly to lower food prices, and partly to lower liquor license fees which resulted in more saloons competing more fiercely for a steady lunch trade. "The best free lunches to be found anywhere in the country are in Chicago, in St. Louis, and in San Francisco," according to Calkins. "The following amount is consumed per day in a Chicago saloon: 150 to 200 pounds of meat, 1½ to 2 bushels of potatoes, 50 loaves of bread, 35 pounds of beans, 45 dozen eggs. . . , 10 dozen ears of sweet corn, $1.00 to $2.00 worth of vegetables." Though the volume of the fare in this particular saloon was unusual, its variety and appeal was not. In middle- and far-western areas, huge herds of cattle and other livestock, as well as a variety of grains and vegetables, could be cheaply raised and quickly brought to market on newly constructed railroads. Saloons of the urban West were thus able to offer meals reminiscent of the traditional cowboy repast, featuring hearty portions of beef or pork supplemented with bread, beans, and greens of various descriptions.[17]

In addition to being influenced by frontier tastes, western saloon lunches in urban areas were often influenced by the ethnic preferences of the neighborhood clienteles they served. In Chicago, for example, a saloon catering primarily to Irish Americans served almost nothing but potatoes, according to Jane Addams of Hull-House. This fact proved a source of confusion for one recently arrived immigrant. "I recall an Italian who, coming into Hull-House one day as we were sitting at the dinner table, expressed great surprise that Americans ate a variety of food," Addams recalled. "A little inquiry showed that this conclusion was drawn from the fact that he lived next to an Irish saloon and had never seen anything but potatoes going in and beer coming out."[18]

In contrast to this Irish establishment in Chicago, George Ade observed, "In a German place you might find blut-wurst or blood sausage. . . . Or the hard and leathery cervelat or summer sausage. The longer it was kept, the more petrified and tasty it became." Also popular in many saloons were German "sardellen," poor cousins of the "aristocratic sardine," which were usually consumed "draped across a slab of rye bread" and, in Ade's opinion, "were more than fish. They were silent partners." The German custom of preparing pickled items such as herring, ham, and pig's feet had actually developed into such a popular fad that it was becoming tiresome, according to one disgruntled contributor to a liquor trade journal in 1913. "One good joint of roast or corned beef is better," he complained, "than a dozen dishes of pickled this, and pickled that, and pickled almost anything that was never eaten in Germany."[19]

To appeal to as many customers as possible, some establishments offered a variety of German, Irish, American, and other dishes. As Ade observed, "Many would have free-lunch specialties for every day in the week, as, for instance: Monday, hot frankfurters; Tuesday, roast pork; Wednesday, roast mutton; Thursday, Irish stew; Friday, baked fish and dressing; Saturday, roast beef and mashed potatoes; Sunday, dry crackers."[20]

Further west in San Francisco, saloon fare was also plentiful and varied. In the early 1900s, sailor Fred Klebingat recalled the delicious "Bull's Head Stew" at the Bulkhead saloon on the waterfront (now Fishermen's Wharf). Another tantalizing specialty was offered at Feige Hansen's saloon, also known as the "Hash House." "It served cannibal sandwiches as free lunch," according to Klebingat. "These were slices of pumpernickel with raw hamburger and a slice of onion on top." Probably his favorite meal was available at an Italian saloon called Sanguinetti's. "At noon there were large bowls of spaghetti and Italian bread set out on the free lunch counter. With each scoop of beer you bought you would receive a couple of pieces of deep-fried fish," he recalled. "How Sanguinetti made money I don't know, but I don't doubt that he did." San Francisco saloongoers benefited not only from the seafood harvests of Italian fishermen, but also from the presence of Mexican immigrants whose influence ensured an abundance of Mexican hot beans on many free lunch counters.[21]

In the South, some saloons offered nearly as sumptuous an array. In New Orleans, for example, "A large table is set out in the saloon, on which are placed trays of cut bread, bowls of butter, salads, and sauces," according to Calkins. "Then there is another table where there is a large tureen of soup, a platter of roast beef, a large dish of rice or baked beans, or hash or mashed potato; there is generally a change every day, and on Friday there are oyster soup and fish." The heavily Catholic heritage of New Orleans, owing to French and Spanish colonial influences as well as Irish-, Italian-, and German-Catholic immigrants arriving throughout the nineteenth century, no doubt explains the custom of serving fish on Fridays. (The baked fish that Ade noted was often served in Chicago saloons on Fridays was probably a similar gesture aimed at that city's large communities of Irish, Polish, and Italian Catholics.) But serving fish was by no means restricted to Fridays. On the contrary, seafood and beans were as regular a feature of lunches in New Orleans as in San Francisco, with the significant difference that in Louisiana the influence of French and African Creole cooking was strongly felt. Thus, many establishments routinely offered red beans and rice, oysters, shrimp, and crab. They also served gumbo, a thick, spicy soup of African origin featuring vegetables as well as seafood, chicken, and/or sausage (a Louisiana tavern specialty since at least 1804).[22]

Bargoers in Atlanta, on the other hand, were not so fortunate. Laws designed to discourage the free lunch trade in saloons forbade hot lunches altogether, and otherwise strictly limited the fare to five items only: cheese, crackers, pretzels, bologna, and pickles. Fortunately for workingmen elsewhere in the South, however, Atlanta was rather a special case. In Baltimore, for instance, the free lunches were described as "abundant" and one of the "principal attractions" of bargoing in that city.[23]

Least attractive were the meals offered by saloons in the East, according to Calkins, where high food prices and high license fees worked against lunch abundance. In Philadelphia, for example, the annual license fee in 1899 was $1,000, which "has so lessened competition that . . . the free lunch is inferior in quantity and quality to that of the saloons of other cities." (In contrast, most liquor sellers in San Francisco paid $84 annually; those who reported quarterly sales under $600 paid no license fee whatsoever.) Like Philadelphia, the free lunch in Boston saloons was often meager, consisting mainly of crackers, pickles, salt fish, and beef tea, though sometimes also including meat stew, steamed clams, and that most famous of Boston staples, baked beans.[24]

Summarizing the typical fare offered in eastern cities such as New York, Philadelphia, and Boston, Calkins wrote, "Usually this lunch is cold. . . , generally made up of the following articles: Bread, crackers, and wafers; cheese, bologna, sausage, wienerwurst, cold eggs, sliced tomatoes, cold meats, salads, pickles and other relishes. The demand is commonly for something sour or salt. The consumption of pickles, salt meats, sauerkraut, and potato salad runs far ahead of anything else." Though Calkins was apparently not much impressed by these offerings, the list seems very reminiscent of a classic New York delicatessen menu and, as such, might seem a rather appealing feast to many. In any case, the influence of German ethnic tastes emerges as clearly in the urban East as the urban West. Such items as wienerwurst, sauerkraut, and potato salad were favorites not just in German establishments, but in eastern saloons generally.[25]

In addition to these cold lunch items, some saloons offered hot food. In one such New York establishment, with a clientele composed mainly of first- and second-generation immigrants of German, Irish, and Italian descent, the saloonkeeper described his hot and cold lunch fare in 1909. "For this hot lunch we had a varying menu of pea soup, chowder, bean soup, lamb stew, beef stew, pork and beans, etc.," he remarked. "There were some ten plates of cold lunch besides, consisting of bologna, liver sausage, spiced fish, pickled herring, smoked or shredded fish, sliced cabbage, onion, bread, pretzels, potato salad, radishes, etc." More commonly, however, hot lunches in eastern saloons consisted simply of soup and bread. Even so, such plain fare could be appetizing. As working woman Dorothy Richardson remarked of the modest hot lunch in Devlin's saloon in 1905, "Whatever the soup was made of, it seemed to me the best soup I had ever eaten in New York." Thus, it was probably true, as Calkins admitted, that "any man not supplied with much ready money, regards even the most meagre free lunch as one of his greatest blessings."[26]

From these descriptions it is clear that the significance of the free lunch was cultural as well as economic. Not only was the meal a considerable bargain, but also it afforded both immigrant and native the opportunity to savor the familiar and sample the new. For immigrant workers wishing to reaffirm their ethnic identity, some establishments offered the sights, smells, and tastes of their native cuisine. For the more adventurous, other saloons specialized in the foods of other cultures or combined the culinary traditions of many. As Upton Sinclair remarked in 1906 of Chicago's barrooms along "Whiskey Row" (Ashland Avenue), "One might walk among these and take his choice: 'Hot pea soup and boiled cabbage today.' 'Sauerkraut and hot frankfurters. Walk in.' 'Bean soup and stewed lamb. Welcome.' All of these things were printed in many languages, as were also the names of the resorts, which were infinite in their variety and appeal." Like the immigrants' heterogeneous neighborhoods, their free lunch counters often displayed a hodgepodge of ethnic influences in which foods both known and exotic were jumbled together in profusion. After repeated exposure to such potpourris, members of different immigrant groups who otherwise shared neither language nor heritage could begin to acquire an appreciation for the culinary traditions of others.[27]

Not just immigrants, of course, but also native-born saloongoers were introduced to ethnic and regional dishes that had an important acculturating influence on their lives. Recalling her childhood in Chicago, Helen Constable described a German saloonkeeper in her neighborhood in the 1910s who enthusiastically sent his favorite German recipes home with his American-born regulars (her father among them) for their wives to try. Similarly, Jack London recalled that San Francisco saloons introduced him to "strange breads" and other "delicious dainties" nothing like his mother used to make. Moreover, while a man might hesitate to enter an ethnic restaurant where he could have difficulty interpreting the menu and would have to commit himself to one particular dish or another, the buffet-style offerings of saloons permitted him to see what he was selecting and to sample odd-looking morsels at will. Thus, both natives and immigrants alike had their palates educated and enriched by the foods available in saloons.[28]

Yet there were some ethnic barriers that not even free food could overcome. In the South, where racial prejudice against blacks was particularly rampant, the institution of the free lunch suffered severely from segregationist attitudes. As Calkins explained, "In the South the Negro problem has its effect upon the free lunch. One saloon kept in Atlanta reported that it did not pay to set out much of a free lunch because the Negro is such a heavy eater that there would be no profit. Again, the white man would not help himself out of a dish which had been used by a Negro, and in many saloons it would be impracticable to have a double counter. For this reason, in saloons which have a mixed trade, the free lunch is inconspicuous."[29]

While it seems doubtful that poor blacks ate more than poor whites, the main point is that the refusal of whites to eat alongside blacks was of a piece with the general policy of maintaining segregated lunch counters and restaurants throughout the South, a policy not rigorously challenged until the 1940s and 1950s. Yet, though blacks were often barred from the barroom's lunch table, some of their favorite dishes were not. The serving of gumbo in New Orleans saloons, for example, reflected the important influence that African Creole cooking had on southern tastes. Further, though blacks might not be permitted to consume saloon food, they could be involved in its preparation, so that their influence might be felt in the kitchen if not yet at the counter. Thus, while the races did not usually mingle at the free lunch table, their tastes sometimes did, perhaps inching forward the process of interracial adjustment even under these most difficult of circumstances.

LUNCH AND THE CODE OF THE CLUB

Though the liquor trade performed an essential role in procuring cheap, plentiful foodstuffs, the resounding success of the free lunch idea ultimately depended on the workingman's voluntary cooperation in buying the requisite nickel beer and not overindulging at the food counter. "There was only one condition attached,—you must drink," as Upton Sinclair remarked. "But all of the men understood the convention and drank; they believed that by it they were getting something for nothing—for they did not need to take more than one drink, and upon the strength of it they might fill themselves up with a good hot dinner." Further, most bargoing folk appear to have observed an unwritten code of honor when it came to how much food they consumed for their nickel. The saloonkeeper trusted his regulars not to take unfair advantage, in return for which they expected him to let them eat in peace. So pervasive was this atmosphere of mutual trust that even gourmands were usually persuaded to exercise some restraint. "No limit is ordinarily put on the amount which a man may eat. A well-dressed or a regular customer is never interfered with. It is only the man who comes seldom or evidently comes for the lunch alone who need fear the eye of the bartender," as Calkins explained. "However, there is a kind of etiquette about the use of the free lunch which acts as a corrective to the greed of some patrons."[30]

Though the saloonkeeper naturally resented the man who ate more than his fair share, he might tolerate this behavior as long as the customer did buy something to drink and did not make a regular practice of overindulgence. "I remember one noon when I had a particularly appetizing hot lunch, a Jewish peddlar came in," as one New York proprietor remarked in 1909. "He ordered a 'schooner' of beer, at five cents. He objected to the foam on the top; he wanted it all beer. Then he sat down at a table, and during the next hour he ate three platefuls of my free lunch, and read all the newspapers in my place." While clearly irritated, this saloonkeeper did not insist that a drink purchase accompany each plateful, though technically he was entitled to do so.[31]

Proprietors might also tolerate minor mooching incidents, particularly if the perpetrators were minors. Jack London recalled that in the early 1880s when he was seven years old, a saloonkeeper in Colma, California, always permitted him to take a free soda cracker whenever his father stopped in for a drink. "Just one soda cracker, but a fabulous luxury," remarked London, who came from a poor farming family. "I would take an hour in consuming that one cracker. I took the smallest of nibbles, never losing a crumb, and chewed the nibble till it became the thinnest and most delectable of pastes." Similarly, John Powers recalled that in Waukesha, Wisconsin, in 1915, he and his seven-year-old friend Melvin "Red" Imig often helped themselves to a free snack or two from saloonkeeper Louie Inzio's lunch counter. "After Red got through selling his newspapers to the men at the bar, we'd always pass by the lunch counter on our way out and quick try to grab a piece of bologna or cheese or something," Powers recalled. "Louie would holler at us—'Get away from there, you kids!'—but we knew he wasn't really mad at us, and time after time we'd manage to swipe some snack or other and then run like hell out the door."

Similar episodes occurred at McSorley's Saloon in New York City. "In McSorley's the free-lunch platters are kept at the end of the bar nearer the street door," recalled regular Joseph Mitchell, "and several times every afternoon kids sidle in, snatch handfuls of cheese and slices of onion, and dash out, slamming the door. This never fails to amuse the old men." [32]

Much different, however, were the free lunch freeloaders, the "deadbeats" and "ringers" who deliberately ignored the rules of etiquette by helping themselves to the food without any intention of purchasing a drink. "The code governing the privileges of the free-lunch department was exacting and was observed by the genteel trade even if ignored by . . . unfortunates who had hit the grit," as Ade observed. "The stony-broke who had seen better days would have died rather than go to a back door and beg for a hand-out but he had no scruples against cleaning the lunch counter. . . , pronging in all directions and trying to get a couple of square meals for an investment of nothing whatsoever." [33] The saloon lunch was understandably a tremendous temptation to the hungry and penniless. Here was an abundance of food laid out in a convenient buffet-style arrangement that meant the freeloader need not directly entreat anyone for a hand-out. In the midst of the noontime confusion, the lunch sponger knew he might grab at least a few bites before he was caught and ejected, by which time the proprietor could hardly reclaim his stolen property. Further, lacking the regular customer's sense of loyalty or responsibility to a particular saloon, the meal moocher might convince himself that his hunger outweighed the proprietor's right to profit, and anyway the few items he pilfered would never be missed.

Rather than resort to thievery, some hungry saloongoers might invoke the venerable custom of clubbing their meager resources toward meals for all. In San Francisco in the early 1900s, for example, Fred Klebingat recalled how he and his seafaring friends managed to come up with the requisite nickel apiece for lunch. "One sailor would have a nickel, the other a dime. A nickel all around!" he recalled. "'What do you fellows say to a fish dinner?' Off we would trudge to the Seawall—three of us with 15c. A long walk, but when we got there Sanguinetti would serve you a scoop of steam beer, some spaghetti and Italian bread, and all the fish you could eat—all for a nickel." The sense of comradeship among these saloongoers prompted them to club together toward a mutually desirable end, and their status as regulars at Sanguinetti's kept them from stooping to deviousness at the lunch counter.[34]

In contrast, there was the testimony of Walter Strauss, a contemporary of Klebingat's in San Francisco, who recalled the attitude of his seafaring friends toward the lunch at the Ensign saloon. This establishment "was a little higher class than the others on the waterfront," according to Strauss, and was therefore not a regular hangout for his group. "When we were broke and hungry, we slipped in the side door to do a little foraging, but we had to watch out for the bartender," he explained. "The restrooms were in the basement and we always went there first. Then we would watch our chance; when the bartender was busy serving customers we would pop out and grab some eats." Not being regular customers of the place, these men apparently regarded its lunch as fair game, though their skulking around by the men's room reveals that they well knew the violation of the club code they were committing. On the other hand, the Ensign was a prosperous enterprise which would hardly suffer much from the "piece of bread and some sausage" they pilfered, and besides, they were hungry.[35]

From the standpoint of saloonkeepers, however, business was business, and the lunch they offered was intended as an incentive to paying customers, not as a bonanza for bums. To prevent such pilfering, according to Ade, some proprietors in the larger establishments hired muscle-bound "bouncers" to eject vagrants, known as giving them the "bum's rush." Others parceled out edibles from behind the bar or supplied tickets to drink-buyers to be exchanged for food at the counter. Still others, like legendary saloonkeeper Malachy Hogan of Chicago, enforced the code of etiquette by personally chasing after violators with a bung starter (a mallet used to open beer kegs). "He could vault over the bar and light on an unwelcome caller with all the destructive effect of a horse lying down on a butterfly," remarked Ade. Most proprietors, however, did not go to such extremes as hiring bouncers, rationing food, distributing tickets, or wielding clubs. Instead they relied on a rough word to the violator to shame him off the premises, and otherwise trusted most of their customers to honor the traditional code of the lunch.[36]

During particularly hard times, some bartenders might even permit a destitute man to eat a truly *free* lunch, especially if he were a former regular now down on his luck. Upton Sinclair provided an

illustration in *The Jungle* (1906). Lithuanian immigrant Jurgis Rudkus, the downtrodden protagonist, "had not eaten since morning,
and he felt weak and ill; with a sudden throb of hope he recollected
he was only a few blocks from the saloon where he had been wont to
eat his dinner." The bartender did indeed remember and indulge
him. "So Jurgis drank a huge glass of whiskey, and then turned to the
lunch-counter, in obedience to the other's suggestion. He ate all he
dared, stuffing it in as fast as he could; and then, after trying to speak
his gratitude, he went and sat down by the big red stove in the middle
of the room." According to Sinclair, however, the motives of such
bartenders were not necessarily philanthropic. On the contrary, the
liquor seller in this case "reflected that [Jurgis] had always been a
steady man, and might soon be a good customer again." Thus, while
the bartender's actions had the appearance of generosity and hospitality, Sinclair insinuated that his gesture was actually prompted more
by a cynical profit motive than by any humanitarian concern.[37] In
fact, such gestures by saloonkeepers very likely involved a combination of marketplace and community values, reflecting the dual nature
of saloon culture generally.

Ironically, the policy of offering the free lunch primarily as a business proposition was probably one of its most appealing features to
working people too proud to countenance outright charity. They
knew a nickel was obviously just a token amount to pay for such
bounty. Yet because it did cost them something, the deadly stigma of
the hand-out was avoided. As Melendy remarked of the saloon free
lunch, "The general appearance of abundance, so lacking in their
homes or in the cheap restaurants, and the absence of any sense of
charity, so distasteful to the self-respecting man, add to the attrac-
tiveness of the place."[38]

The typical workingman's aversion to any enterprise smacking of
charity or reform was a principal reason for the dismal failure of most
philanthropic and religious projects aimed at replacing the food-
dispensing role of the saloon. In New York, for example, Calkins
noted the failure of the "Church Army Tea Saloon" in the late 1890s.
Partly subsidized by private donations (the counterpart of brewery
subsidies for liquor saloons), this "temperance saloon" offered working folk free sandwiches and desserts with the purchase of a five-cent
cup of tea. Unfortunately for the success of the project, nightly religious services were also offered, and "tea missionaries" went about
instructing people on how and why they should brew and drink this

beverage. "The effect of the benevolent and religious features was not helpful," Calkins acknowledged ruefully, and the project soon foundered and died. The great number of similarly failed experiments across the country led him to conclude that "any charitable or religious motive which may lie behind such attempts as these to rival the saloons must be kept well in the background." This had to be done "lest . . . customers be made to fear that they were being patronized, or that some effort was being made, under religious auspices, for their moral improvement."[39]

THE DOWNSIDE OF THE FREE LUNCH

Despite its benefits, the saloon free lunch was open to a number of legitimate criticisms. In the last analysis, the liquor industry was exploiting the plight of the poor and hungry by luring them into barrooms with elaborate spreads and then requiring them to buy drinks for the privilege of eating. This strategy brought many people into saloons who otherwise might not have chosen to patronize them. In Melendy's words, "[T]he temptation to eat in the saloon, and take advantage of the hot lunch served free, is beyond the power of common clay to resist." Not only men, but women and children were drawn into the net and encouraged to overlook and forgive (or perhaps even participate in) the more negative aspects of barlife. As London remarked of himself, "Here was a child, forming its first judgments of the world, finding the saloon a delightful and desirable place."[40]

By tying drink-buying to food consumption, the liquor trade encouraged people to adopt the habit of drinking with meals, and then further encouraged this habit by serving salty foods to increase the desire for drink. "The more lunch the beer-hounds consumed the greater was their enthusiasm for salty food," explained Ade, "and the more pretzels and sardellen they gobbled up, the more enduring became the thirst." Moreover, the habit of drinking with meals did sometimes help foster the habit of drink itself, among both women and men. When New Yorker Dorothy Richardson began accompanying her co-worker Mrs. Mooney to the free lunch at Devlin's saloon in 1905, for example, she confessed that "I, who never before could endure the sight or smell of beer, found myself draining my 'schooner' as eagerly as Mrs. Mooney herself." Similarly, in the early 1900s, Chicago book salesman Vernon Sheldon confided to a fellow worker that he had had to swear off the free lunch when he realized he was beginning to go to saloons more for the beer than the food.[41]

Besides encouraging people to develop a daily drinking habit, saloons were criticized for the sometimes sloppy and unsanitary conditions that attended their free lunch spreads. Exposed plates of food attracted not only barflies, but also houseflies whose role in spreading germs was starting to be recognized at the turn of the twentieth century. Communal serving forks were similarly becoming objects for objection. "Right in the center of the soiled table-cover you might have found a bowl of baked beans and alongside of it a glass of troubled water," Ade explained, "and in the glass were immersed several forks which, the evidence indicated, had been used in hoisting beans." Another source of scandal were the mustache towels often hanging at intervals along the bar handrail, available to anyone and everyone for wiping food and beer foam from the mustaches so often sported in this period.[42]

Most disturbing of all, muckraking progressives like Sinclair charged that meat-packing plants would routinely take spoiled meat, "rub it up with soda to take away the smell, and sell it to be eaten on the free-lunch counters." Whether this practice was as widespread as reformers claimed is difficult to establish. Rumors made the rounds in Chicago by 1910, but they were not so common in other cities such as Boston. In any case, such attacks on the free lunch were part of the larger, more general effort of the progressive movement to establish better public sanitation standards nationwide, culminating in such federal legislative measures as the Pure Food and Drug Act of 1906. Meanwhile, the sanitation argument added fuel to the prohibitionists' fire, strengthening their allegations that the saloon was undermining both the physical and moral health of the nation.[43]

Among saloonkeepers themselves, moreover, there was growing disenchantment with the tradition of the free lunch after 1900. Many complained of the expense and bother associated with setting forth so generous a feast on a daily basis, all for a few measly nickel beers. Some went broke in their food fights with other saloonkeepers. All felt the pinch of ever stiffer competition from commercial restaurants, jobsite lunch wagons, factory cafeterias, philanthropic food-dispensing projects, and home-cooked meals prepared by the wives of increasingly marriage-prone workingmen. Saloonkeepers felt pressure from restauranteur organizations to discontinue their food giveaways. They also felt continuing pressure from temperance advocates, who ironically had helped to create the whole food controversy in the first place by insisting that saloons offer some sustenance to drinkers. As if all this were not enough, the United States became entangled in World War I in 1917. Now the free lunch came under attack as an unpatriotic flouting of food conservation policies (a dastardly conspiracy, some critics charged, of brewers and barkeepers of German descent). At that juncture, even proprietors who had formerly insisted that the lunch was good for public relations were forced to admit that the days of the free food fest were drawing to a close.[44]

When the saloon era died, the free lunch died with it, for never has the postprohibition workingman's barroom offered anything like the bargain that the lunch once represented. Barrooms in the late twentieth century still sometimes offer free snacks such as popcorn or crackers, and some do offer meals, though almost always for a separate charge.[45] Also, some drink parlors of the better sort prepare an elaborate spread of free hors d'oeuvres at "cocktail hour" (usually after 5:00 P.M.). Indeed, this custom is probably the closest surviving relative of the free lunch of the saloon era. But it is not, of course, the same thing. The free food idea might have been borrowed from saloon tradition, but fussy, gourmet-style hors d'oeuvres are really more a part of middle-class "cocktail culture" than they are of working-class barroom culture. Rare is the man who depends on hors d'oeuvres in cocktail lounges for his dinner; common was the man who depended on the noontime offerings in saloons for his lunch. Literally, then, there is no free lunch anymore.

The Free Lunch and Working-Class Culture

For all the controversy surrounding it, however, the free lunch remains one of the most interesting and significant features of American bar lore. Though it was in some respects just an extension of the venerable victualler role of colonial and antebellum innkeepers, its remarkable variety and quantity at such low cost was testimony to the organization and power of the developing industrial order, of which the liquor trade was an important part. Even its detractors had to admit that the barroom lunch, if not literally free of charge or consequences, was nevertheless a terrific bargain. In its heyday, it fed more people more cheaply and copiously than any other public institution, charitable or profit-making. This it did without the taint of charity or the implied insult of moral uplift, while all the same having the practical effect of giving the poor man a charitable leg up. Even with its drawbacks, the free lunch performed an essential economic function in workers' lives.

Equally significant was its cultural role for the many different nationalities crowding into the working-class districts of industrial centers. As anyone who has traveled to a foreign country knows, there are times when one longs to savor the familiar foods of home in the comfortable company of one's countrymen. The ethnic cuisine available in some saloons met this need, helping to assuage the alienation and homesickness felt by many immigrant workers. In other, more cosmopolitan establishments, meanwhile, a multiethnic smorgasbord influenced the tastes of both foreign- and native-born bargoers. Reflecting the cultural pluralism so characteristic of American urban populations, the free lunch often promoted intercultural contact and adjustment by functioning as a kind of public food forum for the rapidly expanding working class.

In addition to its economic and cultural roles, the lunch played its part in the socialization of the workingman. Day after day, the saloon provided an agreeable setting for communal feasts and encouraged the worker to behave conscientiously regarding the unwritten etiquette of the food counter. Like so many other features of barlife, the viability of the free lunch idea was predicated upon the barroom honor code and the regular's sense of loyalty and responsibility toward his clubhouse, its host, and its amenities. Unlike the freeloader and the over-indulger, the regular customer understood that both he and the proprietor contributed and derived something of value from the arrangement. Perhaps more than any other aspect of bar lore, the free lunch exemplified the marriage of marketplace and community values in saloonlife.

Conclusion

> Whatever else the saloon may be or may fail to be, it is, at any rate, the
> poor man's club. . . . Club life has become a social factor of increasing
> importance in all modern society. It meets a need felt by women as well
> as by men. A very large proportion of those people who have the most
> resources in their homes now spend many of their leisure hours in so-
> cial clubs. The poor man, however, finds no resource of recreation and
> change of scene so convenient or so persuasive as the saloon; and the
> saloon, by every possible device, offers itself for the satisfaction of the
> social instinct.
> — Committee of Fifty [1]

According to the Committee of Fifty's study of saloons as
compared with other urban institutions at the twentieth century's turn, the "poor man's club" was extraordinarily well patronized
precisely because it was a *club*. It answered a need felt by most residents of modern American cities for sociability and a sense of connection with others. The club movement, of which the saloon club
was part, encompassed all classes and both genders in towns and
cities everywhere. "The multiplication and development of these
groups . . . has followed naturally the phenomenal growth of urban
population," as Raymond Calkins noted. Groups took shape among
"those whom some common interest unites. Such is the genesis of the
modern club, which forms such a prominent feature of city life." The
trend was universal, it was on the increase, and it largely explained
the popularity of the urban barroom. [2]

CONTINUING CONTROVERSIES

The Committee of Fifty's remarks are provocative on three counts. First, the Committee stresses the link between the city and the saloon. They assert that the sprawling urban environment stimulates a need for social contact, which the working poor successfully satisfy through the formation of grassroots groups like saloon clubs. This observation upsets the claims of modernization theorists that urbanization spells the inevitable breakdown of close social bonds among city dwellers. Much recent research, however, tends to corroborate the Committee's assessment, uncovering much more evidence of community building than of breakdown in America's industrializing era.[3]

In addition, the Committee unequivocally classifies the saloon as a "club." In form and function, they report, it closely resembles most other social organizations of its era. This finding contradicts the prohibitionist view that saloons are simply scenes of drunken chaos lacking any redeeming social importance. While this pejorative view still persists in some quarters today, several recent studies, including this one, present considerable data in support of the Committee's conclusions.[4]

Finally, the Committee points out that the essence of the modern club, including the saloon, is that its membership comprises "those whom some common interest unites." This tendency of people to unite deliberately on the basis of mutual interest is the hallmark of relationships in the urban marketplace, as social theorists since Ferdinand Tönnies's time have argued.[5] The Committee's observation thus challenges the "alternative culture" theory of saloons which emphasizes the primacy of bargoers' communal relationships persisting from the premodern, preindustrial era.[6] The Committee does acknowledge the importance of mutualistic values among saloongoers. Nonetheless, they still insist that the saloon—mutualistic values included—represents primarily a modern response to modern needs. This book adopts and expands upon this view, arguing for the duality of saloon culture in which both mutualistic and marketplace values commingle, just as they do in most other aspects of urban life.

Urban, deliberately created, and dedicated to achieving a mutually agreeable aim, the saloon club as described by the Committee seems to exemplify what scholars now commonly term a "voluntary association." Yet, should the saloon actually be so classified? Most historians apparently think not. Rarely do they even mention saloons when discussing workers' voluntary associations such as unions, lodges, mutual aid societies, political parties, church groups, athletic teams, and pleasure clubs. They note that barroom back rooms often hosted the meetings of these other groups, but seldom do they acknowledge the saloon as a voluntary association in its own right. Is this a case of oversight or overt slight? Why are saloons left out? What are the arguments for and against adding the saloon club to the roster of recognized voluntary associations? An inquiry into this issue will clarify the place of saloons in working-class life as well as the role of the associative impulse in urban American culture generally.

MEMBERSHIP AND VOLUNTARY ASSOCIATIONS

The strongest arguments for classifying saloon clubs as voluntary associations involve two factors: the characteristics of the membership and the custom of clubbing. Regarding membership, recall that this book began by identifying four principal traits which transformed bar customers into regulars and gave their saloons the character of clubs. These traits were constancy of patronage, conformity to barroom conventions, conviviality of comportment, and commonality of background (specifically, the shared factors of gender, age, marital status, occupation, ethnicity, and neighborhood).

Similar traits also characterized the memberships of most unions, lodges, mutual aid societies, and other working-class organizations. Members of these groups displayed constancy in their dues-paying and meeting attendance, conformity to their organizational rules, and commonality in their backgrounds and interests. Conviviality could also be a component, though not necessarily. Some mutual aid societies, for example, were primarily insurance arrangements involving little or no social interaction. But the majority of workers' groups did generate a measure of conviviality during meetings as well as occasional balls, picnics, and parades. Thus, saloon regulars closely resembled participants in other voluntary associations regarding the basic criteria for group membership.

Some historians might object that saloon club members were too dependent on the bar business to qualify as a separate, bonafide "association." It is true that the proprietor looked after most of the regulars' needs, including refreshments, clean-up, overhead, and discipline. He even collected their dues. On the other hand, a great number of recognized voluntary associations were also headquartered in the saloon and depended almost as heavily on the proprietor for the same services. Further, the identification of the saloon club with any particular establishment was by no means complete. Workers might adopt a certain saloon as their clubhouse, but their sense of group identity was self-generated and essentially separate from the individual enterprise that hosted them. If the proprietor went out of business or gravely displeased the regulars, they could take their business elsewhere. In this regard, the saloon club resembled other voluntary associations.

Some historians might also object that the saloon club was not sufficiently organized to qualify. Its membership was, in effect, *too* voluntary to constitute a voluntary association. Yet, as this book has tried to show, there was more method in the regulars' membership and merrymaking than many outsiders might suppose. Further, one wonders if the typical athletic, singing, or pleasure club had an organizational structure very much more sophisticated than the regulars' own.

The very fluidity of the saloon club's structure, moreover, was a principal reason for its mass appeal. For those who wanted latitude in allocating their leisure hours and chafed at the prospect of fixed meeting times, agendas, and hierarchies, the saloon club offered a comfortable compromise. It provided the basic benefits of club membership with a minimum of rigmarole. Yet achieving regular status still required pledging enough commitment to barroom comrades, customs, and the code of the wets to set members apart from nonmembers. Thus, regarding the issue of membership, the saloon club did qualify as a genuine though elemental form of voluntary association.

CLUBBING AND VOLUNTARY ASSOCIATIONS

Another argument for classifying saloon clubs as voluntary associations concerns the custom of clubbing. This basic engine of saloon interaction involved the essence of voluntary association in that each participant contributed willingly and equally toward the group's common objective—in this case, alcohol-enhanced sociability. Further, if traced back far enough, the history of tavern clubbing in fact seems to converge and merge with that of voluntary association.

When the club idea emerged in Englishmen's taverns of the late seventeenth and eighteenth centuries, it was not an isolated phenomenon. On the contrary, it was part of a much larger trend toward voluntary association in an age of expanding economic and social horizons. As trade increased and cities grew, people increasingly looked beyond their traditional social bonds based on kith and kin. They now cultivated new networks based on shared interest, rational choice, and contractual agreements. They did not lose their need for communal ties in this process, however. Rather, their lives assumed greater complexity as they pursued community-oriented relations in some groups and market-oriented relations in others. Sometimes the two orientations overlapped as a group's members discovered the dual benefits of communal companionship and marketplace clout. Variety in purpose, structure, and membership characterized these emergent voluntary associations as people searched for innovative ways to combine and cooperate in the pursuit of shared objectives.[7]

Thus, enterprising Englishmen formed joint-stock ventures like the Virginia Company in which investors made a contract to pool their resources toward the development of fresh markets in the New World. Puritan dissenters established voluntary religious sects such as the Congregationalists who, in New England, made their famous covenant to build a sin-free "citty upon a hill." Political dissenters in America combined into factions and then parties, culminating in the birth of a new political system with the Constitution as its contract and the concept of volitional allegiance at its core. In these various ways, people constructed their own economic, religious, and political networks reaching far beyond those into which they had been born.[8]

Clubbing customs in colonial American taverns were a further manifestation of this impulse toward voluntary association. Urban dwellers gravitated to taverns with the deliberate intention of cultivating relationships with persons of similar socio-economic backgrounds and interests. Sorting themselves out into informal drinking circles, they clubbed resources toward mutually agreeable ends which were customarily sociable but sometimes practical and market-oriented as well. Benjamin Franklin's tavern circle in Philadelphia, for example, delighted in the pleasures of drinking and debating while also pioneering the concept of the lending library. Similarly, in Massachusetts, the congenial tavern companies of Ebenezer Thayer in Braintree and Elisha Cooke, Jr., in Boston gradually developed a political dimension and became instrumental in these men's successful campaigns for government office.[9]

Since taverns were the principal social institutions of the colonial era, they were the places where the club idea found its most important initial expression. By the revolutionary and early national periods, however, clubs of a social nature proliferated well beyond the tavern milieu, as indeed did all other kinds of associations. "Voluntary fire companies, reform-minded benevolent organizations, volunteer militia companies, and literary, artistic, and scientific groups mushroomed. . . ," as Gary Nash has noted, "[f]acilitating interpersonal contact, providing small-scale arenas for self-improvement and mutual reinforcement, and training ordinary people in organizational skills."[10]

By the early nineteenth century, this trend toward voluntary association had become one of the most striking features of American civilization, in the estimation of Alexis de Tocqueville. Traveling extensively in Jacksonian America in the early 1830s, the French historian and social philosopher produced a penetrating analysis of what he viewed as the national culture. He first expressed concern over the pronounced material acquisitiveness that gripped the population. "It is odd to watch with what feverish ardor the Americans pursue prosperity," Tocqueville observed. He attributed their ambition and competitiveness to the fact that in a democracy, unlike an aristocracy, men were equally free to pursue their own self-interest as they liked. Yet he also warned of the dangers inherent in this "individualism born of equality," for if "the inhabitants of democratic countries . . . [do] not learn some habits of acting together in the affairs of daily life, civilization itself [will] be in peril."[11]

Americans had avoided this peril, Tocqueville maintained, by practicing what he called "the art of association" to a degree unparalleled anywhere in the world. "Americans of all ages, all stations of life, and all types of disposition are forever forming associations," he noted. "Americans combine to give fêtes, found seminaries, build churches, distribute books, and send missionaries to the antipodes. . . . Finally, if they want to proclaim a truth or propagate some feeling by the encouragement of a great example, they form an association."[12]

Individuals combined in this way because they recognized that their private interests were often best served through concerted action by like-minded individuals. Tocqueville called this philosophy "self-interest properly understood," and was impressed by how many Americans consciously recognized and articulated its centrality in their culture. The extent to which ordinary citizens embraced the principle was what made them such an instructive example to other nations contemplating a conversion to the potentially anarchic system of democracy. In sum, the Americans, "alone in the world, have thought of using the right of association continually in civil life, and by this means have come to enjoy all the advantages which civilization can offer."[13]

Though Tocqueville apparently steered clear of workingmen's taverns, he would have found ample evidence for his views had he stopped in. Throughout the antebellum period, taverngoers increasingly coalesced into what David Conroy has called "tavern companies" and Elliott Gorn has termed "barroom cliques." These often fiercely loyal peer groups cooperated in endeavors ranging from defending neighborhood turf to staging sporting events to organizing political clubs. They also regularly engaged in communal binges which, W. J. Rorabaugh has argued, represented a collective effort to counteract the anxieties and competitiveness of the rising market economy. Thus, the "art of association" was thriving in workers' barrooms in the decades before the Civil War, whether in rough frontier towns like Denver, Colorado, or burgeoning manufacturing centers like Rochester, New York.[14]

But it was in the late nineteenth and early twentieth centuries that the associative impulse in barlife reached its zenith. With industrialization spreading, immigration soaring, and urbanization transforming both the social and physical landscape, saloons exploded like popcorn all over the workingmen's districts. They were everywhere, they offered comfort and sociability, and workers flocked to them by the millions. In them, the regulars created a form of clublife that celebrated the mores of mutuality and reciprocity while simultaneously incorporating the values and social relations of the expanding urban marketplace.

Should saloon clubs be considered voluntary associations? Indeed they should, though the pronounced duality of saloon culture does make them something of a special case. More than most other voluntary associations, saloon clubs appear to have involved community- and market-oriented values in almost equal measure, which perhaps accounts for the confusion over their proper classification. On the other hand, the presence of both orientations made saloonlife unusually versatile and satisfying on many levels. Indeed, this duality gave saloon culture a hybrid vigor that propelled it to the center stage of male working-class life.

SALOON SWAN SONG

From its rise in the 1870s to its demise in 1920, the saloon managed to serve the many needs of its working-class constituency remarkably well. Workers derived from the lore of the barroom a much-needed sense of shared heritage and common values. Drinking folkways, the free lunch, and the pastimes of storytelling, singing, and gaming helped the regulars find enjoyment and meaning in life. Further, the saloon provided an array of services and comforts which for decades were not readily available elsewhere. That a drink parlor should function in this capacity was in itself a revealing commentary on the condition of American society in its industrializing phase. To be sure, many criticisms could be made of the saloon's makeshift efforts to serve as the poor man's employment bureau, union headquarters, political action center, immigrant way station, banking and credit agency, and neighborhood charity dispensary. Imperfect as these efforts were, however, they filled a void in workers' lives until better solutions in more sober surroundings could be devised.

Yet, by the eve of the First World War, the saloon's formerly firm foundations were beginning to show some significant cracks. Among the many factors undermining the saloon's position were the competition from new forms of amusement like movie theaters, the exodus of older immigrant groups for the suburbs, an upsurge in antisaloon legislation, increasingly cutthroat competition within the liquor industry, the initiation of criminal proceedings against machine politicians, and the drive for wartime preparedness and conservation.[15]

But the unkindest cut came from within.

The difficulty was that the saloon enabled workers to develop the associative impulse to such a degree that eventually they no longer needed the supportive environment of the barroom to sustain it. Thus, although the saloon was a warm nest in which fledgling workers' organizations could take shape and grow, an increasing number of groups such as trade unions and fraternal lodges were outgrowing the need for nurture and were desirous of an independent life of their own. In effect, workers had learned the art of association all too well, at least from the standpoint of the bar trade. The loss of liquor sales and rentals was problematic, but even more serious was the loss of power and prestige that saloonkeepers suffered when they could no longer depend on playing host to the neighborhood's clublife. This phenomenon played an important role in reducing the centrality of the barroom in workers' lives and rendering it increasingly vulnerable to the attacks of its critics.

In the eyes of most regular customers, the saloon never completely fell from grace. On the contrary, many men continued to regard it fondly as their personal club and to patronize it to the end. But something had gone out of the old relationship when the saloon had stood at the center of everything happening in cities across the country. The secret of its success had always been to capitalize on the disorganized state of urban society in general and the working class in particular.

Yet the confused and wide-open urban conditions that had sustained the saloon's immense popularity could not last. It was a great irony, in fact, that the saloon helped along the process of working-class self-organization that would be a major factor in its own undoing. By providing an arena in which laborers could cultivate their common ties and develop solutions to their problems, it effectively hastened the day of its own demise, at least in the form which it had assumed in its glory days. Thus, the saloon was already slipping from its former position of prominence in working-class culture when its history was cut short by national prohibition on 16 January 1920.[16]

The "noble experiment" of prohibition of course proved a disastrous failure in the 1920s and was finally abandoned in the early 1930s.[17] When President Franklin Roosevelt proclaimed the repeal of the Eighteenth Amendment on 5 December 1933, however, he articulated the misgivings of many that this newest noble experiment with alcohol might somehow result in the re-emergence of preprohibition conditions in the liquor trade. He announced that the federal government would hereafter impose stringent codes on the production and sale of intoxicating beverages. He then added, "I ask especially that no State shall by law or otherwise authorize the return of the saloon either in its old form or in some modern guise." While the prohibition against alcohol was to be judiciously lifted, the prohibition against the saloon was to stand. Even after thirteen years of bootlegging, gangsters, and lawless speakeasies, it was still the saloon "in its old form" that Roosevelt singled out for special condemnation.[18]

In the last analysis, however, Roosevelt probably need not have bothered, for workers had long since turned to other institutions for the expanded services which the saloon had once supplied and which had made it so central to their lives. Bar culture there would certainly be, and the camaraderie of the regulars and the lore of the barroom would live on. But the *saloon* was a creature of its time, and its time was past.

Notes

INTRODUCTION

1. W. H. Auden, "September 1, 1939," in *Collected Poems* (New York: Random House, 1945), 57–59.

2. The phrase "saloon period" appears in Robert Popham's fine study of the characteristics and functions of the saloon, as well as its place in the history of taverns worldwide. See Robert E. Popham, "The Social History of the Tavern," in *Research Advances in Alcohol and Drug Problems,* ed. Yedy Israel et al., vol. 4 (New York: Plenum Press, 1978), 277.

3. Herbert G. Gutman, *Work, Culture, and Society in Industrializing America* (New York: Knopf, 1976), 10–12.

4. For useful summaries of alcohol and temperance studies in the United States and abroad, see Susanna Barrows and Robin Room, eds., *Drinking: Behavior and Belief in Modern History* (Berkeley: University of California Press, 1991); and Jed Dannenbaum, "The Social History of Alcohol," *Drinking and Drug Practices Surveyor* 19 (1984): 7–11. Of the many studies of the temperance movement during the saloon period, some of the most useful include Jack S. Blocker, Jr., *American Temperance Movements: Cycles of Reform* (Boston: Twayne, 1989); K. Austin Kerr, *Organized for Prohibition: A New History of the Anti-Saloon League* (New Haven, Conn.: Yale University Press, 1985); Richard F. Hamm, *Shaping the Eighteenth Amendment: Temperance Reform, Legal Culture, and the Polity, 1880–1920* (Chapel Hill: University of North Carolina Press, 1995); Harry Gene Levine, "The Discovery of Addiction: Changing Conceptions of Habitual Drunkenness in America," *Journal of Studies on Alcohol* 39 (January 1978): 143–74; Norman H. Clark, *Deliver Us from Evil: An Interpretation of American Prohibition* (New York: Norton, 1976); James H. Timberlake, *Prohibition and the Progressive Movement, 1900–1920* (New York: Atheneum, 1970); Andrew Sinclair, *Era of Excess: A Social History of the Prohibition Movement* (New York: Harper and Row, 1962); Joseph R. Gusfield, *Symbolic Crusade: Status Politics and the American Temperance Movement* (Urbana: University of Illinois Press, 1963); and Peter H. Odegard, *Pressure Politics: The Story of the Anti-Saloon League* (New York: Columbia University Press, 1928). On women's involvement in the temperance movement, see Barbara Leslie Epstein, *The Politics of Domesticity: Women, Evangelism, and Temperance in Nineteenth-Century America* (Middletown,

Conn.: Wesleyan University Press, 1981); Ruth Bordin, *Women and Temperance: The Quest for Power and Liberty, 1873–1900* (Philadelphia: Temple University Press, 1980) and Bordin, *Frances Willard: A Biography* (Chapel Hill: University of North Carolina Press, 1986).

5. W. J. Rorabaugh, *The Alcoholic Republic: An American Tradition* (New York: Oxford University Press, 1979), ix. Another reason for the scholarly neglect of drinking culture has been the general disenchantment over alcohol reform issues following the failure of Prohibition, according to Barrows and Room, introduction to *Drinking*, 3. For an excellent analysis of the tendency among American reformers and their historians to regard all drinking as "problem behavior," see Joseph Gusfield, "Benevolent Repression: Popular Culture, Social Structure, and the Control of Drinking," in Barrows and Room, *Drinking*, 399–424.

6. W. J. Rorabaugh perceptively analyzes the immense popularity and pervasiveness of drink culture in the antebellum period in *The Alcoholic Republic;* Paul E. Johnson examines workers' resistance to evangelicals' efforts to foist a sober and disciplined regimen upon them in *A Shopkeeper's Millennium: Society and Revivals in Rochester, New York, 1815–1837* (New York: Hill and Wang, 1978). See also Paul Faler, "Cultural Aspects of the Industrial Revolution: Lynn, Massachusetts, and Industrial Morality, 1826–1860," *Labor History* 15 (summer 1974): 367–94. For the postbellum period, Roy Rosenzweig explores the social and economic functions of immigrants' saloons in Worcester, Massachusetts, in *Eight Hours for What We Will: Workers and Leisure in an Industrial City, 1870–1920* (New York: Cambridge University Press, 1983); Perry R. Duis performs a detailed comparative analysis in *The Saloon: Public Drinking in Chicago and Boston, 1880–1920* (Urbana: University of Illinois Press, 1983); Thomas J. Noel discusses saloons in Denver as that city evolved from frontier outpost to urban center in *The City and the Saloon: Denver, 1858–1916* (Lincoln: University of Nebraska Press, 1982); and Elliott West researches the role of barrooms in western towns in *The Saloon on the Rocky Mountain Mining Frontier* (Lincoln: University of Nebraska Press, 1979).

7. Oscar Handlin, *The Uprooted: The Epic Story of the Great Migrations that Made the American People* (New York: Grosset and Dunlap, 1951); John Bodnar, *The Transplanted: A History of Immigrants in Urban America* (Bloomington: University of Indiana Press, 1985). Examples of neighborhood network studies include Judith E. Smith, *Family Connections: A History of Italian and Jewish Immigrant Lives in Providence, Rhode Island, 1900–1940* (Albany: State University of New York Press, 1985); Eva Morawska, *For Bread and Butter: Life-Worlds of East Central Europeans in Johnstown, Pennsylvania, 1890–1940* (New York: Cambridge University Press, 1986); and James Grossman, *Land of Hope: Chicago, Black Southerners, and the Great Migration* (Chicago: University of Chicago Press, 1989). On workplace cultures, see David Montgomery, *Workers' Control in America: Studies in the History of Work, Technology, and Labor Struggles* (New York: Cambridge University Press, 1979); Francis G. Couvares, *The Remaking of Pittsburgh: Class and Culture in an Industrializing City, 1877–1919* (Albany: State University of

New York Press, 1984); Susan P. Benson, *Counter Cultures: Saleswomen, Managers, and Customers in American Department Stores, 1890–1940* (Urbana: University of Illinois Press, 1986); and Vicki L. Ruiz, *Cannery Women, Cannery Lives: Mexican Women, Unionization, and the California Food Processing Industry, 1939–1950* (Albuquerque: University of New Mexico Press, 1987). On leisure subgroups, see Kathy Peiss, *Cheap Amusements: Working Women and Leisure in Turn-of-the-Century New York* (Philadelphia: Temple University Press, 1986); Elliott J. Gorn, *The Manly Art: Bare-Knuckle Prize Fighting in America* (Ithaca, N.Y.: Cornell University Press, 1986); and Gunther Barth, *City People: The Rise of Modern City Culture in Nineteenth-Century America* (New York: Oxford University Press, 1980).

8. For a discussion of schoolyard folklore and its tenacity, see Iona and Peter Opie, *The Lore and Language of School-Children* (Oxford: Clarendon Press, 1972). The phrase "cake of custom" comes from Walter Bagehot, *Physics and Politics* (1872; reprint, New York: D. Appleton, 1906), 27.

9. Representative examples of such sources include William L. Riordon, *Plunkitt of Tammany Hall: A Series of Very Plain Talks on Very Practical Politics*, ed. Terrence J. McDonald (1905; reprint, Boston: Bedford Books, 1994); M. E. Ravage, *An American in the Making: The Life Story of an Immigrant* (New York: Harper and Brothers, 1917); *The Autobiography of William D. Haywood* (New York: International Publishers, 1929); Margaret F. Byington, *Homestead: The Households of a Mill Town* (1910; reprint, Pittsburgh: University of Pittsburgh Press, 1974); Joseph Mitchell, "McSorley's Wonderful Saloon," in *Up in the Old Hotel* (New York: Pantheon Books, 1992), 1–370; Grant Holcomb, "John Sloan and 'McSorley's Wonderful Saloon,'" *American Art Journal*, spring 1983, 5–20; and "The Experience and Observations of a New York Saloon-Keeper as Told by Himself," *McClure's Magazine* 32 (January 1909): 301–12.

10. See, for example, Jack London, *John Barleycorn: Alcoholic Memoirs* (1913; reprint, ed. John Sutherland, New York: Oxford University Press, 1989); Upton Sinclair, *The Jungle* (1906; reprint, New York: New American Library, 1960); Frank Norris, *McTeague: A Story of San Francisco* (1899; reprint, New York: New American Library, 1964); Theodore Dreiser, *Sister Carrie*, ed. Donald Pizer (1900; reprint, New York: Norton, 1970); George Ade, *The Old-Time Saloon: Not Wet—Not Dry, Just History* (New York: Long and Smith, 1931); Travis Hoke, "Corner Saloon," *American Mercury* 23 (March 1931): 311–22; James Stevens, "Saloon Days," *American Mercury* 11 (July 1927): 264–75; and Finley Peter Dunne, "The Power of Love," in Elmer Ellis, ed., *Mr. Dooley at His Best* (New York: Charles Scribner's Sons, 1938).

11. For example, see the propaganda issued by the Anti-Saloon League, which is liberally quoted in Odegard, *Pressure Politics;* also see Kerr, *Organized for Prohibition.*

12. Among the progressive reformers who reported on saloons firsthand were Jacob A. Riis, *How the Other Half Lives: Studies among the Tenements of New York* (1890; reprint, New York: Hill and Wang, 1957); Lincoln Steffens, *The Shame of the Cities* (1904; reprint, New York: Hill and Wang, 1957); Jane

Addams, *Twenty Years at Hull-House* (1910; reprint, New York: New American Library, 1960); Robert A. Woods, ed., *Americans in Process: A Settlement Study* (Boston: Houghton Mifflin, 1902); and Frederic C. Howe, *Confessions of a Reformer* (1925; reprint, New York: Quadrangle, 1967).

13. The "Committee of Fifty for the Investigation of the Liquor Problem" was organized in 1893. Disturbed by contradictory and unreliable statements issuing from both the temperance advocates and the liquor interests, the Committee resolved to produce four fact-filled volumes on the "drink question" in its legislative, economic, ethical, and physiological aspects, as well as a fifth volume summarizing their findings. Of particular significance to saloon historians was the third volume, *Substitutes for the Saloon*, researched under the direction of the Ethical Sub-Committee and written by the Reverend Raymond Calkins. He analyzed detailed information on saloons in seventeen major cities and produced a work that was "not only instructive but vivacious and picturesque," in the estimation of the Committee. Prohibition advocates, on the other hand, were not pleased by Calkins's reluctant conclusion that the saloon was "admirably adapted" to the satisfaction of "the social needs of thousands of our laboring people," and that the "longer one searches for just the right kind of substitute. . . , the more one despairs of finding it." See Raymond Calkins, *Substitutes for the Saloon* (Boston: Houghton Mifflin, 1901), v–xii, 5.

14. For an excellent introduction to current approaches to popular culture in the disciplines of history, anthropology, sociology, and literary criticism, see Chandra Mukurji and Michael Schudson, eds., *Rethinking Popular Culture: Contemporary Perspectives in Cultural Studies* (Berkeley: University of California Press, 1991). Other helpful introductory works include Alan Dundes, ed., *Interpreting Folklore* (Bloomington: Indiana University Press, 1980); Dundes, ed., *The Study of Folklore* (Englewood Cliffs, N.J.: Prentice-Hall, 1965); John G. Cawelti, *Adventure, Mystery, and Romance: Formula Stories as Art and Popular Culture* (Chicago: University of Chicago Press, 1976); and Russel Nye, *The Unembarrassed Muse: The Popular Arts in America* (New York: Dial, 1970).

CHAPTER ONE: *"The Importance of Being Regular"*

1. From "The Poor Man's Club: What It Does," circa 1916, circulated by the Anti-Saloon League and attributed to "An Enlightened Ex-Member" of saloon society, quoted in Peter Odegard, *Pressure Politics: The Story of the Anti-Saloon League* (New York: Columbia University Press, 1928), 46. For more on this powerful temperance group, see K. Austin Kerr, *Organized for Prohibition: A New History of the Anti-Saloon League* (New Haven, Conn.: Yale University Press, 1985); and Richard F. Hamm, *Shaping the Eighteenth Amendment: Temperance Reform, Legal Culture, and the Polity, 1880–1920* (Chapel Hill: University of North Carolina Press, 1995).

2. James Stevens, "Saloon Days," *American Mercury* 11 (July 1927): 264; the Anti-Saloon League, quoted in Peter Odegard, *The American Public Mind* (New York: Columbia University Press, 1930), 179; an anonymous anti-

saloon spokesman, quoted in Royal L. Melendy, "The Saloon in Chicago (Part 1)," *American Journal of Sociology* 6 (November 1900): 291.

3. On the average size of saloon crowds, see Robert E. Popham, "The Social History of the Tavern," in Yedy Israel et al., eds., *Research Advances in Alcohol and Drug Problems,* vol. 4 (New York: Plenum Press, 1978), 283; and George Ade, *The Old-Time Saloon: Not Wet—Not Dry, Just History* (New York: Long and Smith, 1931), 104–5.

4. Royal L. Melendy, "The Saloon in Chicago (Part 2)," *American Journal of Sociology* 6 (January 1901): 462 n; Robert A. Woods, ed., *Americans in Process: A Settlement Study* (Boston: Houghton Mifflin, 1902), 221; E. C. Moore, "The Social Value of the Saloon," *American Journal of Sociology* 3 (July 1897): 4.

5. Some of the best scholarly works in the extensive literature on temperance reform and the antisaloon crusade include Joseph Gusfield, "Benevolent Repression: Popular Culture, Social Structure, and the Control of Drinking," in Susanna Barrows and Robin Room, eds., *Drinking: Behavior and Belief in Modern History* (Berkeley: University of California Press, 1991), 399–424; Jack S. Blocker, *American Temperance Movements: Cycles of Reform* (Boston: Twayne, 1989); Hamm, *Shaping the Eighteenth Amendment;* Kerr, *Organized for Prohibition;* Odegard, *Pressure Politics;* Norman H. Clark, *Deliver Us from Evil: An Interpretation of American Prohibition* (New York: Norton, 1976); James H. Timberlake, *Prohibition and the Progressive Movement, 1900–1920* (New York: Atheneum, 1970); Barbara Leslie Epstein, *The Politics of Domesticity: Women, Evangelism, and Temperance in Nineteenth-Century America* (Middletown, Conn.: Wesleyan University Press, 1981); and Ruth Bordin, *Women and Temperance: The Quest for Power and Liberty, 1873–1900* (Philadelphia: Temple University Press, 1980).

6. Bar titles are listed in Raymond Calkins, *Substitutes for the Saloon* (Boston: Houghton Mifflin, 1901), 8; Bishop Potter is cited in Ade, *The Old-Time Saloon,* 26, 100. It is difficult to know what most saloongoers thought of the phrase "poor man's club," if they knew or cared about it at all. Some must have, or seemingly should have, resented it for the invidious comparison it drew between their institutions and those of the rich. The slang adjective "poor man's" is defined as a "less famous, less expensive, smaller, or less satisfactory version of something or someone," according to Harold Wentworth and Stuart Berg Flexner, eds., *Dictionary of American Slang,* 2d ed., supplemented (New York: Thomas Y. Crowell, 1975), 402. In dubbing the saloon the "poor man's club," the unmistakable inference was that barroom society was an example of poor men trying to do what rich men did better. Consider, however, this enigmatic bit of evidence from New York City. In the Bowery district of the 1890s, an area teeming with the tenement poor, there was a saloon bearing the name "Poor Man's Retreat," according to Calkins, *Substitutes for the Saloon,* 8. Its very existence indicates that at least *these* poor men knew what richer men were saying about them, and they were either amused or belligerently prideful enough to tolerate this ironic use of the characterization.

7. Frederick C. Howe, *Confessions of a Reformer* (1925; reprint, New York:

Quadrangle, 1974), 51, 54; Jack London, *John Barleycorn: Alcoholic Memoirs* (1913; reprint, ed. John Sutherland, New York: Oxford University Press, 1989), 72; Francis G. Peabody, E. R. L. Gould, and William M. Sloane, introduction to Calkins, *Substitutes for the Saloon*, viii; Ade, *The Old-Time Saloon*, 100.

8. *Oxford English Dictionary*, 1888–1928 ed., s.v. "club." See especially verb senses 1, 3, 6, 7.

9. *Oxford English Dictionary*, 1888–1928 ed., s.v. "club." See verb senses 8, 9, 10, and subject branch III, senses 10, 11.

10. *The Autobiography of Benjamin Franklin* (New York: Airmont, 1965), 63–65, 73–75. For more information on the social role of taverns in the colonial and antebellum periods, see David W. Conroy, *In Public Houses: Drink and the Revolution of Authority in Colonial Massachusetts* (Chapel Hill: University of North Carolina Press, 1995); Kym S. Rice, *Early American Taverns: For the Entertainment of Friends and Strangers* (Chicago: Regnery Gateway, 1983); Arthur White, *Palaces of the People: A Social History of Commercial Hospitality* (New York: Taplinger, 1970); Paton Yoder, *Taverns and Travelers: Inns of the Early Midwest* (Bloomington: Indiana University Press, 1968); Harry Ellsworth Cole, *Stagecoach and Tavern Tales of the Old Northwest* (Detroit: Gale Research Company, 1972); and Carl Bridenbaugh, *Cities in Revolt: Urban Life in America, 1743–1776* (New York: Knopf, 1955).

11. *Oxford English Dictionary*, 1888–1928 ed., s.v. "club." See subject branch III, senses 15a and 15b. The club idea is discernible in many voluntary associations of the colonial and antebellum periods. For discussion of these early associations, see Richard D. Brown, "The Emergence of Voluntary Associations in Massachusetts, 1760–1830," *Journal of Voluntary Action Research* 2 (1973): 64–73; Jacquetta Mae Haely, "Voluntary Organizations in Pre-Revolutionary New York City, 1750–1776" (Ph.D. diss., State University of New York, Binghamton, 1976); Anne M. Boylan, "Women in Groups: An Analysis of Women's Benevolent Organizations in New York and Boston, 1797–1840," *Journal of American History* 71 (1984): 497–523; Walter S. Glazer, "Participation and Power: Voluntary Associations and the Functional Organization of Cincinnati in 1840," *Historical Methods Newsletter* 5 (1972): 151–68; John Gilkeson, "A City of Joiners: Voluntary Associations and the Formation of the Middle Class in Providence, 1830–1920" (Ph.D. diss., Brown University, 1981); and Benjamin C. Rader, "The Quest for Subcommunities and the Rise of American Sports," *American Quarterly* 29 (fall 1977): 307–21.

12. Most proprietors of antebellum workers' taverns were independent entrepreneurs with working-class backgrounds and few financial resources. Their furnishings and equipment were usually spare, crude, and locally made. Many establishments contained only a wooden plank for a bar, in addition to a few mismatched chairs, tables, and glasses. Some were housed in wooden shacks; some were "kitchen barrooms" operated out of proprietors' homes; some were adjuncts of other business enterprises such as general stores, barbershops, bakeries, or even candy stores. Not until the 1870s would finer amenities such as massive mahogany bars, mirrors, and billiard

tables become widely available through a combination of brewery financing, expanded railway transportation, and the growth of bar equipment manufacturers like the famous Brunswick Company of Cincinnati. For more discussion of workers' taverns in the presaloon era, see Paul E. Johnson, *A Shopkeeper's Millennium: Society and Revivals in Rochester, New York, 1815– 1837* (New York: Hill and Wang, 1978), 58–59; Roy Rosenzweig, *Eight Hours for What We Will: Workers and Leisure in an Industrial City, 1870–1920* (New York: Cambridge University Press, 1983), 40–45; Elliott West, *The Saloon on the Rocky Mountain Mining Frontier* (Lincoln: University of Nebraska Press, 1979), 26–40; and W. J. Rorabaugh, *The Alcoholic Republic: An American Tradition* (New York: Oxford University Press, 1979), 16–18, 231, 235–36.

13. Ade, *The Old-Time Saloon*, 69. The term "saloon" traces back to 1841, according to H. L. Mencken, *The American Language*, 4th ed., abridged (New York: Knopf, 1980), 167. As Rosenzweig has noted, however, "As late as the early 1870s, the term 'grog shop' seems to have been more common than 'saloon.'" See Roy Rosenzweig, *Eight Hours for What We Will*, 244 n. 36. Further discussion of the terms "saloon" and "grogshop" appears in Elliott West, *The Saloon on the . . . Frontier*, 26–27. In Montana, use of the terms "saloon" and "bar" was forbidden by law after the repeal of prohibition, according to *Fortune Magazine* 10 (October 1934): 102. Referring to drinking establishments in the postprohibition era, Mencken observed, "There is probably not a single undisguised *saloon* in the United States today. They are all *taverns, cocktail lounges, taprooms, grills* or the like. Some are called *bars, lounge bars* or *cocktail bars,* but *saloon* is definitely out." See Mencken, *The American Language*, 167.

14. Moore, "The Social Value of the Saloon," 4–5. For a detailed discussion of the characteristics and functions of taverns from the Bronze Age to the early twentieth century, see Popham, "The Social History of the Tavern," 225–302.

15. Perry R. Duis, *The Saloon: Public Drinking in Chicago and Boston, 1880–1920* (Urbana: University of Illinois Press, 1983), 24–45; Timberlake, *Prohibition and the Progressive Movement*, 104–5. On the history of the brewing industry, see Stanley Baron, *Brewed in America: A History of Beer and Ale in the United States* (Boston: Little, Brown, 1962); Thomas Cochran, *The Pabst Brewing Company: The History of an American Business* (New York: New York University Press, 1948); Ronald Plavchan, "A History of Anheuser-Busch" (Ph.D. diss., St. Louis University, 1969); and Peter Park, "The Supply Side of Drinking: Alcohol Production and Consumption in the United States before Prohibition," *Contemporary Drug Problems* 12 (1985): 473–509.

16. On the relationship of saloons and drink to serious social problems, see Clark, *Deliver Us from Evil;* Timberlake, *Prohibition and the Progressive Movement;* Kerr, *Organized for Prohibition;* Odegard, *Pressure Politics;* Epstein, *The Politics of Domesticity;* and Bordin, *Women and Temperance.*

17. Ade, *The Old-Time Saloon*, 28; Popham, "The Social History of the Tavern," 278.

18. Ade, *The Old-Time Saloon*, 31. This paragraph is based on descrip-

tions of saloon interiors in Calkins, *Substitutes for the Saloon*, 7–19; Melendy, "The Saloon in Chicago (Part 1)," 293, 296, 299; Ade, *The Old-Time Saloon*, 28–33, 35; London, *John Barleycorn*, 21–23; Moore, "The Social Value of the Saloon," 4–5, 10; and Stevens, "Saloon Days," 266.

19. On the alleged brewery-saloonkeeper conspiracy to entrap workers, see Marcus T. Reynolds, "The Housing of the Poor in American Cities," *Publications of the American Economic Association* 8 (March and May, 1893): 33 (quotation); and Robert Bagnell, *Economic and Moral Aspects of the Liquor Business* (New York: Columbia University Press, 1911), 21–22. Police precinct surveys of saloon patronage in Chicago and Boston are discussed in Calkins, *Substitutes for the Saloon*, 353; and Andrew Sinclair, *Era of Excess: A Social History of the Prohibition Movement* (New York: Harper and Row, 1962), 77. For maps illustrating the density of saloons in working-class districts in San Francisco and New York, see the gallery following page 156. Regarding the number of saloons in operation, Jon M. Kingsdale observes that "by 1897 licensed liquor dealers in the United States numbered over 215,000, and unlicensed 'blind pigs' or 'blind tigers' represented an estimated 50,000 additional outlets. . . . Cities without effective restrictions were deluged with saloons: in 1915 New York had over 10,000 licensed saloons, or one for every 515 persons; Chicago had one licensed saloon for every 335 residents; Houston had one for every 298 persons; San Francisco had a saloon for every 218 persons." For additional discussion of saloon statistics as well as the police precinct surveys, see Kingsdale, "The 'Poor Man's Club': Social Functions of the Urban Working-Class Saloon," *American Quarterly* 25 (October 1973): 472–89 (quotation, 472–73).

20. Melendy, "The Saloon in Chicago (Part 1)," 293.

21. Rosenzweig, *Eight Hours for What We Will*, 58; Howe, *Confessions of a Reformer*, 54; Ade, *The Old-Time Saloon*, 41. The saloon's role as a semi-public institution is a principal theme throughout Duis, *The Saloon;* see especially 3–5.

22. *Oxford English Dictionary*, 1888–1928 ed. and 1933 supplement, s.v. "regular." See especially adjective branch A, senses 1a (church) and 7 (army), and subject branch D, senses 2a (church) and 4a (army).

23. Regarding medical regulars, see *Oxford English Dictionary*, 1888–1928 ed. and 1933 supplement, s.v. "regular," especially adjective branch A, sense 6b, and subject branch D, sense 4b. Regarding political regulars, see Mencken, *The American Language*, 168, 169. The athletic regular is defined as "a player on an athletic team who usually starts every game" in *Webster's New Collegiate Dictionary*, 3d ed., s.v. "regular," noun, sense 1d.

24. Regarding business regulars, see *Oxford English Dictionary*, 1888–1928 ed. and 1933 supplement, s.v. "regular," especially adjective branch A, sense 3d; and subject branch D, sense 4c.

25. For a discussion of commercial enterprises with a social dimension, see Ray Oldenberg, *The Great Good Place: Cafés, Coffee Shops, Community Centers, Beauty Parlors, General Stores, Bars, Hangouts and How They Get You Through the Day* (New York: Paragon House, 1989). See also Eric Wolf, "Kinship, Friendship, and Patron-Client Relations in Complex Societies," in

Michael Banton, ed., *The Social Anthropology of Complex Societies* (London: Tavistock, 1966), 10; and Wilbert E. Moore, *Social Change* (Englewood Cliffs, N.J.: Prentice-Hall, 1963), 107–8.

26. Ade, *The Old-Time Saloon*, 105. Ade uses the term "regulars" on pp. 31, 47, 101, 102, 103, 105, 107, 114, 117, 144; the "regular trade," p. 52; a "regular place," p. 130; "regular headquarters," p. 58; "dependable patrons," p. 104; the "dependables," p. 147; "steady patrons," p. 72; and "one of the boys," p. 58.

27. "The Experience and Observations of a New York Saloon-Keeper as Told by Himself," *McClure's Magazine* 32 (January 1909): 306. This saloon-keeper uses the phrase "my regular patrons" on pp. 308, 311; "the best regular patrons," p. 306; "a regular customer," p. 308; "my regular customers," p. 308; and refers to one customer who "came in regularly every afternoon," p. 311.

28. Melendy, "The Saloon in Chicago (Part 1)," 297. Melendy cites the saloonkeepers' use of the term "steady regulars" on p. 297; he himself uses the term "regular customers" on p. 306; and he notes that "each saloon has about the same constituency night after night," p. 293. Further references appear in Calkins, *Substitutes for the Saloon*. He uses the term "regular patrons," p. 6; "regular customer," p. 17; and "saloon habitué," p. 13. He also notes that "many saloons have their own constituency," p. 9, and he refers to saloon patronage as "uniform," p. 20.

29. Regarding the traits of conviviality and commonality, see *Oxford English Dictionary*, 1933 supplement, s.v. "regular," especially adjective branch A, sense 6d, which defines a "*regular fellow* (or *guy*)" as "an agreeable, ordinary, or sociable person." See also Wentworth and Flexner, eds., *Dictionary of American Slang*, 425, adjective, sense 1, which defines "regular" as "[a]greeable, pleasant, friendly, fair; in the same social and economic class and with the same general intellectual level and interests as the speaker; liked by the speaker and not considered superior or inferior to him; generally liked by and acceptable to one's fellow men." Both the aforementioned sources cite the following illustration from F. Scott Fitzgerald, *This Side of Paradise* (1920; reprint, New York: Charles Scribner's Sons, 1970), 47: "I know I'm not a regular fellow, yet I loathe anybody else that isn't." Fitzgerald was referring not to barlife, but rather to collegiate life at Princeton University, and specifically to protagonist Amory Blaine's desire to fit in with the ordinary students versus his impulse to stand aloof as their intellectual superior. Yet the parallel to bargoers and their desire to be "one of the boys" is clear, and Fitzgerald's use of this sense of the term "regular" in print in 1920 indicates its prior currency in oral speech.

30. Ferdinand Tönnies, *Fundamental Concepts of Sociology: Gemeinschaft and Gesellschaft*, trans. Charles P. Loomis (1887; reprint, New York: American Books Company, 1940), 42, 74, 270–72. For a thorough discussion of Tönnies's theories and their application to United States history, see Thomas Bender, *Community and Social Change in America* (New Brunswick, N.J.: Rutgers University Press, 1978), especially 17–18, 33–34.

31. Tönnies, *Fundamental Concepts of Sociology*, 272. Other social theorists

note these two fundamental polarities in human relationships, though they adopt different terminologies and approaches to the issue. For example, such relationships are described by Charles Horton Cooley as "primary" versus "secondary;" by Max Weber as "communal" versus "associative;" by Émile Durkheim as "mechanical" versus "organic;" by Talcott Parsons as "affective" versus "affectively neutral;" by Robert Redfield as "folk" versus "urban;" and by Eric Wolf as "expressive" versus "instrumental." For more on their respective theories, see Charles H. Cooley, *Social Organization: A Study of the Larger Mind* (New York: Scribner's, 1909); Max Weber, *The Theory of Social and Economic Organization,* trans. Talcott Parsons (New York: Free Press, 1964); Émile Durkheim, *The Division of Labor in Society,* trans. George Simpson (New York: Free Press, 1933); Talcott Parsons, *The Social System* (New York: Free Press, 1951); Robert Redfield, *The Folk Culture of Yucatan* (Chicago: University of Chicago Press, 1941) and *The Little Community* (Chicago: University of Chicago Press, 1955); and Eric Wolf, "Kinship, Friendship, and Patron-Client Relations in Complex Societies." For more discussion of these social analysts and their theories of social interaction, see Bender, *Community and Social Change in America,* 8–35, 135–37; and Robert A. Nisbet, *The Quest for Community* (New York: Oxford University Press, 1953), chap. 4.

32. Bender, *Community and Social Change in America,* 137, 43 (quotations).

33. Bender, *Community and Social Change in America,* 141–42. Bender remarks on the dualistic nature of the ethnic mutual aid association (p. 96) as well as the trade union (pp. 115, 120, 136).

34. The most complete articulation of the "alternative culture" theory of saloons appears in Rosenzweig, *Eight Hours for What We Will,* 17–18, 36, 48, 58, 60–61, 64, 183–87, 223. Rosenzweig argues, "An ethic of mutuality and reciprocity that differed from the market exchange mentality of the dominant society prevailed within the barroom," so that while itself "a product of a commercializing society, the saloon became a refuge for values implicitly hostile to such a society" (pp. 58, 61). Kathy Peiss, citing Rosenzweig's study, similarly asserts that saloons "comprised an alternative culture to competitive individualism and the values of the marketplace" in *Cheap Amusements: Working Women and Leisure in Turn-of-the-Century New York* (Philadelphia: Temple University Press, 1986), 25. Jon Kingsdale also characterizes the working-class saloon as an "alternative" to Protestant capitalist values in "The 'Poor Man's Club,'" 472, 484, 487–89. Perry Duis acknowledges duality in saloon culture, though he is more interested in the saloon as a "semipublic institution" and emphasizes the issue of defining and controlling public versus private space in the urban setting. Nevertheless, he sometimes portrays saloon culture as a pocket of resistance to modern marketplace trends in *The Saloon,* 274, 289–92, 295. On the concepts of "alternative" and "oppositional" cultures, see Raymond Williams, "Base and Superstructure in Marxist Cultural Theory," *New Left Review* 82 (November–December 1973): 3–16.

CHAPTER TWO: *"Gender, Age, and Marital Status"*

1. Raymond Calkins, *Substitutes for the Saloon* (Boston: Houghton Mifflin, 1901), 9.

2. The categories of "occupational," "ethnic," and "neighborhood" saloons are employed in William Kornblum, *Blue Collar Community* (Chicago: University of Chicago Press, 1974), 77–81. Significantly, however, Kornblum asserts, "Relatively few of the taverns are pure types; rather, they reflect tendencies to specialize in function. Except for the few taverns which become the headquarters for specific ethnic segments in the neighborhood, or which become the after-work meeting place for specific occupational groups, the distinction between occupational and ethnic taverns should be thought of as a continuum, for many tavern owners consciously attempt to increase their business by appealing to a diversity of neighborhood groups" (p. 80). These three categories also appear in Roy Rosenzweig, *Eight Hours for What We Will: Workers and Leisure in an Industrial City, 1870–1920* (New York: Cambridge University Press, 1983), 53 and 58, though he notes, "Not all saloons fit neatly into these categories. Some Worcester saloons could be simultaneously 'neighborhood,' 'occupational,' and 'ethnic.' For example, Michael Taylor, a former English carpet weaver, located his saloon on Cambridge Street in the midst of fellow countrymen who worked in the nearby carpet mills" (p. 53). I also employed these categories in my early work on saloons, before it became apparent to me that they were not adequate tools of analysis for my purposes. See Madelon Powers, "Faces Along the Bar: Urban Saloon Regulars and Their World, 1880–1920" (Publication F101, Alcohol Research Group, School of Public Health, University of California, Berkeley, July 1979).

3. For an account of the preindustrial apprenticeship system and the artisan ethic of mutuality and pride in craft, see the early chapters of Sean Wilentz, *Chants Democratic: New York City and the Rise of the American Working Class, 1788–1850* (New York: Oxford University Press, 1984); Mary H. Blewett, *Men, Women, and Work: Class, Gender, and Protest in the New England Shoe Industry, 1780–1914* (Urbana: University of Illinois Press, 1988); Paul Faler, *Mechanics and Manufacturers in the Early Industrial Revolution: Lynn, Massachusetts, 1780–1860* (Albany: State University of New York Press, 1981); Alan Dawley, *Class and Community: The Industrial Revolution in Lynn* (Cambridge: Harvard University Press, 1976); Charles G. Steffen, *The Mechanics of Baltimore: Workers and Politics in the Age of Revolution, 1763–1812* (Urbana: University of Illinois Press, 1984); Howard B. Rock, *Artisans of the New Republic: The Tradesmen of New York City in the Age of Jefferson* (New York: New York University Press, 1979); Ronald L. Filippelli, *Labor in the USA: A History* (New York: McGraw-Hill, 1984); and W. J. Rorabaugh, *The Craft Apprentice: From Franklin to the Machine Age in America* (New York: Oxford University Press, 1986). On workplace sociability and the easy intermixture of labor and drink in the preindustrial era, see Herbert G. Gutman, *Work, Culture, and Society in Industrializing America* (New York: Knopf, 1976); W. J. Rorabaugh, *The Alcoholic Republic: An American Tradition* (New

York: Oxford University Press, 1979); Ian Tyrrell, *Sobering Up: From Temperance to Prohibition in Antebellum America, 1800–1860* (Westport, Conn.: Greenwood Press, 1979); Jill Siegel Dodd, "The Working Classes and the Temperance Movement in Ante-Bellum Boston," *Labor History* 19 (1973): 510–31; Mark Lender and James Kirby Houston, *Drinking in America: A History* (New York: Free Press, 1982); and Harry Gene Levine, "The Discovery of Addiction: Changing Conceptions of Habitual Drunkenness in America," *Journal of Studies on Alcohol* 39 (January 1978): 143–74.

4. On the role of the expanding market economy in undermining the apprenticeship system and sharpening class differences in patterns of work, residence, religion, and other areas, see David M. Gordon, Richard Edwards, and Michael Reich, *Segmented Work, Divided Workers: The Historical Transformation of Labor in the United States* (New York: Cambridge University Press, 1982); Susan E. Hirsch, *Roots of the American Working Class: The Industrialization of Crafts in Newark, 1800–1860* (Philadelphia: University of Pennsylvania Press, 1978); Bruce Laurie, *Working People of Philadelphia, 1800–1850* (Philadelphia: Temple University Press, 1980); Paul E. Johnson, *A Shopkeeper's Millennium: Society and Revivals in Rochester, New York, 1815–1837* (New York: Hill and Wang, 1978); Christine Stansell, *City of Women: Sex and Class in New York, 1789–1860* (Urbana: University of Illinois Press, 1986); Thomas Dublin, *Women at Work: The Transformation of Work and Community in Lowell, Massachusetts, 1826–1860* (New York: Columbia University Press, 1979); Jonathan Prude, *The Coming of Industrial Order: Town and Factory Life in Rural Massachusetts, 1810–1860* (New York: Cambridge University Press, 1983); Faler, *Mechanics and Manufacturers;* Dawley, *Class and Community;* and Wilentz, *Chants Democratic.*

5. The impact of large-scale industrialization on employer-worker relations in the late nineteenth and early twentieth centuries and the efforts of workers to resist exploitation and change are discussed in David Montgomery, *Workers' Control in America: Studies in the History of Work, Technology, and Labor Struggles* (New York: Cambridge University Press, 1979); Montgomery, *The Fall of the House of Labor: The Workplace, the State, and American Labor Activism, 1865–1925* (New York: Cambridge University Press, 1987); Daniel T. Rodgers, *The Work Ethic in Industrial America, 1850–1920* (Chicago: University of Chicago Press, 1978); Daniel J. Walkowitz, *Worker City, Company Town: Iron- and Cotton-Worker Protest in Troy and Cohoes, New York, 1855–84* (Urbana: University of Illinois Press, 1978); Steven J. Ross, *Workers on the Edge: Work, Leisure, and Politics in Industrializing Cincinnati, 1788–1890* (New York: Columbia University Press, 1985); Brian Greenberg, *Worker and Community: Response to Industrialization in a Nineteenth-Century American City, Albany, New York, 1850–1884* (Albany: State University of New York Press, 1985); Richard J. Oestreicher, *Solidarity and Fragmentation: Working People and Class Consciousness in Detroit, 1875–1900* (Urbana: University of Illinois Press, 1986); Frances G. Couvares, *The Remaking of Pittsburgh: Class and Culture in an Industrializing City, 1877–1919* (Albany: State University of New York Press, 1984); John T. Cumbler, *Working-Class Com-*

munity in Industrial America: Work, Leisure, and Struggle in Two Industrial Cities, 1860–1930 (Westport, Conn.: Greenwood Press, 1979); and David Brody, *Steelworkers in America: The Non-Union Era* (Cambridge: Harvard University Press, 1960). The struggle of particular unions to cope with the deteriorating condition of wage labor after 1870 is analyzed in Leon Fink, *Workingmen's Democracy: The Knights of Labor and American Politics* (Urbana: University of Illinois Press, 1983); Stuart Kaufman, *Samuel Gompers and the Origins of the American Federation of Labor, 1848–1896* (Westport, Conn.: Greenwood Press, 1973); Nick Salvatore, *Eugene V. Debs: Citizen and Socialist* (Urbana: University of Illinois Press, 1972); Sidney Lens, *The Labor Wars: From the Molly Maguires to the Sitdowns* (Garden City, N.Y.: Doubleday, 1973); Melvin Dubofsky, *We Shall Be All: A History of the Industrial Workers of the World* (Urbana: University of Illinois Press, 1988); and Michael Kazin, *Barons of Labor: The San Francisco Building Trades and Union Power in the Progressive Era* (Urbana: University of Illinois Press, 1987).

6. For discussions of middle-class male gender roles and concepts of manliness, see Elliott J. Gorn, *The Manly Art: Bare-Knuckle Prize Fighting in America* (Ithaca, N.Y.: Cornell University Press, 1986); E. Anthony Rotundo, *American Manhood: Transformations in Masculinity from the Revolution to the Modern Era* (New York: Basic Books, 1993) and Rotundo, "Body and Soul: Changing Ideals of Middle-Class Manhood," *Journal of Social History* 16 (summer 1983): 23–38; Mark C. Carnes and Clyde Griffen, eds., *Meanings for Manhood: Constructions of Masculinity in Victorian America* (Chicago: University of Chicago Press, 1990); Mark C. Carnes, *Secret Ritual and Manhood in Victorian America* (New Haven, Conn.: Yale University Press, 1989); Peter Stearns, *Be a Man! Males in Modern Society* (New York: Holmes and Meier, 1979); Charles E. Rosenberg, "Sexuality, Class and Role in Nineteenth-Century America," in Joseph and Elizabeth Pleck, eds., *The American Man* (Englewood Cliffs, N.J.: Prentice-Hall, 1980); Joe L. Dubbert, *A Man's Place: Masculinity in Transition* (Englewood Cliffs, N.J.: Prentice-Hall, 1979); Peter G. Filene, *Him/Her/Self: Sex Roles in Modern America*, 2d ed. (Baltimore: Johns Hopkins University Press, 1986); John D' Emilio and Estelle B. Freedman, *Intimate Matters: A Social History of Sexuality* (New York: Harper and Row, 1988); and Joseph H. Pleck, *The Myth of Masculinity* (Cambridge: Massachusetts Institute of Technology Press, 1984). Victorian advice manuals on proper male conduct are examined in Michael Gordon, "The Ideal Husband as Depicted in the Nineteenth-Century Marriage Manual," in Pleck and Pleck, *The American Man*, 145–57. For Horatio Alger's description of Ragged Dick's "manly" qualities, see *Ragged Dick and Struggling Upward*, ed. Carl Bode (1868 and 1890; reprint, New York: Penguin, 1985), especially p. 7. On popular images of the successful Victorian businessman, see John G. Cawelti, *Apostles of the Self-Made Man: Changing Concepts of Success in America* (Chicago: University of Chicago Press, 1965) and Matthew Josephson, *The Robber Barons: The Great American Capitalists, 1861–1901* (New York: Harcourt, Brace and World, 1934).

7. Jack London, *John Barleycorn: Alcoholic Memoirs* (1913; reprint, ed. John Sutherland, New York: Oxford University Press, 1989), 104. On working-class male gender roles and conceptions of manliness, see references in this chapter, note 6, to Gorn, Carnes and Griffen, Stearns, Rosenberg, Rotundo, Dubbert, and Filene. See also Michael T. Isenberg, *John L. Sullivan and His America* (Urbana: University of Illinois Press, 1988); Roy Rosenzweig, *Eight Hours for What We Will: Workers and Leisure in an Industrial City, 1870–1920* (New York: Cambridge University Press, 1983); Rupert Wilkinson, *American Tough: The Tough-Guy Tradition and American Character* (Westport, Conn.: Greenwood Press, 1984); and David G. Pugh, *Sons of Liberty: The Masculine Mind in Nineteenth-Century America* (Westport, Conn.: Greenwood Press, 1983). On the concept of "manly honor" in its virile, aggressive sense, see Elliott J. Gorn, "Gouge and Bite, Pull Hair and Scratch: The Social Significance of Fighting in the Southern Backcountry," *American Historical Review* 90 (February 1985): 18–42; and Edward L. Ayers, *Vengeance and Justice: Crime and Punishment in the Nineteenth-Century American South* (New York: Oxford University Press, 1986).

8. The manly code of honor that prevailed in working-class saloons is further discussed in Gorn, *The Manly Art*, 133–36, 252.

9. Travis Hoke, "Corner Saloon," *American Mercury* 22 (March 1931): 311; *New York Times*, 8 September 1892; Elliott West, *The Saloon on the Rocky Mountain Mining Frontier* (Lincoln: University of Nebraska Press, 1979), 45–47; Ade, *The Old-Time Saloon: Not Wet, Not Dry—Just History* (New York: Long and Smith, 1931), 31–32; Hutchins Hapgood, "McSorley's Saloon," *Harper's Weekly* 58 (25 October 1913): 15. See also Joseph Mitchell, "McSorley's Wonderful Saloon," in *Up in the Old Hotel* (New York: Pantheon Books, 1992), 1–370 (especially pp. 3–22). McSorley's is still in operation in New York City. In a recent letter to me, Doug Mitchell of the University of Chicago Press provided an interesting observation on McSorley's fate in the modern era. He wrote, "My best friend, then a student at Columbia, took me drinking there back around 1964–65, when no women were allowed, and the sport was for women to sneak in dressed as men." When I myself visited the famous resort one afternoon in 1992 (sans disguise), it appeared to have been largely taken over by the college crowd. For John Sloan's depiction of McSorley's in 1912, see the gallery following page 156.

Turning now to the subject of barside urination troughs, though they are no longer in use (thankfully!), they can be seen in several establishments in or near the French Quarter in New Orleans, including the Ernst Cafe, 600 S. Peters Street; the Acme Oyster and Seafood House, 724 Iberville Street; and the Country Flame Restaurant and Bar, 620 Iberville Street. My friend Jennie Lou Mintz informs me that a urination trough also survives at Jus-Dale's Bar, Route 73, Skippack, Pennsylvania.

10. For discussion of gender-related bar speech, poems, songs, and art, see Kathy Peiss, *Cheap Amusements: Working Women and Leisure in Turn-of-the-Century New York* (Philadelphia: Temple University Press, 1986), 20, 27; Ade, *The Old-Time Saloon*, 32, 110, 113, 118–33; Hoke, "Corner Saloon,"

314, 322; "The Experience and Observations of a New York Saloon-Keeper as Told by Himself," *McClure's Magazine* 32 (January 1909): 310; and Hapgood, "McSorley's Saloon," 58.

11. Christine Stansell, *City of Women: Sex and Class in New York, 1789–1860* (Urbana: University of Illinois Press, 1986), 20–21, 29–30, 79 (quotations, 20 and 29). On the origin and implications of traditional as well as modern conceptions of women, see Josephine Donovan, *Feminist Theory: The Intellectual Traditions of American Feminism*, rev. ed. (New York: Continuum, 1992).

12. Hoke, "Corner Saloon," 315. On the attitude of women in the temperance movement toward the saloon and its negative consequences for male-female relations, see Barbara Leslie Epstein, *The Politics of Domesticity: Women, Evangelism, and Temperance in Nineteenth-Century America* (Middletown, Conn.: Wesleyan University Press, 1981); Ruth Bordin, *Women and Temperance: The Quest for Power and Liberty, 1873–1900* (Philadelphia: Temple University Press, 1980).

13. For positive as well as negative conceptions of women in saloon lore, see sources listed in this chapter, note 10.

14. Women's activities in the street culture and leisure institutions of the late nineteenth and early twentieth centuries have been examined in Peiss, *Cheap Amusements;* Peiss, "'Charity Girls' and City Pleasures: Historical Notes on Working-Class Sexuality, 1880–1920," in Ellen Carol DuBois and Vicki L. Ruiz, *Unequal Sisters: A Multicultural Reader in U.S. Women's History* (New York: Routledge, 1990), 157–66; Lewis A. Erenberg, *Steppin' Out: New York Nightlife and the Transformation of American Culture, 1890–1930* (Westport, Conn.: Greenwood Press, 1981); Robert C. Allen, *Horrible Prettiness: Burlesque and American Culture* (Chapel Hill: University of North Carolina Press, 1991); Karen Trahan Leathem, "'A Carnival According to Their Own Desires: Gender and Mardi Gras in New Orleans, 1870–1941'" (Ph.D. diss., University of North Carolina, Chapel Hill, 1994); Gunther Barth, *City People: The Rise of Modern City Culture in Nineteenth-Century America* (New York: Oxford University Press, 1980); Mary E. Odem, *Delinquent Daughters: Protecting and Policing Adolescent Female Sexuality in the United States, 1885–1920* (Chapel Hill: University of North Carolina Press, 1995); Beth L. Bailey, *From Front Porch to Back Seat: Courtship in Twentieth-Century America* (Baltimore: Johns Hopkins University Press, 1988); and Ellen Rothman, *Hands and Hearts: A History of Courtship in America* (New York: Harvard University Press, 1987). Contemporary accounts of working-class women and urban amusements include Dorothy Richardson, "The Long Day: The Story of a New York Working Girl" (1905) in *Women at Work,* ed. William L. O'Neill (Chicago: Quadrangle, 1972); Clara Laughlin, *Work-a-Day Girl: A Study of Some Present-Day Conditions* (1913; reprint, New York: Ayer Press, 1974); and Frances Donovan, *The Woman Who Waits* (1920; reprint, New York: Ayer Press, 1974).

15. The side door was also used by men wishing to avoid public notice, as well as by all those wishing to purchase alcohol illegally in defiance of

Sunday closing laws. See Ade, *The Old- Time Saloon,* 20 (illustration), 28; and Jacob A. Riis, *How the Other Half Lives: Studies among the Tenements in New York* (1890; reprint, New York: Hill and Wang, 1957), 13, 92.

16. "The Experience . . . of a New York Saloon-Keeper," 305, 311; Robert Wood, *City Wilderness* (Boston: Houghton Mifflin, 1901), 72; Peiss, *Cheap Amusements,* 28–29; Mrs. Robert Bradford, a Philadelphia social worker, cited in Andrew Sinclair, *Era of Excess: A Social History of the Prohibition Movement* (New York: Harper and Row, 1962), 407.

17. Riis, *How the Other Half Lives,* 29, 124, 163, 171; Rosenzweig, *Eight Hours for What We Will,* 40–45; Perry R. Duis, *The Saloon: Public Drinking in Chicago and Boston, 1880–1920* (Urbana: University of Illinois Press, 1983), 61–64, 106–7; Margaret F. Byington, *Homestead: The Households of a Mill Town* (1910; reprint, Pittsburgh: University of Pittsburgh Press, 1974), 109, 131–32, 136, 149–50, 155–56, 173; London, *John Barleycorn,* 37–40; Calkins, *Substitutes for the Saloon,* 49.

18. Richardson, "The Long Day," 287; Royal L. Melendy, "The Saloon in Chicago (Part 1)," *American Journal of Sociology* 6 (November 1900): 295, 300, and Melendy, "The Saloon in Chicago (Part 2)," *American Journal of Sociology* 6 (January 1901): 441, 445–47; Peiss, *Cheap Amusements,* 51–55, 59, 90–93 and Peiss, "'Charity Girls,'" 159; Thomas J. Noel, *The City and the Saloon: Denver, 1858–1916* (Lincoln: University of Nebraska Press, 1982), 56–57; David Brundage, "The Producing Classes and the Saloon: Denver in the 1880s," *Labor History* 26 (winter 1985): 32; Upton Sinclair, *The Jungle* (1906; reprint, New York: New American Library, 1960), 7–25; Kornblum, *Blue Collar Community,* 23.

19. Calkins, *Substitutes for the Saloon,* 15–19; Richardson, "The Long Day," 257–59; Peiss, *Cheap Amusements,* 28, 53; Duis, *The Saloon,* 186.

20. As Timothy Gilfoyle points out, however, New York after 1896 became a place where saloons and prostitution were very intimately associated indeed with the advent of "Raines Law hotels." He explains, "In 1896, State Senator John Raines introduced and saw passed what he envisioned to be the most far-reaching piece of antivice legislation in nineteenth-century New York." New Yorkers soon discovered, however, that "the Raines Law of 1896, originally intended to suppress prostitution and regulate liquor sales, had done the reverse. The new legislation prohibited Sunday liquor sales everywhere except in hotels with ten or more beds. Instead of reducing the number of saloons, the law simply increased the number of brothels, and saloons subdivided rear and upper parts of their buildings into cheap 'hotel rooms' for illegitimate use." See Timothy J. Gilfoyle, *City of Eros: New York City, Prostitution, and the Commercialization of Sex, 1790–1920* (New York: Norton, 1992), 243–48, 303–6.

21. Calkins, *Substitutes for the Saloon,* 15; Melendy, "The Saloon in Chicago (Part 1)," 299. The callous treatment to which prostitutes in saloon back rooms were sometimes subjected is poignantly depicted in a Eugene O'Neill play set in 1906. See O'Neill, *Ah, Wilderness!* (1933), act 3, sc. 1 and act 4, sc. 3. For discussions of prostitution in the saloon era, see Gilfoyle, *City of Eros;* Thomas C. Mackey, *Red Lights Out: A Legal History of*

Prostitution, Disorderly Houses and Vice Districts, 1870–1917 (New York: Garland, 1987); Ruth Rosen, *The Lost Sisterhood: Prostitution in America, 1900–1918* (Baltimore: Johns Hopkins University Press, 1982); Ruth Rosen and Sue Davidson, eds., *The Maime Papers* (Bloomington: Indiana University Press, 1985); Jacqueline Baker Barnhart, *The Fair But Frail: Prostitution in San Francisco, 1849–1900* (Reno: University of Nevada Press, 1986); Mark Thomas Connelly, *The Response to Prostitution in the Progressive Era* (Chapel Hill: University of North Carolina Press, 1980); Edward J. Bristow, *Prostitution and Prejudice: The Jewish Fight Against White Slavery, 1870–1939* (New York: Schocken Books, 1982); and David J. Pivar, *Purity Crusade: Sexual Morality and Social Control, 1868–1900* (Westport, Conn.: Greenwood Press, 1973). For popular histories of vice districts which include rollicking anecdotes about prostitutes' activities, see Herbert Asbury, *The French Quarter: An Informal History of the New Orleans Underworld* (New York: Knopf, 1938) and Asbury, *The Barbary Coast: An Informal History of the San Francisco Underworld* (New York: Knopf, 1933).

22. Rosenzweig, *Eight Hours for What We Will*, 40–45; Duis, *The Saloon*, 2, 49; M. E. Ravage, *An American in the Making: The Life Story of an Immigrant* (New York: Harper and Brothers, 1917), 124–34; Kornblum, *Blue Collar Community*, 76.

23. London, *John Barleycorn*, 24–25; Hoke, "Corner Saloon," 320.

24. "The Experience . . . of a New York Saloon-Keeper," 311; Stevens, "Saloon Days," 267. The impact of the saloon's male ethic on young boys is also noted in London, *John Barleycorn*, 24–25; Ade, *The Old-Time Saloon*, 6; and Jon M. Kingsdale, "The 'Poor Man's Club': Social Functions of the Urban Working-Class Saloon," *American Quarterly* 25 (October 1973): 485. Regarding the harmful effects of the saloon on impressionable youth, see Norman H. Clark, *Deliver Us from Evil: An Interpretation of American Prohibition* (New York: Norton, 1976); James H. Timberlake, *Prohibition and the Progressive Movement, 1900–1920* (New York: Atheneum, 1970); and Peter H. Odegard, *Pressure Politics: The Story of the Anti- Saloon League* (New York: Columbia University Press, 1928).

25. Riis, *How the Other Half Lives*, 161–62; "The Experience . . . of a New York Saloon-Keeper," 311; Melendy, "The Saloon in Chicago (Part 1)," 300. On the role of urban children in supplementing working-class families' incomes in the nineteenth century, see David Nasaw, *Children of the City: At Work and at Play* (New York: Doubleday, 1985); Christine Stansell, *City of Women: Sex and Class in New York, 1789–1860* (Urbana: University of Illinois Press, 1986), 50–54, 193–216; Charles Loring Brace, *The Dangerous Classes of New York and Twenty Years' Work among Them* (1880, 3d ed.; reprint, New York: Patterson Smith, 1967); and Jane Addams, *The Spirit of Youth and the City Streets* (1909; reprint, Urbana: University of Illinois Press, 1972).

26. Riis, *How the Other Half Lives*, 162. Upton Sinclair made this lurid story the fate of young Stanislovas, a character in *The Jungle* (1906; reprint, New York: New American Library, 1960), 286, 289.

27. Henry Clay Work's "Come Home, Father" appears in Emmet G.

Coleman, ed., The *Temperance Songbook* (New York: American Heritage Press, 1971), 68–69. An excerpt from a similar temperance song, "The Drunkard's Lone Child," is quoted in Ade, *The Old-Time Saloon*, 132. Timothy Shay Arthur's novel, *Ten Nights in a Barroom* (1854), as well as enduringly popular temperance plays such as William Henry Smith's *The Drunkard, or the Fallen Saved* (1844) and Charles Hoyt's *A Temperance Town* (1893), are examined in Russel Nye, *The Unembarrassed Muse: The Popular Arts in America* (New York: Dial, 1970), 29–30, 153–54. Arthur's novel was also adapted to film in the early twentieth century. For more discussion of the antisaloon theme in songs, stories, poems, and plays, see Odegard, *Pressure Politics*, 64–67.

28. The impact of alcoholism on the family during the saloon era is considered in Clark, *Deliver Us from Evil;* Timberlake, *Prohibition and the Progressive Movement;* and Odegard, *Pressure Politics*. The phenomenon of "exoteric" lore is discussed in William Hugh Jansen, "The Esoteric-Exoteric Factor in Folklore," in Alan Dundes, ed., *The Study of Folklore* (Englewood Cliffs, N.J.: Prentice-Hall, 1965), 43–51.

29. Parodies of "Come Home, Father" are discussed in Sigmund Spaeth, *A History of Popular Music* (New York: Random House, 1948), 157; an interview with John Burris Powers (my father, now deceased), in Davis, California, 11 March 1982; and Stevens, "Saloon Days," 264. For more information on American vaudeville and burlesque, see Albert F. McLean, *American Vaudeville as Ritual* (Lexington: University of Kentucky Press, 1965); Robert C. Allen, *Vaudeville and Film, 1895–1915: A Study in Media Interaction* (New York: Arno Press, 1980) and Allen, *Horrible Prettiness;* Barth, *City People;* and Nye, *The Unembarrassed Muse*.

30. Powers interview, Davis, California, 11 March 1982. On the presence of newspapers in saloons, see Calkins, *Substitutes for the Saloon*, 11; and Melendy, "The Saloon in Chicago (Part 1)," 292–93. The increasing size and importance of urban newspapers in the saloon era are discussed in Barth, *City People*, 58–109; Nye, *The Unembarrassed Muse*, passim; and John Rickard Betts, "Sporting Journalism in Nineteenth-Century America, 1819–1900," *American Quarterly* 5 (spring 1953): 39–56.

31. Calkins, *Substitutes for the Saloon*, 47; Melendy, "The Saloon in Chicago (Part 1)," 295. A photograph of the recreational equipment in one Chicago saloon back room appears in E. C. Moore, "The Social Value of the Saloon," *American Journal of Sociology* 3 (July 1897): 9, 11. For an analysis of street corner gangs, see F. Whyte, Jr., *Street Corner Society*, 2d ed. (Chicago: University of Chicago Press, 1955); Joseph F. Kett, *Rites of Passage: Adolescence in America, 1790 to the Present* (New York: Basic Books, 1977); John F. Gillis, *Youth and History* (New York: Oxford University Press, 1981); Nasaw, *Children of the City;* and Addams, *The Spirit of Youth and the City Streets*.

32. Riis, *How the Other Half Lives*, 38; "The Experience . . . of a New York Saloon-Keeper," 307. On the relationship between saloons and the criminal element, see Duis, *The Saloon*, 230–73; and George Kibbe Turner, "The City of Chicago: A Study of the Great Immoralities," *McClure's Magazine* 28

(April 1907): 575 – 92. For more discussion of urban gangs, violence, and crime in the saloon era, see Joseph M. Hawes, *Children in Urban Society: Juvenile Delinquency in Nineteenth-Century America* (New York: Oxford University Press, 1971); Robert M. Mennel, *Thorns and Thistles: Juvenile Delinquents in the United States, 1825 – 1940* (Hanover, N.H.: University Press of New England, 1973); Roger Lane, *Violent Death in the City: Suicide, Accident, and Murder in Nineteenth-Century Philadelphia* (Cambridge: Harvard University Press, 1979); and Eric H. Monkkonen, *The Dangerous Class: Crime and Poverty in Columbus, Ohio, 1860 – 1885* (Cambridge: Harvard University Press, 1975).

33. Settlement Director Harry Ward's work with the "Keybosh Club" is described in Melendy, "The Saloon in Chicago (Part 2)," 444. Regarding the significance of the term "kibosh," see Harold Wentworth and Stuart Berg Flexner, eds., *Dictionary of American Slang*, 2d ed., supplemented (New York: Thomas Y. Crowell, 1975), 302. According to the editors, the phrase "to put the kibosh on" is of Turkish origin and dates to circa 1850. In the opinion of H. L. Mencken, however, the phrase is probably of Yiddish origin and dates back to at least 1836. See Mencken, *The American Language*, 4th ed., abridged (New York: Knopf, 1980), 309, 704; also see William and Mary Morris, *Dictionary of Word and Phrase Origins* (New York: Harper and Row, 1962), 204. For more examples of boys' gangs redeemed from the saloon's influence, see Jacob A. Riis, *A Ten Years' War: An Account of the Battle with the Slum in New York* (1900; reprint, Freeport, N.Y.: Books for Libraries Press, 1969), 162 – 63, 220, 229 – 30. Further information on the settlement movement is available in Mina Carson, *Settlement Folk: Social Thought and the American Settlement Movement, 1885 – 1930* (Chicago: University of Chicago Press, 1990); John H. Ehrenreich, *The Altruistic Imagination: A History of Social Work and Social Policy in the United States* (Ithaca, N.Y.: Cornell University Press, 1985); Judith A. Trolander, *Professionalism and Social Change: From the Settlement House Movement to Neighborhood Centers, 1886 to the Present* (New York: Columbia University Press, 1987); and Allen F. Davis, *Spearheads of Reform: The Social Settlements and the Progressive Movement, 1890 – 1914* (New York: Oxford University Press, 1967).

34. A Keybosh Club member, quoted in Melendy, "The Saloon in Chicago (Part 2)," 444.

35. Pleasure club names are cited in Peiss, *Cheap Amusements*, 59. Peiss notes, "Militia and volunteer fire companies . . . provided structure for the bachelor subcultures of the mid-nineteenth century. By the 1890s, gangs and social clubs had taken over this function" (p. 56). Pleasure club statistics and clubroom activities are discussed in Calkins, *Substitutes for the Saloon*, 49 – 50; and Melendy, "The Saloon in Chicago (Part 2)," 441.

36. Calkins, *Substitutes for the Saloon*, 54 – 54. For a discussion of the impact of marriage on young men previously caught up in "the search for action," see Herbert J. Gans, *The Urban Villagers: Group and Class in the Life of Italian-Americans* (New York: Free Press, 1962), 64 – 73.

37. Kingsdale, "The 'Poor Man's Club,'" 479, 482 – 83; Melendy, "The Saloon in Chicago (Part 2)," 437 – 39.

38. Horatio Alger, *Ragged Dick and Mark, the Match Boy* (1868 and 1867; reprint, New York: Collier Books, 1962), 224 (quotation is from the second novel); Gutman, *Work, Culture, and Society*, 30; Moody Morton, "Man's Inhumanity to Man Makes Thousands Mourn," *The Trestle Board* 4 (April 1897): 178 (quotation). *The Trestle Board* is a publication of the Freemasons.

39. Byington, *Homestead*, 108–9.

40. Frank Norris, *McTeague: A Story of San Francisco* (1899; reprint, New York: New American Library, 1964), 150.

41. Byington, *Homestead*, 113.

42. Statistics are from U.S. Bureau of the Census, *Population, 1920,* 2 (Washington, D.C., 1922), 117, 119, 387; and Gilfoyle, *City of Eros*, 238. According to the census, males also slightly outnumbered females in the general population from 1870 to 1920. The proportion of males increased from 50.6 percent in 1870 to 51.2 percent in 1890, reaching a peak of 51.5 percent in 1910 and then decreasing to 51.0 percent in 1920 (pp. 103–4, 107, 383).

43. John Koren, *Economic Aspects of the Liquor Problem* (Boston: Houghton Mifflin, 1899), 219; Kingsdale, "The 'Poor Man's Club,'" 486; Thomas F. Babor and Barbara G. Rosenkrantz, "Public Health, Public Morals, and Public Order: Social Science and Liquor Control in Massachusetts, 1880–1916," in Susanna Barrows and Robin Room, eds., *Drinking: Behavior and Belief in Modern History* (Berkeley: University of California Press, 1991), 282. Babor and Rosenkrantz's principal sources for their conclusion include John Koren, *Economic Aspects;* Gallus Thomann, *Real and Imaginary Effects of Intemperance: A Statistical Sketch* (New York: U.S. Brewers' Association, 1884); and Horace G. Wadlin, *Relation of the Liquor Traffic to Pauperism, Crime, and Insanity* (Boston: Wright and Potter, 1896). On the difficult life of the unattached boardinghouse lodger, see Mark Peel, "On the Margins: Lodgers and Boarders in Boston, 1860–1900," *Journal of American History* 72 (March 1986): 813–34.

44. Duis, *The Saloon,* 152. Words and music to "Crape on the Door of the Licensed Saloon" appear in Coleman, *The Temperance Songbook,* 63. "The theme of this song," Coleman notes, "was suggested by learning of crape being on the door of a licensed saloon in the southeast section of Washington, D.C." On the history of the jazz funeral in New Orleans, see Jack V. Buerkle and Danny Barker, *Bourbon Street Black: The New Orleans Black Jazzman* (New York: Oxford University Press, 1973), 187–97; and Leroy Ostransky, *Jazz City: The Impact of Our Cities on the Development of Jazz* (Englewood Cliffs, N.J.: Prentice-Hall, 1978), 11–12. The people of New Orleans still observe the tradition of the jazz funeral. In the early 1990s, for example, I participated in a jazz funeral parade in honor of Dizzie Gillespie which began and ended at Trombone Shorty's Bar in the Treme district of New Orleans, as well as another in 1996 for local jazzman Pudd Brown which began and ended at the Palm Court Jazz Cafe in the French Quarter. The latter featured an elegant funeral carriage drawn by black-plumed horses. Other descriptions of barroom regulars honoring the memory of a departed comrade are found in Ade, *The Old-Time Saloon,* 112; and London, *John Barleycorn,* 130.

45. Susan Lebsock, *The Free Women of Petersburg: Status and Culture in a Southern Town, 1784–1860* (New York: Norton, 1984), 17; Nancy Woloch, *Women and the American Experience*, 2d ed. (New York: McGraw-Hill, 1994), 84. Lawrence Stone traces the ideal of companionate marriage to the English upper classes in the eighteenth century in *Family, Sex, and Marriage in England, 1500–1800* (London: Weidenfeld and Nicolson, 1977), chap. 8. After the Revolutionary War, American upper-class families began to embrace the companionate ideal in tandem with notions about "republican motherhood" and the importance of rearing virtuous, civic-minded offspring to guide the new republic. The ideal then filtered down to the American bourgeoisie in the nineteenth century and finally to the American public at large after World War I. It should be noted, however, that many marriages comprised an uneasy blend of traditional and companionate ideals, with older notions about male prerogative and dominance often resurfacing in times of familial conflict. Further, the companionate ideal could itself be a source of discord and unhappiness when husbands and wives discovered they had irreconcilable differences of opinion on important family matters. For more discussion of these subjects, see Woloch, *Women and the American Experience*, 84–88, 93, 271, 408–10, 471; Lebsock, *Free Women of Petersburg*, xviii, 17–18, 28–35, 51–53, 110; Carl N. Degler, *At Odds: Women and the Family in America from the Revolution to the Present* (New York: Oxford University Press, 1980), chaps. 7–13; and Daniel Scott Smith, "Family Limitation, Sexual Control, and Domestic Feminism in Victorian America," in Mary S. Hartman and Lois Banner, eds., *Clio's Consciousness Raised: New Perspectives on the History of Women* (New York: Harper and Row, 1974), 119–36.

46. For more discussion of the contrasts between traditional and companionate marriage, see Woloch, *Women and the American Experience*, 84–88, 93, 271, 408–10, 471; Lebsock, *Free Women of Petersburg*, xviii, 17–18, 28–35, 51–53, 110; Degler, *At Odds*, chaps. 7–13; and Smith, "Family Limitation," 119–36. George E. Bevans's 1913 survey of workingmen's leisure habits in New York city is discussed in Peiss, *Cheap Amusements*, 15, 30.

47. Kingsdale, "The 'Poor Man's Club,'" 486–87; Elsa Marek, quoted in Peiss, *Cheap Amusements*, 27. On domestic violence, see Linda Gordon, *Heroes of Their Own Lives: The Politics and History of Family Violence, Boston, 1880–1960* (New York: Viking/Penguin, 1988); and Elizabeth Pleck, *Domestic Tyranny: The Making of American Social Policy Against Family Violence from Colonial Times to the Present* (New York: Oxford University Press, 1987).

48. On female culture and space, see Carroll Smith-Rosenberg, "The Female World of Love and Ritual," *Signs* 1 (Autumn 1975): 1–29.

49. Ade, *The Old-Time Saloon*, 101.

CHAPTER THREE: *"Occupation, Ethnicity, and Neighborhood"*

1. Raymond Calkins, *Substitutes for the Saloon* (Boston: Houghton Mifflin, 1901), 9–10.

2. On the importance of occupational, ethnic, and neighborhood ties as

linking factors among saloon regulars, see Roy Rosenzweig, *Eight Hours for What We Will: Workers and Leisure in an Industrial City, 1870–1920* (New York: Cambridge University Press, 1983), 53, 58; and William Kornblum, *Blue Collar Community* (Chicago: University of Chicago Press, 1974), 77–81.

3. For more discussion of factors affecting workers' sense of solidarity, see David Montgomery, *Workers' Control in America: Studies in the History of Work, Technology, and Labor Struggles* (New York: Cambridge University Press, 1979) and Montgomery, *The Fall of the House of Labor: The Workplace, the State, and American Labor Activism, 1865–1925* (New York: Cambridge University Press, 1987); Daniel T. Rodgers, *The Work Ethic in Industrial America, 1850–1920* (Chicago: University of Chicago Press, 1978); Daniel J. Walkowitz, *Worker City, Company Town: Iron-and Cotton-Worker Protest in Troy and Cohoes, New York, 1855–84* (Urbana: University of Illinois Press, 1978); Steven J. Ross, *Workers on the Edge: Work, Leisure, and Politics in Industrializing Cincinnati, 1788–1890* (New York: Columbia University Press, 1985); Brian Greenberg, *Worker and Community: Response to Industrialization in a Nineteenth-Century American City, Albany, New York, 1850–1884* (Albany: State University of New York Press, 1985); Richard J. Oestreicher, *Solidarity and Fragmentation: Working People and Class Consciousness in Detroit, 1875–1900* (Urbana: University of Illinois Press, 1986); and Frances G. Couvares, *The Remaking of Pittsburgh: Class and Culture in an Industrializing City, 1877–1919* (Albany: State University of New York Press, 1984).

4. "The Experience and Observations of a New York Saloon-Keeper as Told by Himself," *McClure's Magazine* 32 (January 1909): 306. Fridays were also designated as paydays by many companies. For example, the Carnegie Steel Company in Homestead, Pennsylvania, paid workers every other Friday. Despite this fact, Saturday night was still an occasion for heavy drinking in Homestead, with workers relying on Sundays to provide time to sober up. See Margaret F. Byington, *Homestead: The Households of a Mill Town* (1910; reprint, Pittsburgh: University of Pittsburgh Press, 1974), 37, 149; see also the photograph of a large crowd in front of a Homestead saloon on Saturday night in the gallery following page 156. On changing concepts of time, the separation of work and leisure, and the standardization of daily and weekly work cycles, see Michael O'Malley, *Keeping Watch: A History of Time in America* (New York: Penguin, 1990); David Landes, *Revolution in Time: Clocks and the Making of the Modern World* (Cambridge: Harvard University Press, 1983); Eviatar Zerubavel, *The Seven Day Circle: The History and Meaning of the Week* (New York: Free Press, 1985); Rodgers, *The Work Ethic in Industrial America;* Joseph S. Zeisel, "The Workweek in American Industry, 1850–1956," in Eric Larrabee and Rolf Myersohn, eds., *Mass Leisure* (Glencoe, Ill.: Free Press, 1958), 145–53; and Herbert G. Gutman, *Work, Culture, and Society in Industrializing America* (New York: Knopf, 1976), 68–74.

5. Perry R. Duis, *The Saloon: Public Drinking in Chicago and Boston, 1880–1920* (Urbana: University of Illinois Press, 1983), 233–34, 282; Rosenzweig, *Eight Hours for What We Will,* 117, 119–20; "The Experience . . . of a New York Saloon-Keeper," 306. For more discussion of Sunday closing ordinances, see Gerald W. McFarland, *Mugwumps, Morals,*

and Politics, 1884–1920 (Amherst: University of Massachusetts Press, 1975), 95–101.

6. Benjamin Franklin, quoted in Gutman, *Work, Culture, and Society,* 5. As Gutman notes, "To the owners of competitive firms . . . Blue Monday proved the laziness and obstinacy of craftsmen. . . . To the skilled cooper, the long weekend symbolized a way of work and life filled with almost ritualistic meanings. Between 1843 and 1893, compromise between such conflicting interests was hardly possible" (p. 38).

7. Edward W. Bemis, "Attitude of the Trade Unions Toward the Saloon," in Calkins, *Substitutes for the Saloon,* appendix I, 305 (Lennon quotation), 306 (Bemis quotation). For more discussion of the Saint Monday tradition in western culture, see Douglas A. Reid, "The Decline of Saint Monday, 1766–1876," *Past and Present* 71 (1976): 76–101; E. P. Thompson, "Time, Work-Discipline, and Industrial Capitalism," *Past and Present,* 38 (1967): 56–97; Sidney Pollard, "Factory Discipline in the Industrial Revolution," *Economic History Review,* 2d ser., 16 (1963): 254–71; and James Roberts, "Drink and Industrial Work Discipline in Nineteenth-Century Germany," *Journal of Social History* 15 (1982): 25–38.

8. "The Experience . . . of a New York Saloon-Keeper," 303; George Ade, *The Old-Time Saloon: Not Wet, Not Dry—Just History* (New York: Long and Smith, 1931), 59–60, 106. On the daily rhythm of saloon business, see also Travis Hoke, "Corner Saloon," *American Mercury* 22 (March 1931): 320.

9. M. E. Ravage, *An American in the Making: The Life Story of an Immigrant* (New York: Harper and Brothers, 1917), 129; Royal L. Melendy, "The Saloon in Chicago (Part 2)," *American Journal of Sociology* 6 (January 1901): 496; "The Experience . . . of a New York Saloon-Keeper," 303.

10. "Editorial," *Light* 4 (7 November 1891): 291, quoted in Rosenzweig, *Eight Hours for What We Will,* 51; Raymond Spaulding, quoted in Kathy Peiss, *Cheap Amusements: Working Women and Leisure in Turn-of-the-Century New York* (Philadelphia: Temple University Press, 1986), 17–18; George Kibbe Turner, "The City of Chicago: A Study of the Great Immoralities," *McClure's Magazine* 28 (April 1907): 578.

11. Calkins, *Substitutes for the Saloon,* 20; contemporary observer, quoted in Peiss, *Cheap Amusements,* 16. For discussion of the impact of saloongoing on working-class families, see Ruth Bordin, *Women and Temperance: The Quest for Power and Liberty, 1873–1900* (Philadelphia: Temple University Press, 1980); Barbara Leslie Epstein, *The Politics of Domesticity: Women, Evangelism, and Temperance in Nineteenth-Century America* (Middletown, Conn.: Wesleyan University Press, 1981); James H. Timberlake, *Prohibition and the Progressive Movement, 1900–1920* (New York: Atheneum, 1970); and Norman H. Clark, *Deliver Us from Evil: An Interpretation of American Prohibition* (New York: Norton, 1976). Regarding workers' household budgets in South Chicago, New York City, and Homestead, Pennsylvania, see Kornblum, *Blue Collar Community,* 75; Peiss, *Cheap Amusements,* 23; and Byington, *Homestead,* 154–55.

12. Regarding the flouting of official closing times and the bribing of po-

lice, see Frederic C. Howe, *Confessions of a Reformer* (1925; reprint, New York: Quadrangle, 1967), 50–52; Duis, *The Saloon*, 234; and Ade, *The Old-Time Saloon*, 8 (quotation), 144. "Neighborhood saloons were open from seven or eight in the morning till one o'clock at night and for seven days a week, unless there were a Sunday closing law, in which case one used the Family Entrance," according to Hoke, "Corner Saloon," 320.

13. "The Experience . . . of a New York Saloon-Keeper," 308; Peter Roberts, *Anthracite Coal Communities* (New York: Macmillan, 1904), 233. See also Byington, *Homestead*, 37, 149; and Gutman, *Work, Culture, and Society*, 36–39.

14. W. J. Rorabaugh, *The Alcoholic Republic: An American Tradition* (New York: Oxford University Press, 1979), pp. 149–51, 167–69. For an account of communal binges as periodic public rituals in the antebellum era, see Susan G. Davis, *Parades and Power: Street Theater in Nineteenth-Century Philadelphia* (Philadelphia: Temple University Press, 1986).

15. While Rorabaugh has provided a convincing argument regarding why the communal binge pattern gained popularity in the early 1800s, his assertions regarding its virtual demise by mid-century seem far less tenable. In his view, the group drinking spree had come under so much fire from temperance advocates by 1840 that "it had almost disappeared, while the private, solo binge remained" (Rorabaugh, *The Alcoholic Republic*, 169). Though it does appear that the communal binge was not as common after 1840 as it once had been, the numerous accounts of postbellum payday sprees (as well as other communal drinking occasions discussed elsewhere in the present study) make it difficult indeed to embrace the contention that the phenomenon had "almost disappeared" by the saloon era. Instead, the communal binge pattern continued among working-class saloongoers well into the early twentieth century.

16. Calkins, *Substitutes for the Saloon*, 9.

17. An Italian saloon regular in New York, quoted in Peiss, *Cheap Amusements*, 18; Calkins, *Substitutes for the Saloon*, 9; John Koren, *Economic Aspects of the Liquor Problem* (Boston: Houghton Mifflin, 1899), 238.

18. H. L. Mencken, *Happy Days, 1880–1892* (New York: Knopf, 1940), 254–55; Jon M. Kingsdale, "The 'Poor Man's Club': Social Functions of the Urban Working-Class Saloon," *American Quarterly* 25 (October 1973): 482; Melendy, "The Saloon in Chicago (Part 2)," 438; Bemis, "Attitude of Trade Unions Toward the Saloon," in Calkins, *Substitutes for the Saloon*, appendix I, 307, 311–12.

19. Among the best analyses of the drinking patterns of European immigrants in the saloon period are Rosenzweig, *Eight Hours for What We Will*, 35–64, 93–126, and Duis, *The Saloon*, 143–71. On Mexican drinking patterns, see William and Claudia Madsen, "The Cultural Structure of Mexican Drinking Behavior," *Quarterly Journal of Studies on Alcohol* 30 (September 1969): 701–18. The Chinese are sometimes discussed in saloon literature, though most often in connection with opium dens rather than barrooms. See, for example, Jacob A. Riis, *How the Other Half Lives: Studies among the Tenements in New York* (1890; reprint, New York: Hill and Wang, 1957), 69–

76, and Thomas J. Noel, *The City and the Saloon: Denver, 1858–1916* (Lincoln: University of Nebraska, 1982), 28–29. For an assessment of Native-American drinking, see Nancy O. Lurie, "The World's Oldest On-Going Protest Demonstration: North American Indian Drinking Patterns," *Pacific Historical Review* 40 (1971): 311–32. On African-American drinking, see Denise Herd, "The Paradox of Temperance: Blacks and the Alcohol Question in Nineteenth-Century America," in Susanna Barrows and Robin Room, eds., *Drinking: Behavior and Belief in Modern History* (Berkeley: University of California Press, 1991), 354–75; Noel, *The City and the Saloon*, 26–28; and Duis, *The Saloon*, 157–60.

On the more general subject of immigration during the saloon period, perceptive overviews are available in John Bodnar, *The Transplanted: A History of Immigrants in Urban America* (Bloomington: University of Indiana Press, 1985) and Milton M. Gordon, *Assimilation in American Life: The Role of Race, Religion and National Origins* (New York: Oxford University Press, 1964). Regarding the migration experiences of specific ethnic groups, many excellent scholarly works have appeared in recent decades. On Mexicans, for example, see Ricardo Romo, *East Los Angeles: History of a Barrio* (Austin: University of Texas Press, 1983); Albert Camarillo, *Chicanos in a Changing Society: From Mexican Pueblos to American Barrios in Santa Barbara and Southern California, 1848–1930* (Cambridge: Harvard University Press, 1979); and Mario T. Garcia, *Desert Immigrants: The Mexicans of El Paso, 1880–1920* (New Haven, Conn.: Yale University Press, 1981). On Asians, see Roger Daniels, *Asian America: Chinese and Japanese in the United States Since 1850* (Seattle: University of Washington Press, 1988); Sucheng Chan, *Asian Americans: An Interpretive History* (Boston: Twayne, 1991); and Ronald Takaki, *Strangers from a Different Shore: A History of Asian Americans* (New York: Penguin, 1990). On African Americans, see James Grossman, *Land of Hope: Chicago Black Southerners and the Great Migration* (Chicago: University of Chicago Press, 1989); Peter Gottlieb, *Making Their Own Way: Southern Blacks' Migration to Pittsburgh* (Urbana: University of Illinois Press, 1987); and Joe William Trotter, Jr., *Black Milwaukee: The Making of an Industrial Proletariat, 1915–1945* (Urbana: University of Illinois Press, 1985). On the Irish, see R. A. Burchell, *The San Francisco Irish, 1848–1880* (Berkeley: University of California Press, 1981); Timothy J. Meagher, ed., *From Paddy to Studs: Irish American Communities in the Turn of the Century Era, 1880–1920* (Westport, Conn.: Greenwood Press, 1986); and Lawrence J. McCaffrey, Ellen Skerrett, Michael F. Funchion, and Charles Fanning, eds., *The Irish in Chicago* (Urbana: University of Illinois Press, 1987). On Italians, see Dino Cinel, *From Italy to San Francisco: The Immigrant Experience* (Stanford, Calif.: Stanford University Press, 1982); Donna R. Gabaccia, *From Sicily to Elizabeth Street: Housing and Social Change among Italian Immigrants, 1880–1930* (Albany: State University of New York Press, 1983); and Gary Mormino, *Immigrants on the Hill: Italian Immigrants in St. Louis, 1882–1982* (Urbana: University of Illinois Press, 1986). On Jews, Poles, and other eastern Europeans, see Steven Hertzberg, *Strangers within the Gate City: The Jews of Atlanta, 1845–1915* (Philadelphia: Jewish Publication Society of America, 1978); John Bukowcyzk, *And My*

Children Did Not Know Me: A History of Polish America (Bloomington: University of Indiana Press, 1987); and Eva Morawska, *For Bread with Butter: Life Worlds of East Central Europeans in Johnstown, Pa., 1890–1940* (New York: Cambridge University Press, 1986). Scholarly works adopting a comparative approach include Judith E. Smith, *Family Connections: A History of Italian and Jewish Immigrant Lives in Providence, Rhode Island, 1900–1940* (Albany: State University of New York Press, 1985); John Bodnar, Roger Simon, and Michael Weber, *Lives of Their Own: Blacks, Italians and Poles in Pittsburgh, 1900–1960* (Urbana: University of Illinois Press, 1982); and Joseph Barton, *Peasants and Strangers: Italians, Romanians, and Slovaks in an American City, 1900–1950* (Cambridge: Harvard University Press, 1975).

20. On the "old" versus "new" immigration from Europe, see Gordon, *Assimilation in American Life.* For scholarly works illustrating the phenomenon of "chain migration," see Rudolph J. Vecoli, "The Formation of Chicago's 'Little Italies,'" *Journal of American Ethnic History* 2 (spring 1983): 5–20; Rudolph J. Vecoli and Suzanne M. Sinke, eds., *A Century of European Migrations, 1830–1930* (Urbana: University of Illinois Press, 1991); Caroline Golab, *Immigrant Destinations* (Philadelphia: Temple University Press, 1977); John Bodnar, *Immigration and Industrialization: Ethnicity in an American Mill Town, 1870–1940* (Pittsburgh: University of Pittsburgh Press, 1977); and John W. Briggs, *An Italian Passage: Immigrants to Three American Cities, 1890–1930* (New Haven, Conn.: Yale University Press, 1978).

21. Rudolph J. Vecoli, "The Formation of Chicago's 'Little Italies,'" 5–20. See also Vecoli, "*Contadini* in Chicago: A Critique of *The Uprooted,*" *Journal of American History* 51 (December 1964): 404–16.

22. For a comparison of how Italian and Jewish immigrants in Providence, Rhode Island in the early 1900s gradually built a new sense of national self-identification through mutual aid societies and other activities, see Smith, *Family Connections,* 132–41, 164–70.

23. Kornblum, *Blue Collar Community,* 23.

24. A Croatian church leader, quoted in Kornblum, *Blue Collar Community,* 23. Unfortunately, renewed hostilities in the late twentieth century among Croatians, Serbians, and Slovenians in Europe have no doubt undermined the rapprochement of these groups in America in the early 1900s. For a discussion of Italian and Sicilian immigrants in Boston who gradually blended into a community of Italian Americans from the early 1900s to the 1950s, see Herbert J. Gans, *The Urban Villagers: Group and Class in the Life of Italian-Americans* (New York: The Free Press, 1962), 18. On Italian saloon-keepers' efforts to aid and unite the Italian immigrant community in Denver in the early 1900s, see Noel, *The City and the Saloon,* 60–62.

25. On Irish fraternal organizations utilizing saloons in Denver, see David Brundage, "The Producing Classes and the Saloon: Denver in the 1880s," *Labor History* 26 (winter 1985): 32, and Noel, *The City and the Saloon,* 56–57. On fraternal organizations and social clubs utilizing saloons in New York, see Peiss, *Cheap Amusements,* 89–90.

26. On ethnic drinking preferences, see Rorabaugh, *The Alcoholic Republic,* 109–10, and Duis, *The Saloon,* 146–53; on ethnic free lunches, see Ade,

The Old-Time Saloon, 35, 45–47, and Captain Fred Klebingat, *Memories of the Audiffred Building and the Old City Front* (San Francisco: Mills Ryland Company with the National Maritime Museum, 1983), 10; on ethnic newspapers, see Duis, *The Saloon*, 147, 149; on ethnic music, see Ade, *The Old-Time Saloon*, 119–20, and Kornblum, *Blue Collar Community*, 78; on ethnic games, see Robert A. Woods, ed., *Americans in Process: A Settlement Study* (Boston: Houghton Mifflin, 1902), 206; on St. Patrick's Day, see Ade, *The Old-Time Saloon*, 113–14; and on Irish drinking customs in general, see Richard Stivers, *The Hair of the Dog: Irish Drinking and American Stereotype* (University Park: Pennsylvania University Press, 1976).

27. Noel, *The City and the Saloon*, 65; Calkins, *Substitutes for the Saloon*, 11; Woods, *Americans in Process*, 201; *Skandinavia*, 25 May 1888, quoted in Rosenzweig, *Eight Hours for What We Will*, 50–51.

28. Ade, *The Old-Time Saloon*, 15, 158; F. D. Laubach, cited in Robert E. Popham, "The Social History of the Tavern," in *Research Advances in Alcohol and Drug Problems*, ed. Yedy Israel et al., vol. 4 (New York: Plenum Press, 1978), 288 n; Koren, *Economic Aspects*, 228.

29. Koren, *Economic Aspects*, 228; Ade, *The Old-Time Saloon*, 114; F. D. Laubach, cited in Popham, "The Social History of the Tavern," 287, 288 n; Melendy, "The Saloon in Chicago (Part 2)," 436; E. C. Moore, "One Aspect of Vice," *American Journal of Sociology* 6 (July 1900): 11; Francis G. Peabody, ed., *The Liquor Problem: A Summary of the Investigations Conducted by the Committee of Fifty* (Boston: Houghton Mifflin, 1905), 116; Riis, *How the Other Half Lives*, 45. For an in-depth study of how drinking traditions have contributed to the formation of an ethnic stereotype of the Irish, see Stivers, *The Hair of the Dog*.

30. Will Irwin, "The American Saloon," *Collier's Weekly* 41 (16 May 1908): 10; see also Irwin, "More about 'Nigger Gin,'" *Collier's Weekly* 41 (15 August 1908): 28, 30. In Irwin's article of 16 May, he cited the example of Margaret Lear of Shreveport, a white teenager who was raped and murdered in March 1905 when her walk home from high school "took her past a negro saloon." According to Irwin, "Out of that saloon staggered a negro named Coleman—'drunken,' ran the testimony at the trial, 'on cheap gin.'" Such inexpensive gin was produced by northern distilleries and "sold in the low dives of all the black belt from the Carolinas to Louisiana and Mississippi." Many of the gin bottles featured titles suggestive of the aphrodisiacal properties of the contents, such as "Devil's Island Endurance Gin." Irwin noted that after the drunken Coleman had allegedly assaulted and shot Margaret Lear, "this black brute" was nearly killed by local whites made "temporary brutes" by their outrage. In the end, the Louisiana militia had to be called in to protect Coleman from a lynching until he could be legally executed nine days later. Examples of this derogatory African-American stereotype abound. For instance, see the remark that drink "changed so many negroes into sensual hyenas" in Dr. and Mrs. Wilbur F. Crafts, *World Book of Temperance*, 3d ed. (Washington, D.C.: International Reform Bureau, 1911), 58. See also Alabama Congressman Richmond Hobson's assertion before the House of Representatives in 1914 that "[l]iquor will actually make a brute out of a

negro, causing him to commit unnatural crimes. The effect is the same on the white man, though the white man being further evolved it takes longer time to reduce him to the same level." Hobson, quoted in Andrew Sinclair, *Era of Excess: A Social History of the Prohibition Movement* (New York: Harper and Row, 1962), 29. Despite the alarmist claims of white southerners, there were relatively few habitual drunkards among rural southern blacks in the late nineteenth century, according to the data collected in Koren, *Economic Aspects,* 163, 176–77. For more discussion on this subject, see Herd, "The Paradox of Temperance," 364–68.

31. Timberlake, *Prohibition and the Progressive Movement,* 120 (Mitchell quotation), 121. For more discussion of the role of saloons and liquor in the Atlanta race riot, see Charles Crowe, "Racial Violence and Social Reform: Origins of the Atlanta Riot of 1906," *Journal of Negro History* 53 (July 1968): 234–56.

32. J. F. Clark, quoted in Timberlake, *Prohibition and the Progressive Movement,* 30; Herbert Asbury, *The French Quarter: An Informal History of the New Orleans Underworld* (New York: Alfred A. Knopf, 1938), 388, 393; Riis, *How the Other Half Lives,* 117 (quotation), 118, 161.

33. Sinclair argues that because of white southerners' "fear of the Negro," they had "a special use for prohibition . . . as a method of controlling one of his means of self-assertion. Liquor sometimes gave the Negro the strength to repudiate his inferior status. . . . Thus the Negro should be prevented from drinking alcohol." Further, Sinclair maintains that "Negro and white leaders could join together in the crusade against the saloon, which often incited the racial fears of the South to the pitch of murder." See Sinclair, *Era of Excess,* 29–32. Regarding the number of saloons in the South versus the city of Chicago, see Duis, *The Saloon,* 28. For more discussion of blacks and southern prohibition, see Herd, "The Paradox of Temperance," 354–75.

34. Liquor sales in general stores in the early nineteenth century are discussed in Rorabaugh, *The Alcoholic Republic,* 17–18, 231, 235–36. The rise of the saloon and the corresponding demise of the home-based kitchen barroom are examined in Rosenzweig, *Eight Hours for What We Will,* 40–45. *New York Tribune* editor Horace Greeley's encounter with a liquor-selling grocer in frontier Kansas in the mid-nineteenth century is described in Elliott West, *The Saloon on the Rocky Mountain Mining Frontier* (Lincoln: University of Nebraska Press, 1979), 11–12. African-American leader Frederick Douglass's condemnation of the "liquor license of the road corners grocery" in the South in the 1880s is cited in Herd, "The Paradox of Temperance," 375 n. 73. McTeague's favorite hangout, Joe Frenna's corner grocery with a small barroom in the back, is described in Frank Norris, *McTeague: A Story of San Francisco* (1899; reprint, New York: New American Library, 1964), 14, 110–16. The function of general stores and other "Main Street" businesses as social centers is discussed in Ray Oldenberg, *The Great Good Place: Cafés, Coffee Shops, Community Centers, Beauty Parlors, General Stores, Bars, Hangouts and How They Get You Through the Day* (New York: Paragon House, 1989), 110–18.

35. U. M. Bland, of Bland's Detective Agency, Richmond, to E. J.

Richardson, Superintendent of the Virginia Anti-Saloon League, Richmond, "SUBJECT—Whiskey Selling in Hanover County, Virginia," January, 1905, in Virginia Anti-Saloon League Papers, Folder 7, Manuscripts Department, Swem Library, College of William and Mary, Williamsburg, Virginia. I am indebted to Richard F. Hamm in the History Department of the State University of New York, Albany, for bringing this document to my attention. For the Anti-Saloon League's more typically negative portrayal of blacks, saloons, and drinking, see Peter H. Odegard, *Pressure Politics: The Story of the Anti-Saloon League* (New York: Columbia University Press, 1928), 62–63; and Timberlake, *Prohibition and the Progressive Movement*, 119–23.

36. Bland to Richardson, Virginia Anti-Saloon Papers, Folder 7.

37. Herd, "The Paradox of Temperance," 370; Lawrence W. Levine, *Black Culture and Black Consciousness: Afro-American Folk Thought from Slavery to Freedom* (New York: Oxford University Press, 1977), 200–205. For an analysis of the evolution and role of African-American music in cities, see Burton W. Peretti, *The Creation of Jazz: Music, Race and Culture in Urban America* (Urbana: University of Illinois Press, 1992). On the movement of rural African Americans to southern cities in the nineteenth century, see Peter Rachleff, *Black Labor in the South: Richmond, Virginia, 1865–1890* (Philadelphia: Temple University Press, 1984); Howard Rabinowitz, *Race Relations in the Urban South, 1865–1890* (New York: Oxford University Press, 1978); John Blassingame, *Black New Orleans, 1860–1880* (Chicago: University of Chicago Press, 1973); and George C. Wright, *Life Behind a Veil: Blacks in Louisville, Kentucky, 1865–1930* (Baton Rouge: Louisiana State University Press, 1985). On the "Great Migration" of African Americans to northern cities in the nineteenth and early twentieth centuries, see Grossman, *Land of Hope;* Gottlieb, *Making Their Own Way;* and Trotter, *Black Milwaukee.* Other useful studies include Kenneth Kusmer, *A Ghetto Takes Shape: Black Cleveland, 1870–1930* (Urbana: University of Illinois Press, 1976); Darre Bigham, *We Ask Only a Fair Trial: The Black Community of Evansville, Indiana, 1812–1945* (Bloomington: Indiana University Press, 1987); and Richard W. Thomas, *Life for Us Is What We Make It: Building Black Community in Detroit, 1915–1945* (Bloomington: Indiana University Press, 1992).

38. Levine, *Black Culture and Black Consciousness*, 189.

39. For incidents of racial discrimination and violence in barrooms in Chicago, see Duis, *The Saloon*, 157–58; in Denver, see Noel, *The City and the Saloon*, 26–28.

40. Duis, *The Saloon*, 159–60; Levine, *Black Culture and Black Consciousness*, 200–205.

41. John Marshall Barker, *The Saloon Problem and Social Reform* (Boston: Everett Press, 1905), 49–50. For more discussion of reformers' attitudes toward immigrants and saloons, see Timberlake, *Prohibition and the Progressive Movement*, 115–19; and Noel, *The City and the Saloon*, 65–66.

42. The phenomenon of regional subgroups engaging in an intermediate stage of integration as Italian Americans, Jewish Americans, and the like—as well as the tendency of native-born Americans automatically to group immigrants by their nationality or race—are topics discussed in Smith, *Family*

Connections, 132–41, 164–70. See also Thomas Archdeacon, *Becoming American: An Ethnic History* (New York: Free Press, 1983); Thomas Brown, *Irish-American Nationalism, 1870–1890* (Philadelphia: Lippincott, 1966); Alexander DeConde, *Half-Bitter, Half-Sweet: An Excursion into Italian-American History* (New York: Scribner, 1971); and Michael R. Weisser, *A Brotherhood of Memory: Jewish Landsmanshaftn in the New World* (New York: Basic Books, 1985).

43. Howard P. Chudacoff and Judith E. Smith, eds., *The Evolution of American Urban Society*, 4th ed. (Englewood Cliffs, N.J.: Prentice-Hall, 1994), 136; Royal L. Melendy, "The Saloon in Chicago (Part 1)," *American Journal of Sociology* 6 (November 1900): 291, 294. For further discussion of ethnicity and neighborhood, see Kathleen Neils Conzen, "Immigrants, Immigrant Neighborhoods and Ethnic Identity: Historical Issues," *Journal of American History* 66 (December 1979): 603–15; and Howard P. Chudacoff, "A New Look at Ethnic Neighborhoods: Residential Dispersion and the Concept of Visibility in a Medium-Sized City," *Journal of American History* 60 (June 1973): 76–93.

44. Calkins, *Substitutes for the Saloon*, 9. For more discussion of the relationship between neighborhood saloons and political machines, see Duis, *The Saloon*, 114–42. On the interdependence of machine politicians and working-class voters, see John M. Allswang, *Bosses, Machines, and Urban Voters: An American Symbiosis* (Port Washington, N.Y.: Kennikat Press, 1977). Contemporary accounts of machine politicians' activities in workers' districts appear in Lincoln Steffens, *The Shame of the Cities* (1904; reprint, New York: Hill and Wang, 1957) and William L. Riordon, *Plunkitt of Tammany Hall: A Series of Very Plain Talks on Very Practical Politics*, ed. Terrence J. McDonald (1905; reprint, Boston: Bedford Books, 1994).

45. Riis, *How the Other Half Lives*, 159; Gail Levin, "Edward Hopper: The Art and the Artist" (pamphlet, Whitney Museum of American Art, New York 1981), 3. A photograph of Hopper's painting is included in the gallery following page 156. The striking contrast between saloons and their surrounding neighborhoods is emphasized in Marcus T. Reynolds, "The Housing of the Poor in American Cities," *Publications of the American Economic Association* 8 (March and May, 1893): 33. On housing conditions in urban working-class districts in the late nineteenth and early twentieth centuries, see Stanley K. Schultz, *Constructing Urban Culture: American Cities and City Planning, 1800–1920* (Philadelphia: Temple University Press, 1989); Thomas J. Philpott, *The Slum and the Ghetto: Neighborhood Deterioration and Middle-Class Reform, Chicago 1880–1930* (New York: Oxford University Press, 1978); and Roy Lubove, *The Progressives and the Slums: Tenement House Reform in New York City, 1890–1917* (Pittsburgh: University of Pittsburgh Press, 1962). On workers' efforts to enhance their housing conditions through decoration and spatial organization, see Lizabeth A. Cohen, "Embellishing a Life of Labor: An Interpretation of American Working-Class Homes, 1885–1915," *Journal of American Culture* 3 (winter 1980): 752–75.

46. Jack London, *John Barleycorn: Alcoholic Memoirs* (1913; reprint, ed. John Sutherland, New York: Oxford University Press, 1989), 41, 53, 130;

"The Experience . . . of a New York Saloon-Keeper," 303, 308 (quotation), 309–11; Ravage, *An American in the Making,* 129.

47. Odegard, *Pressure Politics,* 45; John A. Garraty, *The New Commonwealth, 1877–1890* (New York: Harper and Row, 1968), 202; Roberts, *Anthracite Coal Communities,* 236.

48. Roberts, *Anthracite Coal Communities,* 236; Calkins, *Substitutes for the Saloon,* 11; London, *John Barleycorn,* 50–54; E. C. Moore, "The Social Value of the Saloon," *American Journal of Sociology* 3 (July 1897): 8.

49. London, *John Barleycorn,* 124–25; Melendy, "The Saloon in Chicago (Part 1)," 297.

50. Moody Morton, "Man's Inhumanity to Man Makes Countless Thousands Mourn," *The Trestle Board* 4 (April 1897): 180. The *Trestle Board* is a publication of the Freemasons.

51. "The Experience . . . of a New York Saloon-Keeper," 310–11.

52. On the relationship between neighborhood saloons and political machines, see Duis, *The Saloon,* 114–42. On popular participation in politics as a form of collective social ritual, see Michael E. McGerr, *The Decline of Popular Politics: The American North, 1865–1928* (New York: Oxford University Press, 1986); and Jean H. Baker, *Affairs of Party: The Political Culture of Northern Democrats in the Mid-Nineteenth Century* (Ithaca, N.Y.: Cornell University Press, 1983). On the more general subject of urban machines, patronage, and reform efforts, see M. Craig Brown and Charles N. Halaby, "Machine Politics in America, 1870–1945," *Journal of Interdisciplinary History* 17 (winter 1987): 587–612; Bruce M. Stave and Sondra Astor Stave, eds., *Urban Bosses, Machines, and Progressive Reformers,* 2d rev. ed. (Malabar, Fla.: Krieger, 1984); Steven P. Erie, *Rainbow's End: Irish-Americans and the Dilemma of Urban Machine Politics, 1840–1985* (Berkeley: University of California Press, 1988); Allswang, *Bosses, Machines, and Urban Voters;* and Blaine A. Brownell and Warren E. Stickle, eds., *Bosses and Reformers: Urban Politics in America, 1880–1920* (Boston: Houghton Mifflin, 1973). Useful contemporary works include Steffens, *The Shame of the Cities* and Riordon, *Plunkitt of Tammany Hall.*

53. Lloyd Wendt and Herman Kogan, *Bosses of Lusty Chicago: The Story of Bathhouse John and Hinky Dink* (Bloomington: Indiana University Press, 1967), v–xiv. This work was originally published in 1943 as *Lords of the Levee.* Michael Kenna acquired the nickname "Hinky Dink" because of his diminutive size; John Joseph Coughlin was known as "Bathhouse John" because he started out as a Chicago bathhouse "rubber" and later acquired a string of his own establishments. For a photograph of Kenna's saloon, the Workingmen's Exchange, see Turner, "The City of Chicago," 577. For statistics on the deep involvement of saloonkeepers in Chicago and New York politics, see Odegard, *Pressure Politics,* 248. On "Buckley's City Hall," see William A. Bullough, *The Blind Boss and His City: Christopher Augustine Buckley and Nineteenth-Century San Francisco* (Berkeley: University of California Press, 1979), 139–40.

54. Hoke, "Corner Saloon," 314; Calkins, *Substitutes for the Saloon,* 11, 371–72; Wendt and Kogan, *Bosses of Lusty Chicago,* 170, 234, 292.

55. On the Anti-Saloon League, see K. Austin Kerr, *Organized for Prohibition: A New History of the Anti-Saloon League* (New Haven, Conn.: Yale University Press, 1985); and Peter Odegard, *Pressure Politics.*

56. London, *John Barleycorn,* 111–12.

57. On the role of churches in aiding new arrivals in a town to "establish close personal relations quickly," see T. Scott Miyakawa, *Protestants and Pioneers: Individualism and Conformity on the American Frontier* (Chicago: University of Chicago Press, 1964), 214. See also Thomas Bender, *Community and Social Change in America* (Baltimore: Johns Hopkins University Press, 1982), 96–98.

CHAPTER FOUR: *"Drinking Folkways"*

1. James Stevens, "Saloon Days," *American Mercury* 11 (July 1927): 266.

2. Little historical study has been done on the drinking habits of the middle and upper classes in America in the nineteenth and early twentieth centuries. "Our ignorance partly reflects where contemporary observers turned their gaze—downward—but it also reflects the concerns of modern social historians, who have scrutinized the populace far more than the well-to-do," according to Susanna Barrows and Robin Room, eds., *Drinking: Behavior and Belief in Modern History* (Berkeley: University of California Press, 1991), 10. For a general account of Victorian culture, see Peter Gay, *The Bourgeois Experience, Victoria to Freud: Education of the Senses,* vol. 1 (New York: Oxford University Press, 1984) and Gay, *The Bourgeois Experience, Victoria to Freud: The Tender Passion,* vol. 2 (New York: Oxford University Press, 1986). Though I too have focused on working-class rather than middle-class drinking, I have found some useful contemporary sources concerning what I have called the "cocktail culture" of the bourgeoisie. For a discussion of specific cocktails as well as "the vocabulary of bacchanalia," see H. L. Mencken, *The American Language,* 4th ed., abridged (New York: Alfred A. Knopf, 1980), 160–68. Bourgeois drinking preferences and working-class attitudes toward them are discussed in George Ade, *The Old-Time Saloon: Not Wet—Not Dry, Just History* (New York: Long and Smith, 1931), 26–28, 34–35, 38–42, 49, 77–78, 103, 110–15, 125, 155–63; see also Travis Hoke, "Corner Saloon," *American Mercury* 23 (March 1931): 316–18. Jack London's account of the sophisticated drink culture of the Bohemian Club in San Francisco around 1900 appears in *John Barleycorn: Alcoholic Memoirs* (1913; reprint, ed. John Sutherland, New York: Oxford University Press, 1989), 147–48. Also informative is Theodore Dreiser's description of the wealthy "swells" who patronized the fictional "Fitzgerald and Moy's" (modeled after two actual upscale saloons in Chicago in the 1880s, "Chapin and Gore's" and "Hannah and Hogg's") in *Sister Carrie,* ed. Donald Pizer (1900; reprint, New York: Norton, 1970), 32–37, 92–93, 121–22, 127, 189–90, 216–18. On middle-class drinking customs during Prohibition (1920–1933), which involved speakeasies, hip flasks, and bathtub gin, see Andrew Sinclair, *Era of Excess: A Social History of the Prohibition Movement* (New York: Harper and Row, 1962), 230–41. For an account of "cocktail culture" in the

mid-twentieth century, see David Gottlieb, "The Neighborhood Tavern and the Cocktail Lounge: A Study of Class Differences," *American Journal of Sociology* 62 (May 1957): 559–62. Regarding the temperance movement, Don Yoder analyzes teetotalers as a folk group and their antiliquor pronouncements as an example of religious taboo in "Folk Cookery," in Richard M. Dorson, ed., *Folklore and Folklife: An Introduction* (Chicago: University of Chicago Press, 1972), 340–41. For more on alcohol as a religious taboo, see Joel Bernard, "From Fasting to Abstinence: The Origins of the American Temperance Movement," in Barrows and Room, eds., *Drinking*, 337–53. On the striking similarity in appearance and social function of the temperance society and the saloon club, see W. J. Rorabaugh, *The Alcoholic Republic: An American Tradition* (New York: Oxford University Press, 1979), 189; and Roy Rosenzweig, *Eight Hours for What We Will: Workers and Leisure in an Industrial City, 1870–1920* (New York: Cambridge University Press, 1983), 106.

3. London, *John Barleycorn*, 47, 50.

4. Upton Sinclair, *The Jungle* (1906; reprint, New York: New American Library, 1960), 224. For a discussion of how tradition functions to stabilize culture by setting forth rules of socially acceptable conduct, see William R. Bascom, "Four Functions of Folklore," in Alan Dundes, ed., *The Study of Folklore* (Englewood Cliffs, N.J.: Prentice-Hall, 1965), 279–98.

5. The longstanding view that alcohol has beneficial medicinal properties, and the efforts of temperance advocates to discredit that view, are discussed at length in Sinclair, *Era of Excess*, 36–62, 408–12. Sinclair notes the amusing fact that of fifty members of the Woman's Christian Temperance Union polled by the *Ladies' Home Journal* in 1904, three-fourths reported they regularly used patent medicines such as Lydia E. Pinkham's, which contained an alcoholic content of up to one-half pure spirits (p. 407). For more analysis of the controversy over alcohol's medicinal properties, see Harry Gene Levine, "The Discovery of Addiction: Changing Conceptions of Habitual Drunkenness in America," *Journal of Studies on Alcohol* 39 (January 1978): 143–74 (Cotton Mather quotation, 145).

6. The phenomenon of "disinhibition" was discussed during a conference held 11–13 February 1981 in Berkeley, California, and sponsored jointly by the National Institute on Alcohol Abuse and Alcoholism (NIAAA) and the Social Research Group (now renamed the Alcohol Research Group) of Berkeley. For the proceedings of the conference, see Robin Room and Gary Collins, eds., *Alcohol and Disinhibition: Nature and Meaning of the Link*, NIAAA Research Monograph no. 12 (Washington, D.C.: U.S. Government Printing Office, DHHS Publication no. [ADM] 83-1246, 1983). Regarding the "divine madness" allegedly caused by alcohol use, see Bertrand Russell, *A History of Western Philosophy* (New York: Simon and Schuster, 1945), 14–21. For a comparative approach to different cultures' use of alcohol as a social lubricant, see Mac Marshall, ed., *Beliefs, Behaviors and Alcoholic Beverages: A Cross-Cultural Survey* (Ann Arbor: University of Michigan Press, 1979). On the subject of acceptable behavior under the influence of alcohol, see Craig MacAndrews and Robert Edgerton, *Drunken Comportment: A Social Explanation* (Chicago: Aldine, 1969). Regarding popular attitudes in

the saloon era toward the role of alcohol as a social lubricant, see, for example, "The Experience and Observations of a New York Saloon-Keeper as Told by Himself," *McClure's Magazine* 32 (January 1909): 309; Ade, *The Old-Time Saloon,* 93; London, *John Barleycorn,* 53–54, 85–86, 165, 171–73; and Hoke, "Corner Saloon," 320–22.

7. For information on the use of alcohol as an item of barter and remuneration in colonial America, see Rorabaugh, *The Alcoholic Republic,* 62–64. Similar traditions among immigrants in Worcester, Massachusetts, are discussed in Rosenzweig, *Eight Hours for What We Will,* 59–60. For a Marxian analysis of the use of alcohol as a commodity of exchange, see Marianna Adler, "From Symbolic Exchange to Commodity Consumption: Anthropological Notes on Drinking as a Symbolic Practice," in Barrows and Room, eds., *Drinking,* 376–98.

8. Harold Wentworth and Stuart Berg Flexner, eds., *Dictionary of American Slang,* 2d supp. ed. (New York: Thomas Y. Crowell, 1975), 168. Under the entry "Dutch, go," the editors cite the quotation, "We'll go Dutch . . ." from Sinclair Lewis, *Our Mr. Wren* (1914). Since the phrase appears in print in 1914, it can be assumed to have been current in speech before that.

9. Wentworth and Flexner, eds., *Dictionary of American Slang,* 168 (entry under "Dutch book"); London, *John Barleycorn,* 58.

10. Rorabaugh, *The Alcoholic Republic,* 7–10, 100–112; Robert E. Popham, "The Social History of the Tavern," in Yedy Israel et al., eds., *Research Advances in Alcohol and Drug Problems,* vol. 4 (New York: Plenum Press, 1978), 269; Hugh Johnson, *Vintage: The Story of Wine* (New York: Simon and Schuster, 1989), 353–55.

11. Rorabaugh, *The Alcoholic Republic,* 233 (appendix I, table A1.2).

12. Rorabaugh, *The Alcoholic Republic,* 69–74.

13. Rorabaugh, *The Alcoholic Republic,* ix, 233 (appendix I, table A1.2).

14. On the rise of the antebellum temperance movement, see Ian R. Tyrrell, *Sobering Up: From Temperance to Prohibition in Antebellum America, 1800–1860* (Westport, Conn.: Greenwood Press, 1979); Jack S. Blocker, Jr., *American Temperance Movements: Cycles of Reform* (Boston: Twayne, 1989); Jed Dannenbaum, *Drink and Disorder: Temperance Reform in Cincinnati from the Washingtonians to the WCTU* (Urbana: University of Illinois Press, 1984); John Allen Krout, *The Origins of Prohibition* (1925; reprint, New York: Russell and Russell, 1967); and Levine, "The Discovery of Addiction." Regarding the reduction of whiskey production and the destruction of apple orchards, see Rorabaugh, *The Alcoholic Republic,* 10, 90.

15. Alexis de Tocqueville, *Democracy in America,* ed. J. P. Mayer (1835; reprint, Garden City, N.Y.: Doubleday, 1969), 516.

16. Levine, "The Discovery of Addiction," 153; Krout, *The Origins of Prohibition,* 129; Rorabaugh, *The Alcoholic Republic,* 233 (appendix I, table A1.2).

17. Ade, *The Old-Time Saloon,* 136–37; Herbert Asbury, *The Great Illusion: An Informal History of Prohibition* (Garden City, N.Y.: Doubleday, 1950), 62; Rorabaugh, *The Alcoholic Republic,* 109. On the general history of the brewing industry, see Stanley Baron, *Brewed in America: A History of Beer*

and Ale in the United States (Boston: Little, Brown, 1962); Thomas Cochran, *The Pabst Brewing Company: The History of an American Business* (New York: New York University Press, 1948); Ronald Plavchan, "A History of Anheuser-Busch" (Ph.D. diss., St. Louis University, 1969); and Peter Park, "The Supply Side of Drinking: Alcohol Production and Consumption in the United States before Prohibition," *Contemporary Drug Problems* 12 (1985): 473–509.

18. Rorabaugh, *The Alcoholic Republic,* 109–10, 229–30, 233 (appendix I, table A1.2).

19. On the changing drink preferences of Jews and Italians, see Robert A. Woods, ed., *Americans in Process: A Settlement Study* (Boston: Houghton Mifflin, 1902), 204. The increasing tendency of Italians to call for distilled liquors was also noted in Raymond Calkins, *Substitutes for the Saloon* (Boston: Houghton Mifflin, 1901), 20. Similarly, the tendency of younger Jews to indulge in the drinking of hard liquor was lamented in the *Daily Jewish Courier,* 6 March 1914, cited in Perry R. Duis, *The Saloon: Public Drinking in Chicago and Boston, 1880–1920* (Urbana: University of Illinois Press, 1983), 163–64. For more discussion of the "old" and "new" immigration, see Milton M. Gordon, *Assimilation in American Life: The Role of Race, Religion, and National Origins* (New York: Oxford University Press, 1964).

20. Wentworth and Flexner, eds., *Dictionary of American Slang,* 138 ("dago red"); Walton Bean, *Boss Ruef's San Francisco: The Story of the Union Labor Party, Big Business, and Graft Prosecution* (Berkeley: University of California Press, 1952), 120; Calkins, *Substitutes for the Saloon,* 20; *Daily Jewish Courier,* 16 March 1914, quoted in Duis, *The Saloon,* 164; London, *John Barleycorn,* 38, 61–62, 130.

21. Rorabaugh, *The Alcoholic Republic,* 233 (appendix I, table A1.2).

22. "We'll Take the World" and "Marching Onward," in Emmett G. Coleman, ed., *The Temperance Songbook* (New York: American Heritage Press, 1971), 29, 72.

23. "District of Columbia W.C.T.U. Song" and "I'll Be There to Vote," in Coleman, *The Temperance Songbook,* 15–16, 24.

24. Mencken, *The American Language,* 166.

25. Richard O'Flynn, quoted in Rosenzweig, *Eight Hours for What We Will,* 48–49. In Don Yoder's discussion of "American foodways, particularly what we may as well refer to as American 'drinkways,'" he has noted the manner in which Protestant temperance advocates created their own distinctive folk culture based on antidrink sentiments. "Taboos on liquor . . . did not appear until the nineteenth century when the American temperance movement, one of the most curious examples of religious taboo in history, invaded most of the Protestant churches. . . . While certain classes in American society continued to 'drink,' and the 'colonial tavern' in turn became the nineteenth-century 'saloon' and the twentieth-century 'bar,' nondrinking Americans had to find their substitutes." In establishing "temperance houses" and observing the "temperance taboo" with drinks like sarsaparilla, Protestant teetotalers produced a body of traditions which functioned not only as substitutes for profane drinkways, but also "as unofficial Protestant

substitutes for the Catholic sacramentals . . . in much the same way that earlier folk-religious practices served the [medieval] peasant." See Yoder, "Folk Cookery," in Dorson, ed., *Folklore and Folklife,* 340–41. Similarly, Rorabaugh has argued that "[s]ome men sought camaraderie at the tavern, others in their local temperance organization," so that "drinking and abstinence performed many of the same functions in people's lives." See Rorabaugh, *The Alcoholic Republic,* 189. Roy Rosenzweig has noted that Catholic temperance societies in Worcester, Massachusetts, provided "clubrooms with newspapers, domino sets, gymnasiums, card tables, libraries, and even pool tables. . . . To a surprising degree, then, the model for the temperance society was actually the saloon." For more discussion of this point, see Rosenzweig, *Eight Hours for What We Will,* 106. On the role of temperance organizations as social and political rallying points for African Americans in the nineteenth-century South, see Denise Herd, "The Paradox of Temperance: Blacks and the Alcohol Question in Nineteenth-Century America," in Barrows and Room, eds., *Drinking,* 354–75. For an overview of temperance advocates' beliefs regarding alcohol as a religious taboo and abstinence as a form of religious fasting, see Bernard, "From Fasting to Abstinence," in Barrows and Room, eds., *Drinking,* 337–53.

26. Hoke, "Corner Saloon," 316; Ade, *The Old-Time Saloon,* 31, 52; "The Experience . . . of a New York Saloon-Keeper," 301–2, 305, 311.

27. Ade, *The Old-Time Saloon,* 31, 58–59; Hoke, "Corner Saloon," 315–16, 320.

28. Ade, *The Old-Time Saloon,* 114–15; Hoke, "Corner Saloon," 312.

29. Hoke, "Corner Saloon," 318; Frank Norris, *McTeague: A Story of San Francisco* (1899; reprint, New York: New American Library, 1964), 132.

30. Examples of saloon-era toasts appear in Ade, *The Old-Time Saloon,* 150; Hoke, "Corner Saloon," 319; James Stevens, "Saloon Days," *American Mercury* 11 (July 1927): 272; and Norris, *McTeague,* 95–96, 132, 307. Regarding toasts (or "healths") in colonial American taverns, see David W. Conroy, *In Public Houses: Drink and the Revolution of Authority in Colonial Massachusetts* (Chapel Hill: University of North Carolina Press, 1995), 24–25, 27, 30, 33, 40, 51, 57, 160; David Walstreicher, "Rites of Rebellion, Rites of Assent: Celebrations, Print Culture, and the Origins of American Nationalism," *Journal of American History* 82 (June 1995): 44; and Richard J. Hooker, "The American Revolution Seen through a Wine Glass," *William and Mary Quarterly* 11 (January 1954): 64–65.

31. London, *John Barleycorn,* 147–48. According to Hoke, most saloon whiskeys were blends. "There never were more than a few straight whiskeys on the market; they were otherwise blends of various mashes which made either rye or bourbon." See Hoke, "Corner Saloon," 316.

32. Whiskey and water with sugar and bitters "is the basic formula for the old-fashioned; hence, perhaps, its name," Mencken notes in his analysis of the historical usage of the term "cocktail." Regarding origins, Mencken lists no less than seven very different derivations for "cocktail" which various scholars have suggested. For example, some claim that "the word comes from the French *coquetier,* an eggcup, and was first used in New Orleans soon

after 1800." Others insist that "it descends from *cock ale*, a mixture of ale and the essence of a boiled fowl, traced by the OED [Oxford English Dictionary] to c. 1648 in England." Still others maintain that "its parent was a later *cock ale*, meaning a mixture of spirits and bitters fed to fighting cocks in training." At the end of Mencken's list of derivations, he adds parenthetically: "All are somewhat fishy." See Mencken, *The American Language*, 162–63 and footnote 5. The usually unpalatable (and sometimes dangerous) bootleg liquor available during Prohibition, and the use of mixers to disguise the flavor, are discussed in Sinclair, *Era of Excess*, 197–209, 237.

33. Ade, *The Old-Time Saloon*, 56–58; Hoke, "Corner Saloon," 317. Jack London's account of one of his first drinking sprees with a group of California fishermen confirms the appraisals by Ade and Hoke of this masculine mystique. "They were men. They proved it by the way they drank. Drink was the badge of manhood. So I drank with them, drink by drink, raw and straight," he recalled. "I shuddered and swallowed my gorge with every drink, though I manfully hid all such symptoms." See London, *John Barleycorn*, 28–29. Regarding southern whites' belief that gin acted as an aphrodisiac upon blacks, see (but be prepared for some offensive racial stereotypes) Will Irwin, "The American Saloon," *Collier's Weekly* 41 (16 May 1908): 10; see also Irwin, "More about 'Nigger Gin,'" *Collier's Weekly* 41 (15 August 1908): 28, 30.

34. Margaret F. Byington, *Homestead: The Households of a Mill Town* (1910; reprint, Pittsburgh: University of Pittsburgh Press, 1974), 149.

35. From interviews with John Burris Powers (my father, now deceased), in Davis, California, 11 March 1982 and 3 January 1990.

36. London, *John Barleycorn*, 151–53.

37. London, *John Barleycorn*, 153.

38. Hoke, "Corner Saloon," 321. As Hoke wryly added, "The ability to consume large amounts of liquor without being affected by it was greatly admired, simulated and praised. . . , nor was it ever suggested that if they did not feel their liquor they might as well not drink it" (p. 321).

C H A P T E R F I V E : *"Clubbing by Treat"*

1. Jack London, *John Barleycorn: Alcoholic Memoirs* (1913; reprint, ed. John Sutherland, New York: Oxford University Press, 1989), 100–101.

2. London, *John Barleycorn*, 96–97.

3. "The roots of the [treating] custom can be traced as far back as the wassail bowl and loving cup of the fifth-century Saxons, and beyond them to practices of the Egyptians and Assyrians," according to Elliott West, *The Saloon on the Rocky Mountain Mining Frontier* (Lincoln: University of Nebraska Press, 1979), 93–94. See also Frederick W. Hackwood, *Inns, Ales, and Drinking Customs of Old England* (New York: Sturgis and Walton, 1909), 141–52. On antebellum American treating, see W. J. Rorabaugh, *The Alcoholic Republic: An American Tradition* (New York: Oxford University Press, 1979), 16. For a comprehensive account of taverns and drinking customs in cultures worldwide over the centuries, see Robert E. Popham, "The Social History of

the Tavern," in *Research Advances in Alcohol and Drug Problems,* ed. Yedy Israel et al., vol. 4 (New York: Plenum Press, 1978), 225–302.

4. Travis Hoke, "Corner Saloon," *American Mercury* 23 (March 1931): 319; London, *John Barleycorn,* 112.

5. Upton Sinclair, *The Jungle* (1906; reprint, New York: New American Library, 1960), 85. A photograph of some of the forty-eight saloons on Ashland Avenue's "Whiskey Row" appears in George Kibbe Turner, "The City of Chicago: A Study of the Great Immoralities," *McClure's Magazine* 28 (April 1907): 576.

6. Sinclair, *The Jungle,* 217. It should be noted, however, that Sinclair regarded saloongoing as ultimately detrimental to workers' lives for the alcoholism he believed it caused, even though he understood its attractions.

7. Frank Norris, *McTeague: A Story of San Francisco* (1899; reprint, New York: New American Library, 1964), 226, 227.

8. Norris, *McTeague,* 286–88.

9. Hoke, "Corner Saloon," 319. Sociologists have examined the code of reciprocity under the rubric of symbolic exchange theory. See, for example, Marcel Mauss, *The Gift: Forms and Functions of Exchange in Archaic Societies* (Glencoe, Ill.: Free Press, 1954); Émile Durkheim and Marcel Mauss, *Primitive Classification* (1903; reprint, Chicago: University of Chicago Press, 1963); George Homans, *Social Behavior: Its Elementary Forms,* rev. ed. (New York: Harcourt Brace Jovanovich, 1974) and Homans, *Sentiments and Activities* (New York: Free Press, 1962); Peter Blau, *Exchange and Power in Social Life* (New York: Weiling, 1964); and K. Cook, ed., *Social Exchange Theory* (Beverly Hills, Calif.: Sage Press, 1987). I wish to thank Dr. Susan Mann of the Sociology Department at the University of New Orleans for suggesting these references.

10. From a newspaper article in the *White Pine Cone,* 17 August 1883, published in White Pine, Colorado; cited in West, *The Saloon on the . . . Frontier,* 94. Lest anyone should misinterpret the narrator's use of the term "poison" as evidence of an antiliquor stance, I would point out that the term was here being used in jest, just as bartenders often say, "Name your poison."

11. Jacob Riis, *How the Other Half Lives: Studies among the Tenements of New York* (1890; reprint, New York: Hill and Wang, 1957), 57; Sinclair, *The Jungle,* 225.

12. Riis, *How the Other Half Lives,* 57, 58. The fictional character of George Hurstwood, a former manager of an elegant Chicago saloon who was ruined by his illicit affair with Carrie Meeber and his theft of several thousand dollars from his employers, provides a wrenchingly pathetic illustration of such fallen men. For the Hurstwood character and the real-life model for him (the lover of Dreiser's sister), see Theodore Dreiser, *Sister Carrie,* ed. Donald Pizer (1900; reprint, New York: Norton, 1970), 358, 373–88. For more discussion of Dreiser's Hurstwood, see Perry R. Duis, *The Saloon: Public Drinking in Chicago and Boston, 1880–1920* (Urbana: University of Illinois Press, 1983), 58. On the misery and isolation of such marginal men in Boston, see Mark Peel, "On the Margins: Lodgers and Boarders in Boston, 1860–1900," *Journal of American History* 72 (March 1986): 813–34.

13. London, *John Barleycorn*, 41. The correct spelling of the Last Chance proprietor's name was in fact "Heinold."

14. London, *John Barleycorn*, 41. The term "gink" is defined as "[a]ny man or fellow; a guy; especially an old and eccentric or unkempt man," in Harold Wentworth and Stuart Berg Flexner, eds., *Dictionary of American Slang*, 2d ed., supplemented (New York: Thomas Y. Crowell, 1975), 215.

15. London, *John Barleycorn*, 50.

16. James Stevens, "Saloon Days," *American Mercury* 11 (July 1927): 267–69.

17. Hoke, "Corner Saloon," 319. Sometimes even vociferous protestations of drunkenness were not enough to convince fellow drinkers to take "no" for an answer; see, for example, London, *John Barleycorn*, 51; and Norris, *McTeague*, 227–28. In taverns of the early 1800s, "To refuse to imbibe gave 'serious offense,' suggesting a lack of respect and friendship. It was sometimes dangerous," according to W. J. Rorabaugh, who provides several examples in *The Alcoholic Republic*, 151. Similarly, in frontier saloons after 1865, "[T]he man who turned down a free shot risked physical retaliation," according to West, *The Saloon on the . . . Frontier*, 93. Barroom brawls erupting over drinking disputes have been a favorite theme of Hollywood western movies. See, for example, the 1953 western classic, *Shane*, in which Alan Ladd and Ben Johnson repeatedly become embroiled in altercations over saloon drinking, including one fist-fight precipitated by the unforgivable affront of tossing one's drink in the other fellow's face.

18. "The Experience and Observations of a New York Saloon-Keeper as Told by Himself," *McClure's Magazine* 32 (January 1909): 308; Stevens, "Saloon Days," 271–72.

19. Ade, *The Old-Time Saloon*, 110; Hoke, "Corner Saloon," 319.

20. London, *John Barleycorn*, 61.

21. Ade, *The Old-Time Saloon*, 32. Unfortunately for Sullivan, he made a party of victory a bit too often, eventually leading to his defection from the ranks of hard drinkers to become a star lecturer of the temperance circuit. For more discussion of Sullivan as a working-class hero and legendary saloon-goer, see Michael T. Isenberg, *John L. Sullivan and His America* (Urbana: University of Illinois Press, 1988); and Elliott J. Gorn, *The Manly Art: Bare-Knuckle Prize Fighting in America* (Ithaca, N.Y.: Cornell University Press, 1986).

22. "The Experience . . . of a New York Saloon-Keeper," 311.

23. Norris, *McTeague*, 49–50.

24. Frank Roney, *Irish Rebel and California Labor Leader: An Autobiography*, ed. Ira B. Cross (Berkeley: University of California Press, 1931), 226–27. Court sessions and even religious services were sometimes held in early colonial taverns. See David W. Conroy, *In Public Houses: Drink and the Revolution of Authority in Colonial Massachusetts* (Chapel Hill: University of North Carolina Press, 1995), chap. 1; and Popham, "The Social History of the Tavern," 271. On the American frontier in the 1800s, several court trials were held in saloons, according to West, *The Saloon on the . . . Frontier*, 80.

25. Roney, *Irish Rebel and California Labor Leader*, 226–27.

26. Popham, "The Social History of the Tavern," 271; Royal L. Melendy, "The Saloon in Chicago (Part 1)," *American Journal of Sociology* 6 (November 1900): 302; M. E. Ravage, *An American in the Making: The Life Story of an Immigrant* (New York: Harper and Brothers, 1917), 129; "Warner Brothers," *Fortune* 16:2 (December 1937): 111–12; London, *John Barleycorn*, 41.

27. Ade, *The Old-Time Saloon*, 96–97; George Washington Plunkitt, quoted in William L. Riordon, *Plunkitt of Tammany Hall: A Series of Very Plain Talks on Very Practical Politics*, ed. Terrence J. McDonald (1905; reprint, Boston: Bedford Books, 1994), 90; "The Experience . . . of a New York Saloon-Keeper," 304; Hoke, "Corner Saloon," 315.

28. Ravage, *An American in the Making*, 125–27.

29. Ravage, *An American in the Making*, 127.

30. Ade, *The Old-Time Saloon*, 95; Hoke, "Corner Saloon," 315. Frontier bartenders who appeared to keep up with their customers drink for drink "perhaps were employing a familiar deception by drawing upon a bottle of colored water," according to West, *The Saloon on the . . . Frontier*, 61.

31. Ade, *The Old-Time Saloon*, 96; George Hand and M. E. Joyce, quoted in West, *The Saloon on the . . . Frontier*, 60–61. Travis Hoke noted that saloonkeepers sometimes handed out drink tokens to encourage customers to return to their establishments; see Hoke, "Corner Saloon," 315. This practice continues to this day. I have saved drink tokens as souvenirs from George Kaye's Bar, 4044 Broadway, Oakland, California, and Tujague's Bar, 823 Decatur Street, New Orleans, Louisiana.

32. Robert Bagnell, *Economic and Moral Aspects of the Liquor Business* (New York: Columbia University Press, 1911), 22.

33. Raymond Calkins, *Substitutes for the Saloon* (Boston: Houghton Mifflin, 1901), 11.

34. Martin Kelly, "Martin Kelly's Story," San Francisco *Bulletin*, 19 September 1917; Plunkitt, quoted in Riordon, *Plunkitt of Tammany Hall*, 99. Wooing voters by treating was not limited to big city saloons of the era, however. For example, in 1877 in the frontier town of Lake City, Colorado, one newsman remarked, "Nowadays when we see a man 'setting them up,' we involuntarily ask, 'What is he running for?'" From the *Lake City Silver World*, 18 August 1877; quoted in West, *The Saloon on the . . . Frontier*, 82. Nor was the practice of politicians treating to win votes and good will limited to the saloon period. On the contrary, the custom had been common since colonial days, inherited from English drinking tradition before that. On John Adams's disapproval of political treating, see Conroy, *In Public Houses*, 156, 171–72, 196–97, 241, 299. Even the venerable George Washington resorted to generous treating when running for office in the Virginia House of Burgesses in 1758. According to W. J. Rorabaugh, "For his 144 gallons of refreshment," which included "rum, punch, wine, hard cider, and beer," Washington "received 307 votes, a return on his investment of better than 2 votes per gallon." See Rorabaugh, *The Alcoholic Republic*, 152.

35. Riordon, *Plunkitt of Tammany Hall*, 101–2.

36. Riordon, *Plunkitt of Tammany Hall*, 101–2; Lloyd Wendt and Herman Kogan, *Bosses of Lusty Chicago: The Story of Bathhouse John and Hinky*

Dink (Bloomington: Indiana University Press, 1967), 82. This work was originally published in 1943 as *Lords of the Levee.*

37. London, *John Barleycorn,* 78–79. In Charles Dickens's *David Copperfield,* chapter 11, Micawber is described as a character habitually down on his luck but always hovering about, "'in case anything turned up,' which was his favorite expression." For an account of lodging-house voters in Chicago, see Turner, "The City of Chicago," 585. For lodging-house conditions in New York, see Riis, *How the Other Half Lives,* 59–67; in Boston, see Peel, "On the Margins," 813–34.

38. London, *John Barleycorn,* 80.

39. London, *John Barleycorn,* 80–81.

40. London, *John Barleycorn,* 81–84.

41. London, *John Barleycorn,* 78. For discussions of street parading and communal bingeing associated with working-class political participation, see Susan G. Davis, *Parades and Power: Street Theatre in Nineteenth-Century Philadelphia* (Philadelphia: Temple University Press, 1986); Jean H. Baker, *Affairs of Party: The Political Culture of Northern Democrats in the Mid-Nineteenth Century* (Ithaca, N.Y.: Cornell University Press, 1983); and Michael E. McGerr, *The Decline of Popular Politics: The American North, 1865–1928* (New York: Oxford University Press, 1986).

42. Turner, "The City of Chicago," 586; Riis, *How the Other Half Lives,* 66; a carpenter in Janesville, Wisconsin, quoted in John A. Garraty, *The New Commonwealth, 1877–1890* (New York: Harper and Row, 1968), 207.

43. Calkins, *Substitutes for the Saloon,* 15.

44. William D. Haywood, *The Autobiography of William D. Haywood* (1929; reprint, New York: International Publishers, 1966), 229. For more information on Haywood's career in labor activism, see Melvin Dubofsky, *We Shall Be All: A History of the Industrial Workers of the World* (Urbana: University of Illinois Press, 1988); and Sidney Lens, *The Labor Wars: From the Molly Maguires to the Sitdowns* (Garden City, N.Y.: Doubleday, 1973).

45. According to the *Dictionary of American Slang,* noun sense 1, a "sharp" is "[a]n expert, usually at card games or other gambling games; a shark." In noun sense 2, a "sharp" is "one skilled in forms of cheating, especially in sleight-of-hand with playing cards; a crooked gambler; one who seeks to take, or habitually takes, advantage of others." The similar term "shark," noun sense 4, is defined as a "cheater, especially a person who uses his skill in a game to deceive his opponent, as a 'pool shark' or 'card shark.'" The editors add, "The usual method of the shark is to keep his proficiency secret until a novice has been enticed into the game or until the stakes have mounted high, then to use his superior skills to clean out his opponents." See Wentworth and Flexner, eds., *Dictionary of American Slang,* 463.

46. Calkins, *Substitutes for the Saloon,* 14, 158. For more information on gamblers, see John M. Findlay, *People of Chance: Gambling in American Society from Jamestown to Las Vegas* (New York: Oxford University Press, 1986); Ann Fabian, *Card Sharps, Dream Books, and Bucket Shops: Gambling in Nineteenth-Century America* (Ithaca, N.Y.: Cornell University Press, 1990); Herbert Asbury, *Sucker's Progress: An Informal History of Gambling in*

America from the Colonies to Canfield (New York: Dodd, Mead, 1938); and Ned Polsky, *Hustlers, Beats, and Others* (Chicago: Aldine, 1967).

47. John Dos Passos, *Nineteen Nineteen* (1932; reprint, New York: New American Library, 1979), 41, 46. Dos Passos's *Trilogy U.S.A.* includes *The 42nd Parallel* (1930), *Nineteen Nineteen* (1932), and *The Big Money* (1936). On the history of homosexuality and bar culture in America, see Neil Miller, *Out of the Past: Gay and Lesbian History from 1869 to the Present* (New York: Random House, 1995); George Chauncey, *Gay New York: Gender, Urban Culture, and the Making of the Gay Male World, 1890–1940* (New York: Basic Books, 1994); John D'Emilio, *Sexual Politics, Sexual Communities: The Making of a Homosexual Minority in the United States, 1940–1970* (Chicago: University of Chicago Press, 1983); and Lillian Faderman, *Odd Girls and Twilight Lovers: A History of Lesbian Life in Twentieth-Century America* (New York: Viking/Penguin Books, 1991).

48. Case #5564, Alameda County Superior Court, Oakland, California, discussed in Mary E. Odem, *Delinquent Daughters: Protecting and Policing Adolescent Female Sexuality in the United States, 1885–1920* (Chapel Hill: University of North Carolina Press, 1995), 55–56. On dating rituals in the saloon era, see Beth L. Bailey, *From Front Porch to Back Seat: Courtship in Twentieth-Century America* (Baltimore: Johns Hopkins University Press, 1988); and Ellen Rothman, *Hands and Hearts: A History of Courtship in America* (New York: Harvard University Press, 1987). For contemporary accounts of drinking and dating, see Dorothy Richardson, "The Long Day: The Story of a New York Working Girl," in William L. O'Neill, ed., *Women at Work* (Chicago: Time Books, 1972), 258; Riis, *How the Other Half Lives*, 124; Melendy, "The Saloon in Chicago (Part 1)," 300; and Jane Addams, *Twenty Years at Hull-House* (1910; reprint, New York: New American Library, 1960), 151–52.

49. On "charity girls," see Kathy Peiss, *Cheap Amusements: Working Women and Leisure in Turn-of-the-Century New York* (Philadelphia: Temple University Press, 1986), 110–13.

50. Melendy, "The Saloon in Chicago (Part 1)," 300. Such saloon women reappeared in the 1930s after the repeal of prohibition and were known as "B-girls." According to Wentworth and Flexner, eds., *Dictionary of American Slang*, p. 32, noun sense 1, a "B-girl" is "a nonprofessional prostitute who sits in bars in order to meet prospective clients." In noun sense 2, she is a "girl employed by a bar or cheap nightclub, either as an entertainer or as a shill, i.e., as a customer who allows male patrons to buy her drinks. . . . Sometimes the girls receive no compensation but the permission of the owner to use the premises for soliciting." The term was originally "bar-girl," but this form "was almost immediately made archaic by this abbreviated use." Regarding the term "trick," in Wentworth and Flexner, eds., *Dictionary of American Slang*, p. 554, noun sense 1, the definition is a "prostitute's customer; a prostitute's 'sale' or business transaction." The editors cite Louis Armstrong's assertion that the term was common by 1915 in New Orleans. For more information on prostitution in the saloon era, see Timothy J. Gilfolyle, *City of Eros: New York City, Prostitution and the Commercialization of Sex,*

1790–1920 (New York: Norton, 1992); Thomas C. Mackey, *Red Lights Out: A Legal History of Prostitution, Disorderly Houses and Vice Districts, 1870–1917* (New York: Garland Publishing Co., 1987); Ruth Rosen, *The Lost Sisterhood: Prostitution in America, 1900–1918* (Baltimore: Johns Hopkins University Press, 1982); Ruth Rosen and Sue Davidson, eds., *The Maime Papers* (Bloomington: Indiana University Press, 1985); Jacqueline Baker Barnhart, *The Fair But Frail: Prostitution in San Francisco, 1849–1900* (Reno: University of Nevada Press, 1986); Mark Thomas Connelly, *The Response to Prostitution in the Progressive Era* (Chapel Hill: University of North Carolina Press, 1980); Edward J. Bristow, *Prostitution and Prejudice: The Jewish Fight Against White Slavery, 1870–1939* (New York: Schocken Books, 1982); and David J. Pivar, *Purity Crusade: Sexual Morality and Social Control, 1868–1900* (Westport, Conn.: Greenwood Press, 1973).

51. John F. McIntyre, quoted in Richard Barry, "Tango Pirates Infest Broadway," *New York Times*, 30 May 1915, section V, 16. For a discussion of cabarets in the saloon period, including the phenomenon of the tango pirate, see Lewis A. Erenberg, *Steppin' Out: New York Nightlife and the Transformation of American Culture, 1890–1930* (Westport: Greenwood Press, 1981), 79–86 (quotation, 84). See also David Nasaw, *Going Out: The Rise and Fall of Public Amusements* (New York: Basic Books, 1994).

52. The term "operator" was not actually used by saloongoers, to my knowledge. Instead, according to lexicographers, it springs from "W.W. II Army use." All the same, it seems appropriate for present purposes. See "big-time operator" in Wentworth and Flexner, eds., *The Dictionary of American Slang*, 36, noun sense 2.

53. Jane Addams, "Why the Ward Boss Rules," in Riordon, *Plunkitt of Tammany Hall*, 121; Lincoln Steffens, *The Shame of the Cities* (1904; reprint, New York: Hill and Wang, 1957), 205.

CHAPTER SIX: *"Clubbing by Collection"*

1. Raymond Calkins, *Substitutes for the Saloon* (Boston: Houghton Mifflin, 1901), 46–47.

2. "The Experience and Observations of a New York Saloon-Keeper as Told by Himself," *McClure's Magazine* 32 (January 1909): 305.

3. Harold Wentworth and Stuart Berg Flexner, eds., *Dictionary of American Slang*, 2d supp. ed. (New York: Thomas Y. Crowell, 1975), 232 ("growler"); "The Experience . . . of a New York Saloon-Keeper," 305; George Ade, *The Old-Time Saloon: Not Wet, Not Dry—Just History* (New York: Long and Smith, 1931), 76, 86 (quotation).

4. Perry R. Duis, *The Saloon: Public Drinking in Chicago and Boston, 1880–1920* (Urbana: University of Illinois Press, 1983), 103, 105.

5. H. L. Mencken, *The American Language: An Inquiry into the Development of English in the United States*, 4th ed., abridged (New York: Alfred A. Knopf, 1980), 165; Wentworth and Flexner, eds., *Dictionary of American Slang*, 232 ("growler").

6. Mencken, *The American Language*, 165; Travis Hoke, "Corner Saloon,"

American Mercury 23 (March 1931): 315; Wentworth and Flexner, eds., *Dictionary of American Slang,* 232 (Brander Matthews quotation) and 233, 439 (Sinclair Lewis quotation); London, *John Barleycorn: Alcoholic Memoirs* (1913; reprint, ed. John Sutherland, Oxford University Press, 1989), 58.

7. Duis, *The Saloon,* 65–67, 103–5; Wentworth and Flexner, eds., *Dictionary of American Slang,* 439.

8. Roy Rosenzweig, *Eight Hours for What We Will: Workers and Leisure in an Industrial City, 1870–1920* (New York: Cambridge University Press, 1983), 40–45 (quotation, 43).

9. Rosenzweig, *Eight Hours for What We Will,* 42 (quotation), 45; Duis, *The Saloon,* 61–64, 106–7.

10. Margaret F. Byington, *Homestead: The Households of a Mill Town* (1910; reprint, Pittsburgh: University of Pittsburgh Press, 1974), 149 (quotations), 150, 155–56. "In this book," Byington explains, "'Slav' is used as a general term to include Magyars [Hungarians] and Lithuanians, as well as those belonging to the Slavic race" (p. 12 n). For more discussion of immigrant households entertaining themselves with shared buckets of beer, see Kathy Peiss, *Cheap Amusements: Working Women and Leisure in Turn-of-the-Century New York* (Philadelphia: Temple University Press, 1986), 14–15.

11. Byington, *Homestead,* 107–17, 131, 145–68 (quotations, 131, 149). A photograph captioned "Summer Evening in a Court," showing a group of Slavic immigrants engrossed in a card game, appears facing p. 137.

12. Byington, *Homestead,* 109, 113, 132 (quotation), 173.

13. Byington, *Homestead,* 136. For a discussion of preindustrial patterns of work, play, and drink, see Herbert Gutman, *Work, Culture, and Society in Industrializing America* (New York: Alfred A. Knopf, 1976), 3–78.

14. Jacob A. Riis, *How the Other Half Lives: Studies among the Tenements of New York* (1890; reprint, New York: Hill and Wang, 1957), 124. Riis employs the term "can racket" on pp. 29 and 171. For more on beer "rackets," see Kathy Peiss, *Cheap Amusements,* 90–93. Peiss notes that indoor, group-sponsored dancing parties in tenement districts were also called "rackets."

15. London, *John Barleycorn,* 37, 39–40; Calkins, *Substitutes for the Saloon,* 49.

16. An analysis of working-class household budgets and their monthly allowances for alcohol expenditures is presented in Byington, *Homestead,* 82, 84. How treating customs affected the social lives of young women in the working class is discussed in Peiss, *Cheap Amusements,* 51–55.

17. Mrs. Robert Bradford, quoted in Andrew Sinclair, *Era of Excess: A Social History of the Prohibition Movement* (New York: Harper and Row, 1962), 407; Robert Woods, *City Wilderness* (Boston: Houghton Mifflin, 1898), 72; Peiss, *Cheap Amusements,* 28–29.

18. Franklin E. Coyne, cited in Gutman, *Work, Culture, and Society,* 37.

19. Royal L. Melendy, "The Saloon in Chicago (Part 2)," *American Journal of Sociology* 6 (January 1901): 456; Hoke, "Corner Saloon," 320. For a discussion of workplace drinking in the eighteenth century, see *The Autobiography of Benjamin Franklin* (New York: Airmont Books, 1965), 50–52; in the early nineteenth century, see Paul E. Johnson, *A Shopkeeper's Millennium:*

Society and Revivals in Rochester, New York, 1815–1837 (New York: Hill and Wang, 1978), 55–61, and W. J. Rorabaugh, *The Alcoholic Republic: An American Tradition* (New York: Oxford University Press, 1979), 132–33.

20. London, *John Barleycorn*, 47, 130; Louis Armstrong, quoted in Lawrence W. Levine, *Black Culture and Black Consciousness: Afro-American Folk Thought from Slavery to Freedom* (New York: Oxford University Press, 1977), 205; Riis, *How the Other Half Lives*, 135.

21. Ade, *The Old-Time Saloon*, 7; Robert S. and Helen Merrell Lynd, *Middletown: A Study of Modern American Culture* (1929; reprint, New York: Harcourt Brace Jovanovich, 1956), 245; Calkins, *Substitutes for the Saloon*, 50.

22. Riis, *How the Other Half Lives*, 29; Judge Adolph Sabath, cited in Duis, *The Saloon*, 104.

23. Robert E. Popham, "The Social History of the Tavern," in Yedy Israel et al., *Research Advances in Alcohol and Drug Problems*, vol. 4 (New York: Plenum Press, 1978), 286–91; Duis, *The Saloon*, 177; Rosenzweig, *Eight Hours for What We Will*, 51; "The Experience . . . of a New York Saloon-Keeper," 304.

24. Royal L. Melendy, "The Saloon in Chicago (Part 1)," *American Journal of Sociology* 6 (November 1900): 292–93; Calkins, *Substitutes for the Saloon*, 28. Statistics on barroom seating in other cities are cited by Calkins in appendix IV, "Summary of Reports from Ten Representative Cities," 338–85.

25. William D. Haywood, *The Autobiography of William D. Haywood* (1929; reprint, New York: International Publishers, 1966), 58. David Conroy notes that tavern groups in colonial Massachusetts in the late 1600s sometimes drank beer or wine in communal "pots" (usually measuring a pint or quart). He reports that "drinkers often passed pots of drink around or used them as punch bowls would be later." In Boston in 1682, one disapproving traveler observed that "the worst of drunkards may find pot companions enough, for all their [Bostonians'] pretenses to sobriety." See David W. Conroy, *In Public Houses: Drink and the Revolution of Authority in Colonial Massachusetts* (Chapel Hill: University of North Carolina Press, 1995), 39, 41.

26. Duis, *The Saloon*, 177.

27. Calkins, *Substitutes for the Saloon*, 46–47; a German minister, quoted in Melendy, "The Saloon in Chicago (Part 2)," 437.

28. Melendy, "The Saloon in Chicago (Part 1)," 295; Calkins, *Substitutes for the Saloon*, 62.

29. Christine Stansell, *City of Women: Sex and Class in New York, 1789–1860* (Urbana: University of Illinois, 1986), 92; Robert Chapin, quoted in Peiss, *Cheap Amusements*, 118.

30. Melendy, "The Saloon in Chicago (Part 1)," 295; Calkins, *Substitutes for the Saloon*, 55–56, 62.

31. For more information on the Dutch treat, see the entry "Dutch, go" in Wentworth and Flexner, eds., *Dictionary of American Slang*, 168.

32. Calkins, *Substitutes for the Saloon*, 72.

33. Calkins, *Substitutes for the Saloon*, 46–69. Calkins presents more

information on saloon-based organizations in appendix IV, "Summary of Reports from Ten Representative Cities," 338–85.

34. Melendy, "The Saloon in Chicago (Part 2)," 438.

CHAPTER SEVEN: *"Games and Gambling"*

1. Finley Peter Dunne, "The Power of Love," in Elmer Ellis, ed., *Mr. Dooley at His Best*, (New York: Charles Scribner's Sons, 1938), 165. Elliott Gorn has cited a real-life parallel to this Mr. Dooley story, except in reference to the James J. Corbett-John L. Sullivan bout (Sullivan's last) on 7 September 1892. According to Gorn, "The day after the fight William Lyon Phelps, professor of English at Yale, read the daily newspaper to his elderly father, a Baptist minister. 'I had never heard him mention a prize fight and did not suppose he knew anything on the subject, or cared anything about it. So when I came to the headline CORBETT DEFEATS SULLIVAN, I read that aloud and turned the page. My father leaned forward and said earnestly, 'Read it by rounds.'" See Elliott J. Gorn, *The Manly Art: Bare-Knuckle Prize Fighting in America* (Ithaca, New York: Cornell University Press, 1986), 245.

2. On colonial and antebellum tavern games, see Kym S. Rice, *Early American Taverns: For the Entertainment of Friends and Strangers* (Chicago: Regnery Gateway, in association with the Fraunces Tavern Museum, 1983), 111–13; John Allen Krout, *The Origins of Prohibition* (1925; reprint, New York: Russell and Russell, 1967), 13–14, 18, 40–41, 56; Robert E. Popham, "The Social History of the Tavern," in Yedy Israel et al., eds., *Research Advances in Alcohol and Drug Problems*, vol. 4 (New York: Plenum Press, 1978), 272; Paul E. Johnson, *A Shopkeeper's Millennium: Society and Revivals in Rochester, New York, 1815–1837* (New York: Hill and Wang, 1978), 71–73, 77; and Elliott West, *The Saloon on the Rocky Mountain Mining Frontier* (Lincoln: University of Nebraska Press, 1979), 84–87.

3. Roger Caillois, *Man, Play, and Games*, trans. Meyer Barash (New York: Free Press, 1961), 12. See also Johan Huizinga, *Homo Ludens: A Study of the Play Element in Culture* (1944; reprint, Boston: Beacon Press, 1955). Though Huizinga's work is perhaps better known, Caillois's system of classification seems to me more systematic and useful for the analysis of saloon games. For an excellent example of the insights which can be gained by thoroughly analyzing the play element in a culture, see Clifford Geertz, "Deep Play: Notes on the Balinese Cockfight," in *The Interpretation of Cultures* (New York: Basic Books, 1973), 412–53.

4. For a comparison of games of competition and of chance, see Caillois, *Man, Play, and Games*, 14–19, 99–128.

5. Play involving vertigo is discussed in Caillois, *Man, Play, and Games*, 12, 23–26, 81–97, 133–36. The significance of amusement parks in working-class culture in the late nineteenth and early twentieth centuries is discussed in John F. Kasson, *Amusing the Million: Coney Island at the Turn of the Century* (New York: Hill and Wang, 1978) and Kathy Peiss, *Cheap Amusements: Working Women and Leisure in Turn-of-the-Century New York* (Philadelphia: Temple University Press, 1986), 115–38.

6. H. L. Mencken, *The American Language*, 4th ed., abridged (New York: Alfred A. Knopf, 1980), 166–67; Harold Wentworth and Stuart Berg Flexner, eds., *Dictionary of American Slang*, 2d ed., supp. (New York: Thomas Y. Crowell, 1975), 653–54. For a discussion of alcohol and play involving vertigo, see Caillois, *Man, Play, and Games*, 51.

7. Upton Sinclair, *The Jungle* (1906; reprint, New York: New American Library, 1960), 17. The role of music and dancing in working-class culture is discussed in Peiss, *Cheap Amusements*, 88–114. On dancing in colonial and antebellum taverns, see Rice, *Early American Taverns*, 107–10, 113. For more observations on dancing and the pleasures of vertigo, see Caillois, *Man, Play, and Games*, 25, 163.

8. Finley Peter Dunne, "On St. Patrick's Day," *Mr. Dooley on Making a Will and Other Necessary Evils* (New York: Charles Scribner's Sons, 1919), 191–92; *Wood River Times*, 11 January 1882, quoted in West, *The Saloon on the . . . Frontier*, 87. For information on Mardi Gras celebrations during the saloon era, see Reid Mitchell, *All on a Mardi Gras Day: Episodes in the History of New Orleans Carnival* (Cambridge: Harvard University Press, 1995); Samuel Kinzer, *Carnival, American Style: Mardi Gras at New Orleans and Mobile* (Chicago: University of Chicago Press, 1990); and Karen Trahan Leathem, "A Carnival According to Their Desires: Gender and Mardi Gras in New Orleans, 1870–1941 (Ph.D. diss., University of North Carolina, Chapel Hill, 1994). On the centuries-old tradition of carnival in Europe and the undercurrent of social protest in its revelry, see Peter Burke, *Popular Culture in Early Modern Europe* (New York: Harper Torchbooks, 1978).

9. On the attempts of middle-class reformers to exert social control over working-class drinking and revelry, see Joseph Gusfield, "Benevolent Repression: Popular Culture, Social Structure, and the Control of Drinking," in Susanna Barrows and Robin Room, eds., *Drinking: Behavior and Belief in Modern History* (Berkeley: University of California Press, 1991), 404. On the general theme of social control, see Paul Boyer, *Urban Masses and Moral Order in America, 1820–1920* (Cambridge: Harvard University Press, 1978); and William Muraskin, "The Social Control Theme in American History: A Critique," *Journal of Social History*, 2 (1976), 559–68.

10. On the definition of "games" and "play," see Caillois, *Man, Play, and Games*, 3–10; and Huizinga, *Homo Ludens*, 1–27.

11. Robert A. Woods, ed., *Americans in Process: A Settlement Study* (Boston: Houghton Mifflin, 1902), 205; Raymond Calkins, *Substitutes for the Saloon* (Boston: Houghton Mifflin, 1901), 14–15. On the history of gambling and the sporting life in America, see John M. Findlay, *People of Chance: Gambling in American Society from Jamestown to Las Vegas* (New York: Oxford University Press, 1986); Ann Fabian, *Card Sharps, Dream Books, and Bucket Shops: Gambling in Nineteenth-Century America* (Ithaca, N.Y.: Cornell University Press, 1990); and Herbert Asbury, *Sucker's Progress: An Informal History of Gambling in America from the Colonies to Canfield* (New York: Dodd, Mead, 1938).

12. Perry R. Duis, *The Saloon: Public Drinking in Chicago and Boston, 1880–1920* (Urbana: University of Illinois Press, 1983), 239, 246–48;

George Kibbe Turner, "The City of Chicago: A Study of the Great Im-moralities," *McClure's Magazine* 28 (April 1907): 583.

13. Calkins, *Substitutes for the Saloon,* 14.

14. Fabian, *Card Sharps,* 1–2, 112–28.

15. Caillois, *Man, Play, and Games,* 17–18.

16. Calkins, *Substitutes for the Saloon,* 14; Frank Norris, *McTeague: A Story of San Francisco* (1899; reprint, New York: New American Library, 1964), 177.

17. Travis Hoke, "Corner Saloon," *American Mercury* 22 (March 1931): 321. Poker dice is also widely known as "Boss." For more information on poker, poker dice, and backgammon, see Richard L. Frey, *According to Hoyle* (Greenwich, Conn.: Fawcett Publications, 1956), 9–36, 66, 214–20, 226–36. The book title refers to Edmond Hoyle, the English games expert who first codified the rules of many popular amusements in the eighteenth century.

18. On Johnny Powers's saloon and political connections, see Duis, *The Saloon,* 248. For details on the rules, strategies, and odds of craps dice, see Frey, *According to Hoyle,* 214–18. For discussion of the murder ballad "Stagolee," see Alan Lomax, *The Folksongs of North America in the English Language* (Garden City, N.Y.: Doubleday, 1960), 558–59; Greil Marcus, *Mystery Train: Images of America in Rock 'n' Roll Music* (New York: E. P. Dutton 1975), 234; Ashley Kahn, "Stagolee," *Wavelength,* November 1987, 22; Howard W. Odum and Guy B. Johnson, *The Negro and His Songs* (Chapel Hill: The University of North Carolina Press, 1925), 196–97; and G. Malcolm Laws, *Native American Balladry,* rev. ed. (Philadelphia: American Folklore Society, 1964), 89. For another example of a widely sung murder ballad, "John Hardy," which was based on an actual barroom killing over a card game, see Lomax, *Folksongs,* 264, 271–73; and John Harrington Cox, *Folk-Songs of the South* (Cambridge: Harvard University Press, 1925), 176–80. For a general discussion of murder ballads in American folksong tradition, see Olive Woolley Burt, *American Murder Ballads and Their Stories* (New York: Citadel, 1958).

19. Woods, *Americans in Process,* 220; Peter Roberts, *Anthracite Coal Communities* (New York: Macmillan, 1904), 235. Apparently, the rich in their "prominent hotels" did not require protection from the moral evils of slot machines.

20. Calkins, *Substitutes for the Saloon,* 14; Abraham Ruef, quoted in Walton Bean, *Boss Ruef's San Francisco: The Story of the Union Labor Party, Big Business, and the Graft Prosecution* (Berkeley: University of California Press, 1952), 156; Duis, *The Saloon,* 248. Duis notes that some players used marked sugar cubes in place of real dice to aid in the speedy disposal of the evidence in the event of a raid.

21. For a thorough discussion of lotteries and policy, as well as the beginning of middle-class investment in corporate stocks and mutual insurance plans in place of lotteries, see Fabian, *Card Sharps,* 112–28, 142.

22. Fabian, *Card Sharps,* 136, 142; Jacob A. Riis, *How the Other Half*

Lives: Studies among the Tenements of New York (1890; reprint, New York: Hill and Wang, 1957), 117; Woods, *Americans in Process*, 220.

23. Riis, *How the Other Half Lives*, 117; Woods, *Americans in Process*, 220–21; W. E. B. DuBois, cited in Fabian, *Card Sharps*, 141; Duis, *The Saloon*, 248; Jacob A. Riis, *A Ten Years' War: An Account of the Battle with the Slum in New York* (1900; reprint, Freeport, N.Y.: Books for Libraries Press, 1969), 244–45.

24. Fabian, *Card Sharps*, 142–50 (quotation, 149).

25. Riis, *How the Other Half Lives*, 117. For an analysis of the role of omens, divination, and conjurers in nineteenth-century African-American life, see Lawrence W. Levine, *Black Culture and Black Consciousness: Afro-American Folk Thought from Slavery to Freedom* (New York: Oxford University Press, 1977), 55–80.

26. Fabian, *Card Sharps*, 125.

27. Calkins, *Substitutes for the Saloon*, 12; "Practical Temperance," *The Trestle Board* 5 (September 1891): 503; Royal L. Melendy, "The Saloon in Chicago (Part 2)," *American Journal of Sociology* 6 (January 1901): 443–44, 458–59. On the history and policies of the Young Men's Christian Association, see C. Howard Hopkins, *History of the Y.M.C.A. in North America* (New York: Association Press, 1951); Emmett Dedmon, *Great Enterprises: 100 Years of the YMCA of Metropolitan Chicago* (Chicago: Rand McNally, 1957); and Mayer N. Zald, *Organizational Change: The Political Economy of the YMCA* (Chicago: University of Chicago Press, 1970).

28. "Practical Temperance," 503–4.

29. William D. Haywood, *The Autobiography of William D. Haywood* (New York: International Publishers, 1929), 42, 54; James Stevens, "Saloon Days," *American Mercury* 11 (July 1927): 269–70. For a discussion of Mississippi River gamblers and some examples of nineteenth-century dime novels and travelogues in which they appear, see Fabian, *Card Sharps*, 6 n. 9. Dapper cardsharps brought to us by way of Hollywood include Tyrone Power in the movie *Mississippi Gambler* (1953) and James Garner in the television program *Maverick* (1957–1960).

30. Woods, *Americans in Process*, 220.

31. Jack London, *John Barleycorn: Alcoholic Memoirs* (1913; reprint, ed. John Sutherland, New York: Oxford University Press, 1989), 111, 113; Riis, *How the Other Half Lives*, 69; Bean, *Boss Ruef's San Francisco*, 49; Woods, *Americans in Process*, 206; Captain Fred Klebingat, *Memories of the Audiffred Building and the Old City Front* (San Francisco: Mills Ryland Company with the National Maritime Museum, 1983), 7 n.

32. Margaret F. Byington, *Homestead: The Households of a Mill Town* (1910; reprint, Pittsburgh: University of Pittsburgh Press, 1974), 109, 110, 114, 149. The photograph of card-players and onlookers, entitled "Summer Evening in a Court," appears facing p. 137.

33. Woods, *Americans in Process*, 205–6.

34. Woods, *Americans in Process*, 202, 205–6; Riis, *How the Other Half Lives*, 40, 80. Though it is sheer speculation, I will venture a guess regarding

the nature of the "finger game" cited by Woods. My friend George Takash, a regular in 1991 at Salerno's Bar and Restaurant in Berkeley, California, informed me that in the 1960s he observed a finger game popular in the Italian barrooms of Punxsultawney, Pennsylvania. Pairs of old Italian men played what was known as "Rock, Scissors, Paper." At the count of three, each participant formed his hand into either a "rock" (a closed fist), "scissors" (a closed fist with index and middle fingers extended), or "paper" (an opened palm). The winner was determined according to the following formula: "Rock crushes scissors, scissors cut paper, paper wraps rock." I have no direct evidence, however, that this game was similar to the one played by Boston's Italian saloongoers in 1902.

35. Calkins, *Substitutes for the Saloon,* 13, 156–58; Royal L. Melendy, "The Saloon in Chicago (Part 1)," *American Journal of Sociology* 6 (November 1900): 293; William I. Cole and Kellogg Durland, "Report on Substitutes for the Saloon in Boston," in Calkins, *Substitutes for the Saloon,* 326.

36. Calkins, *Substitutes for the Saloon,* 48, 158; Ned Polsky, *Hustlers, Beats, and Others* (Chicago: Aldine, 1967), 31–37, 41, 50. For further discussion of the nineteenth-century "bachelor subculture," see Gorn, *The Manly Art,* 141–42, 181, 208.

37. Polsky, *Hustlers, Beats, and Others,* 41, 50–64; Melendy, "The Saloon in Chicago (Part 2)," 449; West, *The Saloon on the . . . Frontier,* 85. For a discussion of the pari-mutuel system of betting, see Gunther Barth, *City People: The Rise of Modern City Culture in Nineteenth-Century America* (New York: Oxford University Press, 1980), 157.

38. Melendy, "The Saloon in Chicago (Part 1)," 296. A photograph of a saloon back room with gymnastic equipment appears in E. C. Moore, "The Social Value of the Saloon," *American Journal of Sociology* 3 (July 1897): 11.

39. "The Experience and Observations of a New York Saloon-Keeper as Told by Himself," *McClure's Magazine* 32 (January 1909): 306; Calkins, *Substitutes for the Saloon,* 50.

40. Popham, "The Social History of the Tavern," 272; Turner, "The City of Chicago," 590; Barth, *City People,* 184–86, 188–90; Roy Rosenzweig, *Eight Hours for What We Will: Workers and Leisure in an Industrial City, 1870–1920* (New York: Cambridge University Press, 1983), 55; Otha Donner Wearin, *Johnny Heinold's First and Last Chance Saloon,* 2d ed. (Oakland: n.p., 1987), 17. Wearin's pamphlet is available for purchase at this fascinating old saloon, located at 50 Webster Street, Oakland, California. On the meaning of cockfighting in Balinese culture, see Geertz, "Deep Play: Notes on the Balinese Cockfight," 412–53.

41. For an account of eighteenth-century "rough-and-tumble" fighting, see Elliott J. Gorn, "'Gouge and Bite, Pull Hair and Scratch': The Social Significance of Fighting in the Southern Backcountry," *American Historical Review* 90 (February 1985): 18–43. Discussions of the London Prize Ring Rules and the Queensberry Rules appear in Gorn, *The Manly Art,* 75, 204; Michael T. Isenberg, *John L. Sullivan and His America* (Urbana: University of Illinois Press, 1988), 68–69; and Alexander Johnston, *Ten—and Out! The*

Complete Story of the Prize Ring in America (New York: Ives Washburn, Inc., 1927), 12–17.

42. Gorn, *The Manly Art,* 136–47, 252 (quotation); Isenberg, *John L. Sullivan and His America,* 48–55.

43. Isenberg, *John L. Sullivan and His America,* 75.

44. Haywood, *The Autobiography of William D. Haywood,* 59–60. Isenberg confirms the popularity of impromptu barroom bouts: "Some bars offered a roped-off area in the back-room where aspiring pugilists could spar or neighborhood enemies work out some of their antagonisms." See Isenberg, *John L. Sullivan and His America,* 54.

45. On the boxing matches hosted at Harry Hill's and other New York saloons, see Timothy J. Gilfoyle, *City of Eros: New York City, Prostitution, and the Commercialization of Sex, 1790–1920* (New York: Norton, 1992), 225–27; Gorn, *The Manly Art,* 183, 184. Contemporary drawings of bouts in Hill's saloon are reprinted in both Gilfoyle (p. 226) and Gorn (p. 184). Regarding prizefights in frontier towns, see West, *The Saloon on the . . . Frontier,* 86.

46. Riis, *A Ten Years' War,* 258–59. For a discussion of middle-class fans of boxing who extolled its virtues as a manly test of vigor and gamesmanship while deploring its association with gambling and lower-class life, see Gorn, *The Manly Art,* chap. 6.

47. Calkins, *Substitutes for the Saloon,* 165–67; Frederick Van Wyck, quoted in Gorn, *The Manly Art,* 130. For more discussion of bawdy shows featuring women, see Robert C. Allen, *Horrible Prettiness: Burlesque and American Culture* (Chapel Hill: University of North Carolina Press, 1991).

48. Barth, *City People,* 158, 188; West, *The Saloon on the . . . Frontier,* 87; Calkins, *Substitutes for the Saloon,* 13–14. On poolrooms and their use of Western Union to receive telegraphed reports of horse racing results, see Steven A. Riess, "Sports and Machine Politics in New York City, 1870–1920," in Raymond A. Mohl, ed., *The Making of Urban America* (Wilmington, Del.: Scholarly Resources, 1988), 108–11.

49. Barth, *City People,* 163–66; Melendy, "The Saloon in Chicago (Part 2)," 446. See also John Rickard Betts, "Sporting Journalism in Nineteenth-Century America, 1819–1900," *American Quarterly* 5 (spring 1953): 39–56.

50. For more information on the rise of the sports industry and its importance to urban dwellers in the late nineteenth century, see Steven A. Riess, *City Games: The Evolution of American Urban Society and the Rise of Sports* (Urbana: University of Illinois Press, 1991); Benjamin C. Rader, *American Sports: From the Age of Folk Games to the Age of Spectators* (Englewood Cliffs, N.J.: Prentice-Hall, 1983); and Barth, *City People,* 148–91.

51. George Ade, *The Old-Time Saloon: Not Wet—Not Dry, Just History* (New York: Long and Smith, 1931), 93; Calkins, *Substitutes for the Saloon,* 10.

52. Caillois, *Man, Play, and Games,* 19.

53. Huizinga, *Homo Ludens,* 8; Caillois, *Man, Play, and Games,* 6–10, 13, 44, 45, 50, 64.

54. Huizinga, *Homo Ludens,* 12; Calkins, *Substitutes for the Saloon,* 10.

CHAPTER EIGHT: *"Talk and Storytelling"*

1. Royal L. Melendy, "The Saloon in Chicago (Part 1)," *American Journal of Sociology,* 6 (November 1900), 293–94.

2. For a discussion of the role of medieval taverns like Chaucer's Tabard Inn in the social lives of townspeople and pilgrims, see Robert E. Popham, "The Social History of the Tavern," in Yedy Israel et al., eds., *Research Advances in Alcohol and Drug Problems,* vol. 4 (New York: Plenum Press, 1978), 248–54. A fascinating analysis of the oral lore and its social context in Chaucer's work is presented in Carl Lindahl, *Earnest Games: Folkloric Patterns in the Canterbury Tales* (Bloomington: Indiana University Press, 1987). For additional scholarly works on Chaucer, see Derek Brewer, ed., *Writers and Their Backgrounds: Geoffrey Chaucer* (Athens: Ohio University Press, 1975). Samuel Johnson is quoted by James Boswell and cited in Popham, "The Social History of the Tavern," 258.

3. Jonas Green, quoted in Kym S. Rice, *Early American Taverns: For the Entertainment of Friends and Strangers* (Chicago: Regnery Gateway, in association with the Fruances Tavern Museum, 1983), 119; Elise Lathrop, *Early American Inns and Taverns* (New York: Robert M. McBrick and Company, 1926), 280. For a superb study of the New England colonial tavern as a forum for political ideas and organizing, see David W. Conroy, *In Public Houses: Drink and the Revolution of Authority in Colonial Massachusetts* (Chapel Hill: University of North Carolina Press, 1995).

4. Raymond Calkins, ed., *Substitutes for the Saloon* (Boston: Houghton Mifflin, 1901), 11; Melendy, "The Saloon in Chicago (Part 1)," 292–93; E. C. Moore, "The Social Value of the Saloon," *American Journal of Sociology* 3 (July 1897): 8.

5. George Ade, *The Old-Time Saloon: Not Wet, Not Dry—Just History* (New York: Long and Smith, 1931), 111; Perry R. Duis, *The Saloon: Public Drinking in Chicago and Boston, 1880–1920* (Urbana: University of Illinois Press, 1983), 129. For an analysis of Dunne's career and a chronological summary of the content of Dooley pieces from 1893 to 1898, see Charles Fanning, *Finley Peter Dunne and Mr. Dooley: The Chicago Years* (Lexington: University of Kentucky Press, 1978).

6. Jack London, *John Barleycorn: Alcoholic Memoirs* (1913; reprint, ed. John Sutherland, New York: Oxford University Press, 1981), 56–57.

7. Ade, *The Old-Time Saloon,* 116; James Stevens, "Saloon Days," *American Mercury* 11 (July 1927): 269; Jacob A. Riis, *How the Other Half Lives: Studies among the Tenements of New York* (1890; reprint New York: Hill and Wang, 1957), 64, 152.

8. "The Experience and Observations of a New York Saloon-Keeper as Told by Himself," *McClure's Magazine* 32 (January 1909): 310.

9. Ade, *The Old-Time Saloon,* 6, 152–54; Richard M. Dorson, *American Folklore* (Chicago: University of Chicago Press, 1959), 41; Constance Rourke, *American Humor: A Study of the National Character* (New York: Harcourt, Brace and Co., 1931), 36–37. More examples of boastful saloon talk appear in Travis Hoke, "Corner Saloon," *American Mercury* 23 (March

1931): 320–21. For more information on backwoods bravado, see Elliott J. Gorn, "'Gouge and Bite, Pull Hair and Scratch': The Social Significance of Fighting in the Southern Backcountry," *American Historical Review* 90 (February 1985): 18–43. On the American "tall tale" tradition and its manifestations in oral and written sources, see Daniel J. Boorstin, *The Americans: The National Experience* (New York: Vintage Books, 1965), 289–95, 327–37; Henry Nash Smith, *Virgin Land: The American West as Symbol and Myth* (Cambridge: Harvard University Press, 1950), 49–120; John G. Cawelti, *Adventure, Mystery, and Romance: Formula Stories as Art and Popular Culture* (Chicago: University of Chicago Press, 1976), 192–230; Dorson, *American Folklore*, 39–73; and Rourke, *American Humor*, 33–76.

10. Ade, *The Old-Time Saloon*, 32, 110.

11. George Washington Plunkitt, quoted in William L. Riordon, *Plunkitt of Tammany Hall: A Series of Very Plain Talks on Very Practical Politics*, ed. Terrence J. McDonald (1905; reprint, Boston: Bedford Books, 1994), 86. On the popularity of Shakespeare in the nineteenth century, see Lawrence W. Levine, *Highbrow/Lowbrow: The Emergence of Cultural Hierarchy in America* (Cambridge: Harvard University Press, 1988), 13–81; on the popularity of narrative poetry, see Russel Nye, *The Unembarrassed Muse: The Popular Arts in America* (New York: Dial, 1970), 117–37.

12. Ade, *The Old-Time Saloon*, 130; Elliott West, *The Saloon on the Rocky Mountain Mining Frontier* (Lincoln: University of Nebraska Press, 1979), 49; Levine, *Highbrow/Lowbrow*, 4, 14, 15–16. In John Ford's classic western film, *My Darling Clementine* (1946), there is a scene in a saloon in Tombstone, Arizona, in which an itinerant Shakespearean actor, with Doc Holliday's help, recites Hamlet's "To be or not to be" soliloquy, complete with piano accompaniment.

13. Stevens, "Saloon Days," 272.

14. Calkins, *Substitutes for the Saloon*, 10, 54 (quotation). For more discussion of the relationship between neighborhood saloons and political machines, see Duis, *The Saloon*, 114–42. On popular participation in politics as a form of collective social ritual, see Michael E. McGerr, *The Decline of Popular Politics: The American North, 1865–1928* (New York: Oxford University Press, 1986); and Jean H. Baker, *Affairs of Party: The Political Culture of Northern Democrats in the Mid-Nineteenth Century* (Ithaca, N.Y.: Cornell University Press, 1983).

15. On saloongoers' interest in professional sports, see Calkins, *Substitutes for the Saloon*, 10, 13–14. For an examination of the importance of black prizefighters like Jack Johnson and Joe Louis as success symbols in the black community, see Lawrence W. Levine, *Black Culture and Black Consciousness: Afro-American Folk Thought from Slavery to Freedom* (Oxford: Oxford University Press, 1977), 429–40. For a broader analysis of ethnic boxers and their social importance to their constituencies, see Elliott J. Gorn, *The Manly Art: Bare Knuckle Prize Fighting in America* (Ithaca, N.Y.: Cornell University Press, 1986). A fascinating contemporary view of Irish prizefighters is provided in Finley Peter Dunne's columns featuring the fictional bartender-philosopher Martin Dooley in the *Chicago Evening Post*, 27 January 1894 (the

Corbett-Mitchell fight) and 20 March 1897 (the Fitzsimmons-Corbett fight). On the importance of Horatio Alger's "rags to riches" formula in American popular culture, see Nye, *The Unembarrassed Muse,* 62–72.

16. "The Experience . . . of a New York Saloon-Keeper," 310; Hoke, "Corner Saloon," 314, 322. On the disinhibiting effects of alcohol, see Robin Room and Gary Collins, eds., *Alcohol and Disinhibition: Nature and Meaning of the Link,* NIAAA Research Monograph no. 12 (Washington, D.C.: U.S. Government Printing Office, DHHS Publication no. [ADM] 83-1246, 1983). Cultural attitudes about acceptable behavior under the influence of alcohol are discussed in Craig MacAndrews and Robert Edgerton, *Drunken Comportment: A Social Explanation* (Chicago: Aldine, 1969). On different cultures' use of alcohol as a social lubricant, see Mac Marshall, ed., *Beliefs, Behaviors and Alcoholic Beverages: A Cross-Cultural Survey* (Ann Arbor: University of Michigan Press, 1979).

17. Ade, *The Old-Time Saloon,* 130.

18. Robert W. Service's "The Shooting of Dan McGrew" and Hugh Antoine D'Arcy's "The Face upon the Floor" appear in David L. George, ed., *The Family Book of Best Loved Poems* (Garden City, N.Y.: Hanover House, 1952), 417–19 ("McGrew") and 420–21 ("Face"). D'Arcy's "The Face upon the Floor" persists in oral tradition to this day. At the piano bar in the Alley, 3325 Grand Avenue, Oakland, California, one of the regulars, a former Texas Ranger known as "Tex," often recited a version of the poem accompanied by the tinkling "frontier-style" piano-playing of Rod Dibble. My friend Jeannine Hinkel and I first heard Tex perform the piece in 1980, and we heard him perform it again in 1989. "The Shooting of Dan Mcgrew" originally appeared in 1907 in Service, *Songs of the Sourdough,* retitled *The Spell of the Yukon* in later editions. For an account of Service's great popularity in this period, see Nye, *The Unembarrassed Muse,* 128–29. "Dan McGrew" has remained popular. I witnessed a partial recitation of same by "Juke Joint Johnny" Lumsdaine in the Starry Plough Pub, 3101 Shattuck Avenue, Berkeley, California, in February 1989. The recitation was prompted by the several loud "whoops" issuing from a group of drinkers at a nearby table.

19. Ade, *The Old-Time Saloon,* 131.

20. For an explanation of this method of analysis in folklore, see Alan Dundes, "The Hero Pattern and the Life of Jesus," *Interpreting Folklore* (Bloomington: Indiana University Press, 1980), 223–61.

21. On the derelict "sitters" in New York saloons, see Riis, *How the Other Half Lives,* 57–58; in Chicago saloons, see Upton Sinclair, *The Jungle* (1906; reprint, New York: New American Library, 1960), 225.

22. On the development of the "drunkard's confession" as a temperance ritual in the antebellum period, see John Allen Krout, *The Origins of Prohibition* (New York: Russell and Russell, 1925), 184–92; Harry Gene Levine, "The Discovery of Addiction: Changing Conceptions of Habitual Drunkenness in America," *Journal of Studies on Alcohol,* 39 (January 1978), 153–54. On the various therapeutic techniques developed by temperance organizations in America, see Jed Dannenbaum, *Drink and Disorder: Temperance*

Reform in Cincinnati from the Washingtonians to the WCTU (Urbana: University of Illinois Press, 1984); Ernest Kurtz, *A.A.: The Story* (San Francisco: Harper and Row, 1988); and Jack S. Blocker, Jr., *American Temperance Movements: Cycles of Reform* (Boston: Twayne, 1989).

23. For a discussion of the working-class concept of manly honor and gender identity in saloons, see Gorn, *The Manly Art*, chap. 4.

24. On the contrast between "companionate" and "traditional" marriage, see Nancy Woloch, *Women and the American Experience*, 2d ed. (New York: McGraw-Hill, 1994), 84–88, 93, 271, 408–10, 471; Susan Lebsock, *The Free Women of Petersburg: Status and Culture in a Southern Town, 1784–1860* (New York: W. W. Norton, 1984), xviii, 17–18, 28–35, 51–53, 110; Carl N. Degler, *At Odds: Women and the Family in America from the Revolution to the Present* (New York: Oxford University Press, 1980); and Daniel Scott Smith, "Family Limitation, Sexual Control, and Domestic Feminism in Victorian America," in Mary S. Hartman and Lois Banner, eds., *Clio's Consciousness Raised: New Perspectives on the History of Women* (New York: Harper and Row, 1974), 119–36.

25. On the traditional conception of women as "Eve's daughters," see Christine Stansell, *City of Women: Sex and Class in New York, 1789–1860* (Urbana: University of Illinois Press, 1986), 20–21, 29–30, 79.

26. Cawelti, *Adventure, Mystery, and Romance*, 35.

27. London, *John Barleycorn*, 56–57.

28. Stevens, "Saloon Days," 269; William D. Haywood, *The Autobiography of William D. Haywood* (1929; reprint, New York: International Publishers Co., 1966), 57–58. For the use of religious imagery in another miner's complaint against an exploitative employer, see Archie Green, "Marcus Daly Enters Heaven," *The Speculator* 1 (winter 1984): 26–33.

29. On the difficulty of separating fact from fiction regarding the Molly Maguires, see Kevin Kenny, *Making Sense of the Molly Maguires* (New York: Oxford University Press, 1997); Wayne G. Broehl, Jr., *The Molly Maguires* (Cambridge: Harvard University Press, 1964); Anthony F. C. Wallace, *St. Clair: A Nineteenth-Century Coal Town's Experience with a Disaster-Prone Industry* (New York: Knopf, 1987); and Sidney Lens, *The Labor Wars: From the Molly Maguires to the Sitdowns* (Garden City, N.Y.: Doubleday, 1973). On the difficulty of determining the veracity of popular legends generally, see Alan Dundes, "The Hero Pattern and the Life of Jesus,"52.

30. Haywood, *Autobiography*, 58–61. On William "Big Bill" Haywood's own militant activities in the labor movement, see Melvin Dubofsky, *We Shall Be All: A History of the Industrial Workers of the World* (Urbana: University of Illinois Press, 1988).

31. John Dos Passos, *The 42nd Parallel* (1930; reprint, New York: New American Library, 1969), 51; Ray Ginger, *Eugene V. Debs: A Biography* (New York: Collier Books, 1962), 47. For more discussion of Debs's activism in the labor movement, see Nick Salvatore, *Eugene V. Debs: Citizen and Socialist* (Urbana: University of Illinois Press, 1972).

32. Hutchins Hapgood, "McSorley's Saloon," *Harper's Weekly* 58 (25

October 1913): 15. A photograph of John Sloan's depiction of McSorley's Bar appears in the gallery following page 156.

33. Melendy, "The Saloon in Chicago (Part 1)," 294; Frank Norris, *McTeague: A Story of San Francisco* (1899; reprint, New York: New American Library, 1964), 14; Calkins, *Substitutes for the Saloon*, 55; Ginger, *Eugene V. Debs*, 124. Like Pullman, the community of Harvey, Illinois, was originally founded by businessman Turlington Harvey in the 1890s as a "temperance town" free of the menaces of saloons and subversion. Its failure to retain its saloon-free environment is discussed in Ray Hutchison, "Capitalism, Religion, and Reform: The Social History of Temperance in Harvey, Illinois," in Susanna Barrows and Robin Room, eds., *Drinking: Behavior and Belief in Modern History* (Berkeley: University of California, 1991), 184–216. See also James Gilbert, *Perfect Cities: Chicago's Utopias of 1893* (Chicago: University of Chicago Press, 1991).

34. The Irish "98" Club is cited in Timothy J. Gilfoyle, *City of Eros: New York City, Prostitution, and the Commercialization of Sex, 1790–1920* (New York: Norton, 1992), 231. For an analysis of Italian and Jewish mutual aid associations and their role in perpetuating Old World traditions, see Judith E. Smith, *Family Connections: A History of Italian and Jewish Immigrant Lives in Providence, Rhode Island, 1900–1940* (Albany: State University of New York Press, 1985), 124–65. See also Royal L. Melendy, "The Saloon in Chicago (Part 2)," *American Journal of Sociology* 6 (January 1901): 434–35.

35. Duis, *The Saloon*, 149; Stevens, "Saloon Days," 274; John Marshall Barker, *The Saloon Problem and Social Reform* (Boston: Everett Press, 1905), 49–50.

36. On middle-class fears that industrialization and urbanization were undermining traditional American values, see Paul Boyer, *Urban Masses and Moral Order in America, 1820–1920* (Cambridge: Harvard University Press, 1978), especially 189–219.

37. Jo Freeman, quoted in Nancy Woloch, *Women and the American Experience*, 2d ed. (New York: McGraw-Hill, 1994), 518; Melendy, "The Saloon in Chicago (Part 1)," 294. Charlotte Bunch made the same point when she asserted that "there is no private domain of a person's life that is not political, and there is no political issue that is not ultimately personal." Charlotte Bunch, quoted in Sara Evans, *Personal Politics: The Roots of Women's Liberation in the Civil Rights Movement and the New Left* (New York: Vintage Books, 1979), 212. Alice Echols has noted that the radical feminists' technique of consciousness-raising through the discussion of personal problems as political phenomena "did not originate with this group. . . . The proponents of consciousness-raising took their inspiration from the civil rights movement where the slogan was 'tell it like it is,' the Chinese revolution when peasants were urged to 'speak pains to recall pains,' and from the revolutionary struggle in Guatemala where guerillas used similar techniques." See Alice Echols, *Daring to Be Bad: Radical Feminists in America, 1967–1975* (Minneapolis: University of Minnesota Press, 1989), 83–84.

38. Stevens, "Saloon Days," 274–75.

39. M. E. Ravage, *An American in the Making: The Life Story of an Immigrant* (New York: Harper and Brothers, 1917), 128–30; Hoke, "Corner Saloon," 311; Moore, "The Social Value of the Saloon," 8; Melendy, "The Saloon in Chicago (Part 1)," 294; Stevens, "Saloon Days," 275.

CHAPTER NINE: *"Songs and Singing"*

1. Upton Sinclair, *The Jungle* (1906; reprint, New York: New American Library, 1960), 22–24.

2. Sinclair, *The Jungle*, 7–25 (quotation, 23). According to F. B. Haviland of the firm of George T. Worth, which published "In the Good Old Summer Time" in the mid-1890s, "George Evans, the Honey Boy, brought us 'In the Good Old Summer Time,' which was introduced by Blanche Ring, then a girl in her 'teens, in *The Defender.* The song was an over-night sensation." See Haviland, quoted in Isaac Goldberg, *Tin Pan Alley: A Chronicle of American Popular Music* (New York: Frederick Ungar Publishing, 1961), 120.

3. Danny Barker, quoted in Ashley Kahn, "Stagolee," *Wavelength* (November 1987), 22; Alan Lomax, *The Folksongs of North America in the English Language* (Garden City, N.Y.: Doubleday, 1960), 558 ("Frankie," "Ta-ra-raboom-de-ray"). For a general discussion of murder ballads in American folksong tradition, see Olive Woolley Burt, *American Murder Ballads and Their Stories* (New York: Citadel, 1958).

4. John A. and Alan Lomax, *Cowboy Songs and Other Frontier Ballads*, rev. ed. (New York: MacMillan Company, 1938), 417–20 ("The Dying Cowboy"). For additional verses and more discussion of origins, see H. M. Belden, *Ballads and Songs Collected by the Missouri Folk-lore Society*, 2d. ed. (Columbia: University of Missouri Press, 1973), 392–97. Several versions of this ballad, as well as informative liner notes by Kenneth Goldstein, are available on Folkways Record No. 3805, "The Unfortunate Rake."

5. Belden, *Ballads and Songs*, 392. Though Belden presents the lyrics under discussion, he makes no overt mention of syphilis. More graphic is the account in Lomax, *Folksongs*, 363. For information on the use of mercurous chloride as a treatment for syphilis, see Roderick F. McGrew, *Encyclopedia of Medical History* (New York: McGraw-Hill, 1985), 333–34. I wish to thank Jeannine Hinkel, the head medical librarian at Kaweah Delta District Hospital in Visalia, California, for helping me locate scholarly references to the mercurous chloride cure.

6. Lomax, *Folksongs*, 364 (quotation), 385–86 ("The Sailor Cut Down in His Prime").

7. Lomax, *Folksongs*, 193–94, 363 ("The Bad Girl's Lament"), 364 ("St. James' Infirmary"). Lomax notes that the theme of merrymaking mixed with menace and melancholy, often leading to an "enjoyably morbid conclusion," was characteristic of many songs about barrooms and drinking. Americans have long regarded their drinking establishments and the dangers of pleasure with deep-seated ambivalence. Lomax argues that this reflects the tension between the legacy of ascetic puritanism on the one hand, and the

siren call of individual freedom and adventure on the other. Cautionary narratives like "The Bad Girl's Lament" contained just enough reference to risque behavior to make listeners thrill vicariously to a threatened taboo, while still meting out a punishment severe enough to satisfy the moralists of the day. See Lomax, *Folksongs,* 80.

8. Lomax, *Folksongs,* 364, 384–85 ("The Dying Cowboy"); Belden, *Ballads and Songs,* 393.

9. Lomax, *Folksongs,* 80, 362 (Abbott quotation), 363; G. Malcolm Laws, *Native American Balladry,* rev. ed. (Philadelphia: American Folklore Society, 1964), 16.

10. According to Ella Scott Fisher of San Angelo, Texas, in 1910, "The origin of this ballad I have been told was the shooting of Billy Lyons in a barroom on the Memphis levee by Stack Lee. The characters were prominently known in Memphis, Stack belonging to the family of the owners of the Lee line of steamers which are known on the Mississippi from Cairo to the Gulf." Bluesman Danny Barker of New Orleans testifies to the popularity of the song among southern "barroom balladeers." See Fisher and Barker, both quoted in Kahn, "Stagolee," 22. For more information and speculations about the ballad and historicity of "Stagolee," see Greil Marcus, *Mystery Train: Images of America in Rock 'n' Roll Music* (New York: E. P. Dutton 1975), 234; Howard W. Odum and Guy B. Johnson, *The Negro and His Songs* (Chapel Hill: The University of North Carolina Press, 1925), 196–97; Laws, *Native American Balladry,* 89; and Lomax, *Folksongs,* 559. For another example of a widely sung murder ballad based on an actual barroom killing over a card game, see "John Hardy," discussed in Lomax, *Folksongs,* 264, 271–73; and John Harrington Cox, *Folk-Songs of the South* (Cambridge: Harvard University Press, 1925), 176–80. On the significance of "bad men" like Stagolee and John Hardy in African-American lore, see John W. Roberts, *From Trickster to Badman: The Black Folk Hero in Slavery and Freedom* (Philadelphia: University of Pennsylvania Press, 1989); and Lawrence W. Levine, *Black Culture and Black Consciousness: Afro-American Folk Thought from Slavery to Freedom* (New York: Oxford University Press, 1977), 407–20.

11. Lomax, *Folksongs,* 571–72 ("Stagolee").

12. On the performance of "Frankie and Albert" in the Castle Club in St. Louis, see Lomax, *Folksongs,* 558. On the issue of the song's historicity, Sigmund Spaeth reports that in a St. Louis courtroom in 1938, Frankie Baker "brought suit against Republic Pictures for defamation of character and invasion of privacy in a film based on the familiar song. The plaintiff, an elderly Negro woman of apparent sincerity, admitted the nature of her youthful profession and seemed rather proud of having killed a sixteen-year-old colored boy named Al Britt, at 66 Targee St., St. Louis, in October, 1899." The case was dismissed, however, when Republic Pictures presented evidence that the song very likely dated back to the Civil War or earlier, but in any case it was already in circulation by the early 1890s. See Sigmund Spaeth, *The History of Popular Music in America* (New York: Random House, 1948), 206–7. For more speculation on the origin of "Frankie and Albert," see Bruce Redfern Buckley, "Frankie and Her Men: A Study of the Inter-

relationships of Popular and Folk Traditions" (Ph.D. diss., Indiana University, 1962); Laws, *Native American Balladry*, 248; Belden, *Ballads and Songs*, 330; and Lomax, *Folksongs*, 558. For discussion of another love-and-murder ballad apparently based on an actual barroom homicide in 1864, in which a jealous cowboy shot his flirtatious "Star of Banneck" in a Montana dance-hall, see Burt, *American Murder Ballads and Their Stories*, 53–54.

13. Lomax, *Folksongs*, 569–70 ("Frankie and Albert").

14. Lyle Kenyon Engel, ed., *Five Hundred Songs That Made the All Time Hit Parade* (New York: Bantam Books, 1964), 236 ("Ta-ra-ra-boom-der-é").

15. Goldberg, *Tin Pan Alley*, 113–17 (Goldberg quotation, 113; Cohan, 114). The lawsuit over the publishing rights to "Ta-ra-ra-boom-der-é" was brought in England in the 1890s. Goldberg quotes an unidentified newspaper clipping which provided an account of the proceedings: "The fun came in when counsel read the words to the original song, with allusions to Tuxedo and other local American hits. The text and its solemn delivery by the lawyer were irresistibly comic, and the spectators roared, and there was an attempt to join in the chorus, which was sternly repressed by the court" (p. 115).

16. Levine, *Black Culture and Black Consciousness*, 200–202, 204–5 (Armstrong quotation). For further discussion of the evolution and role of African-American music in American cities, see Burton W. Peretti, *The Creation of Jazz: Music, Race and Culture in Urban America* (Urbana: University of Illinois Press, 1992); and Garry Boulard, "Blacks, Italians and the Making of New Orleans Jazz," *Journal of Ethnic Studies* 16 (spring 1988): 53–66.

17. Russel Nye, *The Unembarrassed Muse: The Popular Arts in America* (New York: Dial, 1970), 317, 330–33; Lomax, *Folksongs*, 558. For a discussion of white musicians exploring black music in jazz clubs in the late nineteenth and early twentieth centuries, see Peretti, *The Creation of Jazz;* and Boulard, "Blacks, Italians and the Making of New Orleans Jazz."

18. Lawrence W. Levine, interviewed in the film documentary, *Ethnic Notions* (San Francisco: Marlon Riggs in association with KQED, Channel 9, 1986). For more information on minstrelsy, vaudeville, and burlesque, see Robert C. Toll, *Blacking Up: The Minstrel Show in Nineteenth Century America* (New York: Oxford University Press, 1974); Albert F. McLean, *American Vaudeville as Ritual* (Lexington: University of Kentucky Press, 1965); Robert C. Allen, *Vaudeville and Film, 1895–1915: A Study in Media Interaction* (New York: Arno Press, 1980) and Allen, *Horrible Prettiness: Burlesque and American Culture* (Chapel Hill: University of North Carolina Press, 1991).

19. George Ade, *The Old-Time Saloon: Not Wet—Not Dry, Just History* (New York: Long and Smith, 1931), 119–20.

20. Ade, *The Old-Time Saloon*, 120; Royal L. Melendy, "The Saloon in Chicago (Part 2)," *American Journal of Sociology* 6 (January 1901): 437.

21. Margaret F. Byington, *Homestead: The Households of a Mill Town* (1910; reprint, Pittsburgh: University of Pittsburgh Press, 1974), 37.

22. Royal L. Melendy, "The Saloon in Chicago (Part 1)," *American Journal of Sociology* 6 (November 1900): 304–5; Melendy, "The Saloon in Chicago (Part 2)," 448.

23. Melendy, "The Saloon in Chicago (Part 2)," 437; Peter Roberts,

Anthracite Coal Communities (New York: MacMillan, 1904), 233; Michael M. Davis, quoted in Kathy Peiss, *Cheap Amusements: Working Women and Leisure in Turn-of-the-Century New York* (Philadelphia: Temple University Press, 1986), 91.

24. William Kornblum, *Blue Collar Community* (Chicago: University of Chicago Press, 1974), 78.

25. Kornblum, *Blue Collar Community*, 78. For a discussion of "marginal survival," see Alan Dundes, ed., *The Study of Folklore* (Englewood Cliffs, N.J.: Prentice-Hall, 1965), 240–41 n. 20.

26. Ade, *The Old-Time Saloon*, 128–29. On the history of the Knights of Labor, see Leon Fink, *Workingmen's Democracy: The Knights of Labor and American Politics* (Urbana: University of Illinois Press, 1983).

27. Lomax, *Folksongs*, 410, 412. On the history of the Industrial Workers of the World, see Melvin Dubofsky, *We Shall Be All: A History of the Industrial Workers of the World* (Urbana: University of Illinois Press, 1988); and Sidney Lens, *The Labor Wars: From the Molly Maguires to the Sitdowns* (Garden City, N.Y.: Doubleday, 1973).

28. Harry "Mac" McClintock, quoted in Lomax, *Folksongs*, 410.

29. Lomax, *Folksongs*, 422–23.

30. Lomax, *Folksongs*, 410, 412. For more I.W.W. songs, see *Songs of the Workers: To Fan the Flames of Discontent*, 34th ed. (Chicago: Industrial Workers of the World, 1973).

31. Lomax, *Folksongs*, 423–24 ("Pie in the Sky"); Captain Fred Klebingat, *Memories of the Audiffred Building and the Old City Front* (San Francisco: Mills Ryland Company with the National Maritime Museum, 1983), 15.

32. Goldberg, *Tin Pan Alley*, 173–74. As Goldberg notes, "The Alley would follow the Theater in its procession from Fourteenth to Twenty-eighth to Thirtieth to Forty-second. It still follows the Theater" (p. 108). Other useful histories of popular music in the nineteenth and early twentieth centuries include Spaeth, *The History of Popular Music in America;* and Nye, *The Unembarrassed Muse*, 306–21. On minstrelsy, see Toll, *Blacking Up;* on vaudeville, see Mclean, *American Vaudeville as Ritual*, and Allen, *Vaudeville and Film.*

33. Timothy J. Gilfoyle, *City of Eros: New York City, Prostitution, and the Commercialization of Sex, 1790–1920* (New York: Norton, 1992), 231.

34. Gilfoyle, *City of Eros*, 210, 224–32.

35. Calkins, *Substitutes for the Saloon*, 23.

36. Melendy, "The Saloon in Chicago (Part 2)," 447.

37. Melendy, "The Saloon in Chicago (Part 1)," 298; Spaeth, *The History of Popular Music*, 280, 312.

38. Calkins, *Substitutes for the Saloon*, 13; Travis Hoke, "Corner Saloon," *American Mercury* 23 (March 1931): 313.

39. Nye, *The Unembarrassed Muse*, 316, 318.

40. Hoke, "Corner Saloon," 321; Jack London, *John Barleycorn: Alcoholic Memoirs* (1913; reprint, ed. John Sutherland, New York: Oxford University Press, 1989), 93–94; Ade, *The Old-Time Saloon*, 125.

41. Ade, *The Old-Time Saloon*, 126 ("A Flower"), 128 ("A Boy's Best Friend"); Spaeth, *The History of Popular Music*, 218–19.

42. Goldberg, *Tin Pan Alley*, 96.

43. Ade, *The Old-Time Saloon*, 127 ("Her Eyes" and "Mother and Son"), 128 ("Little Hoop"); Spaeth, *The History of Popular Music*, 249–50.

44. Goldberg, *Tin Pan Alley*, 101; Ade, *The Old-Time Saloon*, 123.

45. Peiss, *Cheap Amusements*, 15–16; Ade, *The Old-Time Saloon*, 124. Hoke also noted that workingmen occasionally wept in saloons, explaining that "any man might attain a crying jag when the right combination of alcohol and circumstances arose." See Hoke, "Corner Saloon," 322.

46. Ade, *The Old-Time Saloon*, 126 ("The Picture"), 128 (quotation); Sigmund Spaeth, *Read 'Em and Weep*, rev. ed. (New York: Arco Publishing, 1945), 160–61; Spaeth, *The History of Popular Music*, 259. Monroe Rosenfeld's career is discussed in Goldberg, *Tin Pan Alley*, 173–74; and Spaeth, *The History of Popular Music*, 230–32.

47. Spaeth, *The History of Popular Music*, 276 (Spaeth quotations), 277 (Dreiser quotation); Ade, *The Old-Time Saloon*, 126 ("Just Tell Them").

48. Ade, *The Old-Time Saloon*, 125; Spaeth, *Read 'Em and Weep*, 151–53 ("My Mother Was a Lady"); Spaeth, *The History of Popular Music*, 272.

49. Engel, *Five Hundred Songs*, 234 ("Sweet Adeline"); Ade, *The Old-Time Saloon*, 191; Goldberg, *Tin Pan Alley*, 94, 124, 257.

50. Hoke, "Corner Saloon," 321.

51. Nye, *The Unembarrassed Muse*, 323.

CHAPTER TEN: *"The Free Lunch"*

1. Jack London, *John Barleycorn: Alcoholic Memoirs* (1913; reprint, ed. John Sutherland, New York: Oxford University Press, 1989), 21–22.

2. R. E. Popham, "The Social History of the Tavern," in Yedy Israel et al., *Research Advances in Alcohol and Drug Problems*, vol. 4 (New York: Plenum Press, 1978), 249–50, 258–62, 272–74. For more information on the role of the tavern in the colonial and antebellum periods, see Kym S. Rice, *Early American Taverns: For the Entertainment of Friends and Strangers* (Chicago: Regnery Gateway, 1983); Arthur White, *Palaces of the People: A Social History of Commercial Hospitality* (New York: Taplinger, 1970); Paton Yoder, *Taverns and Travelers: Inns of the Early Midwest* (Bloomington: Indiana University Press, 1968); Harry Ellsworth Cole, *Stagecoach and Tavern Tales of the Old Northwest* (Detroit: Gale Research Company, 1972); Carl Bridenbaugh, *Cities in Revolt: Urban Life in America, 1743–1776* (New York: Alfred A. Knopf, 1955); and John Allen Krout, *The Origins of Prohibition* (1925; reprint, New York: Russell and Russell, 1967). For older, less analytic works that are nevertheless rich in historical detail, see Elise Lathrop, *Early American Inns and Taverns* (New York: Robert M. McBride, 1926); Edward Field, *The Colonial Tavern* (Providence: Preston and Rounds, 1897); Alise Morse Earle, *Stage-Coach and Tavern Days* (New York: Macmillan, 1900); and S. A. Drake, *Old Boston Taverns and Tavern Clubs* (Boston: Butterfield, 1917).

3. *Oxford English Dictionary,* 1888–1928 ed., s.v. "ordinary." See especially the definition of "ordinary" as a "public meal" in subject branch II, sense 14a. For the use of the term as a synonym for "tavern," see senses 14b (British examples) and 14c (American examples). On the timing of the ordinary (or "dinner"), see Rice, *Early American Taverns,* 86.

4. Lloyd Wendt and Herman Kogan, *Bosses of Lusty Chicago: The Story of Bathhouse John and Hinky Dink* (Bloomington: Indiana University Press, 1967), 19 n. For further discussion of Mackin's free lunch and political ambitions, see Perry R. Duis, *The Saloon: Public Drinking in Chicago and Boston, 1880–1920* (Urbana: University of Illinois Press, 1983), 52. I wish to note that over the last decade, various colleagues have indignantly informed me that the free lunch idea originated not in Chicago, but rather in New Orleans, in Baltimore, and in New York, respectively. On the phenomenon of popular legends and the difficulty of determining their "truthfulness," see Alan Dundes, "The Hero Pattern and the Life of Jesus," *Interpreting Folklore* (Bloomington: Indiana University Press, 1980), 52.

5. London refers to the free lunch in San Francisco in 1883 in *John Barleycorn,* 21–22.

6. By 1909, the major brewing companies owned or controlled approximately 70 percent of the saloons nationwide, according to James H. Timberlake, *Prohibition and the Progressive Movement, 1900–1920* (New York: Atheneum, 1970), 104–6. See also Duis, *The Saloon,* 25–26, 40–45. Laws regarding food in saloons varied tremendously from city to city, depending largely on the strength and strategies of local temperance organizations. In Boston, for example, every saloon was required by its license to offer food, to encourage customers not to drink on empty stomachs. In Atlanta, in contrast, barrooms were forbidden to offer anything but the lightest of snacks, to encourage customers to go elsewhere for meals. See Raymond Calkins, *Substitutes for the Saloon* (Boston: Houghton Mifflin, 1901), 322, 338. As Duis points out, however, the 1875 licensing law in Boston requiring that food be served was difficult to enforce, widely evaded, and finally repealed in 1891. See Duis, *The Saloon,* 52–55.

7. Royal L. Melendy, "The Saloon in Chicago (Part 1)," *American Journal of Sociology* 6 (November 1900): 296–97; "The Experience and Observations of a New York Saloon-Keeper as Told by Himself," *McClure's Magazine* 32 (January 1909): 306. Similarly, Duis notes that the William Davidson Company "specialized in daily service to saloons" in Chicago. See Duis, *The Saloon,* 55.

8. "The Experience . . . of a New York Saloon-Keeper," 305; Calkins, *Substitutes for the Saloon,* 18.

9. Calkins, *Substitutes for the Saloon,* 15; George Kibbe Turner, "The City of Chicago: A Study of the Great Immoralities," *McClure's Magazine* 28 (April 1907): 587.

10. Kathy Peiss, *Cheap Amusements: Working Women and Leisure in Turn-of-the-Century New York* (Philadelphia: Temple University Press, 1986), 53 (Robbins quotation), 28 (Peiss quotation).

11. Dorothy Richardson, "The Long Day: The Story of a New York

Working Girl," in William L. O'Neill, ed., *Women at Work* (Chicago: Quadrangle, 1972), 257.

12. Richardson, "The Long Day," 258–59.

13. Richardson, "The Long Day," 258.

14. Richardson, "The Long Day," 259. Women patronizing establishments where liquor was sold "raised many Boston eyebrows in 1890," according to Duis, and "fostered a rapid increase in the number of tearooms near the turn of the century." See Duis, *The Saloon*, 186.

15. Calkins, *Substitutes for the Saloon*, 338 (Atlanta), 352 (Chicago), 365 (Minneapolis and St. Paul). Calkins based his remarks on reports prepared in 1899 by the Reverend Frank E. Jenkins of Atlanta, Royal L. Melendy of the Chicago Commons settlement project, and Professor F. L. McVey of the University of Minnesota. On the "merchant's lunch," see Travis Hoke, "Corner Saloon," *American Mercury* 23 (March 1931): 313.

16. Royal L. Melendy, "The Saloon in Chicago (Part 2)," *American Journal of Sociology* 6 (January 1901): 455–56.

17. Calkins, *Substitutes for the Saloon*, 18. It may have been, in fact, that saloon fare in the urban West was often better and more bountiful than what cowboys, miners, and travelers could obtain in their rough-and-tumble saloons of the frontier West. "Old, heavily salted meat, beans, and hard bread were served with monotonous regularity" in the early saloons of Denver, for example, according to Thomas J. Noel, *The City and the Saloon: Denver, 1858–1916* (Lincoln: University of Nebraska Press, 1982), 10. This was in contrast to the urban barroom's tantalizing roast beef which, according to Travis Hoke, was "the glory of the corner saloon—the best that could be bought ('saloon cut' was the butcher's synonym for the most expensive) and perfectly cooked." However, as Hoke wistfully added, "But the lunch-cutter shaved exceeding small." See Hoke, "Corner Saloon," 312.

18. Jane Addams, *Twenty Years at Hull-House* (1910; reprint, New York: New American Library, 1960), 102.

19. George Ade, *The Old-Time Saloon: Not Wet—Not Dry, Just History* (New York: Long and Smith, 1931), 45–47; *Champion of Fair Play* 41 (13 December 1913): 7, cited in Duis, *The Saloon*, 56.

20. Ade, *The Old-Time Saloon*, 35.

21. Captain Fred Klebingat, *Memories of the Audiffred Building and the Old City Front* (San Francisco: Mills Ryland Company with the National Maritime Museum, 1983), 6, 8, 10; report prepared by Dane Coolidge, Stanford University graduate student, summarized by Calkins, *Substitutes for the Saloon*, 381.

22. Calkins, *Substitutes for the Saloon*, 17–18. On the serving of African-Creole gumbo (or "gombo") in antebellum Louisiana taverns, see Lathrop, *Early American Inns and Taverns*, 234. Various groups in Louisiana have long contested the proper usage of the label "creole." According to Bennett Wall, "The term *creole*, as used in Louisiana, applied originally to all persons born in the colony or state, irrespective of race, ethnic origin, or social status, but since the Civil War its meaning has been and still is hotly contested. To some it means native colonials of French or Spanish ancestry and their

descendants; to others it refers to persons of color who were free before the Civil War and their descendants. The term has retained its earlier meaning when referring to Louisiana-grown fruits, vegetables, and animals." See Bennett H. Wall, ed., *Louisiana: A History,* 3d ed. (Wheeling, Ill.: Harlan Davidson,1997), 91 n. For further discussion of the controversy surrounding the term, see Arnold R. Hirsch and Joseph Logsdon, eds., *Creole New Orleans: Race and Americanization* (Baton Rouge: Louisiana State University Press, 1992). On the history and techniques of Creole cuisine in Louisiana, see Lafcadio Hearn, *Creole Cook Book, with the Addition of a Collection of Drawings and Writings by Lafcadio Hearn during His Sojourn in New Orleans from 1877 to 1887: A Literary and Culinary Adventure* (1885; reprint, Gretna, La.: Pelican, 1990); *The Original Picayune Creole Cook Book,* 14th ed. (1901; reprint, New Orleans: Times-Picayune Publishing, 1971); and Rima Collin and Richard Collin, *The New Orleans Cookbook: Creole, Cajun, and Louisiana French Recipes* (New York: Alfred A. Knopf, 1975). I wish to thank Dr. Jerah Johnson of the Department of History at the University of New Orleans for bringing the latter three sources to my attention.

23. Atlanta data are from a report prepared in 1899 by the Reverend Frank E. Jenkins, summarized by Calkins, *Substitutes for the Saloon,* 338. Baltimore information is from a report prepared in 1899 by William L. Ross of Johns Hopkins University, summarized by Calkins, *Substitutes for the Saloon,* 341. There is a puzzling inconsistency in Calkins's remarks regarding the free lunch in Baltimore. On p. 341, from which the quotations cited here were drawn, his information regarding Baltimore was based on the firsthand report of Ross, his research assistant. On p. 16, however, where Calkins summarized the reports of many such research assistants across the country, he included Baltimore in his discussion of establishments of the East (not the South) and claimed these saloons (those of Baltimore included) "do not serve a very abundant or very appetizing lunch." Of these two opposite appraisals of the fare in Baltimore, perhaps more credence should be placed in the version presented on p. 338, which was based on Ross's eyewitness account of the situation.

24. Philadelphia and San Francisco data are from the reports prepared in 1899 by E. S. Meade of the University of Pennsylvania, and by Dane Coolidge, a graduate student of Stanford University, both summarized by Calkins, *Substitutes for the Saloon,* 376, 381. Boston data are from William I. Cole and Kellogg Durland, "Report on Substitutes for the Saloon in Boston," in Calkins, *Substitutes for the Saloon,* 322–23.

25. Calkins, *Substitutes for the Saloon,* 16.

26. "The Experience . . . of a New York Saloon-Keeper," 305–6; Dorothy Richardson, "The Long Day," 258; Calkins, *Substitutes for the Saloon,* 16.

27. Upton Sinclair, *The Jungle* (1906; reprint, New York: New American Library, 1960), 84.

28. Chicago information is from an interview with Helen Constable, retired dental hygienist and former Chicago resident, in Davis, California, 28 December 1983. London quotation is from *John Barleycorn,* 21.

29. Calkins, *Substitutes for the Saloon*, 16.

30. Sinclair, *The Jungle*, 84–85; Calkins, *Substitutes for the Saloon*, 16–17.

31. "The Experience . . . of a New York Saloon-Keeper," 305.

32. London, *John Barleycorn*, 21–22; John Burris Powers (my father, now deceased), interviewed in Davis, California, 11 March 1982; Joseph Mitchell, "McSorley's Wonderful Saloon" (1940), in *Up in the Old Hotel* (New York: Pantheon Books, 1992), 22.

33. Ade, *The Old-Time Saloon*, 36–37. Hoke remarked that the free lunch counter was usually "strategically placed far from the door so that a desperado . . . would have to run a frightful gauntlet." See Hoke, "Corner Saloon," 312.

34. Klebingat, *Memories . . . of the Old City Front*, 17.

35. Walter Strauss, quoted in Klebingat, *Memories of . . . the Old City Front*, 9 n.

36. Ade, *The Old-Time Saloon*, 36, 41–43.

37. Sinclair, *The Jungle*, 185–86.

38. Melendy, "The Saloon in Chicago (Part 1)," 297.

39. Calkins, *Substitutes for the Saloon*, 221–22, 224.

40. Melendy, "The Saloon in Chicago (Part 2)," 456–57; London, *John Barleycorn*, 22.

41. On the salty foods served in saloons, see Ade, *The Old-Time Saloon*, 44; Cole and Durland, "Report on . . . Boston," in Calkins, *Substitutes for the Saloon*, 328; Popham, "The Social History of the Tavern," 279; and Hoke, "Corner Saloon," 312, 319. On developing a taste for beer with lunch, see Richardson, "The Long Day," 259; and Vernon Sheldon, a Chicago book salesman and friend mentioned during an interview with John Burris Powers, in Davis, California, 11 March 1982.

42. Ade, *The Old-Time Saloon*, 47; Duis, *The Saloon*, 296.

43. Sinclair, *The Jungle*, 73; Duis, *The Saloon*, 296–97.

44. Duis, *The Saloon*, 55, 296–97.

45. A marvelous exception to this general rule can be found in New Orleans, where neighborhood bars still honor many of the old traditions. On holidays such as the Fourth of July, Thanksgiving, and Christmas, several saloons in my neighborhood—the French Quarter—offer stupendous free feasts to all comers. It goes without saying, of course, that one is honor-bound to purchase a drink or two to wash down such items as Cajun-spiced turkey, ham, barbequed beef, fried chicken, sweet potatoes, corn, and the inevitable red beans and rice.

CONCLUSION

1. Francis G. Peabody, E. R. L. Gould, and William M. Sloane of the Committee of Fifty, introduction to Raymond Calkins, *Substitutes for the Saloon* (Boston: Houghton, Mifflin, 1901), viii–ix.

2. Calkins, *Substitutes for the Saloon*, 46.

3. Modernization theory postulates that as society evolves from simple to complex, rural to urban, and traditional to modern, there are certain

inevitable consequences for human relationships as well as the overall social structure. The forces of modernization—which include such factors as industrialization, urbanization, market capitalism, centralization, and bureaucratization—allegedly have a catastrophic impact on people's ability to cultivate a sense of community. Not only are bonds of physical closeness broken as villages and small towns give way to burgeoning metropolises and sprawling suburbs, but also bonds of emotional solidarity wither in the depersonalized, competitive, alienating atmosphere of the urban-industrial environment. With the rise of modern urban society, kinship ties weaken, neighbors become strangers, and informal, community-oriented institutions are largely supplanted by formal, market-oriented organizations such as business corporations and special interest groups. According to this theory, then, modernizing trends spell the inexorable breakdown of community. For more on modernization theory, see Marion Levy, Jr., *Modernization and the Structure of Societies* (Princeton: Princeton University Press, 1966); Cyril E. Black, *The Dynamics of Modernization* (New York: Harper, 1967); and Richard D. Brown, *Modernization: The Transformation of American Life, 1600–1865* (New York: Hill and Wang, 1976).

Critics of modernization theory have questioned the unilinear, unidirectional nature of this model of historical change. Cultures are assumed to evolve in a straight line from one polar extreme or "ideal type" to another: from purely traditional community to purely modern society. But such logical, well-reasoned abstractions as ideal types and linear evolution do not always correspond to factual reality. Indeed, from the time that modernization theory rose to prominence in the 1960s, historical evidence has been steadily mounting that community can in fact resurge and thrive in urban-industrial environments. For criticisms of modernization theory, see Thomas Bender, *Community and Social Change in America* (New Brunswick, N.J.: Rutgers University Press, 1978), 15–16, 24–29; Joseph Gusfield, "Tradition and Modernity: Misplaced Polarities in the Study of Social Change," *American Journal of Sociology* 72 (1967): 351–62; Dean C. Tipps, "Modernization Theory and the Comparative Study of Societies," *Comparative Studies in Society and History* 15 (1973): 199–226; and L. E. Shiner, Tradition/Modernity: An Ideal Type Gone Astray," *Comparative Studies in Society and History* 17 (1975): 245–52. For historical studies of community building in the saloon era, see, for example, Judith E. Smith, *Family Connections: A History of Italian and Jewish Immigrant Lives in Providence, Rhode Island, 1900–1940* (Albany: State University of New York Press, 1985); Eva Morawska, *For Bread and Butter: Life-Worlds of East Central Europeans in Johnstown, Pennsylvania, 1890–1940* (New York: Cambridge University Press, 1986); and Frances G. Couvares, *The Remaking of Pittsburgh: Class and Culture in an Industrializing City, 1877–1919* (Albany: State University of New York Press, 1984).

4. For numerous samples of the Anti-Saloon League's pejorative views on barlife, see Peter Odegard, *Pressure Politics: The Story of the Anti-Saloon League* (New York: Columbia University Press, 1928). Additional commentary is available in K. Austin Kerr, *Organized for Prohibition: A New History of the Anti-Saloon League* (New Haven, Conn.: Yale University Press, 1985); and

Richard F. Hamm, *Shaping the Eighteenth Amendment: Temperance Reform, Legal Culture, and the Polity, 1880–1920* (Chapel Hill: University of North Carolina Press, 1995). Scholarly studies presenting more positive views of saloonlife include Roy Rosenzweig, *Eight Hours for What We Will: Workers and Leisure in an Industrial City, 1870–1920* (New York: Cambridge University Press, 1983); Perry R. Duis, *The Saloon: Public Drinking in Chicago and Boston, 1880–1920* (Urbana: University of Illinois Press, 1983); Thomas J. Noel, *The City and the Saloon: Denver, 1858–1916* (Lincoln: University of Nebraska Press, 1982); and Elliott West, *The Saloon on the Rocky Mountain Mining Frontier* (Lincoln: University of Nebraska Press, 1979).

5. On market-oriented versus community-oriented relationships, see Ferdinand Tönnies, *Fundamental Concepts of Sociology: Gemeinschaft and Gesellschaft,* trans. Charles P. Loomis (1887; reprint, New York: American Books Company, 1940), 42, 74, 270–72. Other scholars who have followed Tönnies's lead include Charles H. Cooley, *Social Organization: A Study of the Larger Mind* (New York: Scribner's, 1909); Max Weber, *The Theory of Social and Economic Organization,* trans. Talcott Parsons (New York: Free Press, 1964); Émile Durkheim, *The Division of Labor in Society,* trans. George Simpson (New York: Free Press, 1933); Talcott Parsons, *The Social System* (New York: Free Press, 1951); Robert Redfield, *The Folk Culture of Yucatan* (Chicago: University of Chicago Press, 1941) and *The Little Community* (Chicago: University of Chicago Press, 1955); and Eric Wolf, "Kinship, Friendship, and Patron-Client Relations in Complex Societies," in Michael Banton, ed., *The Social Anthropology of Complex Societies* (London: Tavistock, 1966), 10. For more discussion of these social analysts and their theories of social interaction, see Thomas Bender, *Community and Social Change in America,* 8–35, 135–37; Robert A. Nisbet, *The Quest for Community* (New York: Oxford University Press, 1953), chap. 4.

6. The alternative culture theory of saloons exhibits several parallels with modernization theory which, while perhaps unintentional, are striking nevertheless. According to the alternative culture theory, the saloon's communal orientation is attributable to the premodern, preindustrial behavior patterns of its largely immigrant, working-class customers who were as yet imperfectly assimilated into modern industrial society. In other words, the communal values of saloongoers are assumed to be the cultural leftovers of a bygone era. In this view, the saloon is not only an alternative culture, but something of an anachronism as well, a place where communal values live on in marginal survival despite the prevailing market ideology of the world outside. The more American culture moves in the direction of modernity, the weaker communal values become, until at last, presumably, the breakdown of community— as well as bar culture—is complete. For the most thorough presentation of the alternative culture interpretation, see Rosenzweig, *Eight Hours for What We Will,* 17–18, 36, 48, 58, 60–64, 183–87, 223. See also Kathy Peiss, *Cheap Amusements: Working Women and Leisure in Turn-of-the-Century New York* (Philadelphia: Temple University Press, 1986), 25; and Jon M. Kingsdale, "The 'Poor Man's Club': Social Functions of the Urban Working-Class Saloon," *American Quarterly* 25 (October 1973): 472, 484, 487–89. On the

concepts of "alternative" and "oppositional" cultures, see Raymond Williams, "Base and Superstructure in Marxist Cultural Theory," *New Left Review* 82 (November–December 1973): 3–16.

7. For works which explore the significance of community and marketplace orientations, see this chapter, note 5.

8. On the concept of volitional allegiance regarding citizenship and religion from the colonial to the Reconstruction eras, see James Kettner, *The Development of American Citizenship, 1608–1870* (Chapel Hill: University of North Carolina Press, 1984).

9. On Franklin's tavern club and its lending library project, see *The Autobiography of Benjamin Franklin* (New York: Airmont, 1965), 63–65, 73–75. On the tavern-based political factions of Ebenezer Thayer and Elisha Cooke, Jr., see David W. Conroy, *In Public Houses: Drink and the Revolution of Authority in Colonial Massachusetts* (Chapel Hill: University of North Carolina Press, 1995), 197, 238–39.

10. Gary B. Nash, "The Social Evolution of Preindustrial American Cities, 1700–1820," in Raymond A. Mohl, ed., *The Making of Urban America*, 2d ed. (Wilmington, Del.: Scholarly Resources, 1997), 15–36. Nash provides an excellent example of how the community versus marketplace theories of both Ferdinand Tönnies and Thomas Bender can be applied to United States history.

11. Alexis de Tocqueville, *Democracy in America*, ed. J. P. Mayer (1835; reprint, Garden City, N.Y.: Doubleday, 1969), 508, 511, 514, 536.

12. Tocqueville, *Democracy in America*, 513, 517.

13. Tocqueville, *Democracy in America*, 520, 526.

14. Elliott J. Gorn, *The Manly Art: Bare-Knuckle Prize Fighting in America* (Ithaca, N.Y.: Cornell University Press, 1986), 133; Conroy, *In Public Houses*, 156; W. J. Rorabaugh, *The Alcoholic Republic: An American Tradition* (New York: Oxford University Press, 1979), 149–51, 167–69. On drinking in Denver and other frontier towns, see Noel, *The City and the Saloon* and West, *The Saloon on the . . . Frontier*. On drinking in manufacturing centers like Rochester, New York, and Lynn, Massachusetts, see Paul Johnson, *A Shopkeeper's Millennium: Society and Revivals in Rochester, New York, 1815–1837* (New York: Hill and Wang, 1978); and Paul Faler, "Cultural Aspects of the Industrial Revolution: Lynn, Massachusetts, and Industrial Morality, 1826–1860," *Labor History* 15 (summer 1974): 367–94.

15. For more discussion of factors contributing to the saloon's downfall, see Duis, *The Saloon*, 274–303; and Rosenzweig, *Eight Hours for What We Will*, 191–228. Though I am now in the awkward position of disagreeing with myself about some of the conclusions I have previously drawn from my data, I still stand by the data I presented on the saloon's declining centrality in "Decay from Within: The Inevitable Doom of the American Saloon," in Susanna Barrows and Robin Room, eds., *Drinking: Behavior and Belief in Modern History* (Berkeley: University of California Press, 1991), 112–31.

16. The Eighteenth Amendment which put an end to saloons went into effect on 16 January 1920. However, as Andrew Sinclair has pointed out, the "end of alcoholic drink had already been celebrated or mourned three times

before the actual sixteenth of January, 1920. The first funeral orgy had taken place with the opening of wartime prohibition on July 1, 1919. From that date onwards, the people of America were reduced to drinking up the remaining stocks of liquor, for its manufacture was now forbidden. . . . The remaining stocks . . . were drunk up in October, when all drinkers held a wake at the passing of the Volstead Act. The final spree took place over Christmas." See Andrew Sinclair, *Era of Excess: A Social History of the Prohibition Movement* (New York: Harper and Row, 1962), 173–74.

17. For information on the prohibition era, see Sean Cashman, *Prohibition: The Lie of the Land* (New York: Free Press, 1981), and Thomas Coffey, *The Long Thirst: Prohibition in America, 1920–1933* (New York: Norton, 1975). On the controversy over the Eighteenth Amendment's repeal, see David E. Kyvig, *Repealing National Prohibition* (Chicago: University of Chicago Press, 1979).

18. Franklin D. Roosevelt, *The Public Papers and Addresses of Franklin D. Roosevelt,* vol. II (New York: Random House, 1938), 511–12.

Index